Princess Alice

Vermilion Books
The Lives of Remarkable Women

Toni Lopopolo, Executive Editor

St. Martin's Press is proud to announce a series of
biographies of women who have led remarkable and
unusual lives and who, through their work or lifestyles,
have left an indelible mark upon the world. Biographies,
autobiographies, and memoirs—Vermilion Books will
bring to the public, in quality paperback editions, the life
stories of these brilliant and fascinating women.

Straight On Till Morning: The Biography of Beryl Markham
by Mary S. Lovell

Simone de Beauvoir: A Life... A Love Story
by Claude Francis and Fernande Gontier

Sylvia Plath: A Biography
by Linda W. Wagner-Martin

Princess Alice: The Life & Times of Alice Roosevelt Longworth
by Carol Felsenthal

My Life, My Loves: The Memoirs of Alma Mahler
by Alma Mahler

Princess Alice

Carol Felsenthal

St. Martin's Press
New York

Library of Congress Cataloging-in-Publication Data

Felsenthal, Carol.
      Princess Alice.

      (Vermilion books)
       · 1. Longworth, Alice Roosevelt, 1884-1980.
2. Presidents—United States—Children—Biography.
3. Politicians' wives—United States—Biography.
I. Title.
E757.3.F46   1989   973.9′092′4   [B]   88-29840
ISBN 0-312-30222-3   (pbk.)

First published in the United States by G. P. Putnam's Sons, under the title *Alice Roosevelt Longworth*.

ACKNOWLEDGMENTS

I had been warned that, as a Midwesterner, I'd have trouble breaking into the crowd of East Coasters who mixed with Alice Longworth. In fact, I found the Washington/New York powerbrokers, both current and former, to be open and generous with their memories and time. The Oyster Bay Roosevelts are a diverse and charming group. I spoke to nearly every one of them over age twenty-one, and that was more fun than work.

Anyone writing about the Roosevelts comes to owe a large debt to John Gable, a seemingly bottomless source of help and anecdotes. The same goes for Wallace Finley Dailey, curator of the TR Collection at Harvard. I had help from librarians all over the country, but want to acknowledge especially Roxanne Deane, chief of the Washingtoniana collection at the D.C. Public Library.

My thanks to my agent, Philippa Brophy of Sterling Lord Literistic, who believed in this book and didn't give up until she found the right publisher. No one I know is more savvy than "Flip" in the mysteries and irrationalities of the publishing world. Although I didn't always agree with my editor, Faith Sale, I thank her for her guidance, her persistence, and her wisdom. Usually she was right. Thanks also to Faith's very able assistant, Jennifer Barth. And to Liz Cucco, who was always ready to help with unfailing efficiency and good humor.

On the personal side, I want to thank a unique group of relatives—my parents, my husband's parents, and aunts who have picked up my children from school, taken them to assorted lessons, and listened to them when their mother was otherwise engaged. To my friends Rick and Harriet Meyer, also thanks. Not only did they seem interested in my endless tales of missed deadlines, but while they listened they served me and my family Harriet's wonderful food.

Finally, to my husband, Steve, who, by assuming that I can do it, makes me believe that I can.

For my daughters,
Rebecca and Julia

Contents

Princess Alice

1

Alice's Parents

Theodore Roosevelt was bound for Harvard. There was never a question that the intellectually precocious boy, older of two sons, would go to the school that had become an expected stopping place for boys of his social station.

His younger brother would not be following Teedie, as the future president was called in his family, to Cambridge. The problems, physical and emotional, that would lead Elliott to severe alcoholism and death at age thirty-four, practically in the arms of his mistress, were already evident. It went without saying in the mid-1870s that Teedie's two sisters, Anna (always called Bamie or Bye), the eldest of the four children, and Corinne, the youngest, would not be college educated.

Classmates noted that the sickly looking freshman seemed unusually nervous—not surprising, given his determination to please his seemingly perfect father. Theodore Senior was a rare combination of a man of good works and good times. He helped establish the Children's Aid Society, the New York Orthopedic Hospital, the Metropolitan Museum of Art, and the American Museum of Natural History. He also loved to dance and tended to be the last to leave parties. He seemed to have limitless energy—he had none of the health problems that plagued all four of his children—and drove his four-in-hand home in the early morning hours at such a fast clip that his grooms "fell out at the corners." During a stay in Civil War Washington, where he worked in a civilian capacity for the Union side, he so charmed Mary Todd Lincoln that she insisted he accompany her to help select her bonnets.

Although Teedie considered his father's purchase of a Civil War substitute the only flaw in his awe-inspiring character, TR Sr. had his reasons. His wife, Mittie, was Southern-born and would have been devastated by the sight of her husband bearing arms against her own brothers. She was raised in a slave-owning family at Roswell, a sweeping Georgia plantation that Sherman looted on his march to the sea. At the foot of her bed had slept "her little black shadow," also known as "Black Bess," a slave who had been given to Mittie at birth. One of her brothers was the secret agent Admiral James Bulloch, who had "bought, outfitted, and launched" the blockade-running *Alabama*. Another served on the Confederate warship until she was sunk.[1]

Mittie became a casualty of the Civil War—her brothers were permanently exiled to England—salving her wounds by retreating into a daily routine so obsessive that she found it increasingly difficult to emerge from the family's new Fifty-seventh Street mansion. She bathed twice every day, each time ordering her maid to fill the tub twice, once for the wash and once for the rinse. Because she took such precautions before going out—to avoid even a speck of dust she covered herself in a dust coat, veils, and brown paper cuffs[2]—she was chronically late. When she said her prayers a sheet was put down so that no part of her would touch the immaculately clean floor.[3]

Bamie was not quite four years older than Teedie, but because of her mother's disinclination to deal with anything so prosaic as running a house, Bamie had taken over very early on and somehow seemed always middle-aged. Although Bamie was only in her early twenties during Teedie's Harvard years, it was assumed that she was headed to spinsterhood—perhaps because Mittie needed tending to, perhaps because Bamie was homely, especially when in the company of her mother, who was considered one of the two most beautiful women in New York.[4] Mittie's complexion was described as "moonlight white"; Bamie's was unstylishly dark. Mittie's figure was delicate and her gait regal; Bamie's was short, thick through the shoulders, and her gait stooping and hunched. (It was said in the family that she had been dropped on her back as a baby. More likely she had Pott's disease, tuberculosis of the spine.) Yet men and women flocked to Bamie to drink in her charm and intelligence.

Corinne was a spirited, fun-loving, highly sentimental girl, two years younger than Teedie. Under pressure from her family she would soon marry a steady, exceedingly wealthy Scotsman named

Alice's Parents

Douglas Robinson—he was part of a group that bought up all the land for Pennsylvania Station—but the only love of her life remained Teedie, especially when, during Teedie's sophomore year, their father, seemingly a perfect physical specimen, died from bowel cancer at age forty-six.

Theodore—he dropped Teedie after his father's death—was still reeling from the shock when, eight months later, in October 1878, the nineteen-year-old junior met and became fanatically smitten by seventeen-year-old Alice Hathaway Lee. She was tall for a woman of that era (five feet seven inches), willowy, athletically graceful, with blue-gray eyes, long, wavy golden hair, a slightly tilted nose, and a disposition described by friends as "radiant," "enchanting," and "high-spirited." Within her doting family—she was the second oldest of five girls and one boy—she was nicknamed "Sunshine."

All that and a pedigree that even the priggishly snobbish Harvard man—"I stand 19th in the class . . .," Teedie had written home, "only one gentleman stands ahead of me"[5]—pronounced to be perfect. Alice had cousins in the very best of Boston families, including the Cabots and Saltonstalls. Her father, George Cabot Lee, was a partner in Lee, Higginson & Co., the Boston banking and investment firm—as prominent in Boston as J. P. Morgan was in New York or Drexel in Philadelphia.

Theodore met Alice while on a weekend visit to the Chestnut Hill home of his classmate Dick Saltonstall, who easily qualified as one of the "gentlemen sort" that Theodore was so careful to cultivate, having assured his female relatives that, because he knew so little of his classmates' "antecedents," he was going slow in making friends. With Dick*—the seventh generation of his family to attend Harvard[6]—Theodore knew he was on safe ground.

Dick and Alice were first cousins and next-door neighbors. The families occupied sprawling Victorian mansions on Essex Street enveloped by hay fields and orchards and joined by a path. Theodore felt immediately at home in these country homes, which likely reminded him of his own family's tribal gathering spot at Oyster Bay, on Long Island's North Shore.

They spent that first weekend walking and dancing in a group that

---

*Dick would grow up to become the father of Leverett, a future governor of Massachusetts and U.S. Senator.

included Dick and his sister Rose, who was as plain as Alice was pretty. After church on Sunday, Theodore managed to get "Miss Lee" alone for some "chestnutting." Three weeks later he was back, on the pretense of visiting the Saltonstalls. He played tennis and strolled with both girls, having realized that winning Alice meant also courting Rose. On Thanksgiving he returned, again a houseguest of the Saltonstalls. For the first time, Alice allowed him to call her by her given name. That was all the encouragement he needed. Upon returning to Harvard, he vowed in the pages of his diary to "woo and marry her."

Alice was not nearly so eager—perhaps partly because of the peculiar figure her suitor cut. He seemed all gleaming spectacles and teeth, perched on a spindly body. The legend that the sickly Teddy overcame his asthma by transforming his weakling body into broad-chested vigor is overblown. Yes, he worked out incessantly and adhered to a bruising schedule of running, rowing, riding, and boxing. And he was certainly much improved from what he had been at age twelve, when his father warned him that if he did not "make his body," he was on his way to career invalidism. Still, he looked like the kind of boy who was born to be bullied. One of his Harvard classmates remembered him as "thin-chested, spectacled, nervous and frail." The month before he met Alice, Theodore went to northern Maine on his first hunting trip. His guide, a burly outdoorsman named Bill Sewall, described Theodore as "a thin, pale youngster with bad eyes and a weak heart."[7]

Sewall might also have added a high-pitched voice, an irritating stammer as thoughts so outpaced words that the result was an unintelligible explosion, a laugh that, in his mother's words, was like a "sharp, ungreased squeak." The asthma attacks still came, as did attacks of what Theodore called cholera morbus (severe diarrhea). "Very embarrassing for a lover, isn't it?" TR confided to Corinne. "So unromantic, you know; suggestive of too much unripe fruit."[8]

But perhaps not so unromantic as the slight but persistent reek of arsenic that the young lover and naturalist had acquired from years of skinning and viscerating animal specimens. As a boy, Teedie had been the classic nearsighted, bookish, awkward scientist. Stories abound of his furry specimens leaping from food passed at the Roosevelt dinner table; of the cook threatening to quit on discovering that a woodchuck was the source of a "noxious odor" that "permeated the

Alice's Parents

entire house" and that the young master expected her to obey his order to boil it, "fur and all, for twenty-four hours"; of Teedie meeting his mother's friend on a streetcar and, upon absentmindedly lifting his hat, presenting the venerable Mrs. Hamilton Fish with the spectacle of several frogs leaping "gaily to the floor . . ."[9]

Arsenic odor aside, Theodore did care for his appearance. But, typically, he overdid it. Instead of admiring glances, his concern for his clothes and grooming—he parted his hair down the middle— brought barely stifled giggles.

Even before he met Alice Lee, he had begun to dress in a fashion that only he fancied "very swell." Edmund Morris, one of TR's latest and best biographers, wrote that "he agonized for days over his afternoon coat, 'being undecided whether to have it a frock or a cutaway'; and he whined that his washerwoman did not act squarely 'on the subject of white cravats.'" On meeting Alice Lee he adorned himself with cameo pins and fobbed watch chains and "coats rakishly cut away to show off the uncreased, cylindrical trousers of a man of fashion."[10]

To this girl, whom many besides Theodore described as irresistible, the unnervingly intense boy must have seemed far from the ideal suitor, not to mention lifetime mate. A classmate's fiancé described him as "studious, ambitious, eccentric—not the sort to appeal at first." She also told TR's adoring biographer Hermann Hagedorn that "most of his classmates simply did not like him."[11]

Theodore knew that although Alice had no trouble resisting him, she would be unable to resist the charms of his mother and especially of his sisters. In May 1879 Corinne and Bamie came to Cambridge to meet the Saltonstalls and Lees. These sisters who so adored Theodore—Corinne called him "truly the spirit of my father reincarnate"[12] and Bamie noted that "Theodore is the only person who had the power except Father . . . of making me almost worship him"— would do what needed to be done to bring Alice Lee to her knees.[13]

A month later Theodore proposed marriage to the girl, who was not yet eighteen and so not yet officially "out." That Theodore was unhappy with her answer is obvious from his diary. He followed a lifelong pattern of excising from his mind and his writing news that was unhappy or humiliating. He had apparently recorded her answer in his diary that evening but later carefully removed the offending page.

Although Alice had rejected him, she softened it with encouragement to revive his suit the next autumn. Alice Lee had fallen in love with Bamie and Corinne—the latter would become her best friend—but it would take her longer to fall in love with their brother.

He spent most of the summer at his family's country home at Oyster Bay, misnamed Tranquillity, and then, in late August, set out on a hunting trip to Maine. On the way he stopped at Chestnut Hill and found Alice "so bewitchingly pretty"—and receptive—that he could leave her for the wilds "only by heroic self-denial." [14]

Thus further encouraged, he returned to Harvard to complete the conquest. He needed to make the grand gesture, to add flamboyance to his diligence, to overwhelm her with the magnificent style that he fancied he was about to acquire by equipping his horse Lightfoot with a dogcart. He was jubilant on the late September day he called on Alice. If passersby stared with amusement, he assumed that they were admiring his style. "I really think that I have as swell a turnout as any man," he confided to his diary. [15] That was a boast difficult to substantiate because Theodore's dogcart was the first ever seen at Harvard.

One classmate was not impressed. Of Theodore's "turnout" he commented, "not . . . very stylish. . . . in a horse show where the judges were passing upon fine points of equipment and technique, I fear Roosevelt would have been given the gate." [16]

And that, essentially, is what Alice did when the dandified undergraduate pulled up to her house. The words that passed between them went unrecorded, but the fact that Alice's name did not appear in his diary from that day until late November is proof that she easily withstood the dogcart's allure. [17]

With Thanksgiving 1879—the first anniversary of his vow to win Alice—fast approaching, Theodore decided to reenlist the charms of his female relatives. The fact that Alice would be officially launched into society in a matter of weeks, fair game for the inevitable swarm of suitors, filled Theodore with dread. He believed that if he failed to catch her now, she would remain forever beyond his grasp.

Mittie invited Alice, her parents, and Rose to visit in New York on November 2. Two weeks later, Bamie and Corinne visited Chestnut Hill. The Saltonstalls and the Lees gave dinner parties in their honor but *the* event was a luncheon for thirty-four that Theodore hosted at the Porcellian ("Porc" was the most prestigious of Harvard's clubs, which TR had been asked to join shortly before meeting Alice and to which Dick Saltonstall also belonged). Lees, Roosevelts, and Saltonstalls all attended, along with "gentlemen" from Teddy's class.[18]

"Everything went off to perfection"; Theodore wrote of the luncheon, "the dinner was capital, the wine was good, and the fellows all gentlemen." But when he went to Chestnut Hill he found Alice flirtatious, but teasing and ambivalent to his pleas.[19]

At her debut the week after Thanksgiving, Alice treated Theodore as just another of the eligible men who, in the words of a Lee cousin, circled about Alice "as moths to a flame." In fact, he was at something of a disadvantage for, as Alice's older sister observed, Theodore danced "just as you'd expect him to dance if you knew him—he hopped."[20]

In despair, he decided that he had better follow Alice's example and resume his attentions to other girls. On Christmas Eve he called on "at least ten 'very pretty girls,'" among them Edith Carow,[21] an old family friend who had grown up with the Roosevelt children. Edith was Alice Lee's opposite in nearly every way. She was by nature serious, while Alice Lee was gay; a loner, while Alice was gregarious; studious and literary, while Alice was bright and quick but hardly rigorous in her study or refined in her tastes. Moreover, Edith was steady rather than flirtatious and apparently deeply in love with the young man who had been her childhood sweetheart.

Edith and Teedie had had an "understanding" before he left for Harvard, an understanding that was shattered by a bitter argument several months before he met Alice. That Christmas Eve, when Alice seemed to be sliding out of his reach, Theodore wrote of Edith, "She is the most cultivated, best-read girl I know."[22] Those were not the words of a lover, certainly no match for words he would soon write about Alice Lee: "When we are alone, I can hardly stay a moment without holding her in my arms or kissing her; she is such a laughing, pretty little witch."[23]

Then began Theodore's wanderings in the dark. Night after sleepless night he roamed the woods near Cambridge. Finally a classmate telegraphed his family. His cousin, a medical student living nearby, was dispatched to see what could be done. Pages are ripped from Theodore's diaries, scribbles are obliterated by ink blotches. Looking back at this period, he confessed, "I did not think I could win her and I went nearly crazy at the mere thought of losing her."[24]

He never lost hope or his characteristic determination. "See that girl," Theodore said to a friend at a party, "I am going to marry her. She won't have me, but I am going to have *her*." [25]

Still, the Christmas holidays were looking bleak when, unexpectedly, Alice, accompanied by Dick and Rose Saltonstall and Alice's older sister Rosy, arrived in New York. On the day after Christmas, Alice's name reappeared in Theodore's diary, accompanied by the exclamation that they were having "an uproariously jolly time" and that he had been squiring her around town—to the theater, to dinner parties, to a New Year's Day lunch and dance at Jerome Park hosted by Elliott. [26]

Back in Cambridge, Alice remained receptive. The warmth of the Roosevelt women had worked wonders. Alice recognized the extraordinary bond that tied Theodore, prematurely the head of his family, to his sisters and mother. For Alice, herself from a happy and affectionate family, the Roosevelt clan was comforting, like her own, but more exciting. There was a sense of worldliness about the Roosevelts—whose children had already taken two grand tours—that was missing from her own parochial upbringing.

Alice's father, who was born in Boston in 1830, graduated from Harvard in 1850, and died in Boston on his eightieth birthday, was as neat and narrow as his lifespan suggests. He seemed never to have doubted that Boston was the hub of the universe. He was the very model of rectitude, prudence, and stability. Besides being a principal of Lee, Higginson, he was an officer of the Union Safe Deposit Vaults, burrowed in the ground beneath Lee, Higginson's State Street headquarters. The name Lee had become so nearly synonymous with reliability that money invested securely was said to be as "safe as Lee's vaults." He was on the early train for Boston every morning and on the train home every evening, the *Boston Evening Transcript** under his arm, his straw boater atop his closely cropped white hair.

Alice's mother, Caroline Russell Hathaway, came from two of Boston's first families. She was small, resolutely proper, always dressed in black (as opposed to Mittie's white, which she wore even while in mourning for her husband), and always with a slightly worried expression.

---

*The *Transcript* was the society paper, known for publishing in every Wednesday's edition the "most complete genealogy column in existence." [27]

Alice's Parents

The day before his semi-annual examinations, in January 1880, Theodore made his second proposal of marriage. What he would have done had she again rejected him is open to speculation. After his falling out with Edith Carow, he had shot and killed a neighbor's dog that was "bothering" him when he was out for a ride.

His diary is full of news of his triumph: "At last everything is settled . . . after much pleading my own sweet, pretty darling consented to be my wife. Oh, how bewitchingly pretty she looked! If loving her with my whole heart and soul can make her happy, she shall be happy . . . the aim of my whole life shall be . . . to shield her and guard her from every trial."[28]

By February 2 he had bought her a diamond ring. On Valentine's Day, a date that would prove to be pivotal in this young woman's life, her father made the official announcement of the engagement. Theodore gushed to his diary, "I do not think ever a man loved a woman more than I love her; for a year and a quarter now I have *never* (even when hunting) gone to sleep or waked up without thinking of her . . . And now I can scarcely realize that I can hold her in my arms and kiss her and caress her and love her as much as I choose."[29]

Theodore's happiness had a manic edge. Every time he recalled his ordeal he felt a pang of terror. To his cousin he confided, "The little witch led me on a dance before she surrendered, I can tell you, and the last six months have been perfect agony. . . . Even now, it makes me shudder to think of some of the nights I have passed."[30]

"I am so happy that I dare not trust in my own happiness," he wrote. He dared not trust her either. According to one of Alice's cousins, "Roosevelt seemed constantly afraid that someone would run off with her, and threaten duels and everything else. On one occasion he actually sent abroad for a set of French duelling pistols."[31]

Eventually he calmed down to address the problem of persuading Alice's parents to set the wedding date for Theodore's twenty-second birthday, October 27, 1880—an unconventionally short engagement. Actually, Bamie addressed the problem by reassuring the Lees that, during the newlyweds' first winter in New York, they could live with her and Mittie. "I don't think Mr. Lee would have consented to our marriage so soon on other terms," Theodore wrote. "I think Bamie's words had a good deal of weight with Mrs. Lee."[32]

If Theodore had any doubts about Alice's love, they were dispelled by the letters she wrote him from Chestnut Hill (he was in New York, having just enrolled at Columbia Law School): "How I wish it was three weeks from today our wedding day. . . . I just long to be with you all the time. . . . I know you can make me happy and you must never think it would have been better for me, if we had never met, I should die without you. . . ." Four days later she wrote him that she "long[s]" for their wedding and that she will be "the happiest girl that you ever saw." Six days later she beseeched him to "never think that I have the slightest fear of giving myself to you. . . ."[33]

The ceremony was at noon at the Unitarian Church in Brookline, on a perfect New England Indian summer day. "It was the dearest little wedding," wrote a friend. "Alice looked perfectly lovely and Theodore *so* happy and responded in the most determined Theodore-like tones."[34] The reception was held in the Lees' home, which was brimming with music, food, champagne, optimism for the future of the privileged young couple, and good feeling among in-laws. The bride was beautiful, the groom ecstatic.

They spent their wedding night in Springfield, Massachusetts. Theodore's diary contains no details, but for reasons of delicacy rather than dissatisfaction. "Our intense happiness is too sacred to be written about," is all that this proper Victorian gentleman revealed.[35]

The next day they arrived in Oyster Bay for a two-week honeymoon at Tranquillity. As usual, Bamie arranged everything, making sure that the pantry was stocked and that they were greeted by the maid Mary Ann, the cook Kate, and the groom Davis. "There is hardly an hour of the twenty-four that we are not together," Theodore noted. "I am living in a dream land; how I wish it could last forever."[36]

Theodore, who throughout his life would place domestic bliss above any other, reveled in his new role as lord of the manor. (It was during this honeymoon that Theodore decided to become lord of his own manor, choosing, with Alice, the Oyster Bay site for the house that would become known as Sagamore Hill.) Theodore described Alice presiding over the tea kettle "in the daintiest little pink and gray morning dress, while I, in my silk jacket and slippers, sit at the other end of the table."[37] Breakfast was always at ten, dinner at two (often woodcock and partridge), and tea at seven. The hours between were filled with tennis, at which Alice was more than his match, hikes, and buggy rides. They eagerly read the newspapers and in the evening lounged in front of a fire while Theodore read aloud from the novels of Scott and Dickens and the poetry of Keats.

Alice's Parents

On the following Tuesday, November 2, Davis drove his young master to East Norwich, where he cast his first vote in a presidential election, for Republican James Garfield.

On Saturday, November 13, the newlyweds arrived at Mittie's house. For the next two years they lived in private quarters on the third floor, sharing their meals and their lives with Theodore's family.

Was the couple, she finishing her teens and he barely out, happy with one another and with this unconventional living arrangement? According to Theodore's diary—very. "I can never express how I love her," he wrote after their first New Year's together.[38]

If there were any strains, he mentioned them only obliquely. His "teasing, laughing, pretty witch" would "jog" his arm while he was writing, making him feel "rather bad tempered."[39] Soon after his marriage, Theodore, just out of Harvard, had the first of many career crises. Into his college years, Theodore wanted to be a naturalist; a career choice that TR Sr. had endorsed, offering to help him financially, but warning that on a professor's salary, even with infusions of family money, he would have to live modestly. Theodore Senior's death left his son rudderless, but still listing toward this hoped-for career. In July 1877, TR Jr., then at Harvard, published *Birds of the Adirondacks*, a scientific catalogue. Fifteen months later he met Alice Lee, who apparently was not eager to be the wife of an academic or to join Theodore in the three years of academic study abroad that were required for a degree.

At Harvard he had begun to take a mild interest in politics and he enrolled in law school to prepare for public life. In fact, the newlyweds had postponed their "proper" European honeymoon until May so that he would not miss classes. (Between May and October they toured England, Paris, Venice, the Alps, and the Low Countries.)

In addition to his legal studies, Theodore was working on what would become the second of his thirty-nine books, the history of the naval war of 1812. These were his daytime projects. At night, during the season, the young Theodore Roosevelts were an active, almost hyperactive, society couple. Nearly all evenings were filled with dinners, receptions, operas, concerts, theater parties, spectacular balls—including those given by Mrs. William B. Astor, who, with Ward McAllister, ruled "the Four Hundred." The week of January 10, 1881, was typical: On the eleventh there was "dinner at Delanos," at which Theodore sat beside Mrs. Astor. The following night was a theater party and supper; the night after that, a "great ball at the Astors'." On Friday the fourteenth, Theodore, Alice, and thirteen friends took off in a private railroad car for a weekend at Niagara Falls, which Theodore described in his diary as a "perpetual spree."[40]

At the same time, Theodore suffered a nagging restlessness. While he lounged at the head of a female-dominated table, his brother, Elliott, was off in India, on the adventure of a lifetime, hunting elephants and tigers. Each time Mittie read aloud from one of Elliott's letters, Theodore paced. Alice feared that her husband would grab his gun and flee the parlor. When she expressed that fear, he smothered her with kisses. Still, Elliott's letters continued to both enchant and dispirit Theodore and led to recurrences of what he called his "caged wolf" feeling.

When Elliott returned home in March 1882, he moved into a small room off Mittie's, where she fussed over him and checked him at night to be sure he was covered. When he came home from parties late or, as he was increasingly apt to do, not at all, he found that she had left him little notes: "My darling son, I have missed you *all* evening. Sleep well, darling, and call Mother if you wish her."[41]

Alice was content to leave Teddy to his daytime intellectual pursuits while she took lessons at Drina Potter's Tennis School, went to Bible class and sewing circle, held Tuesday afternoon teas, and went shopping with Corinne and on drives with Mittie. On occasion, Alice became exasperated with her husband, when his absorption in his work threatened that evening's social engagement. Owen Wister described Theodore, alone in the library, making sketches for his book, when Alice burst in: "We're dining out in twenty minutes, and Teedy's drawing little ships!"[42]

On the other hand, Theodore's four years of marriage to Alice Lee were hardly intellectually or politically dry. He continued to work on *The Naval War of 1812* during that first social season and on their European honeymoon. When it was published in 1882 it was widely praised, adopted as a textbook by several colleges, and put on board every U.S. Navy vessel. Even today it is considered the definitive work on the subject.[43]

While Theodore would later say that he realized that New York's social whirl, with its Patriarchs' Ball and Family Circle Dancing Class and dinners at Delmonico's that lasted until 3 A.M., "led nowhere," and that he and Alice were an "irresponsible couple,"[44] there is no reason to believe that he didn't enjoy that season as much as she did.

Alice's Parents

In fact, before his engagement to Alice Lee, he described, in a letter to his mother, a typical day: "I get up pretty late and breakfast in the club; at about eleven my horse is before the door and I ride off to Chestnut Hill, Milton . . . and I take lunch there and often dinner and if I get back to Harvard sufficiently early there is sure to be some spree going on; either in the Porc, Pudding, or 'Dickey.'" His engagement calendar was filled with dinners at the Lowells', the Wheelwrights', the Whitneys'. "Mr. Whitney is President of a railroad," he informed his mother, "and he has invited a small party of fellows and girls to go down in a special car to see the boat race at New London."[45]

Once he decided that the law was not for him, nor was his father's type of quiet philanthropy—he had taken TR Sr.'s place on many charity borads—and that social life could never constitute a career, he dropped in at the headquarters of the Twenty-first Assembly District Republican Club, and signed on as a member. Not quite three weeks after his return from his European honeymoon, he was nominated as the district's Republican candidate for the state assembly.

Although the Twenty-first was called the "brownstone" or "silk stocking" district, that referred to its residents, not its representatives. Theodore was as out of place in these smoky rooms as a "Porc" man at a Rotary meeting, but he was no iconoclast. Many others of his class had served in politics, including his own Uncle Robert Barnwell Roosevelt,* who had served in Congress as a Tammany Hall–backed Democrat. Still, Theodore's decision surprised many of his friends. As his sister Corinne recalled, "'politics' was considered as something far removed from the life of any one brought up to other spheres than that of mudslinging and corruption."[46] Theodore considered those words much too mild to describe the new company he was keeping. He judged a third of the members of the Assembly to be crooked and half of the Democrats to be "vicious, stupid-looking scoundrels."[47]

---

*Robert, TR Sr.'s youngest brother and next-door neighbor, later broke with Tammany's Boss Tweed and led the assault against him. Robert was a genuine bohemian (he was fond of showgirls), and had his nephew Theodore, who believed in sexual purity before and after marriage for both men and women, known that Uncle Rob was a bigamist, he would have been horrified. Rob kept an entire second family living a block away from his first.[48] He was also a lawyer (he encouraged Theodore to enroll at Columbia), a crusader for clean government and for jobs for the poor. In their love of the limelight, sportsmanship, and the outdoors, TR resembled his uncle more than he did his own father.

These were certainly not types that would appeal to Alice Lee. Yet she apparently never tried to discourage Theodore from taking this unconventional path. This despite the fact that when, on November 8, 1881, he bested Dr. W. W. Shrew, formerly director of Blackwell's Island Lunatic Asylum, it meant that the young couple, the toast of Manhattan last season, would spend the next season in the dull Dutch burg of Albany, 145 miles from Manhattan.

The new assemblyman went alone to Albany on January 2, 1882. Two weeks later Alice joined him, and together they chose rooms at a residential hotel across the square from the Capitol.[49] TR considered his wife a great asset and regularly invited his colleagues home to meet her. "All of the men were perfectly enchanted with their visit to our house . . . they praised my sweet little wife."[50] Isaac Hunt, one of TR's closest legislative colleagues, recalled that Alice "was a very charming woman . . . I was very much taken with her." This unaffected girl made Theodore—with his gold-rimmed spectacles dangling from a black ribbon, cutaway coat with the ends of its tails almost reaching the tops of his shoes, gold-headed cane in one hand and silk hat in the other—seem slightly more human.[51]

Theodore's first term was a spectacular success. Although after his victory he had assured a friend, "Don't think I am going to go into politics after this year, for I am not," it was obvious that he had found his milieu.[52] He easily won reelection, despite a Democratic landslide on the state ticket, led by the reform candidate for governor, Grover Cleveland.

When the new session opened on New Year's Day, 1883, Theodore—at twenty-four the Assembly's youngest member—was nominated for Speaker. His chances of winning, he knew, were nil, because the Democrats controlled the chamber. As expected, the vote broke along party lines and Theodore was soundly defeated. But he now boasted the important title of minority leader, and reporters began to write of the Cleveland Democrats and Roosevelt Republicans, and Cleveland began calling the man who just a year ago was widely known as "that damn dude" or "Oscar Wilde" or "Jane-Dandy" to his office to confer on legislation. (On TR's debut in the House, the Speaker had characterized Republican strength as "sixty and one-half members.")[53]

That year Alice did not return with her husband to Albany. It is unclear why, although it was typical for assemblymen to leave their families home in the district. TR would not have much time for his "pretty pink baby," * as he had not only the minority leader's post but also four demanding committee assignments. Alice, who after more than two years of marriage still had no baby to fill her time, was undoubtedly bored in Albany, where other members' wives (and girlfriends) would have been unsuitable companions. Also, Alice was now mistress of her own Manhattan townhouse. A month before TR's reelection, the couple moved out of Mittie's into a house on Forty-fifth Street, next door to Corinne and her husband, Douglas.

Theodore would arrive home every Friday afternoon to Alice's whoops of excitement and leave the following Monday. In his diary, he recorded his pleasure in these domestic interludes: "Back again in my own lovely little house with the sweetest and prettiest of all little wives—my own sunny darling. I can imagine nothing more happy in life than an evening spent in my own cozy little sitting room, before a bright fire of soft coals, my books all around me, and playing backgammon with my own dainty mistress." [55]

That first year away from Alice Lee was not nearly so successful as his maiden term. He flipflopped on the five-cent streetcar fare, first supporting and later opposing its reduction from ten cents. He supported the return to public squares of the whipping post (for males only). He grew more intemperate in his denunciations, blasting the Democrats as the party of "Sodom and Gomorrah" and Jay Gould and anyone like him as "part of that most dangerous of all dangerous classes, the wealthy criminal classes." [56] Worse yet, one reporter described him as a "'silly and sullen and naughty' young man who brought 'discredit upon a name made honorable by . . . his father.'" [57]

After the legislature adjourned in May 1883, Alice finally became pregnant. Apparently, Alice's doctor had figured out that before his patient could conceive she needed minor surgery.

If Alice's physical condition was now what she wanted it to be—she wrote Bamie immediately after the doctor's confirmation of pregnancy that the news seemed "too good to be true" [58]—Theodore's was not. He suffered a return of asthma and, perhaps as a result of the excite-

---

* Theodore regularly referred to Alice as "Baby" and, in letters to Theodore, Alice often referred to herself in the third person as in: "your baby wife longs for you so much." Theodore later explained, "She was so young and innocent that I used often to call her my 'baby wife,' but she added to her pretty innocence the sweetness and strength of a true woman." [54]

ment of prospective fatherhood, another bout with cholera morbus, this time including vomiting and cramps. He needed to get in shape for his fight the next fall for a third term in the Assembly, to be followed by his planned second try for the speakership. If the Republicans gained control that November—and there was a good chance they would—Theodore, as minority leader the year before, was the likely choice for Speaker.

Thus he set off on a hunting trip to the Badlands of the Dakotas. On September 3, 1883, he left Alice, nearly four months pregnant, for his 2400-mile journey in search of buffalo. "Sweetest little wife," he wrote her, "I think all the time of my laughing, teazing [sic] beauty, and how pretty she is, and how she goes to sleep in my arms, and I could almost cry I love you so. But I think the hunting will do me good. And I am very anxious to kill some large game." [59]

Alice was back in her old quarters on the third floor of Mittie's house. She and Theodore had let their Forty-fifth Street house to Elliott and his new bride, the beautiful but vacuous Anna Hall. Theodore knew he would be gone more than he would be at home and wanted Alice surrounded by women she loved, including Corinne. After her first baby was born the previous April, she had moved back into Mittie's house so that the new mothers and their babies could be close.

On his return from the Badlands, Theodore plunged immediately into his race for a third term, which he easily won, and into the race for the Speakership, which he lost. (He lost when the Republican boss of New York City, with business behind him, threw his support to a more dependable machine mouthpiece, Titus Sheard, an underwear manufacturer.) TR did, however, get appointed chairman of the powerful Committee on Cities, and held hearings on municipal corruption. He also sponsored what came to be known as the "Roosevelt bill"—a far-reaching reform measure that would give more power to the mayor and less to the aldermen, who, in TR's opinion, were "merely the creatures of the local ward bosses or of the municipal bosses." [60]

Mittie had remarked on how "very large" Alice looked. But Theodore, in the press of work, apparently missed signs—a puffy look around her eyes, seriously swollen ankles—that things were not perfect in this pregnancy. A week before the baby was due he came home from Albany, where he was busy pushing through his anticorruption bills. When he returned to Albany—a five-hour train trip from Manhattan—he wrote her, "How I did hate to leave my bright, sunny little love yesterday afternoon! I love you and long for you all the time, and oh *so* tenderly: doubly tenderly now, my sweetest little wife." In the last letter Alice ever wrote him, she warned, "I am feeling well tonight but am very much worried over . . . your little mother, her fever is still very high and the Dr is rather afraid of typhoid . . . I wish I could have my little new baby soon."[61]

Theodore—who would later leave a seriously ill second wife to go off, as a volunteer, to fight the Spanish in Cuba—kept his nose to his anticorruption grindstone. On Monday, February 11, he was in New York holding hearings. Always sensitive to the significance of particular dates, he had decided that his baby would be born on Thursday, St. Valentine's Day, the fourth anniversary of the announcement of his and Alice's engagement. So certain was he that on Tuesday the twelfth he left Alice to dash up to Albany for a quick check on the "Roosevelt bill."

Soon after his departure Alice Lee went into labor and at eight-thirty that night gave birth to a healthy eight-and-three-quarter-pound girl.[62] The next morning, TR was so informed by a telegram from Bamie delivered to him on the Assembly floor. The new mother was "only fairly well" but that didn't seem to worry Theodore.[63] He had undoubtedly wished for a son, but the brood of children he planned to have by Alice Lee—that summer he had completed purchase of 155 acres in Oyster Bay, on which a twelve-bedroom house was to be built—would surely include plenty of sons.* In the meantime, he was ecstatic. If the baby couldn't be born on Valentine's Day, then she chose a day of even greater significance—the birthday of his hero, Abraham Lincoln. (It was also the sixth anniversary of the burial of Theodore's father.)

He requested a leave of absence to begin that afternoon. First he had to report fourteen bills out of his Cities Committee. As he was finishing, a second telegram arrived that turned his face ashen and sent him dashing to catch the train to New York.

---

*Mittie's sister Anna left an account of the birth: Alice "said when I took her [the baby] from the Dr, 'I *love* a little girl,' because I said to the baby you ought to have been a little boy."[64]

2

The Death of Alice Lee

The train ride from Albany to New York City was a hellish ordeal for twenty-four-year-old Theodore Roosevelt. With New York City shrouded in a traffic-snarling fog—proclaimed "suicide weather" by *The New York Times*—the trip took many more than the usual five hours.[1]

He must have been plagued by recriminations for having left Alice at a time when anyone could see that she was about to have her baby, and when the comfortable routine at Fifty-seventh Street had become so disrupted. Mittie was lying two floors below Alice with what had been diagnosed as a cold but was in fact typhoid. Corinne had gone off with her husband the Friday before for a long weekend in Baltimore, leaving their infant son in Bamie's care. Even the indefatigable Bamie must have been overwhelmed.

As Bamie rushed up the two flights from her mother's room to her sister-in-law's, she faced an immediate problem—finding a wet nurse for the hungry, squalling baby, who was already being called Alice.

Bamie had telegraphed Corinne and Douglas, who reached Fifty-seventh Street at 10:30 on that night of February 13, just about the time that Theodore's train pulled into Grand Central Station. As Corinne climbed the front steps, the door was thrown open to reveal Elliott, a look of terror on his handsome face. "There is a curse on this house! Mother is dying, and Alice is dying too."[2]

By the time Theodore had groped his way from the station to his mother's house, it was nearly midnight, the appropriate hour to arrive at such a macabre scene. The only good news—although Theodore seemed oblivious to the baby and its welfare—was that their baby was healthy and had been taken to Mittie's sister Annie's, where the wet nurse would soon arrive.

Theodore rushed to the third floor and took his wife, now attended by Corinne, in his arms. After hearing the infant sneeze, Alice had pleaded with the doctor, "Don't let my baby take cold," and urged him to attend to the baby before he attended to her.[3] She then fell into what the doctor mistakenly believed was a deep sleep. By the time Theodore arrived, she was already semicomatose and gave no sign of recognition. He held her for two hours, until a message arrived from Mittie's bedroom—the same room in which TR Sr. had died on another February night—that if Theodore wished to see his mother alive he should come down at once. Forty-nine-year-old Mittie, still beautiful, with not a single strand of gray in her ebony hair, died an hour later. The obsessively clean woman had died from ingestion of contaminated food or water.

Theodore returned to Alice, who lingered, unconscious in her bewildered husband's arms, for another eleven hours. She died at 2:00 P.M. on Thursday, February 14—the day that Theodore, in the smugness of inexperience and precocious success, had been so sure would be a day of birth. He drew a large cross in his diary and beneath it wrote, "The light has gone out of my life."[4]

Not only was this Valentine's Day to have been the birthday of his first child, but scheduled for that evening was a public recognition of his brilliance as a legislator. His "Roosevelt bill" was on its way to passage. To help push it through the Assembly a mass meeting of citizens had been called at New York's Cooper Union. Thousands of supporters showed up, among them U.S. Grant, Elihu Root, Professor T. W. Dwight (the founder of Columbia Law School), and Robert Roosevelt, who knew but said nothing of the tragedy that had befallen the young man who was by then so popular that the mere mention of his name brought cheers.

On Saturday, two horse-drawn hearses stopped in front of 6 West Fifty-seventh Street to pick up two rosewood coffins. They were driven the few blocks to the Fifth Avenue Presbyterian Church for a heartbreaking double funeral. Theodore, his face white and expressionless, sat in the front pew with Bamie, Corinne, Elliott, and Alice's father to hear the weeping minister pray for the two women and the four-day-old baby. He prayed also that Theodore would find strength to overcome his double tragedy.

Among the gathering of more than two thousand sobbing mourners were Astors and Vanderbilts, but also Theodore's cronies from Albany, including the former underwear manufacturer and current Speaker, Titus Sheard.

A friend of Theodore's described him as being "in a dazed, stunned state. He does not know what he does or says." When offered words of sympathy, he stared blankly. At home, the family could hear him pacing, alone in his room.[5] His new baby might as well have belonged to one of the maids for all the attention he paid her.

Some of Alice's friends and relatives later complained that the Roosevelt family doctor had been criminally negligent in failing to diagnose Bright's disease, the inflammation of the kidneys that was said to have killed her.* Theodore had no interest in pursuing the complaints. His goal was to shove Alice from his heart, which meant also shoving her from his mind. Seeking redress from the doctor or becoming obsessed about how this tragedy might have been prevented would not help him reach that goal. Filling every waking hour with his legislative work would.

When news of the tragedy reached Albany, Theodore's colleagues responded in an unprecedented manner. After seven teary eulogies—one by a Democrat who declared, "Never in my many years here have I stood in the presence of such a sorrow as this"—the assemblymen unanimously voted for adjournment.[7] They must have been surprised to see Theodore enter the Assembly chamber first thing Monday, just two days after he buried his wife and mother.

He got down to abnormally hard work immediately, bounding into his agenda exactly where he left off, arguing for the "Roosevelt bill" and pursuing his investigation of corruption, which required shuttling between Albany and New York City by night train. Six days a week, he kept the bills pouring out of his Cities Committee, he gave speeches, wrote reports, grilled witnesses, conducted inspection

---

*Bright's disease is an outmoded term for kidney disease in general, covering at least a dozen disorders. At the time of Alice's death, Bright's disease was almost always fatal. Chester Arthur, then President, was suffering from it. When the word leaked out, he was considered as good as dead and, for that reason, among others, was not seriously considered for the 1884 Republican nomination. He would die of the disease twenty-one months after leaving office. Ellen Wilson, Woodrow's first wife, died of Bright's disease (and tuberculosis of the kidneys) while her husband was in office. Northwestern University nephrologist Salim Mujais theorizes that Alice Roosevelt did not have Bright's disease but rather died from toxemia of pregnancy or preeclampsia.[6]

tours. "I have taken up my work again: indeed, I think I should go mad if I were not employed," he wrote a friend.

Many nights the only sleep he got was on the train. "There is nothing left for me except to try to so live as not to dishonor the memory of those I loved who have gone before me," he explained.[8]

Refusing a nomination for a fourth term, he faced only one more wearisome hurdle—he had been elected as a delegate-at-large to the 1884 Republican National Convention in Chicago—before he could flee to the Badlands, where few knew him or his grief. During the next two years, except for frequent trips back East for a dose of civility and sisters, the Dakotas would be his home. He claimed to have thrown over politics for ranching and invested and lost most of his fortune in the process. But he also found a measure of peace— thirteen-hour days in the saddle under the broiling sun, nights falling into an exhausted sleep. Baby Alice, or Baby Lee, as Theodore called her, was now living with Bamie at 422 Madison Avenue,* next door to Mr. and Mrs. Clarence Day, the rambunctious family immortalized in *Life with Father*.

Apparently, Theodore had decided that purging Alice Lee meant purging the blue-eyed, blond-haired baby she left behind. In his letters home from the Dakotas he asked not a single question about his daughter. At times he became very depressed and once assured Bill Sewall, the Maine outdoorsman whom TR had persuaded to join him out West, that he had nothing to live for. "You have your child to live for," Sewall told him. "Her aunt can take care of her a good deal better than I can," Theodore replied.[9]

On a visit to New York in October 1885, Theodore opened the front door of Bamie's house and nearly collided with his childhood sweetheart, Edith Carow, now twenty-four and striking in her un-mined sexuality. Her alcoholic father had died two years earlier, and she was now living nearby, in much reduced circumstances, with her mother and younger sister, Emily. (Besides being a drunk, Charles Carow was a business failure who was forced to rely on the charity of relatives to house and feed his family.) Supposedly, Theodore—who, in the Victorian fashion did not believe in second marriages—had

---

*Shortly after Mittie's death Bamie sold the Fifty-seventh Street house and bought the smaller but fashionably located Madison Avenue house. At Theodore's request, Bamie also sold the little house on Forty-fifth Street that he had shared with Alice Lee.

asked Bamie to warn him when Edith would be dropping in for tea. He was intent on avoiding temptation.

But marry Edith he must. He was young, in love again, and he wanted children. But he didn't want the child who was already born because her very presence screamed rebuke—proof that he was an immoral weakling not worthy of the name and memory of his perfect father. By Theodore's rigid standard, once a man consummated his love, he must remain forever faithful, even if only to a memory, in preparation for meeting the departed in heaven. It would have been as immoral for him to remarry as to have kept a mistress in Albany and then to have returned to his wife's bed after the session adjourned. Besides, every time Edith looked at the blond beauty who so resembled her rival, she would remember that she had been second choice.

On February 14, 1886, the second anniversary of Alice Lee's death, Theodore's diary contained a heart pierced by an arrow—an impassioned heart, not a wounded one. Three months earlier, Theodore had proposed marriage and Edith had accepted.[10]

That Edith had her heart set on Theodore from a very early age is likely. "She was one of those people who made up her mind early that Theodore was whom she wanted," said one relative. "She wanted him very, very much. She was passionately in love with him."[11]

Theodore did not tell his sisters that he and Edith were engaged, probably because he knew that they would not be pleased with the prospect of Edith as a sister-in-law. Bamie and Corinne had recognized that Alice, with her generous, gregarious nature, would be happy to share Theodore with them. (In her note of congratulations to the just-engaged Alice Lee, Corinne wrote, "There is hardly another girl in the world that I would resign him to, but I gladly do so to you, for I know and see that your influence over him is so sweet and lovely.")[12] In Edith, on the other hand, they recognized a possessive, private nature not given to sharing, especially sharing something so precious as the long-awaited Theodore.

Edith knew that the sibling relationship in the Roosevelt family was peculiarly intense and potentially consuming. While Alice Lee had come to the family a virtual stranger, Edith had a years-long relationship with the Roosevelt children that was sister-like in its intimacy. Edith could have predicted that neither Corinne nor Bamie, who would marry some years later, would marry for love because they would remain forever in love with their brother. Edith had witnessed the gushy, even by Victorian standards, verbal and physical exchanges—Mittie called them "melts"—between Teedie and his sisters. While at Harvard, Teedie wrote to fifteen-year-old Corinne, known in the family as "Pussie": "I want to pet you again awfully! You cunning, pretty, little, foolish Puss. My easy chair would just hold myself and Pussie." [13]

In late August 1886, with Theodore beyond civilization in the Badlands, a small item announcing his engagement to Edith Carow appeared in the society columns of *The New York Times*. A week later a retraction, probably placed by Bamie, appeared: "The announcement of the engagement of Mr. Theodore Roosevelt, made last week, and which came from a supposedly authoritative source, proves to have been erroneous. Nothing is more common in society than to hear positive assertions constantly made regarding the engagement of persons who have been at all in each other's company, and no practice is more reprehensible." [14]

In a letter from Theodore—then living at his ranch, the Elkhorn, at Medora, Dakota—to "Darling Bamie," dated September 20, 1886, he admitted that he was engaged. This letter was suppressed by the Roosevelt family for nearly a century, and for good reason. Theodore did more than apologize for having kept his engagement from his sisters. After telling Bamie that he "utterly" disapproved of second marriages, he offered to give her Alice: "As I have already told you, if you wish to you shall keep Baby Lee, I of course paying the expense."

Bamie adored her niece—and Alice returned the affection. In later years she said that Bamie was "the only one I really cared about when I was a child. . . . She was the single most important influence on my childhood." [15] Bamie, then thirty-three with no prospects of marriage, would have been happy to "keep" Alice, and Theodore figured the issue was closed.

Alice was not yet three when she had the first "hazy recollection" [16] of the man who would become such a towering and troubling part of her life. It was Theodore's birthday weekend and he was spending it at Sagamore Hill with his sisters and brother-in-law and the woman he would marry in London two months later.

That Saturday morning the Meadowbrook Hunt, a very tony fox-hunting club that counted among its most dashing members Theodore's brother, Elliott, met at Sagamore. Theodore donned the traditional pink coat and let loose with characteristic abandon, jumping "deadly dangerous" fences, six to the mile, five feet or more in height. He was out in front from the start, heedless of accidents that crushed one rider's ribs and sliced half the skin off his brother-in-law's face. At the five-mile mark TR's exhausted horse tripped over a wall, and horse and rider were thrown into a pile of stones. Theodore was left with a broken arm and a bloody mess of a face. [17]

Alice was waiting at the stable for this strange man who Auntie Bye said was her father. The moment his horse picked himself up, Theodore had resumed the hunt. When he finished, ahead of his rivals, his arm, its fractured bones grating together, dangled at his side "like a length of liverwurst" and his face spurted blood. He described himself, with his clothing hanging in bloody shreds, as looking "like the walls of a slaughterhouse." [18]

When he saw the curly-haired toddler, he jumped off his horse and ran toward her. She ran away, screaming in terror. "To his disgust," she recalled in her memoirs, "I refused to come near him and fled in fright, whereupon he pursued and caught me." [19] In a later account she put an uglier twist on the incident: "I started screaming at this apparition and he started shaking me to shut me up, which only made me scream more. So he shook more. It was a theme which was to be repeated, with variations, in later years." [20]

Theodore and Edith's honeymoon was plagued not only by the presence during part of it of Edith's cranky mother and sister; not only by the newlyweds' anxiety over Theodore's financial difficulties (about 65 percent of his cattle had died as a summer drought was followed by the worst winter in frontier history, resulting in a six-figure loss) [21]; but also by disagreement over what to do about Baby Lee.

That Christmas of 1886 was the first that Theodore had ever spent away from home, and Bamie saw what a difference Alice made. So eager was Bamie to raise Baby Lee that in a letter to Theodore she reminded him of his offer.

Bamie was shocked by her brother's response, which came in a letter from Rome: "I hardly know what to say about Baby Lee. Edith feels more strongly about her than I could have imagined possible.

However, we can decide it all when we meet." [22] In Edith's mind it was already decided.

Edith was determined to keep Alice. Some relatives attributed that determination to Edith's conscientiousness: "She would feel that it was totally wrong for her not to bring up her own husband's child," one explained. [23] Others attributed it to jealousy of her husband's closeness to his sister, who was not only his best friend but also his most trusted political adviser. As distasteful as Edith must have found the prospect of raising Alice Lee's daughter, she found the prospect of providing still another link between brother and sister even more distasteful.

"It almost broke my heart to give her up," Bamie recalled years later. [24] As Alice grew up under Theodore's and Edith's much-less-than-ideal care, she recalled her aunt telling her, "Remember, darling, if you are very unhappy you can always come back to me." Bamie, said Alice, "protected me from my father with his guilt fetish, and from my stepmother." [25]

When the newlyweds returned from their honeymoon in late March 1887, Alice, then three, was waiting on the stairs to meet her new mother. Wearing a dress trimmed in Valenciennes lace, curls "licked and prodded into place," carrying a large bunch of pink roses, she obediently descended into the hall for the greeting. [26]

Now that Edith had the child, she was not sure what to do with her. She and Theodore decided to leave Alice with Bamie for a month while Edith went to visit relatives and TR went to assess the damage to his ranching operation. They had planned to spend the summer at their recently completed house in Oyster Bay, its name changed from Leeholm to Sagamore Hill. Citing Edith's delicate condition—she was already pregnant—it was decided that after Theodore and Edith's return, the little girl should make the first of what would become semiannual visits to her Lee grandparents in Chestnut Hill.

Bamie asked Mrs. Lee to pick up Alice as soon as possible. Then, anticipating a painful farewell, Bamie took off on an extended tour of Civil War battlefields.

Not only was Alice deprived of her beloved Auntie Bye, she was also deliberately deprived of the memory of her dead mother. Theodore set the tone. After writing two valedictories to Alice Lee, he never spoke or wrote her name again. The first valedictory was a single paragraph, entered in his diary a couple of days after her funeral. It is full of dates—her birthday, the day he first saw her, the day they were engaged, the day their engagement was announced, and the day they married. "For joy or sorrow my life has now been lived out," it concluded.[27]

Theodore's final reference to Alice Lee came the next August. He compiled the newspaper clippings about her, the tributes, the words of the sermon preached at her funeral, and his own tribute, and sent it to Putnam's for printing and distribution to family and friends: "She was beautiful in face and form, and lovelier still in spirit; as a flower she grew, and as a fair young flower she died. Her life had always been in the sunshine; there had never come to her a single great sorrow; and none ever knew her who did not love and revere her for her bright, sunny temper and her saintly unselfishness. Fair, pure, and joyous as a maiden; loving, tender, and happy as a young wife, when she had just become a mother, when her life seemed to be but just begun, and when the years seemed so bright before her—then, by a strange and terrible fate, death came to her."[28]

With the exception of a couple of anguished descriptions of her death, blurted out under the Dakota moonlight, for Theodore Roosevelt Alice Lee might as well never have lived. In his posthumous *Autobiography,* he made not a single reference to his "bewitching little sunbeam." * Undoubtedly most readers thought that Edith was his first and only wife. What Alice Lee's daughter thought as she read it can only be imagined.

The silence surrounding Alice Lee destroyed the legacy that, in a more emotionally healthy family, would have been left to the daugh-

---

*Another deep humiliation omitted from his *Autobiography* was that his revered father had hired a substitute to fight for him in the Civil War. Had the purchaser of a substitute been anyone but TR Sr., TR Jr., who believed that fighting for one's country was a man's greatest duty and glory, would have considered it an act of unforgivable cowardice. The only way the son could reconcile idolization of his father with such ignobility was to pretend that his father never did such a thing and to himself perform battlefield daredeviltry that was so fearless as to be downright foolish. To anyone but a warmonger like the son, the father's reasons for avoiding service and the substitute service he took it upon himself to perform would have been perfectly sufficient. Worrying that soldiers were wasting their money on prostitutes, gambling, and drink, TR Sr. drafted and finessed through Congress a bill to establish an Allotment Commission that would collect money to be sent to the soldiers' families. President Lincoln appointed TR Sr. as one of New York's commissioners. His duties exposed him to more frontline fire than many soldiers ever saw.

ter. Gone were the memories that would have allowed the girl who would never know her mother to at least know about her. Alice was left with just a few of her mother's possessions—letters, photos, some jewelry; a collection of poetry that Alice had given Theodore on their wedding day; a lock of her mother's hair snipped by Theodore and given her not by her father but by Mittie's sister Anna.

Unfortunately for Alice Lee Roosevelt, the most lasting legacy was the persistent feeling that she was an outsider—different and less loved than the five children whom Edith would eventually bear. Eighty years later, Alice still recalled the hurt when Ted Jr., born of the honeymoon pregnancy, discovered that she had been suckled by a wet nurse and announced to all that "Sissy had a sweat nurse!"[29]

At the same time that Alice realized that she must never mention her mother's name, her nurse required the little girl to say a prayer for her "little mother in heaven." Only once did Edith ever acknowledge that Alice was getting very confusing signals. "Alice was much surprised," she wrote in an attempt at humor, "to learn that I was not Papa's sister."[30]

As an adult, Alice would blame her father, not her stepmother, for this perverse silence: "My father didn't want me to be a burden . . . a guilty burden . . . on my stepmother. He obviously felt guilty about it, otherwise he would have said at least once that I had another parent. The curious thing is that he never seemed to realize that I was perfectly aware of it and developing a resentment."[31]

The only person who regularly talked to the child about her mother was Auntie Bye, who, almost single-handedly, kept Alice's childhood from sinking into disaster.

3

Life with Father—and "Mother"

The first of many rules that Edith imposed on the undisciplined toddler was that Alice must call her "Mother." Alice complied, although her father's new wife seemed more like a stern governess than a mother. She could certainly not take Bamie's place.

Soon after marrying Alice Lee, Theodore had sold some of his Long Island acreage to Bamie. The plan was for her to build a house adjoining Theodore's, and so to create a lively family compound of the sort that all three had known as children. With Alice Lee's death and Theodore's flight to the Badlands, Bamie took charge of her brother's new house, bringing with her, along with Baby Lee, her inimitable style and love of people and conversation.

In later years, Alice recalled the "wonderful feeling of warmth and ease and hospitality when she [Bamie] was there, which was never quite the case with my stepmother." If Bamie, in Alice's words, "had a genius for making her surroundings agreeable," Edith, who was descended from Jonathan Edwards, the "Great Divine" of Puritan New England, had "almost a gift for making . . . people uncomfortable." [1]

From her earliest years, Alice thrived on large groups, loud talk, shouted opinions, and plenty of tasty food. Edith disliked overindulgence in eating, dancing, talking, or assorted other activities that to most people seemed rather wholesome. She liked quiet, refined conversation—about literature, not politics, which, like business, she thought best left at the office—and she preferred that the group be confined to her immediate family and perhaps one or two of Theodore's special friends, such as Englishman Cecil Spring-Rice or Bostonian Henry Cabot Lodge.

"Springy," as the former was called, had a special place in Edith's affections because he had been best man at her wedding and because he had an intellect so refined that he read Dante and Homer in the original Italian and Greek. While in Washington as secretary at the British Legation, Springy made frequent jaunts to Sagamore Hill. He was one of the few people who appealed to Edith and her step-daughter. Alice remembered him "bringing back handfuls of wild flowers from the park . . . which I used to stick in the cane-bottomed chairs in the nursery, trying to make a cushion of flowers, like something in a fairy tale."[2]

Although in both Lodge's and Alice Lee's veins ran the blue blood of the Cabots, Edith liked him anyway, for his impeccable education and taste. Lodge, who was elected to the House in 1886 and to the Senate in 1892, would do more to advance Theodore's political career than any other person, except Bamie. But of greater interest to Edith was his pure-bred intellect. Alice Longworth recalled years later that Lodge "scorned" Woodrow Wilson, a former president of Princeton University, because "he wasn't really an intellectual like the Boston intellectuals."[3]

Lodge was cold, remote, dry—the sound of his voice was compared to the tearing of a bedsheet—and full of patrician disdain. Edith was among the very few of whose bloodlines and education "Lah-de-dah Lodge," as he was called, approved.

With the exception of such rarefied types, Edith preferred her privacy, and that excluded Alice's beloved aunts. Bamie visited Sagamore Hill once in the summer after Theodore and Edith's marriage, and, although Theodore wrote his sister that he and Edith missed her terribly, no invitation to return was forthcoming. Plans for Bamie to build an adjoining house were no longer discussed.

Alice had no playmates, for Edith's penchant for privacy extended to children. Edith didn't step in to fill the gap. She meant to, but she simply couldn't summon the enthusiasm. "I am trying to make Alice more of a companion . . . ," Edith confided to Theodore. "Alice needs someone to laugh and romp with her instead of a sober and staid person like me."[4]

Edith might have added "sick" to her list of limitations. During the years of Alice's girlhood, whatever lightness remained in Edith's personality was wrung out by persistent childbearing (Ted Jr., born in 1887; Kermit, in 1889; Ethel, in 1891; Archie, in 1894; and Quentin, in 1897) and illness. Edith seemed something of an invalid with her neuralgia and headaches and need for quiet, dark rooms.

The only daily attention that Alice could count on from her step-mother was painful, although in later years much appreciated. While Theodore was ranching in the Dakotas and Alice was in Bamie's care, the two-year-old contracted what was later thought to be polio. It left her with one leg shorter than the other and, because the Achilles tendons in her heels were too short, with her feet sticking out at different angles. Every night before Alice went to bed, Edith would stretch each foot in what Alice recalled as "a steel contraption that . . . resembled a medieval instrument of torture."[5] Edith considered it her duty to do so and never missed a night. She also made sure that Alice wore the ugly, uncomfortable leg braces that the doctor had prescribed. (Not a hint that she had once been crippled remained in adulthood.)

In the months before the birth of Edith's first child, Theodore, who could not decide whether to be a writer, historian, or politician, paid his first gentle attentions to his daughter. He rode her piggyback down to breakfast. On rainy days, he built forts with blocks and, to the little girl's delight, filled them with his personal heroes—Davy Crockett, Daniel Boone, and the giants of the War of 1812.

As Edith approached confinement and her hypochondriacal mother wired that she was too ill to sail, Bamie should have been the natural choice to help. Not only could she comfort Edith, but a sensitive parent would have realized her importance to the toddler Alice, whose already tenuous place in the family was about to be usurped. But Edith decided to summon Mame, the old Irish nurse who cared for her when she was a child. Theodore was left to explain to Bamie, "Mame is devoted . . . to Edith; I do not think there is need of anyone else."[6]

Edith was equally tough on the subject of Corinne. In her opinion, she told Theodore, "we've seen quite enough of Corinne and Doug-las and I don't think we'll ask them down for a while."[7]

Alice never enjoyed the privileged position of being the family baby or center of attention. Ted Jr., born in September 1887, became the object of both parents' adoration—Edith's because he was her first born and Theodore's because he was his heir, his namesake, and everyone's unadulterated joy. (There would be no funeral four days after his birth.)

Alice too was entranced by the baby who "eats Mamma" and whom she pronounced "a howling polly parrot."[8] She pulled her rocking chair close to the baby's crib and announced that she planned to remain there forever. Instead, she was too soon shipped off to her Lee grandparents.

Although the timing of Alice's visits to Chestnut Hill was insensitive—just after acquiring a new mother and just after acquiring a new brother—she soon grew "deliriously happy" as the visits approached. (She spent six weeks a year with the Lees; three in the spring at Chestnut Hill, including Memorial Day, and three in the late fall, at their Beacon Street home in Boston's Back Bay, including Thanksgiving.) "I was treated there as *belonging*," she explained. She later prefaced her joy with the observation that her mother's parents were "perfectly well educated, but without any claims to culture." However, "at least they were *mine* and I didn't have to share them with my siblings."[9]

One glare from Edith was enough to let Alice know that certain behavior would not be tolerated, although soon the discipline, without the undergirding of love, prompted Alice to do the opposite of what Edith wanted. Not only were there no cold stares from her grandparents, but, on arriving, she would dash to the sofa and jump up and down, hoping the springs would break, while the Lees "would merely smile indulgently."[10] That, she admitted, was "something I should never have dreamed of doing at home."[11]

At the Lees', Alice could luxuriate in being the center of attention. All the turkey wishbones at Thanksgiving dinner were saved for her "and my aunts would make heads on them with red sealing wax and dress them like witches for my entertainment."[12] At Sagamore, where she ate many of her spartan meals alone in the nursery, she felt like, and, as Edith's children were born, was sometimes treated as, the least favored.

Not only was Alice given the biggest and sunniest room in the Beacon Street house, but she was also given rides in Grandma Lee's victoria to buy delicious white-frosted cakes. In one room stood a source of endless delight to the child—the dollhouse with its perfect miniature furniture that her mother and aunts had played with as children. When she was six, her Grandfather Lee gave her a dollhouse of her own with furniture that Alice, into her 90s, still enjoyed rearranging—often in the middle of the night. [13]

So inconsolable was Alice when she had to return to Sagamore that Edith complained to Bamie, "I do dread getting her upset from all her sweet little ways by that unavoidable visit." [14] Predictably, there were at least two evenings every year when Alice wept during her dreary supper, comparing the crustless brown bread that Edith served to Grandma Lee's crusty, buttery French rolls.

Although Edith might have served crustless brown bread in any case, the spartan atmosphere resulted partly from the fact that the Theodore Roosevelts had very little money—which came as a surprise to those who remembered Theodore during his Harvard days as a conspicuous consumer whose annual clothing expenditure exceeded some boys' total expenses for four years.

Certainly Theodore Sr. lived the life of a man of great wealth—his father was one of the founders of the Chemical Bank and, at his death, among the five richest men in New York—but his legacy to his four children would not allow them to follow suit. TR Sr. had devoted himself to philanthropy, while his older brother, James Alfred, devoted himself to the family business.* The latter's children would have no financial worries. Each of the former's was left an annual income of about $8000, which was certainly enough to live well at a time when a streetcar conductor earned about eighteen cents an hour, had Theodore Jr. not lost nearly half of his legacy on his ranching venture and put about half of what remained into building Sagamore.

There was a bitter twist to this saga of financial ineptitude, and its victim, Edith, who had to run a household that eventually included six children and several servants—no matter how scarce money became, it apparently never occurred to them to cut household help—on half of what Bamie had when she presided over Sagamore. Meanwhile, Alice got regular and big infusions of cash from her Lee grandparents. From this arrangement sprang another of those sad family

---

*Roosevelt lore has it that when Alexander Graham Bell came to Theodore Sr. seeking money to back his newly invented telephone—Bell hooked it up so that Theodore could talk from his desk to a room down the hall—Theodore pronounced it intriguing as a toy, but with no practical application. [15] Meanwhile, James Alfred consolidated control of the business, shifting his family's interests from the glass import trade to investment banking. Roosevelt and Son became a leading Wall Street investment banking house that, among other things, helped finance the transatlantic cable. [16]

jokes—"We'd better be nice to Alice," Theodore advised. "We might have to ask her for money." *

While Alice was donning expensive clothes—a dress from Stern's for $42, a coat for $45—Edith's children were wearing clothes that were relentlessly made over. While Grandma and Grandpa Lee were buying Alice a pony and a cart, Edith was struggling to reduce her butcher's bill from $165 to $110 a month and her grocer's from $95 to $75 and making her own tooth powder "from ground-up cuttlefish bones, dragon's blood, burnt alum, arris root, and aromatic ingredients." [18]

Naturally, Edith, who paid the bills, passed along her anxiety to Theodore, whom she kept on a strict allowance. "I enclose the Harvard Club bill," she wrote him. "Are your dues ten or twenty dollars? Could you resign?" [19] Edith put family finances above Theodore's climb up the political ladder, much to the irritation of Bamie and Henry Cabot Lodge, who were convinced that the ladder would lead to the White House. (Edith was convinced that it would lead to the poor house.)

Theodore, still wallowing in frustration over the incompatibility of being a breadwinner and a politician, remained Alice and Ted Jr.'s only playmate. He branded their toy horses and cows with the marks of his Western ranches by heating "a wire hairpin red hot." On rainy days they played hide-and-go-seek, with TR hiding in his third-floor gun room: "When we approached in our search he would moan or growl, whereat we would scuttle away and downstairs again in a state of delighted terror." [20]

In 1889, TR was rewarded for campaigning the previous fall for Benjamin Harrison with an appointment as civil service commissioner, at a salary of $3500 per annum. He was thrilled to move to Washington, where he could finally join his friends Henry Cabot Lodge—who was largely responsible for persuading Harrison to make the appointment—and Cecil Spring-Rice. Edith, pregnant again, was not so thrilled and objected to the characterization of the appointment as a "reward." She agonized over how they would pay their bills, given that they would have to rent or buy a house in notoriously expensive Washington. Absorbing his wife's anxiety, TR wrote to

---

* By the time she was seventeen she was receiving quarterly stipends of $500. Grandpa Lee would leave her $50,000 in trust and Grandma would leave her a trust that yielded $10,000 annually. [17]

Bamie: "My career has been a pleasant, honorable and useful career for a man of means; not the right career for a man without means."[21]

But Theodore, who had the financial sense of a teenager, couldn't resist, and the family moved to Washington. He also couldn't resist, after long days at the office, leading his children in games—or, as Alice characterized them, "perfectly awful endurance tests masquerading as games!"[22] It apparently never occurred to him that anyone might lack his sharply honed physical courage or his bottomless need to push himself. Some of these activities terrified Alice to the point of tears; she was in fear almost as much of her father's wrath as she was of the sport itself.

"I was really a physical coward when I was a child," Alice recalled.[23] Not surprisingly, given the ankle-to-knee leg braces she still wore, the half-crippled girl, whom Edith described as looking "white and wretchedly," got no sympathy from Theodore, who had himself so splendidly overcome physical infirmities.

One "game" required her to climb a large oak tree. "The lowest branch must have been fifteen or twenty feet from the ground. Father would get up somehow—a rope would be thrown up to him, and he would then haul the children up, child by child. The lighter, more agile, fearless children put a foot in the noose and hung on. I, heavy, awkward, and timorous, had the rope tied around my fat waist and by the time I reached the branch felt that I had been cut in half."[24]

On Sunday afternoons, Theodore organized point-to-point walks. The rule was that these "scrambles," as he called them, must be executed in a simple, straight line: "over and through—never around."[25] If a tree or a sheer cliff got in the way, the children were expected to climb it. If water got in the way, the children were expected to swim.

She remembered with vivid distaste her father's method of teaching her to dive during the summer, when the family returned to Sagamore. "I can see Father treading water a few feet away from the float, upon the edge of which I crouched trembling, saying, 'Dive, Alice; now, dive!' in a voice of increasing sternness. I would quaver, 'Yes, Father!' and plop in after minutes of hesitation, terror of him finally overcoming my terror of the water. The family used to say that after a diving lesson my tears made a perceptible rise in the tide."[26] As an old lady she remembered TR looking like a "sea monster . . . I cried. I snarled. I hated."[27]

Life with Father—and "Mother"

Edith could be counted on, periodically, to dampen her step-daughter's mood and confidence. If Theodore kept the smallest detail about Alice Lee from flowing naturally into conversation, Edith said only enough to convince Alice that her mother had no intellectual or emotional depth. She let the eight-year-old know that her mother was so stupid that had she lived she would have so bored Theodore that he would have been driven to suicide. She also told Alice that her father had proposed to her before he proposed to Alice Lee. Worst of all, she made a point of telling Alice that her father had wanted to leave her with Bamie.[28]

Usually Edith was more subtle. A frosty glance, a turn of the head, a single word, the tone of her voice—Joseph Alsop, a cousin, once described it as "like the wind from the Arctic"—were sufficient to chill relations.[29]

Alice recalled the infrequent visits of her stepmother's sister Emily, whom Alice described as "one of those wizened virgins from birth. I can still hear my stepmother say when poor Emily requested tea, 'If Miss Emily wants tea, she can have tea. In a thermos. In her room.'"[30]

In 1893, when Alice was nine, Bamie shocked her family and friends by marrying Commander William Sheffield Cowles, a portly, genial naval attaché at the U.S. Embassy in London. As Edith predicted, Bamie did not marry for love. Will Cowles's greatest pleasures were poker and primping in his full-dress uniform. He regularly snoozed through the after-brandy talk at her dinners. But Bamie, then forty, lonely for her niece, and recognizing that Edith's jealousy was there to stay, wanted a child of her own. During the periods when the Roosevelts and Cowles were both living in New York or Washington, Alice learned to escape her stepmother's parlor for her aunt's, where there was "piping hot Earl Grey's tea and lots of paper-thin bread and butter," with hot chocolate and champagne on Sundays.[31]

There was nothing on the horizon to ease Theodore's despondency over money and over Elliott's alarmingly immoral and self-destructive behavior—he was in and out of asylums and suicidal rages, and had impregnated the family maid and been declared legally insane—and it was in that mood that TR made what he soon considered the biggest mistake of his career. In 1894 he turned down an offer to run for mayor of New York as a reformer on the Republican ticket. He had accepted the Republicans' offer eight years earlier, two months before his marriage to Edith, and although he lost in a three-man race—given the configuration of candidates, it was known at the start that he had no chance of winning—that election is still regarded as the cleanest, most issues-oriented mayoral campaign in New York history. This time TR's chances of winning were excellent, and the timing was perfect—he had grown restless in the civil service post.

Theodore, Bamie wrote to Cabot Lodge, believed that this had been "his one great chance & that he had thrown it away." [32] It seems to have been Edith's silent discouragement—which always had a dispiriting effect on her husband—that spurred him to say no.

Edith did not want to uproot her family, which by then included five children, to the even more expensive New York. Also, she had grown to enjoy Washington society, which, for her, included a special place at the feet of the sage of Lafayette Square, Henry Adams— historian, philosopher, and descendant of two presidents. He found her caustic observations much more interesting than Theodore's endless enthusiasms. He once dismissed TR as "a bore as big as a buffalo." [33]

Later, Theodore confided to Lodge, "I would literally have given my right arm to make the race . . . It was the one golden chance, which never returns . . . I have grown to feel . . . that in this instance I should have gone counter to her [Edith's] wishes . . ." [34]

Bamie then wrote an angry letter to her sister-in-law, which Edith apparently destroyed. Bamie, however, did not destroy Edith's reply: ". . . I cannot begin to describe how terribly I feel at having failed him at such an important time," Edith wrote. "It is just as I said to you he never should have married me, and then would have been free to take his own course." [35]

The gloom deepened when the reform candidate, William Strong, a businessman with little political experience, whom the Republicans chose after Theodore declined, won. The new mayor added insult to injury by offering Theodore the post of street cleaning commissioner.

Ten-year-old Alice was unconcerned with her father's disappointments and with the death of Uncle Elliott, who had suffered an attack of delirium tremens in his mistress's apartment, went berserk, tried to jump out the window, and had a fatal convulsion. Alice had her own problem that year: the frequent visits of the just-orphaned Cousin

Eleanor—her mother had died two years earlier—who was Alice's age and a favorite of TR's. While Alice brooded over her father's coldness, she watched him greet Eleanor with a hug so enthusiastic that, according to Edith, he "tore all the gathers out of [her] frock and both buttonholes out of her petticoat."[36]

Alice was too self-absorbed to consider that her father might feel a special responsibility to Elliott's daughter, whose childhood was Dickensian in its bleakness. Eleanor's mother, Anna Hall, was Hudson River gentry and so beautiful that the poet Robert Browning asked if he might sit and gaze while she had her portrait painted.[37] She was also superficial and insensitive—convinced that her only daughter was ugly. She routinely called the child "Granny," and once, as the girl played with another child, turned to Eleanor and remarked in a voice so flat she might have been commenting on the weather, "Eleanor, I hardly know what's to happen to you. You're so plain that you really have nothing to do except *be good*."[38]

After her parents' deaths, all Eleanor had left were memories of the father she still idolized. Many of those memories were painful, such as the one of the time Elliott, three of his fox terriers in tow, fetched his daughter at her Grandmother Hall's, took her for a walk, and, passing his club, left her and the dogs with the doorman, promising to return momentarily. The little girl waited six hours while, upstairs, her father drank himself into a stupor. Before the doorman took her home, she watched her father being carried out.[39]

Life with her grandmother, both of whose sons were drunks, was unrelentingly gloomy. One of Eleanor's uncles, sitting in his bedroom window, amused himself by firing his pistol as she played in the garden. Fortunately, he was too drunk to shoot straight.[40]

Theodore continued for another year as civil service commissioner, until Mayor Strong made him a more attractive offer: the commissionership of the graft-infested New York City Police Department.

Although Edith remained opposed to moving to Manhattan, Theodore prevailed, and in May 1895 he started frenetic work at police headquarters on Mulberry Street. He had watched as his reform efforts during his Assembly days came mostly to naught. He knew that at the core of civic corruption was the Police Department itself, which was closely tied to Tammany Hall and which he described as "utterly demoralized by . . . gangrene . . . Venality and blackmail went hand-in-hand with the basest forms of low ward politics."[41]

Edith remained more concerned about the welfare of her family than the welfare of the city. "Theodore and I will not have two pennies to put together if we stay here," she complained. "It is expensive even to breathe." During that first winter in New York, Theodore was forced to sell a field at Sagamore to his rich uncle, James Alfred. [42]

At least housing was not a problem this time, as Bamie was abroad and they rented her house. Again at Lodge's suggestion, the popular police commissioner—he got gobs of publicity for prowling the streets at night in search of dishonest cops—went on the stump; this time for presidential candidate William McKinley. Theodore was ready to move on again, as he realized that open fighting on the police board—it was deliberately divided between Democrats and Republicans—would make it difficult for him to accomplish much more.

The more deadlocked the board became, the more warmongering its commissioner became. As talk of war with Spain heated up—Roosevelt himself doing much of the talking—he decided that more than anything he wanted to be assistant secretary of the Navy.

Lodge, William Howard Taft, and his Cincinnati friend and neighbor, Maria Longworth Storer, a major contributor to McKinley, worked hard to persuade the new president to give Theodore the low-paying ($4500 annually) but high-profile spot in the Navy Department. They had to work very hard, for McKinley regarded Theodore as a dangerous jingoist whose bellicosity could damage America's delicate relations with Spain.

And so in 1897, despite McKinley's gravest misgivings—"Roosevelt is always in such a state of mind," the president told Taft—the family returned to Washington. [43]

This appointment led straight to the governor's mansion in Albany, to the vice presidency, and then to the White House. TR's work to prepare the Navy for war; his relentless lobbying for the U.S. to declare war against Spain; his decision to quit the Navy Department and go to Cuba; these were the key steps. The Cuban people had been trying for more than two years to throw off Spanish rule, and Lieutenant Colonel Theodore Roosevelt, second in command of a curious collection of cowboys and Harvard boys popularly known as the Rough Riders, meant to help them.

Alice was not home to witness her father's ecstacy at the prospect of

Life with Father—and "Mother"

fighting the Spanish. Two months earlier, the fourteen-year-old was told one February evening that she was being sent, the next morning, to Bamie, who was then living in New York and in the beginning of her first and last pregnancy (Sheffield Jr. was born that fall). "Mother," it was explained, was too sick to contend with Alice's "wild ways" and needed a few months' reprieve from her. Edith had yet to recover from the birth of her last child, born the November before. She was suffering with grippe, acute neuralgia, sciatica, and a fever that, for a month, never dropped below 101. For a couple of weeks it appeared that Edith might die. Several weeks after Alice's exile to New York, Edith was operated on to remove an abscess in her abdomen.

Much as Alice had been missing her aunt, she was horrified at the thought of leaving the Washington social life that she had finally made for herself. Edith did not approve of her friends, although she felt that Alice was probably a worse influence on them than they on her. Alice had become a "guttersnipe" [44] who, in Edith's words, ran the streets "uncontrolled with every boy in town" [45] and who prided herself on being the only female member of an all-boys club. "We met in a stable loft and the boys would come dressed in their sisters' clothes in order to deceive their parents," Alice recalled. "My father opened the door once on a petrified boy struggling to adjust one of his sister's dresses." [46] Having gotten a bicycle from her Lee grandparents, Alice would ride to the top of the hill at Dupont Circle and careen down, her feet on the handlebars where her hands should have been.

Adding to Alice's discontent with life at Auntie Bye's was the frequent presence of cousin Eleanor. One afternoon the fourteen-year-old cousins were in the bedroom when Alice started telling Eleanor what she had learned about sex—from the Bible; "probably nothing more explosive than the 'begat' series . . . when she [Eleanor] suddenly leapt on me and tried to sit on my head and smother me with a pillow, saying I was being blasphemous." [47]

Alice's mood was not lifted by two letters from her father. In the first he described Ted running "about the house with tow-headed Kermit. . . . I have told Ted and Kermit 'Jim' stories, of fearful and wonderful African adventure." Although Ethel and Archie had also been exiled, they were staying with the Lodges, where Theodore stopped by regularly to regale them with readings of Hans Christian Andersen stories. In the second letter, TR told of Ted's meeting with two ex-Confederate soldiers ("with real bullets in them!") and of a visit to the zoo during which Ted was allowed to play with "the coons and with two wee leopard cubs."[48]

On May 6, 1898, TR left his still seriously ill wife and son (Ted Jr. had been plagued by debilitating headaches)—he would say ten years later that "it was a question if either would ultimately get well. . . . I would not allow even a death to stand in my way. . . . I know now that I would have turned from my wife's deathbed to have answered that call"[49]—and led the charge up Kettle Hill that made him the most popular man in New York, and the country. He was a sure bet for governor.

When the family arrived at the governor's mansion on December 30, 1898, money was so scarce that they could not afford to bring their own things to cheer up what Alice later described as the "very dismal" executive mansion. The grim vulgarity of the place irritated Alice, who was increasingly concerned with appearances. But Edith, still concerned with the bottom line, was delighted with Theodore's $10,000 annual salary and the rent-free mansion, no matter how "hideously furnished" Alice pronounced it.[50]

At the core of the mother/stepdaughter relationship was a profound difference. Edith was deeply religious. On any day, Alice might happen upon her stepmother reading the Bible or kneeling in prayer. Alice also read the Bible; she bragged that she had read it through twice by age twelve—she would plow through whole books by candlelight in her room at Sagamore—but her interest was in its language and rhythms. As for Christian dogma, she considered that "sheer voodoo."[51] When dragged to church by Theodore, who searched out a Dutch Reformed church wherever they were living, or Edith, who was rigidly Episcopalian, Alice would read a book or practice her "one-sided nose wrinkle." (A few years later, while perfecting it in church, she heard a woman remark, "Poor President Roosevelt, his daughter has a twitch.")[52]

Perhaps all the forced prayer to "My mother who is in heaven," when no such person was otherwise mentioned, drained religion of meaning for her. She called herself a pagan and meant it.

When Alice turned fifteen it was time for her to be confirmed. She simply refused, and eventually her parents relented (allowing her to be the only one of the six children who was not confirmed). She had been reading Darwin (with whom she shared a birthday) and Huxley and "the idea of accepting the dogma and theology of any religion or 'church' went against the grain." [53] Later she became a devotee of James Frazer's *The Golden Bough* and saw things in terms of classic myths and archetypes. She had also grown extremely superstitious—making "magics" to slay her father's political foes and to put him where she felt he belonged: in the White House.

Instead of insisting that she be confirmed, Edith and Theodore went along with Alice's demand that she be "let loose" in their library. And that constituted her formal education, although throughout her youth she had, in her father, a remarkable teacher. TR's only requirement was that she learn something out of a book every night and tell him what it was in the morning. From him she absorbed unbounded curiosity.

Theodore managed what only the best teachers can—he made learning seem interesting. Although the subjects were ones that were interesting to him and odd choices for a young girl, what was important was his exuberance. ". . . Daniel Boone and David Crockett, and the Alamo . . . the Naval War of 1812 . . . Hampton Roads and the Battle of Mobile Bay, . . . Bull Run, and . . . Gettysburg. He made them sound like sagas. There were tales too of the Indian wars, of the massacre of Custer and his men." [54] Although his choice of poetry was somewhat martial in tone—Theodore would recite British ballads, Longfellow's "Saga of King Olaf," Kipling's poems—he gave his children a love of poetry, and his insistence that they memorize the poems helped them to develop memories as prodigious as his own. (One Roosevelt relative recalled that Alice "used to be able to read a poem once, just any poem once and then she'd be able to repeat it with the book closed.") [55]

Edith had informed Alice the year before that she would be sent, that fall, to Miss Spence's School in Manhattan, a prospect that filled her with horror: "I had seen Miss Spence's scholars marching two by two in their daily walks, and the thought of becoming one of them shrivelled me. I practically went on a strike. I said that I would not go—I said that if the family insisted, and sent me, I should do something disgraceful. Every afternoon I made a point of crying about it. . . . The time for school approached and the sheets and towels . . . were ready, marked with my name, and then suddenly one day the family yielded." [56]

Alice was the only one in her family who escaped regimented learn-ing. Her brothers all started at Groton and went on to Harvard. Ethel was sent to the Cathedral School in Washington, and even boarded there on weekday nights. Cousin Eleanor went to Allenwood, a school outside London where Auntie Bye had also gone.

Edith herself had the most formal kind of education then available to a girl. She graduated from Miss Comstock's School, run by its namesake, who believed that all education should be along religious lines.

Edith was so relieved at finally achieving financial security that she insisted her husband run for reelection. Alice, then sixteen, and much less a tomboy—she was infatuated with her father's Rough Riders and had reveled in her position as "the Colonel's Daughter"—pre-ferred that her father lobby for appointment as governor-general of the Philippines, where she fancied herself "among the palm trees, in a 'palace,' surrounded by young officers in white uniforms." [57]

Then began the talk of Theodore as vice president. McKinley's vice president, Garret Hobart, who had been expected to run again, suddenly died. Party and money bosses who were alarmed at The-odore's progressive—they called them socialistic—policies, espe-cially his plan to regulate large corporations and require that statements of their earnings be made available to the public, saw the perfect opportunity to shelve him in the politically impotent vice presidency.

Alice, who had become very ambitious for her father, felt "deep disgust" at the prospect of him as number two on the ticket—she considered the vice presidency a post of "comic obscurity." [58] So did Theodore's enemy, party boss Senator Thomas Platt, who let the governor know that, if he didn't accept the vice presidential nomina-tion, Platt would prevent his renomination for governor. Platt bragged to reporters that "Roosevelt might as well stand under Niagara Falls and try to spit water back" as try to resist the nomination.

Despite Edith's opposition—as vice president Theodore would earn $2000 less per year than he did as governor and would not be supplied with a house—he seemed to half want it. Although he wrote Lodge that "even to live simply as Vice-President would be a serious strain upon me and . . . especially would cause Edith continual anx-iety about money," he appeared at the Republican National Convention in a broad-brimmed hat "craftily reminiscent of Cuba." As the brass band played the tune that had become TR's theme song, "A Hot Time in the Old Town Tonight," he was nominated by acclamation. Edith was white-faced as the sixteen thousand delegates cheered,[59] and Platt told his friends he wouldn't for anything miss the vice-presidential inauguration, "to see Theodore Roosevelt take the veil!"[60]

Maria Longworth Storer again figured largely. She offered to lease the Roosevelts for the nominal annual sum of $3000 her large Washington house at Seventeenth Street and Rhode Island Avenue—large enough for entertaining and also for the coming-out party that would have to be made for Alice, who would turn eighteen during her father's vice-presidential term.

On November 6, 1900, McKinley and Roosevelt trounced William Jennings Bryan and Adlai E. Stevenson by the largest plurality since U. S. Grant swamped Horace Greeley in 1872.

Alice watched her father's inauguration the following March from a room over Madame Payne's Manicure Shop on the corner of Fifteenth and Pennsylvania. As an open-topped carriage rounded the corner bearing McKinley and his new vice president, Alice's younger siblings leaned so far out the window that they almost tumbled out. Alice sat aloofly. She was busy comparing McKinley's stooping posture and gray complexion with Theodore's military bearing and ruddy glow, and "I wondered, in the terminology of the insurance companies, what sort of a 'risk' he was."[61]

4

The President's Daughter

At the McKinley-Roosevelt inaugural ball, Alice was just seventeen, not yet "out," and humiliated by her dress—"an excessively new white point d'esprit, which I despised. It was like wearing a label that said, 'This person is very young.'" [1] Adding to her humiliation was the presence of the two daughters of Secretary of State John Hay. They were a few years older than Alice and light-years more sophisticated in their old dresses that sent the message that inaugural balls were no big novelty. "Got the oldest thing on I could possibly find to go to the dreadful Inaugural Ball" [2] was what those dresses said to Alice.

At that inauguration she had been a mere observer, longing to join the whirling dancers but not allowed. She watched intensely, perched on the arm of a chair for a better view. For that, she was harshly rebuked because the chair was occupied by the first lady, Ida McKinley. "She was such a pathetic, frail little person," Alice recalled, "I hadn't even noticed she was there." *[3]

If Alice's earliest memory was of fleeing in terror from her father's attentions, her later memories were of trying in vain to get him to pay

---

*Mrs. McKinley, who was epileptic, had a seizure at the ball. When her gown was sent to the Smithsonian costume collection, it had a stain on the satin where she fell. President McKinley had protocol changed so that she always sat beside him at official dinners. If she had a seizure he would drape a handkerchief over her face until she regained consciousness. McKinley conducted the 1900 campaign from his front porch so as to be close to his wife, whom he amused by playing cribbage, while TR tirelessly toured the country. Henry Adams described the tone of the White House during McKinley's presidency as "dust and ashes, with a slight flavor of dish water." [4]

attention. She had begun to sense that her father and stepmother would prefer that she not spend much time at home. (Home was now Sagamore until late September, when the new vice president would move his family into the Storers' Washington house.) It was one of the few times that she would heed their wishes.

That summer she began to socialize with the new-monied sons and daughters of "the Four Hundred," the Newport, Rhode Island, crowd, for whom her parents had the most high-browed, high-minded contempt. The more her parents criticized her new friends, who brazenly disregarded old-monied proprieties, the more Alice sought their company.

In early September 1901, Alice was vacationing in the Adirondacks—she with a group of friends at one resort and her parents, sister, and brothers at another—when word came that President McKinley had died from an assassin's bullet. Theodore left immediately for Buffalo where, within hours, he took the oath of office. For many, the words of party chief Mark Hanna, the man who had pleaded with Platt not to shove Roosevelt into the vice presidency, had come horribly true: "Don't you realize that there's only one life between this madman and the White House?"[5]

Edith was left with the burden of getting back to Oyster Bay with five children, including Archie, who was "miserable with tonsillitis"[6] and Quentin, who was screaming in pain from an earache. She would have to find Quentin a doctor in New York before going on to Sagamore. But first a bumpy cart ride, a train trip to Albany, the Hudson River night boat to Manhattan, the search for a doctor on a Sunday morning, and, finally, on to Sagamore.

Alice offered no help. Although when she heard that McKinley was dead and that her father was president, she admitted to feeling "utter rapture" and to dancing "a little jig,"*[7] she decided to steer clear of Washington. If she felt not quite welcome at Sagamore, she knew she would feel even less welcome at the White House. "It pleased me to pretend that I had ceased to take an interest," she recalled.[8] Determined to reject her parents before they could again reject her, she decided to concern herself exclusively with her own pleasure and pretended that she, like some of her Four Hundred friends, found the

---

*Alice had been casting spells for just this outcome. She took credit for the fact that when McKinley raised his hand to take the oath of office a hailstorm broke out. She would later take credit for the perfect weather of TR's 1905 inauguration.

idea of living in the White House vulgar—that politics was something that the rich left to the workers, just as they left the tasks of picking up their garbage and paving their streets.

She worked herself into a state of defiant indifference. "I neither telegraphed nor wrote to either Father or Mother which I think hurt their feelings." [9] She also noted that neither did her parents "send for me to come to Washington." Obviously she needed to be asked to come, because in the absence of such an invitation she feared that she was not wanted. It was several weeks before she saw her father. She happened to be staying at Bamie's country house, Oldgate,* when the new president happened to stop by.

Apparently, Alice wrote Edith asking if she could come home with her father. "Of course," Edith replied, although she noted in the next sentence that Alice was expected in Boston immediately thereafter. In later letters, Edith suggested that Alice go directly from Newport to Islesboro (another fashionable resort spot), rather than stop at home between, and that after visiting her friend Helen, she immediately visit her friend Jean. [10]

"A shy, uncomfortable child" is how Alice later described herself. She claimed to have been incapable of being "more than an audience" for her younger, more confident brother Ted, who, at age seven, insisted on reciting "The Ballad of East and West" for her father's lunch guest, Rudyard Kipling.

Although this shyness would persist until her death—she never would make so much as a toast, even at a dinner for close friends, much less a political speech—she was quickly developing a flamboyant outer layer, and, to mask the shyness, painting it in harsh colors. Starved for attention at home, her appetite for attention outside was insatiable. Traveling with friends, she appeared on a railroad platform with a boa constrictor wrapped around her neck. Visiting a friend whose father kept a dry house, Alice smuggled in small bottles of whiskey in her gloves and passed them to the men sitting beside her at dinner.

---

*Oldgate, Will Cowles's ancestral home in Farmington, Connecticut, was built in 1660 by members of the Hooker family who founded nearby Hartford. The house's name derived from its front gate, modeled on a water gate on the Thames, and crafted by British prisoners incarcerated at Oldgate during the Revolutionary War. The original kitchen was built by Edith's relative, Jonathan Edwards. Bamie's stunning renovation included a garden by Frederick Law Olmsted.

Soon the press was covering Alice as if it were she who had just become president. Before her father could hold his first regular cabinet meeting, his daughter's name was splashed across hundreds of front pages. In mid-America the very name "Alice Roosevelt," or "Princess Alice," as she was soon dubbed, came to connote something a bit naughty—smoking, drinking, racing a car, betting on the horses. People couldn't get enough of her. John McCutcheon of the *Chicago Tribune* drew a cartoon that likely did not elicit a trace of a smile from Edith. Over a caption reading, "Alice Roosevelt at the Horse Show," crowds of spectators, judges, and even the horses in the ring peer at the box in which Alice is seated, while the band plays, "Alice, Where Art Thou?"—one of the day's most popular tunes. Women across the country had gowns made in "Alice Blue," a postman-blue shade that Alice favored.

When Alice became a regular in the most virulent of gossip sheets, *Town Topics*, Edith was horrified. So widely read was this "Journal of Society" that it was rumored that certain Four Hundred types—William K. Vanderbilt, among them—made "loans" to the magazine's publisher for a guarantee that they would be ignored in its pages.

Edith scorned the very notion of a lady's name appearing in print except to announce her birth, marriage, and death. She was as tireless in her efforts to avoid the public eye as Alice was in hers to catch it. Alice contemptuously remembered Edith "waxing very indignant about having her photograph taken. 'Why do they want to photograph me?' she would say. 'They only need a picture of the President.' The loyal little wife always in the background!" [11] When, as assistant secretary of the Navy, Roosevelt was asked to furnish a photograph of his wife, he told reporters, "If I should, Mrs. Roosevelt would consider my act just grounds for divorce."

The press's appetite for Alice grew even larger when, in late fall 1901, it was announced that she would be the first president's daughter in the nation's history to have her debut in the White House. Alice dreaded her coming-out ball, set for the next January 3 in the East Room. The newspapers were heralding it as the most important social event since the days of Dolly Madison, but to Alice it was shaping up as a series of humiliations—to be played out in front of the carloads of Newport sophisticates she had invited.

Because the hideous East Room, overrun by potted palms, smilax,

ALICE ROOSEVELT LONGWORTH

and circular padded seats, had no hardwood floor—Edith's renovation of the White House was a year away—her guests would have to dance on crash, a coarse fabric whose color Alice described as like "the under belly of a fish." (At a White House dinner a couple of months before, she had persuaded Joe Cannon, later the despotic Speaker of the House, to appropriate money for a dance floor. The bill had passed both House and Senate, but there was not enough time to have the floor installed.)

Even more mortifying than the crash was Edith's refusal to serve champagne. Alice pleaded with her stepmother to follow the example of the mother of Cissy Patterson, a Washington debutante of a couple of seasons earlier. Her mother had thrown lavish parties replete with French champagne. But Edith was adamant, and when Alice scaled down her request to "just a little champagne," Edith still insisted on punch. (At Ethel's White House debut, eight years later, there were, in Alice's memory, "*buckets* of champagne.") [12]

Next Edith vetoed a cotillion or favors. "Other girls had cotillions . . . with ten or twelve figures," Alice whined. [13] On the issue of favors, perhaps Edith remembered that her own father had been unable to afford any debut for her. Spending money on favors was as frivolous as spending it on gambling. Edith knew that Alice had in mind something much grander than trinkets. She coveted the sort of gifts that her friend Jean, the daughter of millionaire Whitelaw Reid,* bestowed on her guests—brocade evening bags, mounted in gold and encrusted with rhinestones and pearls, silver vanity cases, and velvet muffs trimmed with mink or ermine. [14]

Later Alice would sneer at her debut as "the sort of [party] Edith Wharton scoffed at": "I think my coming-out party was a hangover from the brownstone-front existence of my stepmother when they had *little* parties with a modicum of decorous dancing and an amusing fruit punch." [15]

At the fashionable hour of 10 P.M., Alice stood in the Blue Room at Edith's side, as the first lady greeted and then presented to Alice each

---

*Reid, publisher of the *New York Tribune* and defeated vice-presidential candidate on the Harrison ticket, got his millions from his wife, the daughter of one of the wealthiest of the old captains of industry, Darius Ogden Mills. When TR was police commissioner Reid's newspaper had nothing good to say about him, but later the paper became a consistent supporter. The month of Alice's debut, TR appointed Reid ambassador to the Court of St. James's.

of six hundred guests. Both stepmother and daughter were dressed in white, Edith in lace and silk and Alice in demure chiffon appliquéd with white rosebuds. Looking back, Alice described her gown as "a singularly repulsive white number—I would have preferred to wear black." [16] One of the guests, Marguerite Cassini, who had only recently come to know Alice, observed, "Under the lights of the heavy chandeliers . . . the tomboyish-looking girl I have seen around Washington is transformed into an assured, sparkling young woman in a stiff white . . . gown and long white gloves. . . . Her hair is of an indefinite blond and her skin lacks color but her eyes are a queer, attractive long shape, a phosphorescent grayish blue, changing color according to her mood, edged by long black lashes." [17]

Alice led the way to the East Room, where she had her first dance with dashing Major Charles L. McCawley of the United States Marine Corps. Archie Butt would later describe McCawley, his predecessor in the job of military aide to the president, as a socially prominent "cotillion leader." The mostly young crowd danced to such numbers as "Hop Long Sing," John Philip Sousa's "Bride Elect" polka, and a new composition, the "Sagamore Hill Waltz."

Shortly after midnight, Edith led the way to the State Dining Room for a simple buffet. That grim necessity over, the dancing resumed, until 2 A.M., when the Marine Band played the last waltz of the evening, "The Blue Danube."

"I myself enjoyed it moderately," [18] Alice said. One of the guests that evening, cousin Franklin Delano Roosevelt, had a better time: "From start to finish it was glorious," he wrote in his diary. [19] He had danced twice with his cousin. (Eleanor, who was then at school abroad, did not attend.)

Aunt Corinne claimed to have watched Alice have "the time of her life, men seven deep around her all the time." [20] Alice would have quibbled with her aunt's use of the word "men." In her opinion, Franklin and his Harvard pals were merely boys, and boring boys at that.

One smitten Harvard boy named DeLancey Jay, great-great-grandson of John Jay, wrote her love notes on his Harvard A.D. Club stationery (a tactical error because Alice knew that her father had turned down A.D. for Porcellian, which was, in her opinion, the only Harvard club that mattered): "I don't expect you to be crazy about me, but there is something between 'loving it madly' and 'I can't bear it', and you really might find me a pretty decent sort of a friend." He confessed that he had been using her picture, "barbarian that I am, like an idol—it hangs by my bed like an up-to-date madonna or Saint of some kind!" [21]

Alice's debut, instead of launching her into a society full of De-Lancey Jays, confirmed her intent not to waste her time on college boys, certainly not on cousin Franklin, who had occasionally been mentioned as an appropriate match. Alice considered him too much of "a good little mother's boy" and "peevish . . . rather like a single child. . . . He didn't rough it." [22] He liked to sail instead of row, and Alice noted that, while her parents banned such sentimental mush as *Little Lord Fauntleroy*, not only did Franklin read the book but he dressed the part as well.

When Franklin went to Harvard, his mother moved to Boston to be near him. His classmates recognized his wimpishness, Alice said, when they refused to let him into the Porcellian, a club to which his own father belonged. Franklin was, she never tired of saying, the kind of boy whom one "invited to the dance but not the dinner." Franklin was also a prig. When he learned that a relative had married beneath him, he pronounced it "disgusting" and wrote his mother that "although the disgrace to the name has been the worst part of the affair one can never again consider him a true Roosevelt." [23]

Although Franklin was certainly handsome—tall and thin with chiseled features—he was called, wrote Joe Alsop, "'the handkerchief box young man' because his good looks . . . though undeniable, too much resembled the rather awful good looks of the young men then customarily portrayed on presentation boxes of feminine handkerchiefs." [24]

Theodore, who was close to Franklin's mother, Sara, would have been happy if Alice had spent time with Franklin. Theodore was very unhappy that Alice had eyes only for the fast, frivolous, and fabulously wealthy Four Hundred. He apparently never recognized how important a role he played in her choice of companions.

Alice recognized early that her father had rigid notions of how life should be lived—House Speaker Thomas Reed once chided him, "What I like about you, Theodore, is your original discovery of the Ten Commandments" [25]—and so she behaved in a way that was guaranteed to make him pay attention.

Theodore packed every day with physical and mental activity so strenuous that it bordered on the comical—he once rushed into his sister Corinne's house and announced that he was taking a month's vacation and would do nothing during that time except write a history of Oliver Cromwell—while Alice regularly stayed out half the night dancing and slept until noon or later. "Sister continues to lead the life of social excitement," Theodore complained in a letter to his son, Ted Jr., "which is I think all right for a girl to lead for a year or two, but which . . . I do not regard as healthy from the standpoint of permanence." [26]

She was totally dedicated to amusing herself with an intensity that, in a perverse way, showed her to be her father's daughter. "I pray for a fortune," she wrote in her diary. "I care for nothing except to amuse myself in a charmingly expensive way." [27] Although with the Lee money coming every quarter, Alice was well-fixed, she was poor by Newport standards. Lace on a girl's evening gown might cost $2000 and be ruined after a single wearing.

Alice declared that she could make do with $50,000 a year to dress on—equal to Theodore's salary—and dressed as if she had it. The period between her awakening after lunch and that evening's party was often filled with anxiety over how to pay her bills. Most months she spent about a thousand dollars over her allowance. She certainly couldn't seek a loan from Edith, who had warned her that incurring debts was "neither honest nor wise," [28] and who was busy buying muslin so that Alice's maid Anna could make drawers for Alice. ("It is expensive to buy them readymade," Edith explained.) So most months Alice, first promising to reform, would ask her indulgent Grandpa Lee. He would admonish her to change her ways—"You go with people who have money to burn and I fear lead you into extravagances"—and not to "tell your grandmother I sent this." With the thousand-dollar check came a word of encouragement: "You say that you don't really think that you are as bad as you seem. You are not bad at all in my opinion. . . . As you are going to turn over a new leaf and reform, I won't find any more fault with you." [29]

Alice still dismissed the Lees as "middle class"—once making that assessment just after stepping off the Vanderbilts' private railway car—except when they sent money. Then Grandpa became "the little pet." Grandma was more of a problem, and Alice steamed over a letter with which Grandma enclosed a bill for an automobile Alice had bought. Grandpa had offered to pay for it, but Grandma would not let him and declared herself "both annoyed and greatly disappointed . . ." with her granddaughter.[30]

Had TR been privy to these exchanges, he would have totally agreed. His younger, perfectly behaved daughter, Ethel, recalled that the family came to consider Alice "a hellion . . . capable of doing almost anything to anyone at any time. . . . what wickedry she might commit next was felt almost constantly by almost all the family."[31]

The newspapers reported that Alice had been asked to leave Boston's Copley Plaza Hotel for smoking in the lobby. When her father prohibited her from smoking under his roof, she said "very well" and smoked atop the White House roof. She drove her car unchaperoned around Washington, getting stopped at least once for speeding, at a time when automobiles, not to mention female-piloted ones, were so rare that some states had laws that required a man on foot to run ahead of the vehicle waving a red flag.[32] She regularly bet on the horses, bragged about her winnings, and ignored her father's increasingly angry lectures.

Her manners were deplorable. At one White House dinner she ate her asparagus with her fingers without removing her gloves.[33] A friend of Edith's remarked that the presidential daughter was "like a young wild animal that had been put into good clothes."[34]

Although Theodore wondered who in his right mind would want to marry his daughter, speculation over Alice's consort filled columns of newsprint. "The suitors for the hand of little Miss Alice Roosevelt . . . bid fair to become as numerous as the wooers of Penelope," William Randolph Hearst wrote in 1902. He described in gushy detail two all-American boys who were her most "ardent cavaliers." He also slyly hinted at a possible romance with Prince Heinrich (Henry) of Prussia, the brother of the German emperor.[35]

Kaiser Wilhelm II had invited Alice to christen his American-built yacht, the *Meteor*, and had dispatched Henry to witness the festivities. Alice smashed the silver-encased bottle of champagne against the boat's bow and declared, "In the name of His Majesty, the German Emperor, I christen this yacht *Meteor*."*[36] She cut the rope with a

---

*During World War I, the *Meteor* was turned over to the German navy, painted white and christened the *Alice Roosevelt*. For years, it remained the only white ship in the German navy.[37] By World War II, it had fallen into disrepair and into the hands of a Massachusetts junk dealer, who tore out the teakwood decks and silver chandeliers and converted the royal yacht—on which, during her honeymoon, Alice Longworth had sipped tea with the kaiser—into a cargo carrier.[38]

silver hatchet, and the Prince responded with a bunch of pink roses, a kiss on the hand, a toast ("Three hearty cheers for Miss Roosevelt"),[39] and a gold bracelet with the kaiser's miniature set in large diamonds.

The notion of mating the American Princess with the German Prince was irresistible. There was, however, one unmentioned impediment. The forty-year-old prince already had a consort—his wife, Irene, princess of Hesse. Besides, Alice was leaning increasingly in the direction of commoners—Charlie de Chambrun or Nick Longworth. But here stood an impediment also, in the irresistible person of Countess Marguerite Cassini.

"Maggie" Cassini, daughter of Arthur Paul Nicholas, marquis de Capizzucchi de Bologna, count de Cassini, the czar's first ambassador to the United States and a man who was even more pompous than his name suggested (Theodore would grow to despise the very sight of him), was two years older than Alice and much more sophisticated. Ever since she arrived in Washington in 1898, when she was sixteen, she had, by her father's orders, taken over the duties of official hostess of the Russian embassy. In her role as "almost-ambassadress," she spent her days dining with men "twice my age." One of them was Theodore Roosevelt, who, when he met her at an inauguration-eve dinner in 1901, remarked, "It is Anna Karenina!" "Why Anna Karenina, Colonel Roosevelt?" the sultry beauty asked. "There is tragedy in your eyes," he answered.[40]

He probably had something more in mind. When Theodore read *Anna Karenina* some fifteen years earlier he pronounced the book morally suspect and, in a letter to Corinne, described Anna as "being prey to the most violent passion, and subject to melancholia, and her reasoning power is so unbalanced that she could not possibly be described otherwise than as in a certain sense insane."[41]

Not only was the dark-eyed countess the kind of woman who made men—even prudes like TR—feel passionate rather than paternal, but she knew how to flirt, a skill that Alice was eager to acquire. Maggie kept a swansdown puff tucked in her décolletage which she ostentatiously retrieved to powder her nose.[42]

For Alice, the countess held another attraction—she was the subject of some lively scandal, and when cavedwellers dropped her from their calcified guest lists, Alice couldn't wait to be seen in public with her. The girls were soon best friends.

On Count Cassini's arrival in Washington, the budding beauty at his side was introduced to society as the daughter of his dead brother. Later Cassini rushed back from Russia claiming to have adopted the girl. According to rumor, the count had no need to adopt Maggie, as she had always been his daughter—by his housekeeper.*

While society matrons gasped and TR and Edith wished that Alice would find a more suitable friend, such as cousin Eleanor, Alice and the countess had the time of their young lives. Soon added to their group was Eleanor "Cissy" Patterson, three years Alice's senior.

While Alice's bone structure, eyes, and carriage made her beauty endure into very old age, as a young woman she was more tomboy than femme fatale. Her straight back, her lifted chin, her upswept hair, her outdoorsiness, gave her an air of all-American regality.

Her new friends were exotic. Cissy, who was soon to marry an abusive, alcoholic, but sexually passionate Polish nobleman, had blazing red hair and a figure that turned heads—even Theodore's. "Watch the way that girl moves," TR whispered to Alice as Cissy sashayed down a White House receiving line. "She moves as *no one* has ever moved before!"[44]

The men who traveled in this exclusive circle had more than merely the look of experience. One of the regulars was French diplomat Comte Charles de Chambrun, a direct descendant of Lafayette and later Alice's brother-in-law once removed (when his brother married Nick Longworth's sister). When Alice first saw him at the White House, she contemplated a more direct link. But when he returned to Washington as the French embassy's first secretary, it was obvious that he had his heart set on Maggie.

Just about this time, thirty-four-year-old Nicholas Longworth arrived from Ohio to serve his first term in Congress. Nick was a gentleman politician, thanks to his great-great-grandfather, who bought big chunks of the land that became the heart of Cincinnati. Politics for the balding Harvard graduate was an amusing pastime, leaving him plenty of time to pursue his consuming interests—wine, women, and the violin.

Nick was a member of Washington's most exclusive club, the Al-

---

* In Countess Cassini's memoirs, written when she was well past middle age and the mother of clothing designer Oleg and gossip columnist Igor, she gave this version of her roots: Her mother had been in the theater. Because the czar would never have consented to the marriage of one of his diplomats to a singer, the count did so secretly and ordered the child of this marriage to pretend that her mother was her governess.[43]

ibi,* where he played poker and cooked—his specialties included "Toothsome Terrapin," Welsh rabbit, scrambled eggs and small sausages, served with the finest wines and champagnes. The club, located at 1806 I Street in a pre–Civil War townhouse that was once slave quarters, was off-limits to women, except during members' private parties. Nick's guest list often included Cissy, Alice, and Maggie. All three flirted with the impeccably tailored congressman and he, according to Cissy's biographer, "courted all of them, often at the same time." [45]

When Maggie Cassini described her and Alice's friendship as having the "violence of a bomb . . . a combination of two heedless girls who used their position thoughtlessly to impose their fads, their caprices on everyone—a veritable reign of terror," she wasn't exaggerating. James Hazen Hyde, the head of the Equitable Life Assurance Society, decided to give a costume ball in New York in their honor, patterned on the court entertainments of Louis XV. The preparations and the expense—$100,000—were grotesquely lavish. "Say what you want and whom you want," Hyde told them. "'Do you want Melba and Caruso?' . . . We wanted everything and we got it"— including the Metropolitan Opera's corps de ballet and orchestra. "For days," Marguerite continued, "the New York and Washington papers were full of the grandeur it would be. Private trains were bringing people from Boston, Washington, Philadelphia."

On the Tuesday morning of the party, the girls were preparing to leave for New York when Nick Longworth called to invite them to dine with him that evening at the Alibi. They accepted. "To our host in New York," Maggie recalled, "we sent an apologetic last-minute wire, leaving the embarrassed man to explain how he liked the mortifying absence of his guests of honor."

Hyde wasn't the only older gentleman humiliated by the pair. The inventor George Westinghouse also decided to throw Alice and Maggie a ball. "Make your own list," he told them. They did, and the list, Maggie recalled, "was so long that to indulge us he had to build an annex to his already huge ballroom. Men worked overtime, but as the night of the ball neared it became clear the walls would not be fin-

---

*To this day, the Alibi maintains its exclusivity in the same cluttered quarters—its walls covered with drawings of half-naked women—by never admitting to membership more than fifty men—among whom are the chief justice of the United States and the chairman of the Joint Chiefs of Staff.

ished. So from all over the country . . . Mr. Westinghouse ordered
. . . carloads of orchids, and with these he completely blanketed the
unfinished walls. On the night of the ball we seemed to be dancing in
a room hung with exquisite velvet coverings of mauve and purple and
violet. . . . Later in the evening, the lovely blossoms wilted and
drooped." Alice likened the effect to that of a cemetery after a huge
funeral. The girls grew bored in this funereal atmosphere and departed early, "leaving the generous bearded old gentleman wondering, I fear, if his efforts had been appreciated."[46]

In the meantime, Eleanor was busy lecturing her cousin on the
sorts of presents a girl could receive from gentlemen: "Flowers,
books, cards were all possible . . . but jewelry of any kind, absolutely
not. I listened to her earnest discourse, fingering all the while a
modest string of seed pearls that an admirer had given me the week
before."[47]

Eleanor heartily disapproved of Alice. She said so in a letter to her
cousin Franklin, to whom she would soon become engaged. She
described Alice as "crazier than ever. I saw her . . . in Bobbie
Goelet's auto quite alone with three other men!"[48]

One day at the White House, TR was chatting with a fellow Harvard man, Owen Wister—later author of *The Virginian*—when Alice
three times casually interrupted the men's conversation by rushing in
and out of the room. "The next time you come, I'll throw you out the
window," TR admonished his daughter. According to Wister, a friend
asked TR why he couldn't "look after Alice more." "I can be President of the United States—or—I can attend to Alice," TR replied.[49]

But try to attend to—or rather control—Alice he did, because he
was determined to shed the hated title, "His Accidency." The 1904
campaign, when he would run for a term in his own right, was approaching. He could not forget that no previous vice president who
had been elevated to the top by the death or assassination of the
president had ever won a term on his own. He feared that his "hellion
daughter"—whom a newspaper photographer had recently captured
collecting her winnings from a bookie—would prevent him from
grasping the biggest prize of his life.

When news of his daughter's escapades started crowding TR's political accomplishments off the front page, he was left sputtering.
When TR's crusade to regulate railroad rates and to curb the excesses
of the "malefactors of great wealth" was weakened by his daughter's

social ties with the malefactors' own sons and daughters, the "fearful lectures," as Alice described them, increased. He was not happy, for example, that Alice was socializing with Mary Harriman, daughter of one of the principal targets of his trust busting, railroad magnate E. H. Harriman. (Harriman, of Morgan, Hill and Harriman, had masterminded the Northern Securities Company, a huge railroad combine, that could control transport and travel in all of the western half of the U.S. and against which Theodore had an anti-trust suit pending.)

TR wrote Alice, then visiting friends in Newport, a letter so angry that it "scorched the paper on which it was written" as he "enumerated the iniquities that I had committed" and castigated her for her choice of friends and for having stopped writing to the family. Had he told her that he missed her and wanted her home, perhaps she might have swallowed her pride and gone. Instead, the message was, so long as you write, you'll be fulfilling your duty. She was so angry that she finished the job words had begun and burned the letter.[50]

Mary Harriman wrote Alice of the "disappointing news that I can not go to Islesboro [where she was to have met Alice]. . . . It is *too beastly* [underlined twice] for I wanted to do that more than anything this summer. . . . But my family won't allow me to go both to Islesboro and the Adirondacks and the latter I have to do having promised that visit long ago. How do you manage to make your family so agreeable?"[51] Had it not hurt too much to admit it, Alice would have said that it didn't seem to matter to her parents whether she ever stopped at home.

Although Alice enjoyed Islesboro and the Adirondacks, her favorite spot—because TR hated it so extravagantly—was Newport. Grace Vanderbilt, in whose Newport "cottage" Alice frequently frolicked, was hardly the best campaign symbol for the upcoming contest. At one party, Grace was drenched in so many gems that the wonder was she could walk upright: diamonds covered her neck, the back of her head, and even a rose in her corsage, stem, leaves, buds and all.[52] And certainly it was not to Theodore's political advantage when *Town Topics* reported (falsely) that his daughter, wearing only her chemise, had danced on the roof of Grace Vanderbilt's house for the entertainment of young gentlemen.[53]

Theodore complained to his sister Corinne, "Alice has been at home very little—spending most of her time in Newport and elsewhere, associating with the Four Hundred—individuals with whom the other members of the family have exceedingly few affiliations." [54]

Although it seems to have escaped Theodore, Alice spent so much time in Newport because she had no where else to go, except to Auntie Bye's, where she passed many more weeks than she did at home. Edith's letters of this period are full of excuses as to why Alice should not come to the White House: "Quentin has the measles . . . so I did not feel that you ought to come here and I am so happy that Auntie Bye would take you. . . . Call me up on the telephone if you want to speak to me after 10:00." [55] No wonder that when Alice was home and wanted to talk to her stepmother, she described herself as going down "to call on Edith." [56]

She became oddly invisible in the family. When she was eighteen and traveling from Boston to Albany, her train passed through the Berkshires, slowing as it passed a station, "and there on the platform was Father . . . talking emphatically to the people who were crowding around. I tried unsuccessfully to make him see me." [57] In his letters, Theodore hardly counted Alice among the family members. In one letter to Edith he waxed affectionate about every child—except Alice. No wonder she wrote in her diary, "Father doesn't care for me, that is to say one-eighth as much as he does for the other children. It is perfectly true that he doesn't, and Lord, why *should* he. We are not in the least congenial, and if I don't care overmuch for him and don't take any interest in the things he likes, why *should* he pay any attention to me or the things that I live for, except to look on them with disapproval." As an old woman, some seventy years later, Alice Longworth stuck to this view: "I don't think he had any special affection for me. I think he certainly did for my sister Ethel . . ." [58]

Although there was not much bitterness between these half sisters (as old ladies they seem to have grown genuinely fond of one another), it must have been tough on Alice to be, within the family, relentlessly and unfavorably compared to the girl who was by nature so good, so sweet—so different from Alice. According to TR's classification, Ethel was an "asset child" and Alice a "liability child."

The comparisons started early. When Ethel was three, Edith described her as "a general favorite," explaining, "If I lie down on the sofa, she will come and rub my ankles with her pretty little hands." [59] Later, while Alice was leading a social life that even modern parents would consider excessive—White House usher Ike Hoover recalled, "there was never an evening when there was not some party being given in her honor. Sunday was no exception. . . . It would be a wizard indeed who could . . . state just when she went to bed"[60]— Ethel, seven years Alice's junior, was playing surrogate mother to "the boys" at Sagamore.*

While Alice was sleeping off a Saturday-night party—Edith's diary frequently noted that "Alice slept all day"—or gone for the weekend to Newport, Ethel was up early and off to church and then to teach a Sunday-school class of black boys. Theodore, overburdened with paperwork, campaigning, traveling, and his voracious appetite for visiting friends, was delighted that his favored daughter was teaching the less fortunate—as he had done while at Harvard—and that she was such a good companion to Edith.

Ethel was not the only one with whom Alice was unfavorably compared. Corinne was among many who observed that Eleanor was "more like [TR] than any of his children"—left unsaid was that she was especially more compatible with him than was Alice. While Alice devoted herself to her own amusement, Eleanor studied political and social issues so she could discuss them with her uncle. Sixteen-year-old Eleanor piously wrote in the guest book at Bamie's house, "A laborer is worthy of his hire . . ."[62]

It was also said that Alice was more like Edith than any of Edith's own children, certainly more like her than the irrepressibly sweet Ethel. (Edith herself said that Alice resembled her stepmother more than she did her own mother.) Edith and Alice shared razor-sharp tongues and minds and a contempt for Theodore's taste in literature and art.

Theodore "scorned" Edith Wharton, who happened to be Edith's distant cousin, while his wife and older daughter adored her. As to the nearsighted Theodore's taste in art, mother and stepdaughter considered it opinionated and ignorant. They laughed when, during a visit to the St. Louis Fair, Theodore stopped to admire a statue, telling a large crowd that "he considered it a particularly fine Diana. It happened to be Apollo."[63]

---

*According to Ethel's daughter, "Mother kept house at Sagamore while my grandparents were in Washington. She was responsible for all the boys. . . . She was always in charge and she took her responsibilities very much to heart. I have letters of my mother's to my grandparents . . . giving a whole report on what the boys have done, which items had gone to the laundry."[61]

So intolerant of middle-American taste was Edith that, in a letter to Alice, she reviewed McKinley's funeral service, pronouncing it "not particularly impressive" and the music "poor. They had a melodeon like a country Sunday school."[64] Her comment about living in the White House, with its cramped family quarters and hideously Victorian furnishings—"It's like living over the store"[65]—was good enough to have been said by Alice herself. Alice described the White House furnishings as "late General Grant and early Pullman" and she admired her stepmother's efforts to rid the place of some of its more "lugubrious touches such as the acres of plush and the overwrought gilt furniture."[66]

The warmth TR inherited through his mother's Southern blood made him a man who, although he insisted on the social niceties—he would wince if a cowboy with whom he was sharing a blanket called him by his first name or neglected to attach the "Mr." to his last— loved to grasp hands and to administer bruising bear hugs. Edith and Alice, however, shared an aversion to the most conventional forms of physical contact. Alice recalled how much she loved the family breakfasts with "Father . . . in the best of spirits. . . . The only awful part was having to kiss [him]. One tried to aim somewhere on his face but his mustache usually got in the way. He never hung it out to dry and it was invariably wet and smelling of shaving soap . . . The boys got away with just a 'good morning' but Ethel and I had to do the kissing part. She was . . . docile and didn't mind. I minded terribly."[67] Even as a debutante, she didn't like touching her peers because "I didn't like the smell of people. . . . I liked to dance by myself."[68]

It was traditional to open the White House on New Year's Day to any member of the public who was "sober, washed, and free of bodily advertising."[69] A long line snaked through the Blue Room as thousands waited to shake hands with the president and first lady. Theodore enthusiastically grasped hands. Edith clutched a bouquet of white roses so that she would not have to touch the flesh of the plain folk who passed through.

According to Ethel's daughter, Edith "didn't let her emotions be easily seen. . . . I remember my mother saying that she only saw her cry once in her life."[70] Alice, even during periods of spirit-breaking tragedy, was never known to look misty-eyed.

Another quality Alice admired in her stepmother was power. Edith inspired fear in some of the most unlikely people. Even Bamie was said to be a bit afraid of her. And so was Theodore. When TR, at his own table, started waxing effusive, she would order him to keep quiet and he would. "She had a way of doing it so it didn't look rude or strange," explained one TR scholar. "She would just say, 'Now, Theodore' and that was his signal to completely shut up or move to another subject. . . . One time . . . he didn't shut up. She said, 'Now, Theodore' and he didn't heed it. 'Now, Theodore, that is just the sort of thing that makes it so hard for your friends to defend you,'" she concluded, finally silencing him except for his whimper, "Why Edie, I was only . . ."[71]

"He stands in such abject terror of Edith," observed Henry Adams, who found Theodore ridiculous and so thoroughly approved of Edith's dominance. Adams said after one White House dinner that Theodore "talks with all the fluency and *naïveté* of a schoolboy." "Would the President have a ghost of a chance if Mrs. Roosevelt ran against him?" Adams pondered.[72]

But as much as Alice admired her stepmother's power to intimidate, she must often have wished that her father were a bit less awed by her. Alice suspected, for example, that it was Edith who had "suggested" to her husband that Alice be given no official duties at the White House.

When TR did allow Alice to assume a responsible role, it was more likely to be a matter of his political advantage than of her emotional needs. In looking toward the 1904 election, TR saw Mark Hanna, then in the Senate, as a potent rival for the Republican nomination.

When Hanna's daughter Ruth married Joseph Medill McCormick (brother of Colonel Robert McCormick, the future publisher of the *Chicago Tribune*), TR, who hadn't even been invited, decided to go to Cleveland to the wedding. He saw this as the perfect chance to cozy up to Hanna's cronies among the old-line senators, as well as to the father of the bride himself. TR also decided that it would look much less peculiar if Alice were to accompany him and in the process befriend the bride. His daughter's protests that she hardly knew Ruth and felt shy about going, especially without an invitation, got her nowhere. More embarrassing yet, when Hanna died the next year, a timely occurrence that TR certainly didn't mourn, he insisted that Alice go to the Arlington Hotel, the Hannas' Washington home, to pay her condolences to Ruth. Again Alice protested—Ruth "could not possibly at such a time want to see some one whom she knew so slightly"[73]—but in vain.

TR's worries were irrational, especially after Hanna's death, but his mood didn't improve, even after he easily won the nomination. His opponent in the general election was a stodgy, drab conservative named Alton B. Parker—an anti-imperialist at a time when Americans adored Teddy's bust-our-borders approach to foreign policy. Still, Theodore worried that the public would tire of the daily newspaper dose of Alice's escapades and find relief in the colorless Parker and his presumably equally colorless family.

Alice had other matters on her mind, such as Maggie Cassini, who called her relationship with Charlie de Chambrun "a flirtation." Alice knew that he was writing the countess passionate love letters, and that Maggie was beginning to think she might be in love. Although Alice had declared herself in love with Charlie and had predicted that they would soon be engaged, she recognized defeat and turned her attention to Nick Longworth.

Maggie described her feelings for Nick as "un petit béguin . . . a little love rather than a grande passion." Still, she could not sit by and watch Alice capture Nick. "It became more and more fun to tease my friends by trying to take their beaux away from them," Maggie admitted. "I was forever stepping on other people's toes, just to satisfy my tremendous ego."

Taking Nick away from Alice was easy. He had fallen for Maggie with a grand passion, ignited the evening he met her at the marble Massachusetts Avenue mansion of Mrs. Richard Townsend. Mrs. Townsend was the daughter of a congressman who made his millions in coal and in the Pennsylvania Railroad. Said to resemble in her bearing the princess of Wales, she was known for throwing sit-down dinners for a hundred served by troops of liveried waiters chosen for their imposing height.

"Here is someone who wants to meet you," Mrs. Townsend told Maggie. "Be careful; he's dangerous!" Then, turning to Nick, she repeated the warning: "And you be careful because she's *very* dangerous!" Later that evening, "In the middle of a waltz [Nick] asked what flowers I liked best. . . . The next morning, after bringing me my coffee, Marthe [her maid] staggered in with a box the size of a coffin—inside, American Beauties with stems so long they stuck several feet out of the end. Regularly, for over a year these American Beauties came."

Although the newspapers and *Town Topics* reported that Nick could not make up his mind between the two girls—according to Maggie, "People began making bets and opinion swung back and forth like a weathervane depending upon which one of us Nick was seen with last"—Alice could see that Nick would marry Maggie in a minute if she would have him. [74]

Ethel Barrymore, who had joined the circle (she remained a life-long friend of Nick's), was Alice's guest at lunch at the White House. After lunch, they were to go to a matinee with Maggie and Nick. While the latter two waited downstairs, Alice and the young actress took the elevator upstairs to get their hats. Kermit and Quentin deliberately opened the ground floor door so that the descending elevator—self-service and operated by a rope—was trapped, for over an hour, between floors. The girls' screams were drowned out by the boys' roars of laughter. Alice's shrieks grew shriller as she imagined Maggie and Nick flirting in privacy. "Alice," Ethel Barrymore recalled, "was not amused." [75]

Nor was she amused when, as had become her custom, she asked Maggie, in what she hoped was a teasing tone, "Has Nick proposed yet?" In the past, Maggie, with a flip of her hair, had answered no. One day Maggie answered "yes" because the night before Nick had proposed as they walked in Lafayette Square. Alice was crushed: "He [Nick Longworth] is the second person [Charles de Chambrun was the first] that I vowed to have and that she has reft from me," she wrote in her diary. "So I suppose there will be a third. I don't think he should have been as nice to me as he has been . . . oh why am I such a desperate pill?" [76] Alice vowed to "retaliate" and even called Maggie "very cheap" for walking alone at night with a man.

Nick did not give up. He proposed to Maggie again one night as they rode in a sleigh between Chevy Chase and Washington. Something snapped in the harness and Nick got out in the snow to fix it. "'This is the last time I ask,' he said, struggling with the buckle. 'You will give me a sensible answer right now or we stay here until we freeze to death.' 'All right,' I said, suddenly gathering up the reins. 'Here's my answer!' I flicked the horse with the whip, the sleigh bounded forward and Nick was left standing in the snow." [77]

And so ended the congressman's pursuit of the countess—and Maggie and Alice's friendship. Alice was not going to wait around to lose a third man to Maggie's whims and, besides, a world crisis—the Russo-Japanese War—finally intruded on the girls' world.

In February 1904, Japanese warships attacked the Czar's fleet at Port Arthur, after Russia refused to withdraw its troops from Manchuria, which it had occupied in 1900 during the Boxer Uprising in China. The result was a huge loss of Russian ships and lives, and Count Cassini accused TR and Secretary of State John Hay of harboring pro-Japanese views. A series of Japanese victories did not improve Cassini's temper. TR, who wanted the war ended so as not to endanger Hay's Open Door policy in China, started acting as a mediator between Cassini and his Japanese counterpart. But Cassini so feared displeasing his superiors that he would make no concessions. Later that year Marguerite was back in St. Petersburg with her seventeen trunks, her maid, and, within a couple of months, her father.* With Cassini gone, TR was able to bring the belligerents to an agreement, a feat that won him the Nobel Peace Prize.

TR won the 1904 election in a landslide, showing himself to be the most popular president since his hero, Abraham Lincoln, and even eating into the Solid South, the first time a Republican had done so since the Civil War. Outside the South, Parker won not a single state. Alice, who momentarily shed her air of Newport superiority, was ecstatic, calling it a "smashing victory" and describing the celebration on election night as "jubilant."

With her father now the star of the show and she the star of the country, the inauguration was an event to relish, even if some of her Four Hundred friends might consider it all rather uncouth. But then a reprimand from her father changed her mood from buoyant to "resentful." Recognizing friends in the crowd, Alice had "gesticulated exuberant greetings . . . until Father rather firmly told me to sit down. I had not had the slightest idea that I was 'making a show of myself.' . . . He had been greeting friends whom he recognized . . . so why should I not do likewise?" [78] That the world's most shameless publicity hound should balk at sharing a smidgeon of the limelight infuriated Alice.

TR's touchiness persisted even after he was safely ensconced in his own term and even after he had made the startling promise, on the night of his election, that he would not seek a second full term. (Edith said that Theodore "tied with his tongue" the biggest knot

---

*The war was a disaster for the Russians, showing the weakness of the Czarist government and thus helping to precipitate the revolutions of 1905 and 1917, which would leave the Cassinis in abject poverty.

that he "could not undo with his teeth" [79] when he made this announcement, which in effect made him a lame-duck leader, limiting his power with Congress and his party.)

While reading the morning paper, he was distressed to see his daughter's name advertised, along with that of her new friend Ethel Barrymore, as tea pourers for a charity portrait show to benefit the New York Orthopedic Hospital. "Do not like the advertisements of your appearing at portrait show," TR telegraphed his daughter. "They distinctly convey the impression that any person who wishes to pay his $5 may be served with tea by you and Ethel Barrymore. I cannot consent to such use of your name and must ask you not to serve tea. In my opinion managers have shown poor taste in making this use of your name . . ." Alice poured as planned, explaining to Theodore that his telegram had arrived too late. More likely, she chose not to heed it, believing that he was becoming petty in his criticisms. [80]

That incident was one of many that led Alice to the same conclusion: she had to get married so that she would never have to go back to the White House and her father's criticisms.

She was peeved by the announcement later that year that her cousin Eleanor would beat her to the altar—on St. Patrick's Day, 1905—even if Eleanor was getting stuck with silly cousin Franklin. Although Bamie liked Franklin and helped persuade his domineering mother to allow the marriage, many of the other members of the Oyster Bay branch thought Eleanor much too good for him. Corinne's daughter wrote in her diary, "What does she see in him? I don't understand." [81]

Eleanor asked Alice to be a bridesmaid and Alice, realizing that all eyes would be on her rather than on her dowdy cousin, eagerly agreed. Alice took malicious pleasure in the pompous Franklin's insistence that the bridesmaids wear three "Prince of Wales feathers" in their hair in honor of the Roosevelt family crest—a highly dubious artifact, in Alice's opinion. Alice took a dim view of her stepmother's offer to host Eleanor's wedding in the White House, "to do for you as we should for Alice." [82] She was determined to be the first White House bride of that generation, and was relieved when Eleanor decided to marry at a relative's house in Manhattan. Alice was downright jealous when her father offered to give the bride away.

Shortly after the wedding, Alice ran into Franklin in the lobby of a

Boston hotel. The two sat swinging their heels on a trunk in an alcove outside Alice's room drinking green mints and feeling "like leprechauns on a roof. Somehow Eleanor got to hear of it and was very annoyed and said to Franklin, 'No one would know that you were her cousin. You were seen going to a woman's room. I think it would be a good idea if you and Alice didn't see each other for some time.'"[83]

That hardly mattered to Alice, who, with both Maggie and Cissy in Eastern Europe—Cissy married Count Gizycka in April 1904 and moved to Poland—finally had Nick to herself. She declared herself in love and accepted Nick's invitation to visit Rookwood—the Longworth estate set on two hundred forested acres in Cincinnati—as the guest of his sister Nan Wallingford. The visit was set for early June 1905, when Nick knew that Rookwood's real mistress, his mother, would be abroad.

Susan Longworth, widowed for fifteen years, hoped, indeed expected, that her only son and the most beloved of her three children, would never marry. If anyone was going to keep house for "Colie," as Nicholas Longworth III was called in the family, she would. She saw herself and her son as companions and confidants, together growing older and more eccentric as her two daughters, devoted to their mother and brother above all else, fawned over the matriarch and the sole Longworth heir. Oddly, it seems not to have disturbed Susan that this bachelor son would therefore produce no Nicholas IV, or at least no legitimate one.

Mrs. Longworth and her daughters had taken a house on Beacon Street in Boston so that they could be near Nick while he was at Harvard. When he was elected to his first term in Congress, his mother followed him to Washington, renting a house for the two of them on the corner of Eighteenth and I streets.

Alice's first visit to Cincinnati passed without a proposal. The twenty-one-year-old was aching to get married—she even consulted a fortuneteller, who predicted that she would be married by age twenty-two—partly because she fancied herself in love with Nick but mostly because she wanted to escape her family. "I think I might well have gone abroad . . . if I hadn't married," she said later.[84] Alice soon saw a way to get a proposal.

In the early years of the century Congress took a long spring-to-fall recess. Congressmen who didn't need to work for a living cast about for some amusing way to pass the months. In 1905 there was an especially appealing prospect—a trip to the Far East, led by Secretary of War William Howard Taft, that would last from late June to late October. It was officially billed as an inspection tour of the Philippines,* but street-smart reporters called it by its right name—a junket.

Alice's parents happily gave her their permission, figuring that the long trip would provide a respite from reading about their daughter in the morning paper. Alice suggested to Nick that he might like to join her, putting Taft, whose wife was to remain at home, in the awkward position of chaperoning the wayward children of two very close friends. (The Tafts and Longworths were old friends from Cincinnati. Nick was Taft's congressman.)

The secretary of war, who adored Nick's mother and sisters, did not approve of Nick's "Un-Ohio-like sophistication." He told his wife—who strongly disapproved of both Nick and Alice—"I know that she and Nick indulge in conversations on subjects that are ordinarily tabooed between men and women much older than they are and indeed are usually confined to husband and wife." [85]

Before Taft agreed to preside over the original "Love Boat," he sought the approval of Susan Longworth. He warned her that if Nick and Alice sailed together they would certainly return an engaged couple. Mrs. Longworth laughed and assured Taft that Nick was "a thoroughly confirmed old bachelor." [86]

During the last days of June, a group of eighty congressmen, wives, friends, and servants boarded a train bound for San Francisco. From there, they would catch a steamer for the ten-day crossing to Japan. Apparently thinking that he might keep Alice and Nick apart, Taft arranged for a private railroad car, on which six of the party, including Alice and excluding Nick, were invited. The rest followed in regular cars. En route to San Francisco they received news of the death of Secretary of State John Hay. Alice worried only that her father might call Taft home and cancel the trip.

* Five years earlier, McKinley had appointed Taft the first civil governor of the Philippines. His mission had been to end military rule of the islands, which had been ceded to the United States following the Spanish-American War, and to prepare the Filipinos for self-government. Before Taft left in 1904 to become Roosevelt's secretary of war, he promised the people, whom he called "our little brown brothers," that he would return with a delegation of congressmen to see the new Philippine legislature in action. Roosevelt was eager for Taft to fulfill this promise and even more eager for him to stop in Tokyo to sound out the Japanese about their interest in the Philippines.

ALICE ROOSEVELT LONGWORTH

Alice set off in grand style, accompanied by her maid, Anna, three flat trunks, two steamer trunks, suitcases, bags, hatboxes, and a special container for her sidesaddle[87]—although she would soon pack that away and shock her fellow voyagers by riding astride. By the time they reached Manila, Anna had suffered what appeared to be a nervous breakdown—probably a result of endless packing and unpacking and the elaborate care that Alice's wardrobe required. She might change, within the day, from white linen traveling suit, to bathing costume (a silk or mohair dress, high necked, with sleeves and long black stockings), to riding habit, to evening gown, all requiring appropriate underclothes (including petticoats with lace and embroidered ruffles and small trains), hat, shoes, handbag, parasol, jewelry, and hair ornaments. While Anna was given a few days respite, Alice was attended to by Taft's own valet, who undoubtedly found the girl a relief compared to the perpetually sweating, three-hundred-plus-pound cabinet secretary, whom Alice described as "enormous in white duck."[88]

For Alice, who had never been west of the Mississippi, much less to Europe,* even the train ride was exciting. TR and Edith's hopes that Alice and the headlines would enjoy a brief separation were soon dashed. If anything, this junket, so full of exotic people, places, and possibilities, generated more press coverage.† Even her luggage was "listed in breathless detail."[89]

Alice soon supplied the press with more meaty material. The last day on the train was the Fourth of July and Alice set off firecrackers on the back platform and shot her revolver at the telegraph poles.[91] No sooner did the party arrive at San Francisco's Palace Hotel than she

---

*Three years earlier, Alice was set to go to London for Edward VII's coronation, but the news of her departure sparked so much criticism that Theodore canceled the trip. The controversy centered on what the American Princess's exact rank would be. Only the offspring of officially recognized sovereigns could be seated in Westminster Abbey, and some of TR's critics thought he was getting dangerously close to fancying himself just that. The following year, Edith, fearing that "too much fuss" would be made over her stepdaughter, vetoed an invitation from the governor of Jamaica. Alice, who considered herself dull and unattractive, said a fuss was just what she was looking for.

†Alice's adventures were reported in newspapers worldwide, generating stacks of fan letters—for example the following from a man named Hanssen in Denmark: "To Denmark the fame of your beauty and endowment has come. . . . I promise you that if you fulfill my prayer [to send a photo] I shall protect and keep holy your image."[90]

The President's Daughter

slipped out of the view of Taft and her chaperon, Mrs. Newlands, the wife of the senator from Nevada. She headed for Chinatown, notorious for its opium dens and off-limits to any girl with even the slightest pretense of respectability. Theodore's reaction when he, along with millions of Americans, read of Alice's adventure, went unrecorded.

On July 8, the entire party boarded the *Manchuria*, described in the press as a "floating palace," for the ten-day crossing to Japan, to be broken midway by a stop in Hawaii. Alice, who had no fear of Taft—she considered him ineffectually amiable and servile—derailed Taft's plan to separate her from Nick. Taft was surprised to find them together at his table in the ship's dining room.

In Hawaii the band played "Alice, Where Art Thou?" following "a rather expurgated hula." Alice asked if she could see "a less *jeune fille* version" and not only saw it but performed it. She further shocked her fellow passengers by lingering too long with Nick and a few others on the beach at Waikiki. "I missed the boat at the wharf . . . so in a launch with Nick . . . I pursued the *Manchuria* out into the open Pacific."[92]

Alice simply ignored her chaperones, even the imposing Miss Mabel Boardman, later the head of the American Red Cross who bulldozed Clara Barton into retirement (she was so tall and regal that it was said that the prince of Wales once mistook her for his mother). Alice's indiscretions continued. She jumped—dressed in a white linen suit—into a canvas pool that had been rigged up on the *Manchuria*'s deck, and lured Bourke Cockran, a Tammany congressman, whose oratory was said to rival William Jennings Bryan's, to join her. Alice could not understand why the papers splashed the story on their front pages. (As she told Bobby Kennedy years later, "Had I jumped into a swimming pool *without* my clothes, *that* would have been outrageous.")[93]

While her husband junketed, Mrs. William Howard Taft vacationed in England. On her trip back to Washington she had trouble getting her baggage back to the boat. Afraid that her trunks would be left behind, she announced, "I am the wife of the Secretary of War." No one was impressed. In desperation, she added, "You know, William Howard Taft—the man who is escorting Miss Alice Roosevelt in the Orient." Suddenly her baggage practically flew to the boat.[94]

In Japan, the Taft party was treated like conquering heroes or visiting royalty. The emperor fawned over Princess Alice, whose father, he thought, was about to let him get away with the lion's share of the spoils of war. The emperor tried to install Alice in a palace, but the American minister insisted that she stay at the American legation. "We drove through crowded streets . . . jammed with cheering citizens, brass bands, and hundreds of Japanese banner-bearers," she recalled. ". . . Crowds were on the platforms to shout, *Banzai!* as we passed." *[95]

Alice ignored Taft's distaste for her habit of smoking in public. She kept her cigarettes in the compartment of a gold vanity case meant for hairpins. In Korea, she made an unplanned impression: "Someone had spilled a whiskey and soda on me, and as I got off the train with my small black dog under my arm, my cigarette case as usual dropped spilling its contents at the missionaries' feet. So I arrived in an atmosphere of alcohol and tobacco."[97]

In the Philippines, they were greeted by tribesmen, including the sultan of Sulu, "wiry, savage looking, little Malays . . . in their best costumes." The sultan proposed marriage, telling Alice that his subjects were so devoted to her that if she would remain he would make her his sultana of the Sulu archipelago. Alice responded, "In a harem? As his seventh wife?"[98]

Alice preferred Nick, and around this time they reached an understanding, although the official announcement would await their return to Washington. Taft's entreaties to Alice, "I think I ought to know if you are engaged to Nick," were met with the reply, "More or less, Mr. Secretary, more or less."[99] To her friends, Alice expressed some doubts. She asked the young American minister in Japan, Lloyd Griscom, "Do you see that old, bald-headed man scratching his ear over there?" "Do you mean Nick Longworth?" he asked. "Yes," she answered. "Can you imagine any young girl marrying a fellow like that?" "Why, Alice," Griscom replied. "You couldn't find anybody nicer." In her diary, she was much more passionate: "I love you with everything that is in me Nick, Nick, my Nick."[100]

Actually, Nick was beginning to panic at the prospect of ending his bachelor days and so was Alice, who could not forget that she was

*Their reception was much less grand when part of the party—Taft and most of the delegation returned home from Hong Kong while Alice, Nick, and a few others continued to Peking—stopped in Japan en route home. The treaty ending the Russo-Japanese War had just been signed, and Japan felt it had been denied its just due. Overnight, TR went from hero to villain, and Alice was advised to pretend to be an "itinerant Englishwoman."[96]

second choice and that, before this trip, Nick would occasionally neglect to call or write for days at a time. While in Korea, Alice wrote him a note that she never sent: "Your losing your temper and getting these uncontrollable *dislikes for me* has got to stop. You say that it is because I get on your nerves. If that is the case it is . . . the pot calling the kettle black, as no one could accuse you of over-refinement in words or deeds." [101]

The meeting with the empress dowager vastly improved Alice's mood. Seventy years later she still wore the gowns made from the empress's gift—rolls of the finest silk, brocaded with gold. Alice's relatives liked to joke that all that loot—which also included two rings, a pair of earrings, some white jade, a white fox and an ermine coat—was what kept the empress so high in Alice's opinion that she ranked her with Catherine the Great, Queen Elizabeth I, Queen Hatshepsut, and Cleopatra as history's greatest women rulers.

Alice's relatives also liked to joke that she admired the empress because she was so ruthless in her climb from the emperor's favorite concubine, to his secondary wife, to empress. To keep her place on the Dragon Throne she did away with two weak emperors, one her own son and the other her nephew.

Alice accepted the empress's invitation to spend the night in the Summer Palace before her presentation at court early the next morning, while the others stayed fourteen miles away in Peking. Alice was announced by the chamberlain, a eunuch, who slithered on his belly toward this woman whom Alice recalled as having "palpable" power and a "cruel, thin mouth, turned up at one corner, drooping a little at the other." [102] The empress then kicked him until he rolled over like a dog and exited the same way he entered. [103]

After the presentation came the garden party. While the others were expected to walk, Alice was seated on a yellow tasseled and cushioned chair, carried on the shoulders of eight bearers and surrounded by "chattering court officials and eunuchs." The empress's interpreter was Wu Ting Fang, whom Alice knew from his days in Washington as minister. "He stood between us, a little to the side, but suddenly, as the conversation was going on, the Empress said something in a small savage voice, whereat he turned quite gray, and got down on all fours, his forehead touching the ground. The Empress would speak; he would lift his head and say it in English to me; back would go his forehead to the ground while I spoke; up would come his head again while he said it in Chinese to the Empress; then back to the ground would go his forehead again." (When Alice later described this scene to her father, he suggested that "it might have been to show us that this man whom we accepted as an equal was to her no more than something to put her foot on.")[104]

In Tokyo, en route to the seaport city of Yokohama, where those still traveling on the junket would board ship to San Francisco, they met E. H. Harriman, who had been looking over railroad properties in Manchuria. He and his wife were traveling with their own party, which included a much more junior member of the Four Hundred, Bertie Goelet—a young man who was even richer than most of the sort who so irritated Theodore. The Harriman group joined the congressional group and they sailed together on the *Siberia* on October 13.

Then came the sort of frivolous prank that so exasperated Theodore, who with the rest of the world, read of it in the newspaper. Goelet bet Harriman that the *Siberia* could not beat the record set by the *Korea* of making the west-to-east trip in ten days. To Theodore, this was an utterly wasteful dare. It was one thing to row faster than another man, or to ride a horse faster, and to do it no matter how miserable the weather—but to lounge aboard a luxurious ship, drinking, dining, and dancing, while the crew toiled and for its sweat gained nothing but a big tip, was ludicrous. It was just what one might expect from the likes of Harriman.

Harriman won, as the *Siberia* bested the *Korea*'s record by twenty-seven seconds. No sooner had they docked than Harriman leaped into another challenge—beating the previous rail speed record between San Francisco and New York. The railroad tycoon ushered a select group, including Alice and Nick, into his private train, ahead of which raced a pilot engine whose sole function was to make sure that the route was clear.

Theodore was outraged by the overheated news dispatches describing his daughter traveling in velvet, mahogany-paneled, gold-plated luxury as the guest of a man whom he considered a criminal. TR telegraphed Harriman and ordered him to slow down. Even Harriman, whom Alice described as not so much hungry for the "pomp" of great wealth as he was hungry for "power," could not ignore the president.[105]

Alice had often had trouble keeping her mind on the complicated social and political problems of the countries she visited. Always first on her mind was the loot that was hers for the grabbing. Willard Straight, a friend who observed her in Korea—he was secretary to the U.S. minister in Korea—wrote a poem about Alice's greedy romp through the Far East and titled it "Alice in Plunderland."

When she landed in San Francisco on October 26, 1905, the day before Theodore's birthday, he was greeted with an unexpected present—the assumption that he would pay the duty on twenty-seven boxes of Alice's spoils.

A month later, he was greeted with another present—second-term Congressman Nicholas Longworth III, thirty-six years old and a fellow Harvard graduate and "Brother Honorary of the Porcellian Club," stood in TR's study and formally asked the president's permission to marry his daughter. Meanwhile, Alice was in her stepmother's bedroom trying to summon up the courage to tell her.

Alice later described herself as feeling "shy and self-conscious" about telling the family that she was engaged. "I had the perfectly unwarranted feeling that they might be 'sentimental' about it" [106]— unwarranted because Edith was as likely to have grabbed Alice and kissed her as she was to have stood up at an official White House dinner and belted out a song.

There was another reason why Alice stalled for four weeks and then told her stepmother the news while she was brushing her teeth. Alice wanted her to "have a moment to think before she said anything." [107] She feared that her stepmother might blurt out how bad a choice Nick was, having earlier warned Alice, "You know, your friend from Ohio is a very heavy drinker." [108]

So worried was Alice about parental approval of the match that this girl, who so loved to eat and had only recently shocked Edith's friends by appearing at a tea with a sandwich in one hand and a spare in the other, had lost twenty pounds and appeared pale and agitated. Alice needed approval from Edith and Theodore because she wanted a White House wedding. Also, had the president and/or first lady showed the slightest sign of balking at her wonderful son, Mrs. Longworth, who controlled the family fortune, would have tied the purse strings into a knot.

Alice was finally forced to disclose her engagement because the newsapers were about to do it for her. Since the couple's return from the Far East, rumors of the engagement had been daily front-page fare. Finally the editor of the *Chicago Tribune* sent its Washington Bureau Chief an ultimatum: "Is Alice Roosevelt engaged or is she not?" The bureau chief wired back, "She went out driving with Nick Longworth this afternoon, without a chaperon. If they are not engaged they ought to be." [109]

On December 13, the president and first lady invited Susan Longworth to lunch at the White House. On the morning of December 14, the *Tribune* anounced the engagement.

Of the three parents, TR, a notorious poor judge of character, was the only one who was pleased about the match.

5

The Longworth Family

In its day, the Longworth clan was as prominent as any in America and more colorful than most. Its American patriarch, Nicholas Longworth I, started the country's first major winery, befriended Lincoln, Longfellow, and Lafayette, and became the richest man west of the Alleghenies and the second richest in the country, behind John Jacob Astor.

The family came from Worcestershire, England, and later London. Francis Longworth, proprietor of a house near the Globe Theater, decided he had had enough of the stench of a nearby beer garden and accepted a land grant from Queen Elizabeth I, making him the proud master of a castle in Ireland.

In 1747 Francis's grandson left Ireland for the settlements of Newark, New Jersey, where he lived in "good credit and repute" as the king's magistrate. His son, Thomas, followed him as prosperous magistrate until the Revolution, when he was chased out of Newark barely two steps ahead of an angry mob. Thomas had remained loyal to the king, and, as descendant Clara Longworth de Chambrun [Nick's sister] later complained, every loyalist "who refused to betray the trust placed in him was declared a 'traitor.'"[1]

The Thomas Longworths soon found themselves in very reduced circumstances, as the revolutionary government seized most of their property. By the time Nicholas was born, in 1784—the year the new United States ratified the peace treaty with England—the family was so hard hit by fines and confiscations that Nicholas's future course was set. He would seek his fortune elsewhere.

At age twenty, Nick headed for Sea Island, where his brother had established himself as a captain whose main cargo allegedly consisted of African slaves. Clara claimed that Nick soon left because he had fallen in love with the daughter of a Carolina plantation owner, but so despised slavery that he couldn't marry a girl whose family fortune depended on it.* Another descendant claimed that Nick left "with a very angry father after him" when he "got a young lady in trouble."[2]

Nick's next stop was Pittsburgh, where he caught a flatboat to Cincinnati, arriving in the fledgling settlement—population under one thousand—in 1804. He had barely a penny in his pocket, but he did have a letter of introduction to a prominent judge, a former neighbor of Nick's parents', who, by espousing the patriots' instead of the king's cause, had prospered. After six months of apprenticeship, Nick hung out his shingle in a little house on Second Street. Three years later he married a widow named Susan Howell—daughter of Captain Silas Howell, one of the city's earliest settlers, who had served under George Washington and was an aide-de-camp to Lafayette.

Nick had a quality that would not be passed down to his male descendants—he wanted to make lots of money, and quickly. He realized that in Cincinnati, founded a few years after his birth, there were ample opportunities, for the town, which sits on the banks of the Ohio River, had the potential to become a thriving port. (The population would grow more than two hundredfold in the sixty years after Nick's arrival.) Before the first steamboat docked, Nick began acquiring land.

He made it known that he would accept land in lieu of payment for legal services. He successfully defended one man accused of horse stealing. "If you can collect two secondhand [gin] stills, left for debt in Joel Williams' waterside tavern, you are welcome to them," the penniless client told him. Williams, who planned to build a distillery, was not eager to relinquish the stills. In their place he offered Nick a thirty-acre lot, admitting that it was "not worth shucks," but might eventually be worth the price of the copper in the stills. Nick grabbed the lot, located in what is now downtown Cincinnati, and valued, fifty years later, at $2 million.[3]

---

*So progressive was Nick that, according to family lore, Harriet Beecher Stowe based a scene in *Uncle Tom's Cabin* on a real act of Nick's courage in hiding a runaway slave. "Once liberated," wrote Clara, the slave "remained in his protector's family as a faithful 'body-servant.'"

The Longworth Family

Nick soon gave up the practice of law to devote himself to his real estate investments, art, gardening, and his belief in the interplay between moral and physical health. (When he died in 1863 he was searching for a cure for cancer.) The latter two passions led him to plant grapevines on the hills along the Ohio River. Nick was appalled by the amount of hard liquor consumed by workingmen and urged them to forsake their "red-eye" for wine. "He realized the value of pure wine in the development of brain cells and tissues," wrote Clara.[4]

He imported hundreds of Germans to plant, tend, and harvest the vines of Catawba grapes that produced a sort of pink champagne called sparkling Catawba. By the middle of the century, Ohio was the country's largest wine producer.

Convinced that his Catawba compared favorably to European vintages, Nick sent samples to Queen Victoria and to his friend Longfellow. The poet was so impressed that he wrote an ode to Catawba wine, in which he dubbed Cincinnati "the Queen of the West, in her garlands dressed."

Nick was undersized, homely, and dressed in shabby all-black suits, with notes pinned to his cuffs to remind him of chores and appointments. He walked with his head down, whittling soft pine with his pen-knife. When he arrived at his office he would invariably find some poverty-stricken soul searching for money or a job. The more unappealing the supplicant, the more likely Nick was to help.[5]

He was also a patron of struggling artists including, prior to the Civil War, a black painter and a woman artist who described him as "a little bit of an ugly man. . . . His manners are extremely rough and almost coarse."[6]

Susan and Nick had three daughters and one son, Joseph; the latter born in 1813 and the grandfather of the man who would marry Alice Roosevelt. As befitting a man of so much property, Nick finally bowed to his daughters' wishes and traded way up from the modest house he and Susan bought as newlyweds. The new place was a colonial mansion with the imposing name Belmont. Located on fashionable Pike Street, in what is now downtown, it was considered the finest home in all Cincinnati. Set on wide expanses of lawn and garden, with its portico reached by marble steps, it resembled the White House, with which it shared an architect.

Strangers who toured Belmont's renowned gardens—which Nick

opened to the public, even announcing in the newspaper the blooming of an exotic cactus—often mistook Nick for a hired hand. When Abraham Lincoln was in Cincinnati arguing a case, he visited Belmont, where he saw a shabby little man puttering around in the garden. "My good man, do you think your master would allow me to look around the gardens?" The man tipped his hat and said, "Certainly, Sir." Lincoln tipped him a dollar, never knowing who he was.[7] (Longfellow, Trollope, Dickens, Thackery, and Lafayette also visited Belmont.)

When Nick's son Joseph married Ann Marie Rives in 1841 and brought her north from her family's beloved Virginia plantation, he showed none of his father's hesitation about marrying a slave-owner's daughter. As Americans, the Rives were older by a century than the Longworths, having settled in the Virginias during the Cromwellian period. In the family of Joseph Longworth, as in the family of the elder Theodore Roosevelt, cousins, nephews, and in-laws found themselves fighting on opposing sides in the Civil War—an upheaval to which Joseph seemed largely oblivious.

Although he dabbled a bit in managing his father's investments, Joseph never worked. Instead he read, collected, traveled, endowed art schools, museums, and orchestras, staged amateur theatricals for his children and grandchildren, painted, planted trees, and entertained the likes of Emerson, Thackeray, Wilde, and Presidents Garfield and Hayes.

Soon these pleasant pastimes would be enjoyed amid surroundings even grander than Belmont's—the sloping and forested terrain of the family's new home, Rookwood (so named because of the area's large population of crows). Annie had grown increasingly homesick for the sort of open life she had loved as a girl. She wanted their three children, Landon (who died in early manhood), Nicholas II, and Maria, to experience the freedom of country life. When cholera struck, leaving more than forty downtown residents dead, she insisted that the family move to the country (even though officials assured the city's "good" families that casualties were high only among recent immigrants from Ireland and Germany).

There was no need to buy land, as two hundred acres on the eastern hills—only four miles from the city but considered country— were already in the family, given by land grant to Silas Howell. Joseph designed a house that Alice Longworth later described as "*enchanting*, it was so awful. . . . It was built in the very worst Victorian tradition and was definitely out to impress. It was a series of brick boxes connected by a large 'Italian style' brick tower." [8]

Nevertheless, the children grew up happily at Rookwood, raised by a father—their mother died early—who was as unpretentious as he was philanthropic. He was fat and, like his father, unusually short and ill-kempt in baggy clothes. For his trips to the city, he relied on streetcars and before them on omnibuses. [9]

Joseph had a positive disdain for money. "I cannot bear . . . being infested with money," he used to say. When money came in from his father's investments, he proclaimed it "excess income" and used it to endow the Cincinnati Art School. He was one of the founders of the Cincinnati Symphony Orchestra, and he gave a huge parcel of family property to the city. That land is now called Eden Park. [10]

The character in a family of characters was the only daughter, Maria, recalled by a descendant as "kind of a wild gal for those days." [11] Even the dreamy Joseph noticed, and to keep her out of trouble he gave her the resources, including an abandoned riverbank schoolhouse that he bought at a sheriff's sale, to launch what became the world-renowned Rookwood Pottery.

Rookwood's first kilns were drawn in 1880. Nine years later Rookwood was a profitable concern, having been launched at the height of a fad for china painting. The pottery suffered during the depression and went bankrupt in 1941, but today Rookwood pieces bring very high prices.

When Maria Storer started Rookwood she was twelve years into a rocky marriage to George Ward Nichols, a colonel in the Union army, who was handsome, fiery, accustomed to barking orders and having them obeyed. Maria was also used to being boss and so the marriage was never peaceful.

Family gossip has it that while the Colonel lay on his deathbed in 1885, Maria was already having an affair with Bellamy Storer, said to be "the handsomest man in southern Ohio." He became her second husband six months after the death of her first. Although Bellamy was very tall and she was tiny, according to one relative, "She could lead him around with a ring in his nose." [12]

She also spent great chunks of the family fortune in efforts to influence Washington policy and appointments. It was Maria Longworth Storer who lobbied her old friend William McKinley—to whom she had given a $10,000 campaign contribution—to give the assistant Navy secretary post to her new friend Theodore Roosevelt. In addition she founded the Cincinnati summer opera and the May Festival, by convincing Theodore Thomas that if he would conduct the orchestra she would raise the money to back it and to build the Music Hall.

Maria's brother Nick II was a lawyer, a judge, and a man who much preferred such hobbies as woodcarving, paddle boating, and photography to working. In 1883, two years after winning a seat on the Ohio Supreme Court and just thirty-eight years old, he retired. He continued, however, to dispose of some of the Longworths' best income-bearing lots, the proceeds of which he gave to the art school.

When Nick II died in 1890—his daughter Clara blamed a chill that he caught while attending a gubernatorial inauguration in a "driving rain and sleet"[13]—he left a forty-five-year-old widow with a set of imposing bloodlines and a single interest: the only man left in her life, her son Nicholas III. Susan Walker Longworth, born in 1845 in Cincinnati, was the daughter of the founder of the Cincinnati Law School. Judge Timothy Walker was a direct descendant of Elder William Brewster, who sailed on the Mayflower and, as a leader of the Pilgrims, helped establish the Plymouth Colony.

Susan was close to her daughters, Clara and Nan, but there was never a doubt that she would sacrifice their interests for Nick's. And Clara, the younger of the two, had plenty of interests. She wrote several books on Shakespeare in both English and French, two volumes of autobiography, a biography of her brother, and a history of Cincinnati. She had a degree from the Sorbonne and was one of the few women to be made a knight of the Legion of Honor. Newsman Frank Waldrop, who knew her as an old woman, said she was as "homely as a mud fence, but she was . . . smart as a whip."[14]

Like her mother, Clara apparently had little resentment of her role, abnormal even for those times, as the indefatigable booster of her brother. She struggled to become accepted as a serious Shakespeare scholar at the same time that she filled her books with catty comments on the inferiority and frivolity of her sex and, like her mother, strongly opposed women's suffrage. Despite her interest in public affairs—she signed letters to the editor with the pen name "Clarence Brownfield"—she praised her congressman brother for being "always ready to discuss his point of view with those who were really interested in a subject, even should the questioner be a woman . . ." [15]

In her worshipful biography of her brother, *The Making of Nicholas Longworth*, published two years after his death (and so reminiscent of Corinne's biography of TR), Clara wrote of the joy that greeted the birth of the family's first born: "When sisters arrived, they fell in quite naturally with a tradition firmly established . . . that all that was best in life must be reserved for [Nick]." [16]

Not surprisingly, Susan Longworth and her daughters greeted news of Nick's marriage to Alice Roosevelt with dread. They had too much invested in this man, whom Clara called the "first born of Israel," [17] to see him come under the influence not only of this girl, who obviously didn't know the meaning of the word subservience, but, worse yet, under the influence of that compelling creature whom all the world called "Teddy."

Even Clara admitted that Nick, who followed his father to Harvard, was a mediocre student. In Nick's day, she explained, "moderation" was the fashion: "I remember that those who did more than was necessary to pass examinations honorably were stigmatized by their fellows as 'Greasy Grinds.'" [18] Nick was so proud of his mediocre record that he pasted in his college scrapbook a note from his professor of political economy: "I regret to be obliged to say that I do not think you are performing . . . in a systematic manner." [19] (During TR's Harvard days it was also de rigueur to earn nothing higher than the "gentleman's C." Still, the future president could not restrain himself. TR not only ran to classes when his more elegant classmates ambled, he also leaped to his feet to shout questions at professors, until one shouted back, "See here, Roosevelt, let me talk. *I'm* running this course.") [20]

To Nick, being a "good sport" was the top priority—a goal for which he almost gave his right arm. During his initiation into DKE, Nick's soon-to-be fraternity brothers branded him with lighted cigars, causing nicotine poisoning and fears that amputation would be necessary. "To be a 'good sport,'" Clara explained approvingly, "was a thing that he demanded of himself." [21]

Although the family vineyards had been destroyed in the 1860s by phylloxera (plant lice), Nick III grew up guzzling the lore, history, and romance of wine making. By the time he reached Harvard, he was guzzling more than lore. He had become a connoisseur of wine

ALICE ROOSEVELT LONGWORTH

and a fledgling alcoholic. Joining the Porcellian, a club whose major activity was drinking,* turned Nick from fledgling to confirmed.

Nick's one serious interest was the violin. He was first violinist and often soloist with the college orchestra. His college scrapbook is full of rave reviews, but it also contains the hand with which he won a poker game—ace, queen, king, jack and ten—"Hand held by N. Longworth Jr., December 10, 1887." [22]

Although Nick was short, he was fastidious about his dress and is best remembered at Harvard for redesigning the commencement costume, which then required full evening dress. He complained that he would be "god damned if he was going to look like a French waiter at breakfast." [23]

After graduation in 1891, Nick spent one year at Harvard Law School, reluctant to leave his college friends. But "for the sake of old traditions," [24] he finished at the Cincinnati Law School, which had been founded by his grandfather and where one of his professors was William Howard Taft.

Nick then took on a task that soured him forever on practicing law. He tried to untangle his mother's estate from his Aunt Maria Storer's. He was soon looking for more lively work and leaning in the direction of politics. Although friends and family professed to be horrified by the very thought, politics was a natural choice. His own father had run for a seat on the Ohio Supreme Court.

Still Nick's relatives gasped with high disdain reminiscent of that voiced by TR's a decade earlier. Clara recalled family members solemnly warning that Nick "could not touch pitch without being defiled."† When Nick joined the Young Men's Blaine Club,‡ a cell of Ohio boss George B. Cox's machine, friends lamented, "The name of Longworth should never be connected with that of . . . Cox." [26]

---

*It was said that the reason Harvard president Charles Eliot had refused to join the Porcellian was that it was the most intemperate of the college's clubs.

†Corinne Roosevelt Robinson wrote in strikingly similar terms of her brother's decision to devote himself to politics: "At that time, even more than now, 'politics' was considered as something far removed from the life of any one brought up to other spheres than that of mudslinging and corruption." [25]

‡James G. Blaine, Speaker of the House, senator, secretary of state, was known during his 1884 run for the presidency as "the continental liar from the state of Maine" because of some questionable financial dealings. Although TR supported a reformer over Blaine in the 1884 race for the Republican nomination, when the reformer lost at the convention, TR proved himself a good party man by supporting Blaine.

The Longworth Family

While Nick became an obedient cog in the state Republican machine, marching in torchlight parades, pulling voters out of their houses to vote Republican, and in general showing mindless obedience to Bosses Cox and Hanna, his mother was able to profess pride in her "statesman" son without ever acknowledging the existence of such low types. As Alice later observed, Cox and Hanna "were never invited to the house in Cincinnati. I don't think old Mrs. Longworth knew anything about bosses and things like that." *[27]

In Nick's first race for the Ohio House he was defeated—not surprisingly, as the reformers, or "mugwumps," were in control that year, and Nick had entered the race knowing his chances of winning were slight. Cox showed his gratitude to this surprisingly tractable rich boy by making sure that Nick won in 1899.

After serving in the Ohio House, Nick moved up to the state senate. When, in 1902, Charles Taft, William Howard's brother, † decided not to run for a second term representing the First District in the U.S. House, Nick was his obvious successor and, again with Cox's help, the easy winner.

Nick, who was as much a dandy as the young TR, was as incongruous a sight in Columbus as TR had been in Albany. In the lower house of Congress, hardly a hotbed of sartorial splendor, Nick was equally conspicuous. As Archie Butt noted in his description of a White House diplomatic reception, "It was noticeable how few Congressmen there were in line. . . . It made the reception all the more brilliant, for the fewer Congressional people there are at these receptions, the fewer incongruous costumes there are to be seen . . ."[29]

Nick, as it happened, was there that night, and even Butt couldn't have faulted his costume. (Or his dancing. Countess Cassini, among others, described Nick as the best dancer she'd ever known.) Nick often appeared at late-night sessions of the House still dressed in his

---

*In that regard, and many others, she resembled Franklin Roosevelt's mother. Joe Alsop wrote of Franklin inviting the political powerhouse Huey Long to dine at Hyde Park. To avoid an argument with Mama, he gave her no warning. "Seeing 'the Kingfish' at her own table was too much for Mrs. . . . Roosevelt, and she retaliated. In a stentorian whisper audible to the entire table, she inquired blandly. *Who is the awful man* sitting next to Franklin?' "[28]

†Charles, a pillar of Cincinnati society—he had major investments in the city's baseball team, streetcar lines, opera house, leading hotel, and newspaper—made large annual contributions to his brother Will's household, allowing the future president and chief justice to pursue his career as a judge, cabinet member, and politician.

evening clothes and looking as if he had walked out of a Gibson illustration. His supporters once bashfully asked him if he could please refrain from wearing spats on the House floor, as "some of the plainer fellows don't know what to make of them." He couldn't, he told them, and continued to favor patent leather shoes, brown spats, a walking stick, and a hankie that matched his socks.

Elegant as he was, Nick III could not escape the Longworth looks. What one noticed first about him was how bald and how short he was. He came by the latter naturally. Nick I's only elective office had been that of fence viewer, a task he shared with a man named John Kilgour. The two were described in doggerel:

> *For Kilgour, straight, and slim, and tall,*
> *Could gaze severely over each wall,*
> *While Nicholas, rather short and small,*
> *Spied through the holes where pigs might crawl.* [30]

Joseph Longworth told of his humiliation when "the clerk in a clothing store responded to his request for flannel trousers by yelling through a speaking tube: 'Say, Bill, send down a pair of . . . *short fats.*'"[31]

Still, Alice seemed to have found Nick as attractive as any man. Possibly, his stature and the fact that he looked older than his years reminded her of her own five-foot-eight-inch father.

When Nick announced his engagement, Susan Longworth, who believed deeply in propriety, must have wished that she had ordered her son to stay home and look after family affairs. For had Nick not gone to Washington, he probably would have remained her Rookwood companion and, if he married, he would have chosen some appropriately docile Cincinnati heiress.

A year before her son's marriage, Susan got a taste of things to come. For the benefit of visitors to Washington during TR's inauguration, the Inaugural Committee had put placards on buildings of historic interest and on houses in which prominent people lived. Alice recruited her friend, Bertie Goelet, and they ordered his valet, who could draw, to copy the official placards, but to add unofficial information supplied by Alice. Congressman Bourke Cockran, whom Alice described as a "professional Irish sympathizer," was to get a shield that informed the visitor, "Here lives the Irish Ambassador. All he

Theodore Roosevelt, Sr., was, in his son's eyes, nearly perfect—a rare combination of a man of good works and good times. *(Sagamore Hill National Historic Site)*

Theodore Roosevelt's mother, Mittie, was a Southern-bred beauty. She died on the same day, in the same house, as her daughter-in-law, Alice's mother. *(Sagamore Hill National Historic Site)*

Eighteen-year-old Theodore Roosevelt *(left)* poses with his sister Corinne *(seated on the ground)*, his brother, Elliott, and his childhood sweetheart, Edith Kermit Carow, who, ten years later, would become his second wife. *(Sagamore Hill National Historic Site)*

Alice Hathaway Lee at the time Theodore Roosevelt fell in love
with her. She died two days after her daughter, Alice Lee, was born.
(Sagamore Hill National Historic Site)

Alice Lee Roosevelt, one
year old. *(By permission of the
Houghton Library, Harvard
University)*

Theodore's sister Anna—
Alice's beloved Auntie
Bye, who seemed headed
for spinsterhood—adored
"Baby Lee" and longed
to raise her as her own.
*(Sagamore Hill National
Historic Site)*

The Roosevelt family in 1895: *(from left)* Theodore, Archie, Ted Jr.,
Alice, Kermit, Edith, Ethel (Quentin would be born in 1897).
(Sagamore Hill National Historic Site)

Even as first lady, Edith Kermit Roosevelt avoided publicity—as assiduously as her stepdaughter courted it. *(Sagamore Hill National Historic Site)*

"Princess Alice," daughter of the president, became the rage of the entire country. Songs were written for her, colors named after her, and descriptions of her escapades plastered over front pages of newspapers from coast to coast. *(Sagamore Hill National Historic Site, photo by Frances Johnston)*

Nicholas Longworth, his bride, and her father all look glum just after the wedding ceremony in the White House East Room. Edith disapproved of the groom, who she thought drank too much and had too many women. *(UPI/Bettmann Newsphotos)*

needs is an Embassy." *The* Mrs. Townsend, who had introduced Nick and Maggie Cassini and who often invited foreigners to her dinners, was to get a shield in front of her mansion that read, "Dagoes Boarding-house." There were many others, equally tasteless, and, apparently realizing this, Bertie backed out, refusing to let his valet release the signs to Alice, who was raring to put them up herself. He did give her one, however, which she hung outside the house that Nick shared with his mother. It read simply, "I live here, Nicholas Longworth." [32]

When Nick's secretary informed Susan of the offensive sign, she ordered him to remove it "and at once!" As he was about to do so, Alice appeared, "shrieking not to touch it." [33] In the meantime, Nick arrived and the horrified Mrs. Longworth watched as Alice maneuvered him to stand in the window directly over it, "unconscious it was there, while the sightseeing stages passed, looked, and then shouted with laughter." [34]

If the first lady of Rookwood didn't approve of Alice, then neither did the first lady of the White House approve of Nick. Edith didn't like much of anything about him, including his friends, whom she considered "totally worthless, rich and frivolous." [35] It was not only his reputation for having too many drinks that troubled her but also his reputation for having had too many women. It was known that he had been in love with department-store heiress Mary Leiter, who became Lady Curzon. He had been engaged to Nancy Astor's older sister, Irene, who later married Charles Dana Gibson and became the Gibson girl. Worse yet, Edith, who had herself experienced the humiliation of being tossed aside for a more vibrant woman, heard that at the time he became engaged to Alice, he was already engaged to a Cincinnati girl named Miriam Bloomer.

By any measure, Nick's morals left much to be desired, and the wonder is that the prudish TR—whose morals were straight out of a Victorian primer—consented to the marriage. Most likely TR, who did not allow even the mildest sexual jokes or innuendoes to be made in his presence, was the only politician in town who hadn't heard the stories about Nick's womanizing.

There is also the inescapable fact that TR gave few signs that he cared much about his oldest child—certainly not to the extent that he was preoccupied at that time by Ted Jr.'s poor academic performance at Harvard.

ALICE ROOSEVELT LONGWORTH

On the surface—and that was as deep as TR cared to go—this was an appropriate match. That Nick was fifteen years older than Alice (and only eleven years TR's junior) suggested something different to him than it did to Edith. TR felt that Nick's greater maturity would improve his chances of controlling Alice.

TR also considered Nick a serious politician. The president could look at Nick and, to some extent, see himself—the privileged, Harvard-educated young man, whose options for filling his pockets or time were many but who chose to lend his educated mind to lifting government out of the pigsty.

He was pleased with Nick's family ties, including his generations-old link to the Tafts, to Harvard College—Nick's great-great grandfather had been president—and to the Mayflower. The Rives blood in Nick's veins was especially impressive. If an American aristocracy was not a contradiction in terms, this grand old Southern family, which undoubtedly triggered in TR nostalgic memories of his mother, was it. Although he had since had a falling out with her, he had to admit, if only to himself, that Nick's Aunt Maria Storer played a key role in his becoming president at age forty-two.

But most important to TR was the wonderful fact that Nick was "Porc." When the engagement was announced, TR wrote to Kaiser Wilhelm II, "Nick and I are both members of the Porc, you know." [36] In later years, Alice would claim that she might otherwise never have met Nick. "My father told me that a new congressman was coming in from Ohio . . . who . . . was Harvard and was in the Porcellian . . . He was just the opposite of my father, except that he was Harvard and in the Porcellian." [37]

Although it is hard to imagine it today, making "Porc" and so joining a brotherhood that included Charles Sumner, James Russell Lowell, and Oliver Wendell Holmes, was, for many of its members—men who would go on to win the nation's highest honors—the single most important achievement of their lives. Owen Wister said that not even the success of his novel *The Virginian* had meant so much to him. Franklin Roosevelt, who was rejected by the Porcellian, even though his own father was a member, confessed to Bamie's son that not making "Porc" had been the biggest disappointment of his life. [38]

It surely also occurred to Theodore and Edith that Alice, who would have almost no inheritance from the Roosevelts, was lucky to get a man who had, in Edith's opinion, a "comfortable income according to our not over-ambitious ideas." [39] Alice was mixing in a mate market in which she lacked the means to compete. While she was looking for a husband, so were girls like the daughters of Ogden Mills—heir to the Mills Bank, Comstock Lode, and Santa Fe Railroad fortunes—one of whom, Beatrice, married Lord Granard, a member of the British aristocracy. Beatrice once invited Alice to go on a shopping trip, explaining that her father "has promised to buy me a tiara for little dinners." "A tiara for *little* dinners . . . ," Alice joked. "Heaven knows what she had for the big ones."[40]

While the idea of marrying the president's daughter may have intrigued some impoverished minor nobleman, TR would have vehemently protested, as he despised the fashion of ambitious mothers auctioning off their daughters to the highest titled bidder. (He was outraged when Alva Vanderbilt shoved her tall and lovely Consuelo into a marriage with the short, arrogant duke of Marlborough.) Besides, for the nobility, no matter how minor, what counted in the end was the bottom line (the duke, for example, ended up with $10 million of Vanderbilt money), and Alice's was paltry in comparison to others that were available.

Most pure-bred American boys who had the money and time to keep up with Alice were more likely to court and flirt with her than to propose to her. She was simply too wild, too much the attention grabber, and, in combination with her father, more than a poor husband could stand up to. He would have to be the kind of man with enough self-esteem to be willing to go through life as "Alice's husband" or "Teddy's son-in-law."

Also, marrying Alice constituted a full-time job. When one eligible man of that era was asked if he was going to marry a particularly feisty young woman, he replied, "No, I rather think I'll have a career of my own."[41]

Nick knew what he was getting into and forged ahead anyway. He certainly had ample warning. "I took the unfortunate man I was engaged to . . . to a pet shop one day and I put a snake around my neck," Alice recalled. "When I looked around, Nick wasn't there. I went outside and saw him down the street looking sick. If he and father hadn't belonged to the same club . . . I think he would have called it off."

One night, soon after TR became president, a young farmer, Henry Weilbrenner of neighboring Syosset, Long Island, arrived at Sagamore Hill. He told the Secret Service man at the gate that he had an appointment with the president, who wanted him to marry Alice. The guard sent him away, but Weilbrenner returned fifteen minutes later, and when asked again what he wanted, snapped, "None of your damned business!" Theodore, who had been working in his study, came out to see what the noise was about. "There he is now!" the would-be suitor screamed as he whipped his horse toward the house, at which point the alarmed Secret Service agent wrestled him to the ground. On the floorboards of his buggy lay a pistol. To his friend John Jay, Theodore described the man as a "poor, demented creature." For his family he had a different comment: "Of course he's insane. He wants to marry Alice." [42]

6

The White House Wedding

In the days before the wedding of the century—called for noon on Saturday, February 17, 1906—the newspapers shamelessly whipped up front-page stories out of the smallest detail. The *New York Sun* breathlessly revealed that "the bride's bouquet will consist of lilies and white orchids, but Mr. Longworth has not taken anybody into his confidence in this respect." On the same day, the competing Hearst paper, the *New York American*, uncovered "an accurate picture of the marvelous trousseau including the details of the wedding gown." [1]

The newspapers covered pages with speculation on the configuration of the wedding party, the itinerary of the honeymoon, the value of the gifts that poured into the White House. All this at a time when domestic and world news was breaking at an unprecedented rate—the Panama Canal, for example, was finally under construction, after decades of failed attempts. TR's role in pushing this vital passage between the Atlantic and Pacific was highly controversial. Some thought it unseemly that when Colombia, on whose territory the canal would be built, proved intransigent in negotiations with the United States, the United States supported a rebellion that led to Panama's independence from Columbia and then hastily negotiated with the new Panamanian government for rights to build, own, and operate the canal.

Had the White House been bombed by angry Colombians, no doubt the lead story would have featured the effect on Princess Alice's nuptials. When Alice and Nick went to New York to shop and visit friends, they were mobbed by gawkers and reporters—as if they were royalty or stage stars. Theodore Roosevelt's daughter would not be the first White House bride—Andrew Jackson's niece had been married there in 1832; Ulysses S. Grant's daughter in 1874; and, in 1886, the rotund, middle-aged Grover Cleveland married the young and lovely Frances Folsom—but Alice was by far the most magnetic.

She was also the most materialistic. The girl who was still counting up her "plunder" from the Far East junket of a few months before was even more grasping in the matter of wedding gifts. She would accept almost anything, although she preferred it to be diamond covered. The flow of loot, reported in unstinting detail, led TR to declare a ban on all gifts from foreign governments—but, fortunately for Alice, the most sumptuous had already arrived.

King Edward VII sent a gold snuffbox with his miniature set in diamonds on the lid. The French government sent a Gobelin tapestry. The German kaiser sent a bracelet with his miniature encrusted with diamonds, which, Alice dryly noted, were smaller than those in the bracelet he gave her when she christened his yacht. Pope Pius X sent a mosaic representing the great paintings in the Vatican. The Cuban government sent a string of pearls that were valued, at the time, at $25,000. (For the pearls, which Alice wore until her death, she had Senator Lodge to thank. He had learned that the Cubans, who wanted to give something very special to the daughter of the man they credited with ridding their country of Spanish rule, had settled on a set of bedroom furniture laden with semi-precious stones. Lodge gasped at the very idea of such ostentatiously poor taste and suggested that "Miss Alice would prefer a set of pearls.")[2]

"I had about the sort of presents that any girl gets from her relatives and friends and friends of the family; with the exception of a few from foreign potentates," Alice wrote, presumably with a straight face.[3] White House Chief Usher Ike Hoover, repeating a remark he heard, offered a more realistic assessment: "'It is enough to make one an anarchist,' for it is entirely too much to be given to one person."[4] Indeed, besides the foreign tributes, hundreds of more conventional gifts of sterling silver, crystal, china, arrived daily from congressmen, Supreme Court justices, and cabinet secretaries. Some of these were quite valuable—for example, a gold puree set with sapphires and diamonds from Mayor Fleischmann of Cincinnati. All gifts were numbered and placed in a White House room that was kept under continuous guard.*

*When Mrs. Longworth was nearing ninety, Selwa Roosevelt took it upon herself to sort through her aunt's belongings, hoping to relieve Alice's granddaughter of the inevitable—

The White House Wedding

Military aide Charlie McCawley joked in the weeks before the wedding, "Alice will accept anything but a red-hot stove and will take that if it does not take too long to cool." [7] Indeed, Alice mostly ignored her father's ban. Unfortunately, she could not ignore his horror at a plan, announced in the papers, by which Alice would receive a gift of cash—$800,000—raised by a group of Americans. He announced publicly that his daughter could not accept the money.

On the wedding day, the *Washington Post* devoted its entire front page and much of the inside of its first section to the story, with its overheated headline bannering, "On a Sun-Kissed Day in Room Abloom, the Eyes of the World Beholding Alice Roosevelt, the President's Fair Daughter, Becomes Mrs. Nicholas Longworth." *[8] The *Washington Evening Star* devoted three almost-full pages to the affair. Its headline writer showed no restraint: "Happy the Bride the Sun Shines On; Brilliant Ceremony in the East Room of the White House; Miss Roosevelt and Mr. Longworth; The President's Daughter United to the Man of Her Choice; Bishop Satterlee Officiates; A Distinguished Company Witnessed the Marriage—the Elaborate Toilets of the Ladies—the Reception Afterward—Congratulations and Good Wishes." The *Sunday Star* boosted sales by offering a special supplement, a "handsome enlarged reproduction of [Alice's portrait] in photographic tints. . . . The picture . . . is printed on the best paper, and will be suitable for framing." [9]

By 11 A.M. there was barely standing room on the White House grounds as peddlers pushing peanuts, popcorn, balloons, and souvenirs hawked their wares to those not fortunate enough to be invited inside. Alice, who had just awakened, gazed sleepily out her bedroom window at this circus scene, noting that the first of the thousand invited guests had already begun to arrive. Among those carriages

---

death, estate taxes, and the chore of organizing some seventy years of stuff. Selwa found stacks of wedding presents still in their wrappings. "I think that's significant," she said. "It shows how little she cared about possessions." [5] Not exactly. The "big tag" items were not relegated to storage, just the conventional ones. Alice was much different from her mother, who gushed to her fiancé, "Just think Teddy we have got 79 presents; I had them all out this afternoon for different people to see." [6]

---

*That headline is carved in lead in the lobby of the *Post*'s new building, along with other such momentous headlines as "Allies Land in France," "President Kennedy Shot Dead; Lyndon Johnson Sworn In," and "The Eagle Has Landed: 2 Men Walk on Moon."

pulling up early was cousin Franklin's, who, eleven months earlier to the day, had married cousin Eleanor. At Franklin's side was his mother. Eleanor could not be seen in public as she was pregnant and a few weeks away from confinement.

Edith was exasperated with Alice, who seemed in no hurry to get out of her nightgown and into her wedding gown. The first lady decided that her stepdaughter was exercising one last act of rebellion by being late for her own wedding.*

Already in the East Room, inspecting the flowers, was the meticulously dressed Nick Longworth and his best man, Bostonian Thomas Nelson Perkins. The two had been Harvard classmates, as had their fathers. Nick wore a black Prince Albert frock coat, over a white Marseilles waistcoat, a pearl gray cravat tied in the puff style, with a moonstone stick pin inserted in its exact center, patent leather shoes, a white boutonniere, pearl gray gloves.

Most girls would have been up early to dress, as merely getting into the elaborate gown with its "regulation court train" (it would double as a court gown for her presentation, during her European honeymoon, at the Court of St. James's) could consume most of an hour— not to mention the time required to construct a pompadour with a foundation firm enough to support masses of orange blossoms and a voluminous veil. But Alice simply couldn't work up much enthusiasm. "I wasn't excited," she later recalled. "I wasn't nervous. It was another big party, and I had been to big parties." [11]

She had little desire to be seen in her wedding gown, which, like her debut gown, she dismissed as demurely dowdy. She had wanted it made of the empress dowager's gift of precious silks, but TR insisted on domestic material and manufacture. The princess–style gown was made in Patterson, New Jersey, of white satin trimmed with the point lace that had adorned her mother's and grandmother's wedding dresses. Orange blossoms bloomed—not only in her hair but also in the lace at her shoulders and on the silver brocade slippers.

She was to meet her father in the upstairs hall at two minutes before noon to descend together in the elevator. But the pompadour,

---

*While having tea with Lady Bird Johnson at the White House in January 1964, Alice described Edith's anger on that morning fifty-eight years earlier. Lady Bird, whose own daughter was married in the White House, wrote in her published diaries that she felt complete sympathy with Edith. [10]

just as Edith warned, proved recalcitrant. On this unseasonably warm day, the overdressed guests, packed wall-to-wall, sweated in the flower-festooned East Room as the Marine Band played and the clock struck twelve. Nick's sister Clara described the scene as bristling with "officialdom"—nearly the entire Congress, Supreme Court, diplomatic corps—and so hot that when one of the wives of a cabinet officer "fell into an alarming swoon," she almost landed on Clara who was "wedged among a group of 'Cabinet Ladies.'" [12]

Finally father and daughter stepped out of the elevator. Nick's eight ushers—one of whom was Lieutenant Douglas MacArthur—escorted the bride and her father to the East Room, where they were joined by military aides. As the Marine Band blasted the grand march from *Tannhäuser*, ushers and officers formed an aisle down which TR and Alice passed to the improvised altar. Waiting to perform the ceremony was the bishop Washington, the Right Reverend Henry Yates Satterlee, who, one guest complained, conducted the service in the voice of an auctioneer. [13]

When Alice and her father reached the raised platform before the altar, the president placed his daughter's hand in Nick's and stepped down, to stand near Edith. To the bishop's question, "Who will give the bride away?" Theodore made no audible answer. Uncharacteristically, the man whom Alice later charged with wanting to be the bride at every wedding and the corpse at every funeral remained a spectator until the service's end.

The star of the show was Alice, and that was just as she intended. Not a single bridesmaid joined the procession. Competing with her father would be tough enough, she figured, without inviting other pretty girls to share the limelight. She recalled cousin Eleanor's wedding at which she and five other girls served as bridesmaids, effortlessly upstaging the gawky bride. Not only that, but TR, at his gregarious best that day, had stolen the scene. Alice had watched as he gave away his dead brother's daughter, kissed her, slapped the groom on the back and said heartily, "Well, Franklin, there's nothing like keeping the name in the family." With that, he stomped off to the dining room, the guests at his heels, and bride and groom were left standing alone. [14]

Edith's face remained impassive during the ceremony. She wore a brown brocade dress that her biographer called an "unfortunate choice" as it "accentuated her tired pallor." When the ceremony ended, intimates who knew of the strained relations between them were taken aback when Alice rushed to Edith with her "arms out-stretched" and "Edith rose in some surprise." Alice placed her hands on Edith's shoulders and "affectionately kissed her."[15]

If father and daughter hugged and kissed, no reporter noted it. It was reported only that the president looked uncharacteristically glum that day—still worried about Ted Jr.'s miserable performance at Harvard—and that he wasn't wearing his accustomed buttonhole. There seemed to be no joy for him in what he never tired of saying was the second most joyous day in a person's life, exceeded only by the birth of children.

In the official wedding photograph, taken after the ceremony, TR looked cheerless, Nick sad, and Alice apathetic. Edith looked no way at all, as she presumably chose not to be included in the portrait. Alice described herself as fluctuating between "animation and grimness on my wedding day."[16] The accent should be on the latter. She later described the East Room, awash with Easter lilies, azaleas, American Beauty roses, and white rhododendrons, as looking "like a funeral parlor."[17] Decades later, at the White House wedding of Richard Nixon's daughter, a reporter asked Alice if Tricia's wedding brought back any memories. "Not a goddamn thing," she snapped. There was, she said, "one thing" that she "relished" about her wedding—the presents.[18]

After the last guest passed through the receiving line, Alice and her "particular friends" went to the Family Dining Room for breakfast. Meanwhile, Edith and Theodore took about sixty of their friends to the State Dining Room. The remainder of the crowd settled for a buffet lunch in the Green Room.

Later in the afternoon Alice produced the day's only showstopper. She grabbed Charlie McCawley's sword and flamboyantly sliced through the wedding cake.

She was shortly put in her place when the "Brothers Immediate" of the Porcellian showed her the door so that they could hold a club meeting in the Family Dining Room. Lewis, the Porcellian's black steward, whose father and grandfather were stewards before him, had, as was the custom, attended the wedding. Despite raised eye-brows, TR put Lewis in "complete charge of the champagne." He switched to hard liquor for the Porc meeting.

Alice could no longer delay two unpleasant tasks: changing into her hideous "muddy-beige" going-away dress and saying good-bye to the family. She thanked Edith effusively for the beautiful wedding, declaring that she had never had so much fun. She was stunned by Edith's response: "I want you to know that I'm glad to see you go. You've never been anything but trouble."

As the newlyweds left the White House from the garden side, Alice's brothers showered them with rice and, when the supply ran out, with black beans.[19] They drove in an electric brougham to Friendship, the John R. McLeans' spectacular estate, located just above Georgetown on Wisconsin Avenue. The McLeans were old family friends. He owned the *Cincinnati Enquirer*, the *Washington Post*, Washington's gas company, its street railway system, and one of its leading banks, and she was a Beale, a member of the highest stratum of Washington society and dubbed by Henry Adams as Washington's "reigning empress."[20] Their "farm," Friendship, at which Mary Leiter also honeymooned, was known for its sumptuousness and privacy. The entire eighty-acre estate was enclosed by a high stone-and-iron wall.

After two days at Friendship, Alice and Nick were driven in one of the McLeans' "big Mercedes" to the train station at Alexandria—chosen in hopes of avoiding crowds—where they boarded a private railroad car to Miami. From Miami they took a boat to Key West, and from there another boat to, of all places, Havana—the jumping-off point for a two-week official (they were almost always accompanied by Edward Morgan, U.S. minister in Cuba, and Morgan's secretary, Willard Straight) tour of the scenes of her father's greatest triumph.

The Longworths would take the regulation European honeymoon in June, but still the decision to go to Cuba, undoubtedly Alice's, was a curious one. Despite her exotic Far East trip, she was relatively untraveled, and Cuba was a country that she had already visited in 1902. Nick surely would have preferred to visit a city with an opera and/or a symphony.

Besides, the trip would firmly put Nick in his place—as Alice's husband and TR's son-in-law. Everywhere they went, Alice was the celebrity, her absent father the hero, and Nick, a sort of gentleman-in-waiting. No setting could have served to so starkly accentuate the differences between the men. While Rough Rider TR was leading the country into the age of imperialism, Nick had been playing gofer for Boss Cox, toiling at the most mundane ward work, with the goal of making it to Columbus, Ohio, as a machine member of the House. He was not among the many Harvard graduates who signed on as Rough Riders.

On her first trip to Cuba, Alice had seen only Havana. This time she, Nick, Morgan, and Straight boarded a private train for Santiago, then went by boat to Daiquiri, and then by horse over the Rough Riders' trail to San Juan Hill. They were accompanied by a mule laden, appropriately, with daiquiris.

Alice, who had expected a mountain and found a hill, was disappointed: "The reality was quite different from the Spanish war scenes of my imagination. . . . There were mountains in the distance, but such elevations as we encountered were hardly more than mildly sloping hills." [21] By the time they returned to Santiago, the newlyweds had had the first argument of their marriage.

On March 4 they arrived back in Washington, at the house on the corner of Eighteenth and I that Nick had shared with his mother. Susan Longworth had retreated to Cincinnati, leaving Alice, for the first time in her life, with domestic responsibilities. Unlike her younger sister, Ethel, who had learned from her mother, Alice hadn't the vaguest notion how to run a household, which in her case meant managing servants. "I still tremble when I think of her face to face with the practical details of life," Edith said at the time of Alice's engagement. [22]

After lunch at the White House, Nick and Alice found themselves without a dinner invitation. For the first time since their marriage they had dinner alone at the table over which Susan Longworth had so competently presided. Months passed before they were again alone. They were entertained so often that a local cleaner and dyer advertised that he had cleaned, "fifteen hundred pairs of Alice Longworth's gloves." [23]

If their trip to Cuba was a poor send-off to a marriage, the two-month honeymoon in Europe was worse. When Alice's father married her mother, they spent a couple of weeks alone at Oyster Bay and the next May sailed for Europe and a private honeymoon. Not only were the Longworths accompanied by Alice's sour maid, Anna, but they were entertained by so many kings, queens, and lords that on her return home, Alice declared, "If I see one more King I'll have him stuffed." [24]

Their honeymoon became an official tour fraught with political implications. They sailed, Alice complained, on the "antiquated *St.*

Louis of the American Line . . . The foreign lines had . . . the best boats, but it was considered 'better politics' for us to travel on an American ship."[25] Upon landing at Southampton on June 10, they went to London and immediately faced the "serious ordeal" of a crowd and "a perfect battery of cameras" in front of Dorchester House, the Park Lane mansion of the American ambassador Whitelaw Reid, with whom they were staying.[26]

The Reids so aggressively took charge of Alice and her schedule that she might have been a teenager traveling with her maid and her dapper, bald-headed uncle. Soon after the couple returned to Washington, Edith received a twenty-eight-page typed report, marked "personal," that described in the most tedious detail Alice's activities and deportment. Nick was barely mentioned. At the opera, "Mrs. Longworth was received at the Royal entrance," Reid wrote, "and there was a tremendous crush as we drove up, which the police handled very well, though the crowd broke through the instant we had got inside the door. . . . On her appearance in the box, Mrs. Longworth was received with applause . . . and throughout the evening she was kept under the [eye] of a score or two of opera glasses all the time."[27]

When Alice met King Edward, Reid added, she made her "prettiest courtesy"; when she was presented at Court, "the Royalties spoke afterwards in an admiring way of her appearance." The ambassador also noted that at a party the Reids threw in honor of the newlyweds, with "a brilliant company" (of nearly two thousand), the Reids received the guests, while *the* guest of honor was embarrassingly absent. Reid explained, his disapproval lurking between the lines, that the Longworths had gone out and were "somewhat delayed in getting back; but Alice soon found her place beside Mrs. Reid at the head of the staircase, so that her absence was only noticed for a little while."[28]

Alice had been in London only two nights when she sat between King Edward and the duke of Marlborough at a dinner that also included Winston Churchill and his mother, Lord Curzon ("Poor Lady Curzon was not able to come," Reid noted), and a host of mistresses of the robe and lords of the admiralty, including one with the wonderful name Lord Tweedmouth. Enrico Caruso sang at the after-dinner musicale. And that was followed by a supper, which, Reid noted, the king also attended.

For Reid, who had been raised on a farm but who developed serious airs while spending his father-in-law's millions, the fact that the king stayed until 1:00 A.M. was a major coup, which he partly credited to Alice's charms. Reid also noted in his most smarmy tone, "I might whisper in great confidence that the most prominent of these [American men who lobbied to get invited to this dinner] was Mr. Pierpont Morgan, who did not speak for himself, but whose friends did speak for him rather . . . persistently! He was invited only to the reception afterwards, and he came covered with orders in honor of the King . . ."[29]

Alice so intrigued the duke of Marlborough that he invited the Longworths to have lunch with him at his palace. The king also wanted to see more of Alice. He commanded the Longworths' appearance for lunch in the royal pavilion at the Ascot races. Alice had only a moderately good time. When she returned two days later for the Great Cup Day, this time to have lunch with Lord and Lady Churchill, she had a much better time.

Toward the end of June the Longworths left Dorchester House for Kiel and a visit with Kaiser Wilhelm II, with whom they went to the yacht races and took tea on the *Meteor*, the yacht that Alice had christened four years earlier. They also visited his sons, the German princes, whom Alice described as "friendly as puppies," as she played follow the leader with them on the royal tennis court.

On the Longworths' return to London, they were presented at the Court of St. James's in Buckingham Palace—Alice wearing her wedding dress and Nick wearing court breeches, a concession to monarchical custom for which he was harshly criticized in the American press.

Alice recalled waiting in an anteroom and inhaling "the closeness of the atmosphere, the slightly pervasive smell of nervous sweat and mothballs." At 10:30 P.M. the strains of "God Save the King" signaled that the Royal Highnesses had arrived. The lord chamberlain and assorted functionaries, carrying white wands, entered the room backward, facing the king and queen and attending them to their places on the thrones.[30] "Then one was announced, went in, curtsied, and went out," Alice recalled—not nearly as appealing as the empress dowager's violent court.

Nick and Alice's last day in London was July 4, the day of the traditional reception at Dorchester House for all Americans who happened to be in London and who looked, in Reid's words, "at all suitable." Upward of three thousand people, including her father's adversary William Jennings Bryan, attended. Alice "faithfully shook hands steadily for over two hours."

The next day Nick and Alice left by train for Paris. They again had official lodgings—this time in the U.S. Embassy with Ambassador and Mrs. Robert McCormick, whose son would grow up to publish the *Chicago Tribune.* Staying with the McCormicks was awkward— Mrs. McCormick, who was Cissy Patterson's aunt, was a notorious social climber, a highly dissatisfied wife, and, like her husband, a heavy drinker—but the Longworths had more awkward meetings in store.

Their next stop was lunch with Nick's aunt and uncle, the Bellamy Storers, who had rented a house in Versailles for the summer. Aunt Maria and Uncle Bellamy had been conspicuously absent at the wedding of their nephew and the girl they had known since she was five, when her father became civil service commissioner and moved his family to Washington. When Edith and the children were in Oyster Bay, Theodore took most of his "spare" meals at the Storer home. It was there that he met two men who were to figure so prominently in his future—William McKinley and William Howard Taft.

Maria Storer considered herself responsible for Theodore's ascent to the White House. No sooner had he arrived there than she told him that she expected him to appoint Bellamy secretary of the Navy or secretary of war or, if neither of those, then ambassador to France or England. Realizing that Bellamy's most compelling qualification was that he looked the part, TR was in a tough spot. Finally he appointed Bellamy ambassador to Austria-Hungary.

That second-rate appointment was not exactly what Maria had in mind, but it was something and it left her free to pursue her other great goal—to see the pope name an American cardinal. To the horror of the Longworths, Maria had converted to Catholicism. She set Bellamy to the outrageously improper task of lobbying Pope Pius X to give a cardinal's hat to her friend, Archbishop Ireland of St. Paul, Minnesota. In an audience with the pope, Bellamy, claiming to be speaking for TR, quoted the president as saying that he "desires emphatically for Msgr. Ireland all the honors of the Church . . ."[31] TR angrily recalled Bellamy. Maria ended her friendship with TR and devoted herself to blackening his name.

This humiliating end to Bellamy's—or rather Maria's—diplomatic aspirations occurred just at the time of Nick and Alice's wedding. By the time Nick—whose mother was among Maria's closest friends— and Alice arrived for lunch, Maria was busily compiling for publication her collection of "Dear Maria/Dear Theodore" correspondence, in which, in accompanying comment, she charged TR with being a traitor, "a dangerous influence," and a child.[32]

She also told the following story: "Mrs. Roosevelt, like the rest of us, looked upon Theodore as a child. When Archie was a few weeks old, she left Washington with the five children and all the servants to go to Sagamore and open the house for the summer. 'Will Mr. Roosevelt let you go alone?' I asked. 'For heaven's sake,' she answered, 'don't put it into Theodore's head to go too; I should have another child to take care of.'"[33]

Lunch, Alice recalled, with the restraint typical of her mild memoirs, was "rather strained."[34]

The newlyweds' next stop was at the house that Clara and Adelbert de Chambrun, married five years before, had taken that season in the Rue de Varenne. "Bertie" de Chambrun was the son of a diplomat who had come to Washington in Lincoln's time, a great grandson of Lafayette, older brother of Charlie, and a major in the French army. Bertie was a good-natured fellow, prone to following his wife's political enthusiasms, not nearly so bright as she and much less polemical. Like so many men, he was half in love with his famous sister-in-law. When Bertie's friend Archie Butt lost patience with Alice, who, he complained, had insulted him one time too many, he vowed to have nothing more to do with her and told Bertie of his resolution. "We were playing golf, and he [Bertie] laid aside his club and went into hysterics, saying that he had made up his mind to do the same thing many times and that he as frequently changed his mind when she was ready for him to change it. . . . He bet me six balls that I would be in her house before January the first."[35] Bertie won.

Clara was not nearly so dazzled by her new sister-in-law. It wasn't only that she preferred to keep Nick in the family, but Clara also had a visceral dislike for Alice's father. A few years later, when her good friend Taft—to whom she would later dedicate a novel—had his famous falling-out with TR, the dislike would erupt into violently anti-TR broadsides. In her published writings, Roosevelt was an egotistical hothead, and a phony to boot.

At the time Alice and Nick arrived at the de Chambruns', Clara was busily circulating the following anecdote, told her by the hardly disinterested Bellamy: When, several years earlier, Theodore arrived at the Storers' Washington home for dinner, Bellamy told him, "We are not going to be alone, as I had hoped, Theodore. A young man from Cincinnati who is doing some reporting up at the House, is coming. I hope you won't mind." "I can't say that I want to see any callow youths," Theodore whined. "I came for a talk with you." "Albert is a fine fellow," Bellamy assured him, "you will appreciate him. . . . He is a son of Murat Halstead; you know all about him, he edited the old *Cincinnati Commercial.*" "Never heard of him or his paper," Theodore said sourly, "but if I must talk to this fellow, tell me something about the sheet." "Why the *Commercial* has always been the most influential Republican organ in southern Ohio, perhaps in the country," Bellamy assured him. "It was Murat Halstead who started the campaign against the idea of Grant's third term."

"Presently," Clara continued, "Albert entered and Mr. Storer began to make a formal presentation. With hands raised to impose silence, Mr. Roosevelt stepped forward and seized the newcomer's palm. He had the art of seeming to make his glasses sparkle with a warmer cordiality than can be found in most human eyes. 'No one need introduce the son of Murat Halstead to me—that would be too great an injustice to his father!' 'Why, Sir, were you acquainted with my father?' inquired Albert, somewhat startled but not as much so as the rest of us. 'Know Murat Halstead? Is there any good American who does not? Why I don't believe you, yourself, can admire him as I do; I doubt whether you know what he did for this country.' Then, as Albert opened his eyes wider and wider, Mr. Roosevelt exclaimed, 'Why he was the man of all others who awakened the public to the iniquity of a third term for Grant.'"[36]

Having survived the Storers and de Chambruns, Alice was in for a third ordeal. From Paris, she, Nick, an unidentified "old friend," and Anna drove to Bayreuth for a heavy dose of opera. While music was the most serious passion of Nick's life, Alice was nearly as unmusical as her father. As a child, forced to go to symphony concerts, she would tune out the music by reading or reciting poetry to herself. For this woman, who claimed that her favorite musical instrument was the banjo and for whom serious music meant Strauss waltzes, Sousa marches, and her father's Rough Riding theme song, "A Hot Time in the Old Town Tonight," the Bayreuth round of the *Ring, Tannhäuser,* and *Tristan* was, as she said, "something in the nature of an endurance test."[37]

The Longworths sailed home on August 4 on board another American steamship, the *St. Paul.* The "honeymoon" was definitely over. After a brief stop in Oyster Bay they were off to Rookwood and the beginning of the end of their marriage.

7

A Marriage Made—and Unmade— in Washington

Alice started as a reasonably good political wife. In 1906, with the campaign for Nick's third term about to start, she told a reporter for the *Cincinnati Enquirer,* "I would be very glad to try to assist my husband to return to Congress if he would permit me." [1] He was thrilled to have her, for her presence meant that he drew the biggest crowds of any congressman running that year and that he got state-wide, not just local, recognition. There was even talk of Nick as a dark horse candidate for governor.

Their first campaign stop was Columbus, where Nick spoke and Alice unveiled a McKinley monument. "The park in front of the State Capitol was so packed with people curious to see us," Alice recalled, "that they surged up against the low grandstand and we had to rescue fainting women and were nearly mobbed while getting away from the place." [2] One headline exactly captured Alice's value: "Alice Makes Politics Fashionable in Cincinnati." [3]

Theodore was genuinely proud of his daughter's role in her husband's victory that November and wrote her: ". . . let me congratulate you and Nick with all my heart upon the successful way in which both of you have run your campaign. I tell you I felt mighty pleased with my daughter and her husband—especially comparing them with certain other American girls and their spouses, as for example, the Duke and Duchess of Marlboro, of fragrant presence!" [4]

Once her interest in politics was kindled, Alice was smitten. But she was soon drawn more to her father's fortunes than to her husband's. While Nick wedged his congressional duties into a life of

undirected frivolity—of drinking and, rumor had it, other women—
TR was running the country and, so it seemed some days, the world.
The family that Alice had done her best to avoid was now the focal
point of her life. Every day, between tea and dinner, she was at the
White House talking politics.

The girl who had seemed so singlemindedly hedonistic became
one of her father's most valued sources of information and advice.
Theodore recognized that, of his children, she had the most political
savvy. Because of her contacts and charm—outdistanced only by
TR's own—she grew into one of his best lobbyists. As his friend
Lodge and his sister Bamie became less available for reasons, respec-
tively, of politics and health, Alice was the person with whom he most
enjoyed talking things over. (As TR moved to the left, Lodge remained a mainstream Republican. Bamie, whose political judgment
was better than her brother's—"If Auntie Bye had been a man, *she*
would have been President," Alice later said *⁵—was spending more
time in Farmington, crippled by a combination of rheumatoid arthritis
and spinal disease.)

Having impulsively promised on election night 1904 that he would
not seek another term—he neglected to consult with Bamie—TR
was now in the throes of choosing a successor. He wanted Elihu Root,
who had been his secretary of war and of state, as well as a friend of
his father's. Root had a slashing wit, an unbeatable intellect, but also
conservative leanings and a corporate law practice that would have
outraged Theodore's progressive supporters.

By 1907 the president had settled on Alice's Far East chaperon,
Secretary of War William Howard Taft. Although confident that Taft
would carry out his policies, TR worried that the genial fat man didn't
have the backbone to lead. Theodore asked Alice—then recuperating
in the White House Lincoln Room from an appendectomy that had
been performed a few days earlier in the Queen's Room—to grill Taft
about an upcoming campaign speech. To that end, Theodore brought
Taft to Alice, who recalled, "I can see the Secretary, perfectly enormous . . . saying with a slow rumbling chuckle, 'Well, I thought I
would talk about the Philippines,' whereat there was a roar of protest
and ironic mirth from Father and me. Indeed I was so emphatic that
one of the stitches in my scar broke."⁶

* During his first term, the president so often walked over to Bamie's house on N Street to
mull over ideas, policies, and appointments that it became known as the "Little White
House."

A Marriage Made—and Unmade—in Washington

By 1908, when Nick was running for reelection to a fourth term, he had begun to wander, and so had Alice—away from the campaign trail. She explained that she found being a captive audience to the same campaign speech unbearably boring, and accompanied him only occasionally, when he specially requested her to. Had Nick cared to make such a request, he would have had to look for her in Oyster Bay, where her father was apparently never boring, or at Auntie Bye's in Farmington. She left Nick campaigning in Cincinnati and went east two or three times a month.

Noticing the frequent separations, her friends concluded that Alice—who once said that she would marry the next [wealthy] man who asked her so she could stop worrying about paying her bills—had married Nick for his money. They speculated that she was now bitter that the vaunted Longworth millions had disappeared into taxes, philanthropic commitments, Nick's taste for high living, and a long line of men who didn't care to work for a living.

Although Alice later claimed that she was "never terribly in love. . . . It just came time to get married. . . . Nothing very exciting about it. I was interested in politics, so I thought marrying a politician would be much better than marrying someone else,"[7] these were the much later words of a woman who had been deeply hurt by her husband's infidelities. Alice had started out very much in love with Nick. Maggie Cassini had seen it in "the way she was always in her gayest . . . spirits when he was around; the way she always suggested including him in all our plans . . ."[8] Even Edith, shortly before the wedding, noticed that "Alice is really in love and it is delightful to see how softened she is."[9]

While Archie Butt noted that Alice "still seems to be in love with him; certainly no other man in the world would suit her as well," he had noted earlier that Nick was increasingly showing his preference for nights out with the boys, and, some whispered, the girls. Alice and several of her friends were coming to his house for a Saturday-night poker game, Butt explained, "to even things up with her husband for leaving her alone."[10]

Alice, proud and stubborn, reacted to Nick's abandonment just as she had reacted to her father's—by pushing him out of her mind and heart. Butt recalled a dinner in June 1908 at which one of the guests "offered to make a bet with any one that no one at the table could name all the States of the Union. . . . I . . . left out eight; General Edwards failed to mention five. . . . Alice Longworth came nearer than any one else, naming 45 states and two territories, thus missing one state only. . . . She left out the one of all others she had ought to name first, namely, that from which her own husband is a Representative—Ohio." [11]

That campaign year found Alice preoccupied with nursing grudges against Taft, who easily beat William Jennings Bryan to win the election. (Not only that, but Taft surpassed her father's 1904 popular vote.) She couldn't bear the thought that her esteemed father would soon leave the White House to "that lump of flesh." She acted as if TR had been anointed rather than elected.

When Theodore heard rumblings that President-elect Taft, despite his promises, would recall Henry White, the man TR had appointed to replace Robert McCormick as ambassador to France, he dispatched Alice to find out if there was anything to the gossip. Alice soon learned that Mrs. Taft had never forgiven White, who, when he was stationed at the U.S. embassy in London, had, presumably inadvertently, sent the honeymooning Tafts tickets to the Royal Mews (stables) rather than to the House of Commons, as they had requested. "Alice, knowing me as well as you do, you could not think me capable of doing such a thing for such a reason," Taft responded. [12] Not long after that he fired White.

Alice now knew that she was dealing with someone much balkier than Taft himself. Having pushed her reluctant husband into the White House,* Mrs. Taft vetoed his cabinet appointments—she slaughtered one with the comment, "He is perfectly awful and his family are even worse" [13]—and later attended almost every important White House meeting and, according to White House Chief Usher Ike Hoover, "would even walk in on private conferences . . . unannounced." [14] Alice quickly perfected her takeoff of what she called Mrs. Taft's "hippopotamus face."

*Will Taft's goal was to be a Supreme Court justice, but his wife's was to be first lady. In 1904, when TR lured Taft back to Washington to be secretary of war, the president's purpose was to have Taft in place to accept the first Supreme Court vacancy. Nellie Taft refused to see the appointment as anything but a stepping-stone to the White House. The appointment, she said, was "much more pleasing to me than the offer of the Supreme Court appointment because it was in line with the kind of work I . . . expected him to have . . ." When TR offered Taft a spot on the Court, she refused to let him take it. "Ma wants him to wait and be President," one of his sons explained. When someone asked later, "Who thought of Taft for President?" Nellie snapped, "I did." [15] Nellie did not have long to enjoy her position. Ten weeks after Taft became president, she suffered a stroke that paralyzed her speech, movement, and power for most of her husband's term.

A Marriage Made—and Unmade—in Washington

On March 3, 1909, the evening before Taft's inauguration, Edith and Theodore hosted a dinner at the White House to welcome the Tafts to their new home. The guest list included newly elected Senator and Mrs. Root, Archie Butt, who was about to take over as Taft's military aide, Mabel Boardman, Alice and Nick, and Bamie and Will Cowles.

As usual, TR led his guests over a mind-whirling variety of subjects. Edith, who had enjoyed the role of first lady, was dressed in black; Nellie, triumphantly, in white. Root—although four years later he would support Taft when TR tried to wrest the presidency back from him—hated to see Roosevelt go. Alice and Butt reported that they saw Root's tears drop in his soup. Alice never would have given Nellie the satisfaction of even a fleetingly glistening eye. Besides, Alice had something else in mind.

When the ladies retired to the library after dinner, Alice looked out the window and gloated, "It's snowing!" She then slipped into the garden and buried a "bad little idol" that she hoped would bring ill-fortune to the new tenants of 1600 Pennsylvania Avenue.[16]

Inauguration day weather was as miserable as anyone could remember—the snow continued to fall, the temperature plunged, and seventy-mile-per-hour gusts leveled telegraph and telephone poles.[17] For the first time since the inauguration of James Madison a century before, the ceremony had to be held indoors in the Senate chamber.

Alice never got over having to leave the White House. She wanted a ninety-nine-year lease on the place, it was said, without too much exaggeration. She was enraged by Nellie Taft's offer to send her a ticket for the inaugural lunch. "Instead of taking it as obvious routine, I flew shouting to friends and relatives with the news that I was going to be allowed to have a ticket to permit me to enter the White House—I—a very large capital I—who had wandered in and out for eight . . . winters!"[18]

While TR, not ready to make the transition into private life, went off on a big game expedition to Africa, Alice readied herself to pounce on anyone who dared even mildly criticize him. Archie Butt observed that, although no longer the daughter of a sitting president, Alice "is still the drawing card in Washington society, and people will forsake palaces and feasts to have a crust of bread with her." She had made it fashionable that summer to sit under the broiling sun at Fort Meyer watching the Wright brothers fly. She brought a "teabasket" full of gin fizzes, which she served to those who visited her in her motor car. [19]

She refused to go to an elegant party at the home of Larz Anderson, a relative of Nick's and then ambassador to Japan. "She heard of his criticizing her father," Butt noted, "and that is the one unpardonable sin in her eyes." [20] Instead she went to Butt's house to play poker, rendering Anderson's party a failure and the informal gathering at Butt's the hit of the social season.

When Grandpa Lee died in March 1910—Grandma would follow a few years later—Alice's only reaction seemed to be concern for how many dollars she would get, when, and the wish that Grandpa had been more of a "modern businessman."

Later that spring, still in her mourning clothes, Alice went to London, without Nick, to meet her parents for King Edward's funeral. This was the first time she had seen TR since Taft's inauguration—he had been traveling for over a year in Africa and Europe—and she wasted no time in apprising him of Taft's deficiencies. The two stayed up talking late into the night.

In July she took a much more mundane trip with Nick—to the state Republican convention, at which the party's nominee for governor would be chosen. Nick, who made the keynote speech, was very interested in running for governor—a goal that appealed to a sufficient number of delegates to make him a serious contender. Nick had told Alice a year before their marriage that he hoped to be governor of Ohio. Then she smiled admiringly; now she grimaced.

Nick recognized that the time was right for such a move. His congressional career seemed stalled. After four terms, he could not shake his reputation for using the House as a "rich man's hobby." He seemed unable to win recognition for much besides his fancy waistcoats, his status as Alice's husband, and his unbroken record of never having sponsored a bill of any importance.*

But in 1910, the factor most ominous for Nick's future was that he had been on the losing side of a battle then considered to have repercussions more far-reaching than any in the House's history; a

*One bill bearing his name required the government to purchase homes abroad for its ambassadors and ministers. On hearing him argue for his bill, several colleagues remarked, "Longworth must be contemplating a foreign appointment." [21]

A Marriage Made—and Unmade—in Washington

battle that would determine whether the House's power resided in the Speaker or was more democratically distributed among the members. Speaker Joe Cannon exercised such iron control over the House that his name had entered the political lexicon—"Cannonism"—as a synonym for despotism. Nick had signed on the previous March as one of "Uncle Joe's" chief lieutenants in his failed last grasp for power. That move had made Nick, at age forty-one, seem one of the discredited old guard, instead of one of the young insurgents who were forcing fresh air into a chamber too long polluted by Uncle Joe's tobacco juice, cigars, and stifling autocracy.

Cannon, a Republican from Illinois, had become Speaker in 1903, the year that Nick started his first term. There would be no more unlikely House allies until Nick's friendship, several years later, with John Nance ("Cactus Jack") Garner, a Texas Democratic who later became Speaker and FDR's vice president. Nick liked to joke that nature was to blame for his own bald pate, whereas Uncle Joe's taste was to blame for his scraggly whiskers, his clothes that looked as if they had fallen upon him out of a tree, and his appalling manners. When Cannon arrived late at a White House dinner in honor of His Imperial Highness Prince Tsai Tao, Archie Butt asked the Speaker if he might introduce him to the evening's guest. "You mean for me to go over there to meet that Chink?" Cannon asked loud enough for the prince to hear.[22]

It wasn't Cannon's bad manners that were noticed—in the Congress of those days he was hardly unique. What was noticed—and feared—was the Speaker's ruthlessness in controlling the House. Not only had he appointed himself chairman of every committee, including the all-powerful Rules Committee, but all House members, one journalist wrote, "were his creatures," allowing him to tower "above the House like Gulliver in Lilliput." Cannon also controlled committee appointments—those selected either voted Joe's way or lost their appointments—and debates—he decided who would speak and who wouldn't.

As the Progressive movement heated up, the time was right for toppling this dictator. George Norris, a Republican-Progressive from Nebraska, introduced a resolution demanding that committee members be elected by the House and that members then choose their own chairman. It passed, and that marked the beginning of the end for Uncle Joe. Next Norris, with the help of Democrats and insurgent Republicans, stripped Cannon of the source of his power—the chairmanship of the Rules Committee.

This defanging consumed three days of the bitterest battles seen in Congress since the Civil War. When Nick was summoned to Cannon's office, he found the carpet covered with cigar butts and the Speaker pacing "like a caged lion." Cannon ordered Nick on scouting duty, recognizing that Nick was well liked by both insurgents and stand-patters. "You Can't Help Liking Nick"[23] was how one headline writer put it.

But nothing, not even Nick's charms, could save Cannon. When the battle ended, this man whom one observer likened to an "old gray wolf at bay,"[24] a man who had once inspired fear, was jeered at by Norris as "a senile old man who was filled with venom . . . because of the crushing defeat that he had suffered as the result of his tyranny."

While many of those who fought Cannon went on to greater glory in the Senate, Nick's career seemed over. So the governorship looked particularly attractive. Nick knew that the post was a political plum: being the young governor of a state that had already produced six presidents meant that inevitably he would be considered a prospect for the White House. If Nick stayed in the House, with Cannon ousted as Speaker and his replacement, Champ Clark, a leader in the anti-Cannon crusade, Representative Longworth would be lucky to get even the most insignificant committee assignment.

But Alice was not interested. She did nothing to help, nor did she request her father's help. "Nick did not want the nomination," she later claimed. "He enjoyed the work in Congress . . . The governorship was not in line with his plans."[25]

Not in line with her plans, maybe. Archie Butt wrote to his sister-in-law that summer of 1910 that "Alice had threatened that rather than permit Nick to be nominated for governor she would smoke in the streets and thereby defeat his nomination." President Taft observed after a golf game with Nick that the usually unflappably good-natured congressman was "a little disgruntled because he was not nominated."[26] (To Nick's chagrin, the Republicans instead nominated Warren Harding, editor of the *Marion* [Ohio] *Daily Star*, whose most compelling qualifications were his good looks and his ambitious wife.)

Alice, who preferred that Nick run for the Senate, was unwilling to

A Marriage Made—and Unmade—in Washington

get stuck in another governor's mansion. She had dismissed Albany, during her father's term as governor, as strictly parochial, but Albany was Paris compared to Columbus, Ohio. Besides, when her father was governor of New York she was a young teenager. Now she was an adult who had fashioned for herself an unconventionally pleasant life in a city that could be stifling in its social rules. By being what Butt described as "a rule unto herself," she had bypassed the tedious part of official Washington life. While other matrons who failed to involve themselves in the ridiculously time-consuming task of making and receiving calls * were socially blacklisted, Alice was not only forgiven but actively courted by nearly every hostess in town.

Alice claimed that she had tried it, but had soon concluded that "the Washington mania for calling and being called on is a thing that no sane human beings should let themselves in for." (She explained that she had to cancel her day "at home" because it "amounted to keeping open house for the passers-by. Sightseeing stages actually used to stop and let off their passengers, who would come in, wander around, have tea, and occasionally depart with a souvenir . . .")[27]

Alice didn't let it go at that. She thumbed her nose at the ninnies, such as cousin Eleanor, who got tangled in this "pointless waste of time,"[28] by founding and leading a group called the "Night Riders"—her characteristically perverse version of a hallowed custom. She and her pals, all on horseback, had taken to galloping into the front yards of friends and acquaintances between 10 P.M. and 1 A.M. As Archie Butt described it, "Howls and cat calls continue until the house is opened and the refreshments are served . . . At first there was some criticism of the Night Riders, but now the highest social honor one can have is a raid from the Night Riders led by the intrepid Alice."[29]

---

* Consider these labyrinthine guidelines on "Calling" from *The Social List of Washington, D.C.*, popularly known as *The Green Book:* After specifying which days to call on which officials—for example, wives of Representatives on Tuesday; wives of cabinet members on Wednesday—it advises: "When calling on a man, his wife and daughter under 21, you leave two cards of your husband's, one of your own, and two of your daughter's. When calling on a man and his wife, you leave two cards of your husband's and one of your own. Or one double card (Mr. and Mrs. John W. Smith) and a card of your husband's . . ." The advice continues with incomprehensible directions on leaving "double cards," leaving multiple cards at the homes of debutantes (the configuration depends on whether it is a first call, whether there is an older daughter in residence, etc.), and turning down particular corners of cards.

Although Nellie Taft would have liked to cut Alice permanently from the White House guest list, the new president adored her and, after Nellie's stroke, Alice was often seated at the president's right. He considered her wit and repartee brilliantly unorthodox and smiled indulgently even when, at one dinner, she arrived after him—"an unpardonable offense in official Washington," according to Archie Butt.[30] In 1911, shortly before even Will Taft could no longer excuse Alice's nastiness about him and his family, she went to a party in the White House garden. According to another guest, the wife of a congressional colleague of Nick, Alice wore flesh-colored stockings, an electric blue satin gown, and "held the very scant skirt quite high, and when the band played, kicked about and moved her body sinuously like a shining leopard cat."[31] At a diplomatic ball she did the turkey trot with a cigarette hanging from her lips.[32]

She was, as cousin Eleanor often said, not very nice. More than a few Washington matrons were waiting anxiously for Alice to be tempered, bloated, and confined by motherhood. But, although her father's views on a woman's highest calling were well known—he preached that the woman who shirked motherhood was as ignoble as the man who shirked war—Alice remained trim and wild.

TR also preached against birth control as "race suicide," yet it was whispered that his daughter used contraception. Her gynecologist, a German woman named Sophie Nordhoff-Jung, who performed the White House appendectomy, was happy to so advise her famous patient. Eleanor was typical of women of that era—six pregnancies followed by abstinence. Although Eleanor would have had six more babies before asking Alice for advice, Nick's sister Nan, already the mother of three, wrote to her sister-in-law begging her to send "one of those cunning labor-saving devices" so that she might save her "tottering reason."[33]

Although Alice encouraged her father to break with Taft, she showed political judgment better than his when she advised him not to challenge Taft for the 1912 nomination. "I did not believe it possible that he could win the nomination in [the] face of the power a President has, to take it himself through control of the National Committee, influence over officeholders and by patronage."[34] She even wrote to Edith advising her to use her influence.

But once he decided to run, she supported him with unflagging

A Marriage Made—and Unmade—in Washington

energy and loyalty, which was certainly understandable in a daughter. But it was not so understandable for a daughter to place her father's career over her husband's. Nick was in a terrible dilemma. His wife's father was fighting one of his family's closest friends and his own constituent. Nick was solidly in the Taft wing of the Republican party—too conservative temperamentally and politically to support a man who was committing the heresy of challenging a sitting member of his own party—but Nick knew that the very day he came out publicly for Taft, his own wife would come out publicly for her father. Then everyone would know what he knew—that he could not control her and that, in humiliating opposition to current decorum, she would direct her loyalty to whomever she pleased.

Nick also knew that no matter how many primaries TR won, Taft would emerge victorious at the convention. He hoped that his father-in-law would then decide to support Taft against the common Democratic enemy, or at least to stay at Sagamore and keep his mouth shut. But Nick, who got along well with TR—the men respected one another as politicians and TR was still innocent of Nick's philandering—knew his wife's father too well to believe that he would ever support Taft or keep quiet. Nick predicted that TR would grab the Progressive banner and form a splinter party. That third party would undoubtedly enter its own candidates for Congress, meaning that Nick would have to run against two candidates—a Democrat and a Progressive. The latter would wear the banner of Nick's own father-in-law, not to mention his wife. If that happened, Nick vowed, he would withdraw from the race.

In March 1912, Alice rushed to Sagamore to confer with TR on his strategy for besting Taft in the primaries. While Nick continued his nightly habit of dining out, followed by poker and parties, Alice, who declared herself "sick with apprehension," stuck by the telephone logging returns. The night of the Illinois primary, April 9, she kept a line open to her closest friend, Mark Hanna's daughter Ruth McCormick, whose husband represented a Chicago congressional district and whose interest in politics was as obsessive as Alice's. Alice was thrilled by TR's easy win and watched with delight as four days later he won in Pennsylvania.

Two days later there was sad news for both camps. The ugly battle between these presidents had left Archie Butt, who felt loyalty to and affection for both, exhausted and depressed. Taft noticed his aide's suffering and suggested that before the fall campaign he go to Europe for a rest. Unfortunately, Butt booked his return passage on the *Titanic* and, chivalrous to the end, went down as he helped women and children board the lifeboats.*

On April 30, Massachusetts primary day, Nick went to a dance at the White House. Because his wife was no longer welcome there, he took his sister Nan, who was one of Taft's most ardent supporters. Alice much preferred to stay home, hounding the AP for totals. When Nick and Nan returned, the latter reported with undisguised glee that TR would not get more than six of thirty-six delegates.

The young Mrs. Longworth barely avoided coming to blows with Nick's sisters. While Alice declared her father "the one really great man in this country," Clara attacked him as a man who was sick with personal ambition. Alice had to suppress her desire to punch Clara in the nose. "I was so full of bottled up savagery that I very nearly became ill," she recalled. "Food choked me and I existed principally on fruit and eggs and Vichy. I had a chronic cold and cough, indigestion, colitis, anemia and low blood pressure—and quite marked schizophrenia."[36] Edith complained to Ethel that Alice arrived at Sagamore "talking like molasses blobbing out of a bottle and rocking as if she were a boarder in a summer hotel."[37]

Prior to the Ohio primary, Taft announced, "The vote in Ohio, my home state, will be the decisive one, and will settle the question of the nomination." TR won easily in Ohio, with thirty-seven out of forty delegates. Nick, who was in Cincinnati, called Alice in Washington and urged her not to join him as "the feeling there was unbelievably bitter." Alice happily complied.

In the thirteen states that chose delegates through primaries, TR won 278 delegates; Taft only 82.[38] Alice rushed to Sagamore to savor the victory with TR. To her delight, she found Edith upstairs with a

*Born in Augusta, Georgia, in 1865, Archibald Willingham Andrew Brackenbreed Butt was of distinguished colonial stock. He was every inch the Southern gentleman and a favorite riding and walking companion of both TR's and Edith's. Butt had, among other qualities that appealed to Edith, impeccable, uncompromising taste. Theodore had ordered the outside of the president's house painted white and had "The White House" printed on official stationery. When Butt decided to stay on as military aide to Taft, he did so with one private reservation. If the Tafts reverted to the old habit of calling the president's house by "the hideous name 'Executive Mansion,' " . . . I will leave of my own accord, for it will mean that there is something fundamentally wrong with them. Bad temper I can stand, but not bad taste."[35] Later—presumably after Taft decided to stick with "White House"—Butt became the new president's constant companion.

A Marriage Made—and Unmade—in Washington

headache, so she had her "very darling father" all to herself. They plotted strategy for that month's Republican convention.

On the eve of the convention's start in Chicago, TR delivered a rousing speech climaxing in what became one of his most famous lines: "We stand at Armageddon, and we battle for the Lord." Earlier that day, he had asked Edith and Alice to edit the speech. They cut some parts but wisely left in that line, which even "pagan Alice" found stirring.

Despite that exhilarating start, things were going just as Alice and Nick had predicted. Taft was able to get his man, Elihu Root, elected temporary chairman. Root then as consistently approved the credentials of Taft delegates as he rejected those of TR delegates. Believing that they were being "steamrolled," Alice and Ruth and Medill McCormick were reduced to showing their anger at Root* by rubbing together pieces of sandpaper to imitate the noise made by a steamroller. Medill's *Chicago Tribune* carried a banner across every page warning, "THE EIGHTH COMMANDMENT: THOU SHALT NOT STEAL."

When Alice wasn't heckling Root, she was scurrying from the floor to her father's rooms at the Congress Hotel. One evening they discussed the circumstances under which he would bolt the party—if the credentials committee confirmed what they considered to be fraudulently seated delegates. With Root and also Lodge—who remained a regular Republican, loyal to, if not admiring of, Taft—in the enemy camp, Alice was practically living in TR's hotel room.

She saw Nick when she could and, unfortunately for him, was at his side in the Ohio delegation when Harding, who had lost the 1910 governor's race and was now one of Taft's most avid supporters, approached Nick with a deal—the statehouse in exchange for Nick's support of Taft. Exceeding his reputation for obtuseness, Harding made the offer to Nick while Alice sat at his side. Harding had barely finished when Alice cut him off, informing him loudly and coldly that Nick would not accept "favors from crooks"—here referring to the fact that Harding had been a leader in the state convention which, despite TR's decisive victory in the Ohio primary, gave the state's delegates-at-large to Taft. Alice recalled that "at intervals, for the

---

* Root's rock-ribbed Republicanism made it impossible for him to support the insurgent, but he was never comfortable abandoning TR. He would later cry to a friend, "I care more for one button on Theodore Roosevelt's waistcoat than for Taft's whole body." [39]

next twenty-four hours, Nick and Julius Fleischmann [a former Mayor of Cincinnati and, with money from his family's yeast business, a wealthy "sporting friend" of Nick's] pleaded with me to see Harding, to say that I was sorry, that I had not meant to say that he was a crook. But that was what I had meant to say, so I did not see him."[40]

Besides, Nick was hardly first on her mind. She vowed with the Progressives in TR's camp not to let Taft get away with "thievery." As Taft was being nominated, "We left the Coliseum while the seconding was going on to . . . hurry to . . . the 'Rump' convention— and a great and thrilling meeting it was. There were a spirit and buoyancy . . . that were an odd contrast to what we had left behind— the sullen, shame-faced, obedient regulars" (in which group she included her husband). At the Progressive meeting—preliminary to a convention in August—"every one was chockablock with a sort of camp-meeting fervor, cheering, emotional. We were out to 'battle for the Lord' with a vengeance."[41]

Alice couldn't wait for the convention of what was now called the Bull Moose party. Nick, his gubernatorial hopes shattered, still hoped for reelection to Congress and feared that Alice's presence would seriously erode his chances. TR agreed with Nick, and at a meeting on the piazza at Sagamore, the two men "held a sort of court of justice on me. It was decided that it would not be fair to Nick for me to go to the convention. . . . I was so sorry for myself that I was sniffling."

Later the sniffles turned to fury—mostly directed at Nick, who was suffering bouts of severe indigestion. "As the time approached for the Progressive convention the papers were full of all the excitement I was missing. I used to have ignoble thoughts of goading Nick into doing something that would justify me in packing my bag and hopping a train to Chicago."[42]

Instead she went to Newport to visit the Cornelius Vanderbilts, "a visit," she blithely admitted, "that was not well looked on in a political year, as in those days Newport was supposed to be the Mammon of unrighteousness in the eyes of the Middle West, and a stink in the nostrils thereof."[43] Although Nick loved this sort of champagne-soaked extravaganza, he could not join her and expect to get reelected. He knew that Alice would not forgo the trip for his sake. So Alice went to Newport while Nick went to Islesboro to stay with the Dana Gibsons.

A Marriage Made—and Unmade—in Washington

The press coverage of the Vanderbilts' "fancy-dress ball" spread to newspapers across the country, with Alice's presence featured, because, with Grace Vanderbilt, she led the cotillion. So elaborate was this ball, with its series of quadrilles, each requiring a change into Oriental or Russian or gypsy or Persian costumes, that in the days before, Alice recalled, the guests were "drilled and rehearsed like professionals."

Sometime during the evening—the dance lasted well past dawn— Alice went to her room, which was being used as a cloakroom, to fix her make-up. She heard a man's voice behind her say, "If you don't mind, I'll take some of your powder." The man, dressed in a sumptuous Chinese robe, proceeded to powder his nose. This was Englishman F. E. Smith (later Lord Birkenhead and a great friend of Winston Churchill), who before the night was out would make the famous toast, "To the intoxicating women and the intoxicated men of Newport." This was not exactly an evening of wholesome good fun, and Grace Vanderbilt, whose "diamonds blazed like a prairie fire," was hardly the sort of "Amerikun" whom TR and Nick recognized as essential to the candidate who wanted to win elections.

Shortly after TR was formally anointed as the Bull Moose candidate, he summoned Nick to Sagamore and assured him that he would not authorize a Progressive candidate to run from the first Ohio district. TR went so far as to urge Nick, "You let me know how matters are in your district and I will try to smash up any Roosevelt creature who antagonizes you."[44]

Unfortunately, this was a promise that TR could not keep. Certain of his supporters snatched Nick's fate out of TR's hands by tapping Millard F. Andrew to run in the first Ohio district as a Bull Mooser and then carefully watching that the chief Bull Moose make no concessions, not even to his own son-in-law. For the first time in his career, Nick faced a tough fight. He feared that Andrew would attract enough Republican votes to throw the election to the Democrat, Stanley Bowdle.

Although Alice got stuck that summer in Newport instead of Chicago, she did get to the Windy City in October, three weeks before the election, when TR, on his way to give a speech, was shot by a deranged saloon keeper. The bullet would have been fatal had it not been deflected by his steel spectacle case and the thickly folded typescript of a speech, which, despite a bullet lodged in his chest and blood flowing, he insisted on giving. His rousing speech delivered, he was taken by train from Milwaukee, where the shooting occurred, to Mercy Hospital in Chicago, where Alice met him.

En route to Chicago from Cincinnati, where Alice was staying with Nick's unbearably disagreeable relatives, she canceled all her promises to keep out of the campaign. With TR temporarily sidelined and the Longworth women doing everything short of giving speeches for their "pet great man"—they were, for example, busily collecting funds to be used to instruct voters at the polls, "in order that they should be sure to vote for Taft"—Alice was desperate to help her father.

Between stints beside her father's hospital bed, Alice went to hear TR's Bull Moose running mate, Hiram Johnson, speak at Chicago's Coliseum. Earlier in the campaign, when TR was speaking in Cleveland, Nick had asked her not to go, "as it would be sure to get in the papers and would not look well for me to go hear Father and seem to ignore the First Ohio District." Then she agreed to stay away, but now she decided that even Ohio was no longer off-limits. Again she went to hear Hiram Johnson—this time in Nick's own back yard, Cincinnati—and, worst of all, she accepted Johnson's invitation to sit on the platform.

Nick was outraged. His mother and sisters were nearly homicidal—precisely the reaction Alice hoped for. For Susan, having Alice in her house was like having to be hospitable to an enemy agent. For Alice, having to tolerate her mother-in-law's assertions that the man whom Alice considered little more than her father's stooge was the greatest president since Abe Lincoln; that the man who, in Alice's opinion, had been put in the White House by TR, owed nothing to Roosevelt, was unbearable.

Alice took enormous pleasure in antagonizing that "amazing old female." She knew that Susan opposed women's suffrage,* so she considered becoming a suffragette, "just to spite her." She was pleased to learn that Susan's friends felt sorry for her. "They were resentful on her account that she had to have in her house a nonconforming daughter-in-law who obviously would have preferred to be elsewhere; who had little respect for 'the family position.'" [45]

---

*Despite the fact that the Bull Moose platform contained a suffrage plank, Edith opposed the vote for women; so did cousin Eleanor. Alice supported suffrage, although she certainly didn't work for it. To her, the suffragettes were another source of amusement.

A Marriage Made—and Unmade—in Washington

With Alice's appearance at the Bull Moose rally, her lack of respect for any Longworth's position, including her husband's, was out in the open. "I was with father and against Nick," she later cheerfully confirmed. "Thoroughly enjoyable. Mother-in-law business and all that coming in." One relative of Alice's put it this way: "It was as if Alice was saying, 'I'm going back to my family. Screw you.'"[46] The Sunday before Election Day Alice and Nick had a bitter argument, and it was about this time that Alice told her family that she wanted a divorce. "Although they didn't quite lock me up," she recalled years later, "they exercised considerable pressure to get me to reconsider."[47] (As president, TR had supported a national movement for more rigid divorce laws.)

November 5, 1912, was not a good day for TR or Alice or Nick. By splitting the Republican vote, TR and Taft gave the election to the Democrat, Woodrow Wilson. The same pattern in the first Ohio district resulted in Nick's first congressional defeat.

There was a big difference, however. In relative terms, Nick lost by a much smaller margin—a mere 101 votes—and Nick's mother and sisters were perfectly justified in saying, as they did, that Nick had been defeated by his own wife. Bowdle, the Democrat, polled 22,330 votes; Longworth 22,229; and Andrew, the Progressive, only 5771—but more than enough to give the Democrat his slim margin of victory.* (So slim was the margin that Nick demanded a recount, which took six agonizing days and resulted in precisely the same totals.)

Alice Longworth later bragged about having caused her husband's defeat, pointing to her appearance with Hiram Johnson. "I figured I was worth at least [101] votes in Cincinnati."[48] Nick's mother and sisters were inconsolable. Not only had Taft lost—and come in a humiliating third, carrying only Utah and Vermont, after "the Moose," as Clara called TR—but so had Nick, and this, they feared, and he agreed, spelled the end of his political career.

At the time of the 1912 debacle, Clara was awaiting her husband's recall to France. In the meantime, rather than watch those strange creatures known as Democrats celebrate Wilson's inauguration, they followed Taft to Saint Augustine for "a regular 'bat' of golf and bridge" and nonstop bitterness toward TR and his daughter. "You

---

*Nick would get back at Bowdle in 1914 when the Progressive movement was considerably weakened. He beat Bowdle by some 7000 votes, with the Progressive polling only about 700.

know the French proverb," Clara told Taft, "'a country deserves the government that it has.' Let us be thankful that we have not deserved the Moose!"[49]

As for her sister-in-law, Clara vowed to pretend that she didn't exist. In the second volume of Clara's memoirs, she mentions Alice only once. In her biography of her brother, not a single photograph of this eminently photogenic woman breaks the monotony of blurry shots of tangentially related people or scenes.

During the campaign, Nick's other sister, Nan, had written Taft, "You stand for everything I'd like to fight and work for."* When Roosevelt made one of the biggest blunders of the campaign and probably of his career—he advocated the right of the voters to recall judicial decisions that they feel are "in defiance of justice"—he alienated not only Wall Street moguls and editorial writers, but also former allies such as Lodge and Root and some Progressives, such as the man who was to become such a close friend of Alice's, Senator William E. Borah of Idaho. Nan, who had grown weary of listening to Alice joke that she had "married into a family of lunatics," was thrilled with TR's radical judicial recall proposal. She wrote to Taft, "I could hardly resist wiring her . . . 'Who's loony now?'"[51]

After the election, Nan was so bitter that Taft counseled her to calm down: "I am afraid that your nerves are overwrought and that you have allowed yourself to become too greatly excited and too deeply interested." Still, Nan managed to get in her last lick. She ordered her chicken pox-infected child, "Be sure to kiss Aunt Alice."[52]

Alice later claimed that she felt sorry for her husband: "Nick's position, surrounded by furious females pulling him in opposite directions . . . was calculated to drive him quite mad." She added, "I have never been so sorry for any one. . . . It was particularly hard on him that I was, of course, single-minded in enthusiasm for anything that Father decided to do."[53] But on another occasion she recalled his defeat in these words: "It didn't hurt him in the least. He felt terribly about it, but it was all right."

* Shortly after the 1912 convention, Nan sent Taft some verses she had written to stir up the "workmen" vote and to belittle TR's rousing line, "We stand at Armageddon, and we battle for the Lord": "All say with one accord / That I must have at least three terms / To battle for the Lord / 'Thou' means the other fellow / When I say 'Thou shalt not steal.' / . . . Their naked thefts of delegates / I greatly have deplored; / But, *I'm* justified in stealing, / For I battle for the Lord."[50]

A Marriage Made—and Unmade—in Washington

It was not "all right." Nick was miserable in his defeat, especially because it came at a time when he was beginning to shed his rich-boy image. Through canny and uncharacteristically energetic maneuvering he had grabbed a spot as one of only seven Republicans on the House Ways and Means Committee and had become a leader on the tariff issue. (He believed in high tariffs to protect U.S. industry.) He had much to do with framing the new tariff bill, which would have carried his name had he not lost the election.

Not surprisingly, he began to take out his disappointment on Alice. Within a week of his defeat, he was getting drunk during the day, not showing up for dinner, while Alice stayed in bed with her new addiction—history books. Edith noted that on a post-election visit to Sagamore, Alice looked "horribly ill and worn and has a dreadful time with Nick. He can't seem to face his defeat." Three weeks after Wilson took office, Alice arrived at Sagamore for Ethel's spring wedding with a "dark blue satin and dingy yellow" gown. Edith ordered her back to New York to buy something "light and becoming." [54]

There was nothing light about her mood. She somehow had not counted on the fact that Nick's losing this race meant that she would lose her lively Washington life and instead get stuck at Rookwood. Nick refused to go to his sister-in-law's wedding. He sent no congratulatory telegram and claimed that floods in Ohio prevented him from coming. "Unfortunately, we did not care," Edith wrote, "but poor dear Sister was deeply hurt." As usual, Edith's sympathy extended only so far. Five months later Alice was back at Oyster Bay for Ted Jr.'s birthday and was, Edith complained, "very spiteful with everybody. It is very hard for her having Nick out of politics, but not fair to come to stay at Sagamore and visit it on the family." [55]

Both Alice's and Nick's moods would have turned even darker had they realized that Taft had come close to appointing Nick minister to Alice's beloved China. The President changed his mind when Mrs. Taft exercised her veto.

Out of office, with no occupation to fill his days, Nick revived a boyhood fondness for picnicking at the top of a hill overlooking the junction of the Ohio and Little Miami Rivers. This was the country in which Nick's great-grandfather had planted his vineyards; a cavelike excavation that Nick I had used as a wine cellar remained. While Nick took his guests—who invariably included a selection of attractive women—to the cave to begin drinking the wines and champagnes that he carefully selected from his Rookwood cellar, Alice, on the summit, cooked the chops.

A Roosevelt cousin by marriage was invited to one of these picnics. She recalled Nick, who had become openly, belligerently unfaithful, stretched out on the grass holding hands with a girl. As Alice walked by, the girl called out, "Oh, hello, Mrs. Longworth."[56] Shef Cowles recalled Nick "without hesitation lying happily with his arm around a very pretty girl. Not the same one all the time."[57]

8

A Love Affair with Borah

The settings for Nick's sexual trysts became increasingly inappropriate, and his conquests included women from Alice's own circle. Nick rekindled his flirtation with Cissy Patterson, by then a flamboyant divorcée. While Alice and her father plotted against the new object of their hatred, Woodrow Wilson, Nick squired Cissy around town.

Alice looked the other way, but she could not avoid a scene that occurred at a party in her own house. The bathroom door was opened, the light turned on, and there on the floor, drunk, were Nick and Cissy making love.[1]

Nick managed to win back his seat in 1914, without Alice's help. She was busy with her father's political goals. The two had become a very noisy opposition to the infuriatingly cerebral Wilson. The Wilsons invited Alice to a reception early in the administration, but never invited her back after they heard that she had been snickering at the man whom she scorned as a "pedantic professor" and a "Presbyterian minister," and at his daughters. She would not see the inside of the White House until Wilson left office in 1921.

Drunken poker parties remained Nick's greatest pleasure. In 1915, when Warren Harding came to Washington as a senator, he and Nick found that they had much in common—a taste for liquor, gambling, and sex whenever and wherever the opportunity arose. Alice was not pleased to find a new Senate couple among the regulars at Nick's poker nights. The senator was distasteful enough, but his wife, Flo, was unbearable. She was called the Duchess, Alice recalled, "presumably after the one in *Alice in Wonderland* rather than any grandeur on her part." Nick was delighted to have her, for she tended bar. According to Alice, "Harding and Nick and the others would say when they wished another drink, 'Duchess, you are lying down on your job.' And Mrs. Harding . . . would obediently get up and mix a whiskey and soda for them."[2]

Flo Harding, the daughter of the leading banker in Marion, Ohio, and some eight years older than the man she called "Wur-r-ren Ha-ar-r-ding," was a woman born to garner Alice's contempt. While Warren was having sex on desk tops, Flo was plotting his political advancement. "I have only one real hobby," she confessed. "It's my husband." In a little red book she recorded the names of those who had not been civil to her and Warren Harding since they came to Washington. Alice's name was undoubtedly in the book, because, while the Hardings came often to the Longworths', Alice refused to set foot in their house until their address was 1600 Pennsylvania Avenue.[3]

Alice found her greatest pleasure in rushing to Congress to watch Wilson deliver his State of the Union address—previously presidents sent their messages to be read—so she could intensify "the dislike and resentment I felt by hearing him speak rather than waiting to read it in the papers."[4] She had a doll with Wilson's visage carved out of wood, stuck pins in it, and hurled it onto the White House lawn.

In Theodore's opinion, and therefore in Alice's also, Wilson was the lowest form of life—a man who ran away from war. When in May 1915 a German submarine, without warning, torpedoed the British liner *Lusitania*, killing 1198 passengers, 128 of them Americans, TR declared it "murder" and called for war. Wilson went into seclusion and emerged with a diplomatic note of protest to Germany, then another and another. When Alice told her father that still another note had been sent, he asked her, "Did you notice what its serial number was? I fear I have lost track myself, but I am inclined to think it was No. 11,765, Series B."[5]

Alice hoped against hope that the Republicans would nominate her father in 1916, but too much bitterness lingered from 1912—even Wilson credited TR with making his victory possible by splitting the party—and the nod went instead to Supreme Court Justice Charles Evans Hughes. As much as Alice despised Wilson, she took perverse pleasure in his narrow defeat of Hughes, as she was bent on vengeance against the Republican party for bypassing her father.

Alice was also becoming increasingly nasty on the subject of Eleanor and Franklin, whom Wilson had appointed to her father's old position, assistant Navy secretary. Alice howled when *The New York Times* printed an interview with Eleanor on the subject of wartime money-saving hints: "Mrs. Roosevelt on her pledge card said that there were seven in the family, and that ten servants were employed. Each servant has signed a pledge card, and there are daily conferences. . . . 'Making the 10 servants help me do my saving has not only been possible, but highly profitable,' said Mrs. Roosevelt today."[6]

Alice also watched with glee as Eleanor rushed around town making those stupid calls. One week she made sixty and said she envied the independence of her cousin Alice, who was "too much interested in the political questions of the day to waste her time calling on women."

It was because of the "endless hours" it took Eleanor "to arrange my calling list" that she finally hired a secretary, an aristocratic—descended from members of the Continental Congress—but impoverished beauty named Lucy Mercer. Alice quickly realized that Franklin was having an affair with Lucy and did everything she could to encourage it. She called Franklin to tell him, "I saw you 20 miles out in the country. You didn't see me. Your hands were on the wheel, but your eyes were on the perfectly lovely lady."[7]

Alice tirelessly spread a story that cast Eleanor in a particularly silly light: "Dearest Eleanor. She has always been such a help to Franklin. Do you remember once—just once—she let Franklin stay at the Montgomery Country Club after she went home at 10:00. When he arrived at five in the morning, flushed with excitement, and wine and the dawn he found dear Eleanor asleep on the door mat. He had forgotten to give her the key and she did not want to wake the servants."[8] Alice knew that Eleanor left the party because she suspected the affair and that her way of reproaching Franklin was to rise from the door mat "looking like a string bean that had been raised in a cellar."[9]

Still, Eleanor invited Alice and Nick to her "solemn" Sunday night dinners, at which, Alice later said, "one was usually regaled with crown roast, very indifferent wine, and a good deal of knitting . . ." Alice reciprocated by inviting Franklin and Lucy—but not Eleanor—to her parties, at which the entree was saddle of lamb, the wines the finest, the conversation the most brilliant, and the dinner partners the most beautiful. Alice excused herself by claiming that Franklin "deserved a good time. He was married to Eleanor." [10]

Then Alice made sure that Eleanor knew that her husband was in love with Lucy. Eleanor later told Franklin about meeting Alice at the Capitol. Alice tried to tell her a secret, Eleanor said, but she refused to listen. "I don't believe in knowing things one's husband doesn't want one to know."

As Alice was aware of Eleanor's history of male abandonment—she had wept on Ethel's shoulder after she became engaged, "I shall never be able to hold him. He is so attractive"—Alice's attempted confidence was, even for her, unusually cruel.

On April 9, 1917, three days after Congress declared war on Germany, Theodore arrived in Washington to stay with Alice while he begged Wilson to allow him to raise a division of reconstituted Rough Riders. Alice drove him to the meeting, which had been set up by Franklin, who maintained cordial relations with his famous cousin (although Theodore was disappointed that Franklin didn't resign his post and join the military). Congress had authorized TR's request to take his volunteers to France, the public loved the idea, and French Prime Minister Georges Clemenceau wrote Wilson an open letter urging him to send TR—"it will gladden their [French soldiers'] hearts." But Wilson, who dismissed TR as "a great big boy," said no. TR now called Wilson an "abject coward" and "internal skunk in the White House."

Alice's house became for her father what Bamie's had once been. (By then Bamie was confined to a wheelchair and increasingly deaf.) During one visit, Alice gathered for her father an audience of thirty-three newsmen, assorted Army and Navy officers, ambassadors, Supreme Court justices, and politicians of both parties.

During that first summer of the war, when every society matron, able-bodied or otherwise, did "war work," Alice gave it a brief fling and then announced that she had contracted a rare and untreatable malady that she dubbed "canteen elbow." [11] Meanwhile Eleanor worked all day and half the night at the Red Cross Canteen—once cutting her finger to the bone and slogging on anyway, and another time, after spending a steaming day and night toiling in a tin shack that served as a canteen, remarking, "I've come to the conclusion that you only feel heat when idle." [12] Alice spent her evenings going to parties for the members of the high commissions from the Allied powers, lively affairs that sometimes ended in poker games. [13]

She did, however, do one piece of war work, of which, to her delight, Eleanor thoroughly disapproved. She joined forces with cousin Franklin to bug the room in which the estimable Bernard Baruch was allegedly conducting a love affair with a woman who was a friend of Alice's. Franklin had become suspicious that Baruch, then chairman of the War Industries Board, was passing government secrets to his amour, who was then allegedly passing them to an uncle in Bucharest. The result, supposedly, was the sinking of some Allied ships by German submarines.

The suspected spy was a beautiful blonde named May Ladenburg, the daughter of a senior partner in the German/New York banking house of Ladenburg, Thalmann and Co. "All I was being asked to do was to look over transoms and peep through keyholes. Could anything be more delightful than that?" Alice later asked.[14] Actually Alice's assignment, as someone familiar with the layout of May's house, was to advise the military intelligence agents where to place the bugs.

Alice, Franklin, and several agents then listened to the lovers' conversation from a stable adjoining May's studio. "We did hear her ask Bernie how many locomotives were being sent to Rumania . . . In between the sounds of kissing. . . . Of course we were doing a *most* disgraceful thing in the name of looking after the affairs of our country, but it was sheer rapture!"[15] Predictably, what Alice pronounced "sheer rapture," Eleanor pronounced "*most unjust* to poor May Ladenburg."*[16]

Alice's attentions were soon turned back to her father, who was stuck in an uncharacteristic torpor as all his sons donned uniforms and he sat unoccupied. He was also mourning the death of British Ambassador Cecil Spring-Rice, who, during the Wilson administration, had been unceremoniously recalled to England. Friends insisted that he died of a broken heart. Wilson did not like "Springy," whom he called "that highly excitable invalid."[17]

Alice wanted to make sure that in 1920 the Republicans didn't

---

*Apparently, Eleanor, who, before the New Deal, was a committed anti-Semite, didn't feel sorry for Baruch. She had complained in a letter to her mother-in-law about having to go to a party for him: "I'd rather be hung than seen" there. "Mostly Jews." Two days later she was still complaining: "The Jew party [was] appalling. I never wish to hear money, jewels and . . . sables mentioned again." May Ladenburg later became Mrs. Preston Davie, a member of the extreme right wing of the Republican Party, and, not surprisingly, a zealous FDR-hater.

again pass her father by. She started early to lay the groundwork for his candidacy, successfully lobbying for a TR admirer as Republican national chairman. She lured her father from Sagamore to Washington as often as she could, and it was in her house that he wrote the proposal for "rapid victory and peace with honor" that was later adopted as part of the Republican platform.

As Wilson formulated what would become his League of Nations, Alice and her father were ready to pounce, but only Alice had the energy. In February 1918 TR was admitted to Roosevelt Hospital* in New York, close to death as an abscess in his right leg and two in his left ear spread poison through his body. Alice installed herself in the hospital and left only to sleep. She answered the telephone, briefed reporters, and relentlessly lambasted Wilson's plan for an international cooperative body that would provide for the defense of all its members and that, TR feared, would lull the United States into thinking that it no longer had to prepare for its own defense. He could not countenance any plan in which the United States had to depend for its safety on the likes of such proposed League members as Germany and Russia.

TR recovered, and the next October Alice was at his side at Sagamore when he wrote a speech denouncing Wilson—made more poignant by the death the previous July behind German lines of his youngest child, Quentin. As he finished each page of the speech, to be delivered at Carnegie Hall on October 28, he passed it to Alice. She predicted that this speech, which was received with shouts of support, would be the start of a triumphant return to the White House.

Just over two months later, on January 6, 1919, the sixty-year-old former president died in his sleep at Sagamore. There was no more bitter disappointment in Alice's long life. Her father would certainly have won the 1920 Republican nomination, which, that year, was tantamount to winning the election. Wartime tragedies and sacrifices had made the Democrats deathly unpopular.

Alice believed that Wilson's snubs had hastened her father's death, and she was determined to exact revenge. "I never forgive the per-

---

*Opened in 1871, the hospital was founded with money left by James Henry Roosevelt, great-grandson of the founder of the Hyde Park branch. James Henry was sensitive to the sufferings of the sick, having been crippled by polio exactly a century before the same disease crippled Franklin. [18]

sons who injure those I love," she declared. She would see to it that Wilson's cherished League met with overwhelming Senate rejection. She became irrational in her hatred. When Wilson returned from Paris, where he had gone to promote the League that he piously proclaimed "the only hope for mankind," Alice went to the station to count how many people showed up to greet him. She was happy to see only "a sparse crowd" that engaged in "very little cheering." She got out of her "motor and stood on the curbstone to see the Presidential party pass, fingers crossed, making the sign of the evil eye, and saying 'A murrain on him, a murrain on him!'"[19] She spread the crackpot charge that League supporters were being used in Wilson's scheme to become president of the Federation of the World.

On the other hand, she led the battle against the League with such determination and effectiveness that she was dubbed "the Colonel of Death." Although her role has been almost entirely overlooked by historians, nearly all of them male,* she was in the front line of the fight, whether plotting strategy with her new friend, Senator William Borah, Republican of Idaho, or dispatching notes to the Senate floor for Lodge, who led the anti-League forces, or threatening Senators who appeared to be wavering in Wilson's direction. That included Lodge, who was showing alarming tendencies to compromise. On those occasions Alice would loudly greet him, "Good morning, Mr. Wobbly." She carried around with her a "revenge list" of other Senators who showed signs of becoming even slightly reconcilable.

She regularly stayed at the Senate until 3 A.M., often with Ruth Hanna McCormick, whose husband Medill, then in the Senate, was a full-fledged irreconcilable, and returned six hours later to resume monitoring the debate. When League supporters claimed on the Senate floor that had TR lived he would have supported the League, it was up to Alice, scribbling notes to Lodge, to brand that a lie. (They cited TR's call, on accepting the Nobel Peace Prize, for a "League of Peace." Alice pointed out that her father's concept contained the strong proviso that America must remain militarily prepared to defend herself and that he had relegated Wilson to the group of "foolish, weak, or timid characters who have not the will and the power to prepare for their own defense.")

*When asked about Alice's contribution to the defeat of the League, Arthur Link, the dean of Wilson scholars and editor of the Wilson papers at Princeton, responded, "I think it is extremely peripheral. I've never seen her name mentioned."[20]

ALICE ROOSEVELT LONGWORTH

By March 1920, fifteen months after TR's death, Alice and a group of irreconcilable senators, including Bill Borah, put the next-to-the-last nail in the League's coffin and the first nail in Wilson's. During the battle he suffered a stroke from which he never recovered. He died four years later. Alice boasted of having broken his spirit, and his heart, just as he had tried to break her father's. She smiled at Wilson's warning to his countrymen that the United States's rejection of the League would "break the heart of the world."

Alice's battalion celebrated each Senate victory with a party at its Colonel's house, joined by Senators Lodge, Harding, and Borah. Flo Harding scrambled the eggs.[21]

When Eleanor found a love letter from Lucy, she offered Franklin "his freedom" or agreed to stay with him "for the children's sake," if he would promise never to see Lucy again. He would have grabbed the divorce offer, despite his mother's threat to disinherit him and despite the fact that divorce would have killed his political career, but Lucy was a devout Catholic and marriage to a divorced man was impossible.

In July 1920—a year and a half after TR's death—Franklin, to all appearances a happily married family man, was chosen by the Democrats as their vice-presidential candidate. (James Cox, Governor of Ohio, was the party's presidential nominee.) Alice was horrified, for she was determined that the next Roosevelt in the White House would be Theodore Roosevelt, Jr., not the "prissy" boy whom Alice and her cousins had called "Feather Duster" because "he pranced around and fluttered."[22]

Alice was especially galled, for had her father lived, he would have been the Republican candidate and there would have been no reason to give Franklin the nomination. Alice was not alone in thinking that the Democrats chose Franklin for one reason only—his name. They were hoping to exploit the Roosevelt image, again popular after Wilson's "pussyfooting" through the war.

To add insult to Alice's injury, Cox and her cousin made support of the League their main campaign issue, and Franklin toured the country claiming to be TR's political and spiritual heir, evoking his name, stopping at western towns where TR had hunted, appropriating TR's gestures and his very vocabulary. Suddenly Franklin's speeches were sprinkled with "bully" and "pussyfooting" and "square deal." Worst of all, Franklin claimed that the same reactionary Republicans who opposed TR's progressivism were now opposing the League.

Republican strategists worried that the voters might believe Franklin and that some Bull Moosers might even vote for him. And so the legitimate heir, Ted Jr., was assigned an unsavory task—to trail his cousin around the country warning voters that the only thing Franklin and Theodore had in common was a last name. When Franklin finished speaking, TR Jr. would mount the podium and denounce his cousin as a "maverick" who did not wear "the brand of our family." Franklin was furious, and his mood was not improved when Nick Longworth called the candidate a "denatured Roosevelt."

(So began the break between the Hyde Park and Oyster Bay branches. Franklin's mother was so "wild" over Nick's remark that, when asked why the Oyster Bayers were so antagonistic toward her son, she replied, "It must be because our side . . . has all the looks!") [23]

The *Chicago Tribune* picked up the theme by calling Franklin "the one-half of one percent Roosevelt. . . . Franklin is as much like Theodore as a clam is like a bear-cat. . . . If he is Theodore Roosevelt, Elihu Root is Gene Debs, and Bryan is a brewer." [24]

That year's Republican convention, which had been ready to nominate TR by acclamation, was, after his death, deadlocked. Alice watched in horror as Harding—the man who, in 1912, had called Taft "the greatest progressive of his time" and TR "every kind of traitor from Benedict Arnold to Aaron Burr"—got the nomination, and went on to win in the landslide that she felt belonged to her father.

Despite the fact that Alice thought Harding unfit to head a Moose lodge, much less the country, his victory held some satisfaction. First, it was lovely to watch cousin Franklin get trounced, then embark on an unsuccessful career in business, and even to watch him get crippled by polio the next summer. Also, Harding had tried to mend fences with Alice. He had led the fight in the Senate for approval of her father's plan to take his Rough Riders to France. Soon after Harding's inauguration, he appointed TR Jr. assistant Navy secretary, thus, Alice hoped, launching him on the road to the White House. But Alice wasn't taking any chances about Ted's following their father's progression from assistant Navy secretary to New York governor to president. Before agreeing to support Harding, she extracted a promise that he would back Ted as a gubernatorial candidate in 1924.

Still, for the party of Theodore Roosevelt to give the reins to "a slob" who would become best known for the Teapot Dome scandal and for entertaining his girlfriends in White House closets, while First Lady Flo pounded on the door, infuriated Alice. "My God," she said, "we have a President . . . who doesn't even know beds were invented—and his campaign slogan was 'Back to Normalcy!'"* When invited upstairs where, during these prohibition years, liquor was openly served, Alice found that what had once been her father's study was now "filled with cronies . . . trays with bottles containing every imaginable brand of whisky stood about, cards and poker chips ready at hand—a general atmosphere of waistcoat unbuttoned, feet on the desk, and the spittoon alongside."[26]

Alice was delighted to have her brother Ted and her sister-in-law, Eleanor Alexander Roosevelt, whom Ted had married eleven years earlier, living in Washington. The sisters-in-law were close, although, in many ways, TR Jr.'s wife was more like the other Eleanor Roosevelt. During World War I, Eleanor Alexander worked for the YMCA and managed to slip out of New York aboard a ship bound for France, just as she knew orders were imminent forbidding wives from joining their husbands overseas. This girl from a privileged background, who had never washed a dish in her life, was soon running a canteen, with her characteristic high energy and competence.

Still, during Ted's tenure in the Navy Department, the sisters-in-law were often seen attending Senate hearings together. Yet close relatives report that Alice "made every effort to have her brother meet all kinds of women" and encouraged him to have affairs.

Many people noticed that, when Bill Borah got up to denounce Wilson and his League, Alice watched him as she used to watch her father. Borah was not a handsome man. He was coarse-featured and burly, but unequivocally masculine, square-chinned—with a dimple—and the most powerful orator in the Senate. It was said that he alone could bring senators to their feet in spontaneous applause. He

*When Francis Russell's biography of Harding, *Shadow of Blooming Grove,* was published in 1968, it appeared, because of a lawsuit filed by Harding's nephew, without the love letters the president had written to one Carrie Phillips. Russell protested the court order by leaving blank spaces in the text where excerpts of the letters were to have appeared. Someone at McGraw-Hill, knowing of Alice's distaste for Harding, sent her the deleted portions, from which she would read to entertain her friends. Columnist Tom Braden recalled Alice's pleasure in reciting Harding's "absolutely puerile stuff . . . high school pornography."[25]

A Love Affair with Borah

resembled her father—physically and in his seriousness of purpose, his preparation, his propensity for greatness. He was the polar opposite of her husband.

Nick was the House's good old boy—first and last a team player, more interested in the fortunes of his party and his beloved House than in his personal glory. Borah was aloof and contrary. A famous story had Borah riding a horse in Rock Creek Park and Coolidge expressing amazement that the senator was willing to go in the same direction as the horse. He was also unsociable—known in Capitol social circles as a recluse. While Nick was loved by his colleagues on both sides of the aisle, Borah was described by Hiram Johnson as being "as responsive as cold marble," full of "suspicion . . . selfishness . . . and peculiar secretiveness . . ." and "anything but popular among his fellows . . ." [27]

Borah was also a man of enormous power. "Borah, today, is the biggest figure in the Senate, by far," Johnson added, "and I believe his words carry to a much greater extent than those of any other man in Washington, save the President." [28] Borah would get still more power when, in 1924, he headed the Senate Foreign Relations Committee.

Alice continued to frequent the Senate even after the League battle was over. One day when Borah was speaking she lingered until mid-afternoon, arriving home to find her invited luncheon guests very irritated. They had arrived, on time, an hour earlier. One year she went to New York for Christmas and planned to stay over New Year's, but rushed home when she heard that Borah would be holding forth.

She almost never went to Nick's House. Nick liked to lecture the members of the "so-called lower House" to take pride in being part of what he pronounced "the great dominant legislative assembly of the World." But Alice agreed with two prominent newsmen who described the House as "a cross between a troop of monkeys and sheep," with members who "are the lowest common denominator of the ignorance [and] prejudices . . . of their districts . . . the greatest organized inferiority complex in the world." [29] While the Senate debated the great issues of the nation and the world, Alice described going to the House to find "a rag bag of exhausted, frowzy legislators . . . having what the old doorkeeper called a 'social session.' A Y.M.C.A. man was standing in front of the rostrum leading singing— every one joining in—the Marine Band going full tilt." [30]

Nick was in his element. He radiated a joy in living that made him loved by his colleagues, as well as by the corps of Washington milkmen who, as dawn broke, greeted him by his first name as he staggered to his car. Nick loved playing string quartets, but got just as much pleasure from entertaining his drunken friends with his "fiddle" between his knees or behind his back, or from playing the piano with an orange. He could often be found at a local saloon arm in arm with his friend H. L. Mencken singing, "Down Where the Wurzburger Flows."[31] "I can remember him in the back room of this house," said Shef Cowles, "standing next to the piano and playing a tune with his right hand at the same time he was singing . . . and the words were disreputable. He had a wonderful pornographic sense of humor."[32]

Whereas Alice, like her father, and like that enigmatic senator from Idaho, enjoyed nothing more than a political or intellectual discussion, Nick much preferred bawdy jokes and stag parties. "All of . . . Nick's friends were sort of middle-aged drunkards," Alice said, ". . . they thought it manly or something."[33]

By then Nick and Alice were married in name only. It was even reported in that era's best-seller, *Washington Merry-Go-Round*, that the two went "more or less his or her own way."[34] From Nick's family, Alice was totally estranged. When Susan Longworth died in 1921, Nick wrote Clara, then living abroad, "Alice arrives tomorrow, she was anxious to come before but we thought it best not."[35]

While Nick was breaking the law at the Harding White House, Alice, according to close relatives and friends, was breaking her marriage vows. The affair with Senator Borah was, in the words of one niece, "common knowledge. Even my mother knew it . . . there is no question that she was."[36] That same niece recalled Alice visiting her parents, as usual, without Nick and at a time when the couple was to be separated for an extended period. The maid who normally unpacked guests' suitcases was unavailable and so Alice's sister-in-law took over. To her horror, she found a diaphragm in Alice's bag.[37]

A cousin, Tish Alsop, recalled that "there was always family gossip about Borah. I remember I was there [at Alice's home] with another cousin . . . for tea and . . . there was absolutely stunned silence— [the cousin] turned to Mrs. Longworth and said, 'Is it true that you had an affair with Senator Borah?'" Tish recalled Alice's response as "just giggling."[38]

Journalists knew. It was hinted at discreetly in the most respectable papers and maliciously in the least. Hope Miller recalled that when she first came to Washington, "everybody called her Aurora Borah Alice."[39]

Politicians also knew. John Gable, a Roosevelt scholar and head of the Theodore Roosevelt Association, was assured by Hamilton Fish, a New York congressman and Borah adviser, that there was an affair.[40] The late Senator Frank Church of Idaho, who, like Borah, headed the Senate Foreign Relations Committee, told Borah biographer Robert Maddox of the affair: "Church told me directly that that was the case. . . . He said that this was simply known to be true, both from his connections in Idaho and older senators . . . in Washington."[41]

Those who knew Borah only by his carefully cultivated public image were surprised at the affair. He sold himself as a loner who shunned Washington social life in favor of returning to his modest Connecticut Avenue apartment, his wife, Mary, who was known as "Little Borah," a home-cooked meal, usually including his favorite, onion soup, and a long night of poring over books and papers.

Hiram Johnson was not at all surprised. While Borah was nurturing this brooding loner image, he had been accepting all of Alice's invitations and most of another admirer, Cissy Patterson's. Many nights he never returned to his books or his wife. "Your mother has conceived a terrible prejudice against him," Johnson wrote his sons. "Mrs. Borah left for the west and Borah was alone here for some months. Your mother and I did everything in our power to get him to come out . . . to see us. . . . There was always a pretext of some sort why he could not come, in the background being his expressed desire not to go out . . . something of the recluse attitude. Mother discovered, however, that during the times he was telling of what a recluse he was . . . he was dining . . . at other places where he was invited."[42]

Usually with pretty, adoring women. Borah's voracious sexual appetite was among Washington's worse-kept secrets. "His promoters liked to refer to him as the 'Lion of Idaho,'" said biographer Maddox, "but . . . more cynical people referred to him as the 'Stallion of Idaho.'"[43] Although they didn't publish it in their books on Borah—because Mrs. Borah was still alive—two Borah biographers, Marian McKenna and Leroy Ashby, traced Borah's ending up in Idaho at all to a misadventure with a young woman.[44]

Borah, who was born in Illinois and educated in Kansas, had decided, in 1890 when he was twenty-five, to practice law in Seattle or

Portland. But before he was able to head out of Kansas, he allegedly got a young woman pregnant and had to leave town in a hurry—so much of a hurry that he had only enough money to get him as far as Boise. According to Harry Shellworth, whose father, a lobbyist for mining and timber interests, was Borah's closest political adviser, "Borah got off the train completely broke and slept in my grandfather's coal bin. The following morning my grandfather asked him, 'Why don't you take a look at Idaho? It's got a great future.'"[45]

There were similar rumors surrounding Borah's marriage to Mary ("Mame") McConnell, the daughter of Bill McConnell, a former Idaho governor. According to Marian McKenna, "the rumors . . . were that it was a shotgun wedding, that he got her pregnant and she had an abortion. I tried to drag this out of the man who was her physician at the time . . . I asked him the question point blank, 'Did Mary Borah have an abortion before she married him?' He wouldn't answer me. I have ever since been convinced that the reason he wouldn't was because . . . in those days if the abortion was performed in a certain way it meant that the woman could never have children. Her father was furious and made Borah marry her."[46]

In fact, the Borahs never had children and maternal-minded Mary instead surrounded herself with canaries—thirty-two yellow birds flying unrestricted around the Borah apartment. (She almost died from parrot fever, a pneumonia-like illness transmitted to humans by infected birds.) "Mrs. Borah always reminds me of these canaries, with her fluffy yellow hair, bright eyes, and quick movements," one journalist wrote.[47] She spent her spare time, of which she had plenty, caring for shell-shocked soldiers, who called her Aunt Mary.

Marian McKenna, who interviewed Mary Borah several times, recalled her as "the flightiest numbbrain there ever was. She knew absolutely nothing about politics and wasn't even interested."[48]

The relationship was a peculiarly distant one. Leroy Ashby recalled sifting through several hundred boxes of Borah's papers and sensing a great distance in the letters. "At one point she went on a fairly long trip to California. He stayed back in Washington. . . . The letters are very strange. . . . He had dictated them. His secretary had typed them, with her initials at the bottom and very formal . . . no sense that he really missed her. No information about what he was doing back in the nation's Capitol."[49]

No wonder. Borah's habit of finding sex outside marriage was long established. The senior Harry Shellworth was the first newsboy on the streets of Boise. He would sell the Idaho *Statesman* from three in the morning until sunrise in the area around the "sporting houses," of which there were twenty-eight—providing both women and liquor.[50] Fred Kohlmeyer, a professor at Illinois State University who interviewed Shellworth, noted after the interview in a memo to his colleague Leroy Ashby: "Harry Shellworth—newsboy in downtown Boise when Borah was in the statehouse—Borah spent *every* [underlined twice] night in a *cathouse*. Newsboy would know where to find him. Borah's philosophy: 'Better to pay for it before than afterwards.'"[51]

Alice was not alone in vying for Borah's charms. Cissy Patterson, who had already emerged victorious in the fight for Nick, was now intent on adding Borah to her conquests.

Cissy first met the Idaho senator at a party at Alice's house. Before long the two were seen riding in Rock Creek Park. Cissy could not keep quiet about the affair, going so far as to report that Borah slept in his underwear. She also circulated around town the details of an amusing skirmish with Alice. Borah arrived for a party at Alice's house, as usual without his wife, and soon disappeared with Cissy. The next day Alice's maid found several of Cissy's hairpins in the library. Alice sent them to her rival, along with a note that said, "I believe they are yours." Cissy promptly wrote back, "And if you look up in the chandelier, you might find my panties."[52]

Borah, who had presidential ambitions, was not amused. Cissy was proving too indiscreet for his own good. During the 1920 Republican convention in Chicago, Cissy wrote an article for Hearst's *Chicago Herald-Examiner* that was headlined "Borah is Countess Gizycka's Hero." She gushed over his "leonine profile" and his "magnetic speaking voice" in language that was nakedly affectionate. Borah warned her to keep her passion to herself. Then the influential *Chicago Tribune*, which was owned by Cissy's brother and cousin, and undoubtedly read by almost every delegate, ran an editorial critical of Borah. Borah assumed—incorrectly—that Cissy had prevailed on her brother to run the editorial to repay Borah for his humiliating criticism.[53]

Soon after that, Borah was firmly in Alice's salon—and bedroom. Alice had won the battle over Borah, but Cissy refused to gracefully withdraw. She soon published her first novel, *Glass Houses*, which scandalized and titillated Washington society. It featured characters who were transparently Alice, Borah, and Cissy, and it graphically described the bitter struggle between the women for the undeserving senator's affections. *

Although Nick was faithful to no one woman, he too had a special friend—a grande dame named Alice Dows, four years older than Alice Longworth—who had a gorgeously decorated house on O Street in Georgetown and a husband, Tracy Dows, who conveniently stayed on the family estate in Rhinebeck on the Hudson,† thus leaving his wife to indulge her passions for flowing chiffon gowns, serious music, and for the Capitol's most gifted amateur musician, Nick Longworth. The Dowses were an old Hudson River family—the land was in Alice's family since the 1600s—and very close friends of Sara Delano Roosevelt and her son Franklin. As president, FDR frequently visited the Dowses' estate. When Alice Dows became a genuine widow in 1937, she often came to dinner at Hyde Park. [55]

Marian Christie, a friend of the Dowses' children, recalled going to tea at the Georgetown house. She naturally headed for the drawing room, to find the door closed and her friends' shrieked warning: "No, no we must have our tea in the upstairs sitting room." On leaving, Marian asked, "Should I say good-bye to your mother?" and they insisted, "No, no, no! The door of the drawing room is locked." Occasionally she would catch a glimpse inside and see that it was "filled with flowers and an open fire and Mrs. Dows in a trailing chiffon tea gown and then the beaus would come and she'd lock the door." [56]

Although, in recalling Mrs. Dows, women tended to describe her as comically buxom and flirtatious, men described her in variations of FDR's son Elliott's words: "so beautiful . . . extremely regal in her bearing." [57] Nick enjoyed her physical attributes and her coquet-

---

*Cissy came off as the heroine and Alice and Borah as despicable cads. Cissy's character is the beautiful, independent daughter of a Wyoming politician-rancher. She is having an affair with a burly, slovenly, and unprincipled Western senator; at the same time, she starts an affair with a French diplomat. Watching this is the Alice character, a vicious and vindictive Washington hostess, who lusts after the powerful senator. He is murdered by the loyal foreman of the Cissy character, who then marries the handsome diplomat, leaving the Alice character with nothing but her venom. [54]

†Her son was Olin Dows, an artist who painted the murals in the Rhinebeck and Hyde Park post offices. He also wrote a book about his family's relationship with the FDRs entitled *Franklin Roosevelt at Hyde Park*.

tishness, but most of all he enjoyed her worshipful attitude toward his music. For all his clowning around, Nick was a serious musician. Efrem Zimbalist and Leopold Stokowski later praised his playing, the former saying that with a little more practice Nick could have been among the world's greatest violinists.

He certainly received no encouragement from Alice, who early in their marriage infuriated Nick by leaving the room when he played his violin after dinner. In the twelfth year of their marriage, Alice complained to Auntie Bye, "Nick is so 'temperamental' that I have to exercise the utmost discretion about who I ask to hear [him play]. His little visage becomes lineless with hate at the sight of certain people." Gore Vidal would later describe Alice as "an enemy of music (save for 'Hail to the Chief')" [58] and she would describe Nick's musical evenings as boring to the point of "stupefaction." [59]

If Alice Longworth was bored to the point of stupefaction, Alice Dows, who helped to start the National Orchestra, was transported to the point of ecstasy. She often attended Nick's musical evenings (at which one might find Fritz Reiner or Efrem Zimbalist or Ethel Barrymore), and often gave the evenings at her home. Like Nick, she was an intimate friend of the violinist Zimbalist and his wife, soprano Alma Gluck. Alice Dows recalled one night when "the Zimbalists were staying with me and Nick came to dinner. Afterwards we four sat in the library dimly lit with one lamp and the fire. First Zimbalist played, then handed his fiddle to Nick, then Zimbalist again. . . . I shall never forget that evening." She later recalled qualities of Nick's that emerged while he played: "those . . . occasions when music stirred him deeply and brought out a hidden shyness he could at all other times conceal." [60]

The affair became so public that Drew Pearson and Robert Allen in *Washington Merry-Go-Round* referred to Alice Dows as one of "Nick's girls." [61] When she died, she left Gore Vidal, a young friend of hers, one of her most precious possessions—a copy of Clara's biography of Nick with a four-leaf clover pressed against the page on which "Mrs. Tracy Dows" made her entrance. [62]

To the end of her life Alice Dows cast Nick in the role of sensitive, unworldly artist. To Alice Longworth, Nick's unworldliness was limited to money. He was quickly dissipating what remained of his inheritance. According to a friend, Alice "hated the drinking parties . . . with Nick living way beyond his means. . . . This caused her constant anguish about having to produce this sort of life and that he didn't realize that he was just pouring it down the drain. The poker parties would start before dinner, then they'd have a sumptuous dinner and they'd go on all night. She would go to bed. But then a whole new set of servants would come in and serve breakfast."[63]

While Nick was considered the best host in town, H. L. Mencken was among many who found it hard to take Nick seriously once the party ended and most of the rest of the world got to work. "I am off for Washington to see Nick Longworth," Mencken wrote his fiancée, "and try to put in some licks for San Francisco as the scene of the Republican National Convention. . . . If Nick is sober, I may be able to do something. But probably not."[64]

In Nick I's day, the thousands of vineyards planted on the hillsides above the Ohio River gave the region the look of Germany's Rhine. In Nick III's day, that glory was reduced to Nick bootlegging wine in his bathtub. (At least Nick was not a hypocrite. While many of his colleagues publicly praised Prohibition and privately passed the bottle, Nick opposed Prohibition on the House floor.)

Alice started out on Nick's side of Prohibition, but she soon switched because "I saw a great deal of drunkenness and it disgusted and angered me. . . . If the people I knew got drunk, I did not really mind, I merely did not wish to see them and associate with them . . . It was to me merely a question of taste and tipsy people bored me."[65]

Not only did Alice have to contend with alcoholism in her husband and among friends, she also had to deal with a deep strain in the Roosevelt family. As a child, she had listened at keyholes to whispered conversations about her father's brother, Elliott, who, like Nick, started drinking well before he turned twenty-one. In her own generation, her brothers Ted and Kermit were heavy drinkers, and so were her first cousins, Auntie Corinne's sons. In 1909 cousin Stewart had fallen to his death from the window of his Harvard room. The boy had taken a snifter of brandy at each corner window until he came to the third corner and toppled out. His brother Monroe was, according to a recent biographer of the Roosevelts, "an alcoholic whose personality and life seemed to be a carbon copy of the doomed Elliott Roosevelt." Monroe was Alice's exact contemporary, the baby with whom she was to have shared the Fifty-seventh Street nursery, until Alice Lee's death destroyed those plans. (It is fascinating that Corinne, in the face of the alcoholism of at least two of her sons and one of her brothers, would write in her preposterously Pollyannaish biography of the other brother: "It has been my great good fortune to have been associated with men of great self-control as regards drink.")[66]

Alice could not hold Harding to his promise to help Ted Jr. win the gubernatorial nomination; the president died suddenly in August 1923. Instead she besieged one of New York's U.S. senators—a family friend named James Wadsworth—to help ensure it. Ted was indeed nominated, quit the Navy Department, and watched as a towering obstruction blocked his path to the statehouse.

The previous January a scandal had broken in Washington that was quickly dubbed "Teapot Dome" and that, until Watergate, was the most shocking example of abuse of office in American history. At the request of Secretary of the Interior Albert Fall, Navy Department officials had transferred to the Interior Department some naval oil fields at Teapot Dome, Wyoming, which Fall then leased to oil baron Harry Sinclair. When the leases were signed, Sinclair sent Fall a thank-you note with a check for $68,000. Before the Senate investigation ended, many careers were ruined, including that of Ted's boss, Navy Secretary Edwin Denby, and, of course, that of Fall, who later went to prison.

Among the spiciest of the Teapot Dome revelations was the alleged involvement of Ted and his younger brother Archie. Not only had Ted been a Sinclair director before the war, but it was his banking firm that helped finance Sinclair Oil. But Ted, with an eye toward a future in politics, had long since severed all ties to Sinclair—except that in 1919 he had asked Sinclair to give a job to his brother, who had been severely wounded during the war.*

When Sinclair's secretary, G. D. Wahlberg, told Archie about the $68,000 check, which he claimed to have actually seen, Archie resigned from the company and went to the Senate investigating committee without waiting to be subpoenaed. He became the prosecution's key witness.

Ted supported Archie's efforts and convinced Wahlberg to tell the

---

*Archie had been filled with shrapnel during World War I—his kneecap was shattered and one arm was so badly broken that the nerve was severed—and declared 100-percent disabled. During World War II, he was hit by a grenade in the same knee and also contracted malaria—putting him among the handful of people totally disabled in both wars. He was a two-time recipient of the Silver Star.[67]

committee what he had told Ted. But with Sinclair's lawyer staring coldly at him and with the fear of losing his job hanging over him, Wahlberg testified, "No, Senator. Mr. Roosevelt is mistaken. I never mentioned a check for $68,000. What I said was that Mr. Sinclair had sent Secretary Fall a present of six or eight cows and bulls."

A member of Congress had demanded Ted's resignation, even though Ted had argued against transferring the land to Interior and since then had not been consulted on the leases. He claimed to have known nothing about them until the story broke, when he came home in the deepest gloom and informed his wife that his career was over. Not only had he secured the job for Archie, but he owned one thousand shares of Sinclair stock, and the stock jumped ten points on the strength of the transfer. Ted was relieved to learn that his wife, who had taken over the family finances, had sold the Sinclair stock, and sold it at a loss. Eventually both brothers were not only absolved of any complicity in the scandal, but were credited with helping to crack it. [68]

Cousin Eleanor chose to ignore that fact. Since Franklin's paralysis from polio three years earlier, she had been campaigning vigorously for Democrats, and now she assigned herself the task of shadowing cousin Ted. Atop her car she had mounted a giant tea kettle that spouted both steam and the message that Ted was corrupt.

Alice was furious, and the war between the branches was now openly declared. Eleanor later admitted in her autobiography that this was a "rough stunt," but first blamed it on Franklin's manager Louis Howe. Farther on in the same book she boasted, "I thought up some of the best stunts that were undertaken. . . . The recent Teapot Dome scandal—with which Theodore Roosevelt Jr. had nothing to do—had created much excitement" and so the campaign "capitalized" on this. "In the thick of political fights one always feels that all methods of campaigning that are honest are fair . . ." [69] (What was "honest" about pretending that TR Jr. participated in Teapot Dome is not clear.)

Ted narrowly lost to Al Smith and forevermore Alice blamed Eleanor. Ted would make one more unsuccessful stab at getting the gubernatorial nomination, but his political career was effectively ended. "Like the Republican elephant I am," Alice vowed, "I never forget." [70]

*   *   *

A Love Affair with Borah

Alice had been married for eighteen years when, late in the summer of 1924, a reporter for the *Washington Post* shocked the capital by revealing that forty-year-old Alice Longworth was pregnant. (Alice had earlier told "Silent Cal" Coolidge, with whom she knew her secret was safe. Alice had befriended the taciturn president—she once went to a Dempsey-Carpentier prize fight with him—whose dry-as-dust wit she found amusing, despite the disdain of some of her society friends for the cold, plain New Englander. Henry Cabot Lodge sneered that Coolidge was the kind of man who lived in a two-family house.)

Entering middle age, Alice, who often said that she would try anything once, was apparently genuinely pleased at the prospect of motherhood. She figured that after the baby grew, it might become an amusing person to have around. Almost immediately she cast herself in the role of grandmother—a role that would allow her to enjoy the child without getting trapped in daily routine. Referring to the hormonal changes of menopause, she cheerfully called herself a "glandmother."

Among the most surprised at Alice's news, and not happily, was the widowed Edith Kermit Roosevelt. *"Bouleversé,"* she wrote in her diary. In a letter to Bamie, Edith wrote of her upcoming trip to Cuba: "Alice's news was rather a blow, and I daresay a few days at sea are good for me."[71]

The Washington gossip mills were running overtime trying to identify the father. Speculation ranged from Senator Borah to serious talk that Alice had been artificially inseminated.[72] There was scarcely an insider who entertained the possibility that Nick was responsible. Gossip had it that Alice had barred him from her bed. Eventually they moved into separate bedrooms. "I just don't believe that she and Nick were even sleeping together," said one relative. "He was an alcoholic. . . . That doesn't make for a vast amount of sex life. . . . I think she was repulsed by him."[73] Other gossip had Nick sodden to the point of impotence. "He was a drunk and nobody ever thought him capable of having a child," said one Washingtonian who grew up near Alice on Dupont Circle.[74]

In late January 1925, Alice went to Chicago and checked into the Drake Hotel to await the birth. Undoubtedly recalling the disaster of her own home birth, she wanted the best hospital and obstetrician she could find. On Ruth McCormick's advice, she decided to have her baby at the Chicago Lying-In Hospital under the care of the famous Dr. Joseph B. DeLee, who had delivered Ruth's children.

DeLee, now considered one of the fathers of modern obstetrics, opened his first hospital—a clinic for the poor—in 1895 in a stove-heated basement flat on Newberry and Maxwell Streets. He did not want Alice Longworth as a patient because he did not want to become known as an obstetrician to the famous. While he would stay up all night with a girl from the ghetto and charge her nothing, he is said to have "soaked" Alice in the amount of $4000.[75] So nervous was he about caring for his famous patient that he booked passage out of the country in case something went wrong.[76]

As the first and most of the second week of February passed, Alice, who, like her father, attached great significance to particular days of the year, was feeling wary. Her own birthday was February 12; the seventeenth was the nineteenth anniversary of her marriage to Nick, but the day most loaded with meaning was Valentine's Day, the fourteenth—the forty-fifth anniversary of the betrothal of Alice Lee and Theodore Roosevelt and the forty-first anniversary of Alice Lee's death.

The baby, a girl not immediately named but dubbed "the Valentine's Baby" in newspaper headlines, was born on Saturday, February 14. With Alice in the hospital were her stepmother, her brother Kermit, and Ruth McCormick. Nick, who was about to start his campaign for Speaker of the House, was in Washington, but boarded a train and arrived at the hospital Sunday morning.

Lying-In officials announced that the baby weighed six pounds, eight and one-half ounces and was a "normal healthy infant." To Dr. DeLee's relief, the mother was in very good condition, although she would later liken having a baby to "trying to push a grand piano through a transom."[77]

Nick returned to Washington, but Alice, the baby, and Miss Dorothy Waldron, whom Alice hired away from the hospital to become her private baby nurse, returned to the Drake. They stayed in Chicago longer than planned so Alice could comfort Ruth, whose husband, Medill, a manic-depressive, an alcoholic, and a just-defeated candidate for renomination to the Senate, had committed suicide. When Alice, Miss Waldron (whose name Alice soon shortened to "Waldie"), and the baby returned to Washington in early March, troops had to be called out to control the crowds of the curious who jammed the streets from Union Station to the Longworth home on M Street. (Later in 1925 the Longworths moved into their Massachusetts Avenue home.)

Rumors about the baby's patrimony did not stop after the birth, nor even after it was clear that the Speaker-designate (Nick would be sworn in as Speaker in December) was crazy about the baby. Nick took the teasing good-naturedly, although it was reported that "it even became essential for Nick Longworth to knock down a member of the august Alfalfa Club [an all-male club whose members come from the top strata of the three branches of government and major corporations] . . . because of insinuations on this subject."

Although many people expected that the baby would be named Alice, the new mother declined a Roosevelt (or a Longworth) family name and instead decided to give the girl the biblical name Deborah. According to Hope Miller, Nick put a stop to that selection: "With all the gossip going around, why would you want to name her 'De-Borah?'"[78] Instead Alice named her Paulina after St. Paul, who was her—and Borah's—favorite character in the New Testament. Alice chose that name, she explained, so that the child could "have a personality of her own"[79]—a comment that in retrospect sounds ironic, as Alice relentlessly squelched her daughter's individuality.

Alice let it be known that, had the baby been a boy, its name would have been Paul—a curious revelation that buttressed the rumors that this was not Nick's child. Presumably he would have wanted to give a son the name Nicholas Longworth IV or to have named him after his beloved grandfather, Joseph.

On Nick's first viewing of the baby, he remarked, "She looks so much more like a Roosevelt than a Longworth, but she's young yet." Actually she looked neither like a Longworth nor a Roosevelt, but a lot like a Borah. Marian McKenna recalled that Ray McKaig, an Idaho Progressive who traveled the state drumming up political support for Borah, showed her a picture of Paulina and asked, "If you don't think she's the spittin' image."[80] Friends and relatives who knew Paulina as a girl and young woman, often mentioned her "round Borah-like face."

Alice responded in the only way she could. She suggested that the baby bore a striking resemblance to Uncle Joe Cannon.

She then proceeded to ignore the baby, leaving her to Waldie's care. Alice had never pretended to like babies, and often told a story of the time she and a British friend compared notes on the most unappetizing meal they had ever eaten. He mentioned a cauldron of monkey stew complete with floating monkeys' hands. "They looked like the hands of little babies," he told her. "That wouldn't bother me," Alice replied. "I don't like babies." [81] That this was her own child made no difference.

Waldie had been a Red Cross nurse during World War I, then worked at various New England hospitals before ending up at Chicago Lying-In. Friends of Alice remembered Waldie as unattractive, short, wide, and usually wearing "a funny looking little hat." [82] But she was devoted to Paulina and cared for her in a way that was beyond Alice's capabilities.

Nick, given the rumors, his new duties as Speaker, his continued drinking and philandering, might have been excused for ignoring the child. But it was soon clear that Nick and Paulina adored one another. Paulina's patrimony didn't matter much to Nick, who, in the words of one friend of Paulina, "probably just liked children and knew he wasn't having any and just liked this little girl." [83] Nick, who had a near idyllic childhood, was not burdened with Alice's insecurities. He was free to fall in love with Paulina, and he did. "He probably would have adored to have had children and could see that this little girl wasn't getting any attention from his wife," said a friend of Alice. [84]

He nicknamed her "Kitz" and took her with him to the House whenever he could wrestle her away from Waldie. One touching photo shows Nick getting out of his car at the Capitol holding Paulina, who looks to be four or five months old. As she grew older, he had regular luncheons for her in the Speaker's dining room, complete with her favorite dishes. [85] He once adjourned a full day's session in order to attend her birthday party, and on another birthday sat Paulina in the front row of the Speaker's gallery and smiled broadly when Congressmen stood and applauded her. "Paulina comes to the office with Nick nearly every Saturday," Nick's secretary reported. "He sends in for members to come and pay their respects. Democrats as well as Republicans and they are all charmed to meet her." During the 1928 inauguration, Nick organized a party for the three-year-old in his inner office, with guests including the son of a senator, the daughter of the German ambassador, and a full-blooded Indian. [86]

As fastidious as Nick was about his grooming, with Paulina he was lovingly indulgent. Waldie once rushed to Nick's study to find Paulina standing in a chair beside him "with a bowl of powdered sugar. She was making sugar cakes on top of Nick's bald head, moistening them with spit and patting them flat with the handle of a teaspoon."[87]

Paulina idolized her father. Nick's secretary described the Speaker holding Paulina in his arms in his inner office and "showing her off to a lot of members. To test her baby observation, he said, 'Kittsie, show Daddy Col. Lindbergh's picture.'" She searched the photo-covered walls until she found one of "Lindy . . . which Col. Lindbergh had autographed when he was in one day.* She responded without difficulty and then glancing at the photograph above it, said eagerly . . . 'And here is Daddy's Capitol.'"[88]

Nick was thrilled with his new duties as a father and as the Speaker, but he was not imbued with a new seriousness of purpose. He was, to Alice's disgust, the same old Nick. The Republican Speaker's best friend was the Democratic Minority Leader John "Cactus Jack" Garner, "a semi-barbarian from the wilds of Texas," in the words of one journalist.[89] "Longworth is an aristocrat. I am a plebian,"[90] Jack Garner explained, and anyone who saw the two, who had both entered the house in 1903, did not need to be told. Cactus Jack, who often went unshaven and whose heavy gray eyebrows stood on end, appeared to have chosen Uncle Joe Cannon as his sartorial model.

The pair also had poker and drinking in common—and they did both in a House room officially known as the Henry Clay Room and unofficially as the "Board of Education." The name of the hideaway—which went to the Speaker as a "perk" of office—derived from Nick's first public office on the Cincinnati school board and also from the practice of taking neophyte members there to be "educated" on how to vote on a particular issue. In the process, Nick, Jack, and their cronies enjoyed endless rounds of bourbon, branch water, and poker.†

---

*Nick and Alice were close friends of the aviator who, in 1927, made the famous nonstop, solo flight across the Atlantic.

†House historian Raymond Smock identified the room as H-128, one flight down from the House chamber. It has high ceilings, decorated in the 1860s by the artist Brumidi,[91] a big table, a couch, overstuffed chairs, a desk, telephone, and well-stocked icebox. Harry Truman went there to drink bourbon with Sam Rayburn. It was in H-128 on April 12, 1945, that Eleanor Roosevelt finally found Truman to inform him that FDR was dead and that he was president.[92] H-128 attracted some bad publicity in 1976 when it was alleged that its couch was being used for something more exotic than napping.

Nick and Jack's routine never changed. At precisely 5:00, Garner, whom House Doorkeeper Fishbait Miller called "one of the most determined boozers the Capitol has ever known," [93] would signal Speaker Longworth with the words, "Let's cut this stuff out, it's time to strike a blow for liberty." The four bells would ring and off they'd go to their hideaway, Garner, who carried a snifter to help him get through the day, often stumbling down the stairs.

The two were so close that they were harshly criticized for perverting the two-party system and for "fraternizing with the enemy." Every morning, Nick, in his official Speaker's limousine, picked up Cactus Jack for the ride to the Capitol. Although Garner often reviled Longworth on the House floor as "that bald-headed coot," everyone realized that the Democrat was just going through the motions. They couldn't hide the fact that they were just good old buddies who, in journalist Neil MacNeil's words, would go to their hideaway to "have a bottle of booze and divvy up the whole place." [94]

Given the fact that during the mid-1920s Alice shared a house with the Speaker of the House, a bed with the chairman of the Senate Foreign Relations Committee, and a bantering friendship with Calvin Coolidge—she was said to be the only person who could get Coolidge to perform anything even vaguely resembling a banter*—Alice was far and away the most powerful hostess in Washington.

Not surprisingly, Jack and Ettie Garner were not a couple whom Alice cared to include in her glittering dinner parties. Although Garner had now become a multimillionaire through investments in real estate, banks, pecan farms, and poker games, he was known as a prodigious cheapskate and a man who treated his wife like a slave. They lived in a residential hotel, and during his entire congressional career, Ettie served as his secretary, his laundress, and his cook. (She installed a small stove in one of the rooms in the Capitol so she could cook his meals without neglecting her office chores.)

While he was Speaker, Nick was still climbing out a rear window of the Massachusetts Avenue house to visit the daughter of an ambas-

---

*At a White House luncheon Alice sat at Coolidge's right, a National Committeewoman from Nebraska sat on his left. Coolidge's very few words were all directed at Alice, despite the committeewoman's repeated attempts to engage the president. At the end of the luncheon she turned to Coolidge and said, "Mr. President, I made a bet with one of my girlfriends back home that I could get you to say more than three words." He looked her in the eye and said, "You lose" and left the table.

sador whose embassy roof adjoined the Longworths' roof.[95] Fishbait Miller, who came to the House two years after Nick's death but who accumulated forty-two years of service and endless stories about Nick from other members, pronounced him "one of the greatest woman-izers in history on Capitol Hill." In one of those stories a man who waits to see the Speaker picks a cigarette from a box on Nick's desk. "Oh, I don't think you are going to like that cigarette," Nick's secretary warns. It was a condom disguised as a cigarette.

Fishbait's favorite story has the Speaker sitting in the House library, "reading a Cincinnati . . . newspaper . . . when a brash congressman thought he'd make a splash by putting down the Speaker on his womanizing. 'Mr. Speaker,' he said, 'I've always wanted to say something to you but I've never caught you when you were not busy. Your pretty bald head reminds me of my wife's behind. Is it all right if I rub my hand across it? Then I'll be sure.' Without waiting . . . he . . . rubbed his hand all the way across Longworth's bald head and said, 'Yes, it does feel like my wife's behind.' He looked around at his audience a bit smugly as he waited for Longworth to explode. But he didn't. Instead, Longworth lifted his own hand and ran it across his own head thoughtfully. 'I'll be damned if it doesn't,' he said. The brash congressman went slinking out of there and stayed out of sight for some time."[96]

Still, Nick was the Speaker of the House, and after Coolidge's announcement in the summer of 1927 that he did not "choose to run," there was talk of Nick as the Republican nominee. The convention was wide open. Coolidge, despite his disclaimer, was hoping to be drafted and did not designate a successor. One newspaper headline asked, "Will Princess Alice Return to the White House?"[97]

Nick had written his sister that he had "a real horror of the Presidential bee; I have seen it ruin too many good men." But in a later letter he pompously informed her, "I cannot help realizing that I may be called upon to undertake the great adventure."[98]

He was not called, and Alice, much as she would have loved to return to the White House, was not surprised that Nick's name was not even put into nomination. Hoover, who had never been elected to anything, got it on the first ballot.

It was about this time that Bill Borah said of his own presidential prospects: "I'd rather be right than president." It was also about this time that Alice was quoted as saying about "an eminent political personage"—almost certainly her husband—"He would rather be tight than president." [99]

In 1928, as usual, Alice did not campaign with Nick. She was, however, Ruth McCormick's closest counsel in her successful race for a House seat. Ruth was mainly interested, though, in 1930, when she hoped to regain her late husband's Senate seat. Ruth wanted the seat so desperately that she spent some $300,000—part of it from her personal fortune—to win the nomination. She was accused of trying to buy the seat and one of her loudest critics was the notoriously frugal William Borah.

On the morning of August 5, 1930, an editorial appeared on the front page of the *Washington Herald*, signed by Cissy Patterson, who had recently become the paper's editor-in-chief. It was so obviously a product of personal vindictiveness that it shocked Cissy's brother, publisher of the *New York Daily News*, but it titillated Washingtonians who knew of Cissy's affairs with Nick and Borah, and it delighted *Herald* owner William Randolph Hearst, because it sent circulation soaring.

"The news is that Mrs. Alice Longworth will not only be the confidential adviser to Mrs. Ruth Hanna McCormick, but that she will campaign publicly for her lifelong friend. Interesting but not true. . . . Mrs. Longworth gives no interviews to the press. Mrs. Longworth cannot utter in public. Her assistance will, therefore, resolve itself, as usual, into posing for photographs."

The wire services picked up the story and it was soon front-page news around the country. A few weeks later Cissy leveled another blow, this time getting to the point of what was really bothering her. "Some weeks ago, I wrote that Alice Longworth had no real gifts to bring to Ruth Hanna McCormick's camp. Ruth . . . is Alice Longworth's close friend. I was in error. . . . Senator Borah, another *close* friend of Alice Longworth, has said if Ruth McCormick is elected he will vote to unseat her because of her excessive campaign expenditures. Mrs. Longworth may now present her real gifts. She may use her political influence of which the country has for so long heard so much. She may soften this decision of the frugal gentleman from Idaho. . . . But it is for Alice to come now bearing her offerings . . ."

Ruth lost the election, but her adviser, Alice Longworth, would soon have her own chance to run for office. And Cissy would soon have another chance to attack.

9

The Life of Paulina

The last time that Paulina went to her father's beloved House, on March 4, 1931, was also the last time that Nick went there. At his request, Waldie took the little girl to watch the adjournment of the Seventy-first Congress and the openly emotional, wildly affectionate tribute to its Speaker. It was, wrote AP reporter Bess Furman, a "House windup that has never since been equaled." According to Nick's secretary, "The House membership rose to its feet, wildly beating its hands and from the Democratic side of the aisle came several prolonged rebel yells that added to the general excitement. Nick stood and waited for it to subside, getting redder and redder with pleasure and gratification."[1]

"Perhaps this is the last time I will address you from this rostrum," Nick said, referring to the fact that it was uncertain whether the Republicans would control the House in the next session. The deepening depression had cost the party so many seats that its eyelash majority was threatened with extinction after the special elections, scheduled in several districts, were held. "The decision lies with none of us here," Nick added. "It is a decision which lies with an all-wise Providence. . . . With whatever Providence may decree I am abundantly satisfied."

Then the fun began. "The Marine Band marched in," Furman wrote. "Along came a men's chorus from the Interstate Commerce Commission and a mountaineer radio orchestra. The great chamber was filled with back-home melodies, sung by one and all: *Old Kentucky Home, On the Banks of the Wabash, Maryland.* Representative Fiorello H. La Guardia [Nick was a regular at the Democrat's spaghetti dinners] led the Marine Band. . . . Representative William P. Connery, Jr. . . . one-time vaudeville actor, strutted his stuff. Representative Ruth Bryan Owen [William Jennings Bryan's daughter] sang *Pack Up Your Troubles,* and everyone joined in the chorus. And Speaker Longworth came down from his pedestal to play a little wheeled-in piano in accompaniment to Representative Clifton A. Woodrum of Virginia, who sang . . . *Carry Me Back to Old Virginny.* . . . Everybody sang *God Be With You Till We Meet Again."* [2]

Nick was genuinely loved by his colleagues. A journalist who covered the House in the years when Nick was Speaker, wrote, "Longworth has the human affection of the House of Representatives as really no other Speaker in our times has had it. If Longworth should ever die, there would be more cheeks wet with true physical tears for him than for any other public man." [3] The Democratic whip offered this tribute: "There are a lot of Republicans we could do without, but you are not one of them, Nick. You're just a natural human being."

With that, Nick, who had a slight cold, left to visit a poker pal, Laura Curtis, in Aiken, South Carolina, where her husband was a long-time member of the exclusive winter colony. The cold soon turned to pneumonia. Two days later Dr. R. H. Wild, another ensconced member of Aiken society, was issuing alarming health updates.

The death watch over the Speaker became national news, with President Herbert Hoover asking to be kept informed and newsmen from every major paper trampling the lovely lawns and gardens of the twenty-room "Curtis cottage." As Nick lay dying, his friend William Castle, a State Department official, noted in his diary: "The moment Nick got pneumonia everybody said, 'It is the end.' No man can possibly be as rum-soaked as he was and live through a disease of that kind." [4] Alice left Paulina at Rookwood—the six-year-old was attending elementary school in Cincinnati—and hurried to Aiken.

In the meantime, Cissy Patterson ran a front-page photo of the Speaker in better days with Mrs. Curtis on his arm [5]—implying sexual involvement. As was often the case, Cissy was only half wrong. Nick was to have met Alice Dows at Laura's house. According to Virginia Blair, a former social secretary to Laura Curtis, "Laura promoted that affair because she didn't like Alice, or let's say they were friendly enemies." Laura, Ginny added, had another boyfriend at the time.

Laura Curtis had a checkered marital history. She was twice divorced from Mr. Curtis, a wealthy lawyer, and, according to a friend, "was really kicking her heels up."[6] Nick and Laura had become friends because they shared interests in Republican politics and poker, not necessarily in that order. It was said that the best games in Washington were played in Laura Curtis's house at 1925 F St., with regular players including, besides Nick, Vice President Charlie Curtis (no relation), Secretary of War (and donor of the Davis Cup) Dwight Davis, and others of equal stature and poker prowess. "God, the money that changed hands," recalled Ginny Blair. "I know because I used to write the checks."[7] Drew Pearson and Robert Allen dubbed Mrs. Curtis the "patron saint of those who play for a thousand-dollar limit" and described the parties as "always wringing wet and usually terminated in a poker game, although frequently not until Nick had yielded to a demand that he play his violin."[8]

Mrs. Curtis, who later remarried to become Mrs. Gross, had long ties to the Roosevelt family. Her father had been governor of Minnesota; when McKinley appointed him director of the Census (he was later president of the Tabulation Machine Company, IBM's corporate ancestor), Laura, whose godfather was Mark Hanna, used to go to the White House to play with Ethel Roosevelt.

Newsmen knew before Alice did that Nick had died. They had made a deal with Dr. Wild that he would raise a corner of the window shade at the moment of death. Alice was elsewhere in the house when the shade was raised at 10:52 A.M. on April 10. She chose not to sit with Nick during his final hours, as he lay under an oxygen tent.

Alice declined the offer of a state funeral for Nick, perhaps because she felt he didn't deserve the honor or perhaps because she didn't want to pretend, in the most public of forums, to mourn a man whom she had long since ceased to respect.

A government-provided train arrived in Aiken to transport the body to Cincinnati for the funeral and burial. Lest the elegant Nick make his final journey in government issue, the private car of Senator Charles Clark, son of a Montana mining magnate who had been one of the most vociferous opponents of TR's conservation policies, was attached.[9] In that funeral car also rode Nick's valet—who kept a teary watch over several suitcases of the Speaker's wardrobe—and, according to Gore Vidal and others, Alice Dows.

Vidal, who befriended Alice Dows in later years, wrote that she accompanied Nick's body at the invitation of Alice Longworth. "Oh, it was very moving," Dows told Vidal. "Particularly the way Alice treated me, as if *I* was the widow, which I suppose I was." [10] Vidal claimed that "Alice Dows was very fond of Alice Longworth who reciprocated; happy that Nick had so splendid and available a friend." [11] The bitterness toward Nick that Alice Longworth later revealed suggests that Alice Dows, and Vidal, may have misinterpreted things.

Despite the widow's desires, the funeral turned into a star-studded event. Herbert Hoover came—an unusual gesture because then, as now, attending funerals was invariably palmed off on the vice president, especially when the funeral was hundreds of miles away. There was standing room only in the Christ Episcopal Church in downtown Cincinnati. As President Hoover, Vice President Curtis, Nick's friend Will Rogers, Sam Rayburn, congressmen and senators from across the nation, and former first lady Edith Roosevelt watched in amazement, Alice Dows, veiled and gowned in black, bid Nick a final farewell. "The service was just ending," one friend of Alice Longworth's recalled, "when she walked alone down the aisle and laid a small bunch of violets on the coffin, while everybody stared, they couldn't believe it, and walked slowly back. . . . It was the worst taste I've ever seen." [12]

At graveside—Nick was buried between his father and grandfather—Alice left the black crepe veil thrown back from her face as if to dare anyone to notice that she hadn't shed a tear. Among the pallbearers were Thomas Nelson Perkins, who had been Nick's best man, and Charlie McCawley, who, as White House military aide, had escorted Alice to the altar.

Alice, who still hadn't acknowledged her wedding gifts, was coldly methodical about acknowledging the thousands of condolence telegrams, notes, and flowers. At the bottom of each written message— many of which promised that Nick would "meet the angels in heaven" or beseeched Alice to find solace in Jesus—she described the gift ("basket of roses and pink snapdragons") and noted that the sender should get "card only." [13]

One friend of Alice's recalled seeing the new widow at a dinner at the Hungarian legation. "Nick Longworth hadn't been dead very long. It was a huge dinner party and Mrs. Longworth was there. I was horrified that she was out to dinner. I rather shuddered to myself. Yet

I remember looking at her and thinking, 'Never have I seen such a relieved widow in all my life.' . . . She probably hated Mr. Longworth in the end. . . . I have a feeling she hated him." [14]

That summer of 1931, Alice had real reason to grieve. Auntie Bye, who had long been confined to a wheelchair and who was so deaf that visitors had to speak to her through an "acousticon box," died. Franklin's mother, Sara, was among the last to visit her before she slid into a fatal coma.* After Bamie's death, Alice observed, "One of her friends was once talking to me about her. 'She has no looks. She is very nearly ugly—she is almost a cripple, and yet no one for a moment thinks of these things. One is only aware of her charm.' Until he spoke of her in that way, I do not think that I had ever realized that she was not beautiful." [15]

Nick had been dead barely a week when Republican party leaders urged Alice to run for his seat. Nick, who had not lost a congressional race since the disaster of 1912, usually won by a 30,000-vote margin. But in 1930, Nick's margin slid to a mere 3000 votes. Party leaders were understandably concerned about losing the seat because a Democratic victory in the special election meant the parties would be tied at 217 votes each, with the balance of power residing in a Farmer-Laborite from Minnesota.

Alice was a sure-bet victory and House Republicans pleaded with her to accept the nomination. One Wisconsin Republican issued an open appeal. [16] She refused to budge, and the Democrats won control of the House, making Nick's drinking buddy, Jack Garner, the new Speaker.

Alice later offered various explanations for her decision: shyness about public speaking, revulsion at the prospect of joining other House widows who "were using their husband's coffins as a springboard into the Senate or the House"; [17] her lack of campaigning skills—"I was never any good at remembering names and that's fatal in politicians." [18] (In a rare burst of honesty, one reporter observed

---

* Sara had adored Mittie Roosevelt and Mittie's daughter Bamie was Sara's lifelong friend. It was at one of Bamie's dinners that Sara met James Roosevelt, her much-older widower husband. Bamie was in the bridal party and was the only female relative Sara invited to be with her while she gave birth to Franklin. Franklin's godfather was Bamie's brother (and later Eleanor's father), Elliott.

that Alice "would make . . . a rotten candidate because she doesn't like people and won't shake hands. Can you imagine Alice Longworth going around kissing babies?")[19]

At the time, the only explanation she offered was that she wanted to remain in her own house, in order to care for her daughter. Those who watched the relationship between Alice and Paulina knew that Paulina would have been much better off if Alice had devoted herself to congressional duties.

Alice often compared the fate of the Longworths to that of the Ambersons in Booth Tarkington's famous novel. Both families were victims of changing times and men who didn't change with them. Alice used to call the few acres of Rookwood that her husband was able to hang on to (to meet tax obligations he was forced to sell the rest to subdividers after his mother's death) Amberson Island. (On Susan's death, all that remained of Nick I's millions was $800,000, which she left in equal parts to her three children.)

Within a few years of Nick's death, Alice too made a deal with the subdividers. As she closed the house for the last time, she burned most of Nick's papers. The furniture and even Joseph Longworth's lovingly collected paintings (Alice complained that Joseph had such a poor "nose" for value that he had collected contemporary German paintings instead of the much more valuable French) were relegated to storage. Alice left Cincinnati, which she had taken to calling "Cincin-nasty," and never looked back. Friends said that she had always "hated" the city. Rookwood was eventually torn down.

She also burned Nick's most precious possession—his Stradivarius violin—an act of senseless destruction that shows just how deep ran Alice's hatred and hurt. Even then a Stradivarius was extremely valuable, and Alice's finances were in miserable shape. *[20]

Nick left Alice close to a million dollars—but that included, besides his depression-ravaged stocks, Rookwood and the house on Massachusetts Avenue. Once the lawyers' fees, taxes, and Nick's considerable debts were paid, there wasn't much left. "He paid no attention at all to money in his life," explained Joe Alsop, "and he'd been overspending fearfully so Alice Longworth had to buckle down

*Nick's violin, made by the celebrated Italian violin maker, dated from 1690. Antonio Stradivari made some 1200 violins in all, and only about half are believed to have survived. In 1987, a Stradivarius dating from 1716 sold at auction for $726,000.

and pay off the debt. If she hadn't she would have had to sell stocks at the bottom of the market." [21]

In late 1931, Maxwell Perkins, the Scribner's editor whose stable of authors included Thomas Wolfe, Ring Lardner, F. Scott Fitzgerald, and Ernest Hemingway, suggested that Alice write her memoirs. "I've never written anything longer than a postcard," [22] she replied. Yet she reluctantly signed a book contract, admitting that she was writing "for profit, not literature." She told friends that she hated writing *Crowded Hours*, which is obvious on every dull page.* The book is so lacking in bite that it might have been written by a promotion man for a government bureau. One of the more curious aspects— and there are many; for example, she barely mentions her father's death and never mentions her daughter's birth or Nick's death—is the gentle light in which she portrays Edith. Or maybe not so curious, because presumably Alice did not want to hurt the 72-year-old Edith's feelings, if for no other reason than that she hoped to be treated fairly in Edith's will. (She wasn't. When Edith died in 1948, she left her stepdaughter a token $1000—$500 less than she left her maid—and a John Singer Sargent painting of the White House. Her estate of over $400,000 was divided among her surviving children and daughters-in-law.)

When Perkins asked Alice to write a second volume, undoubtedly hoping that she would find her voice and that she would become more personal, she told him, "I shall never write another book. My vocabulary is too limited." [24] It wasn't her vocabulary that was limited; it was her writing skill—and courage. Many of the stories in *Crowded Hours* she told again to Michael Teague forty years later. As he committed them to print a year after her death they sparkled. What she put on paper herself might have been written by any Cincinnati matron. "There never were more delightful evenings," she wrote of Nick's musical gatherings. "We never wanted any one who was not a good listener or performer. If our guests showed signs of becoming conversational while the real music was going on, they were shut up in the

---

* *Crowded Hours* did make it to the bestseller list, buoyed by good reviews from people who must have been reviewing Alice rather than her book. "If Catherine de Medicis had kept a diary," one critic wrote, "I'll wager it would read a lot like *Crowded Hours*." Walter Lippmann assured Alice that the book "really is a fascinating story, a kind of American fairy tale which fascinated me from beginning to end. . . . And every professor of history for a hundred years will have to read it." [23]

dining-room." The same evenings told to and rendered by Michael Teague: "Anyone caught starting a conversation during the music was shut up in the dining-room. Once in a state of boredom bordering on stupefaction I said to the ardent music lover sitting next to me, 'Isn't it extraordinary to think that Mozart never composed anything exclusively for the viola?' He looked perplexed for the rest of the evening." [25]

In 1932 Speaker of the House Cactus Jack Garner was running for president. As William Randolph Hearst's candidate and with the news magnate's influence, Garner won primaries in Texas and California. Competing with Garner for the prize was none other than cousin Franklin, who had accepted the crippling effects of polio and risen above them to serve as governor of New York. He needed those blocs of votes. Eventually Hearst directed Garner to release his California delegates to FDR. Hearst thoroughly distrusted Franklin but was afraid that the Democrats would nominate a man he distrusted even more—the Wilsonian internationalist Newton Baker.

Garner knew that he would end up on the ticket as the candidate for vice president, a position he dreaded, figuring he'd have more power—and more fun—as Speaker. He told a friend that the vice presidency was "not worth a pitcher of warm piss." [26]

Alice agreed completely; at the same time, she knew the presidency was worth a whole lot, and it was sheer torture to contemplate watching Franklin, instead of TR Jr., move from the governor's mansion to the White House, skipping the indignity of the vice presidency.

Republicans in North and South Dakota—where her father was still a folk hero—and in Nebraska made another stab at getting Alice to run for office—this time as Hoover's running mate. (The current vice president, Charlie Curtis,* was bored with the office and was

---

*Curtis, half Kaw Indian, had longstanding ties to the Longworths. As a member of the House in 1905, he joined Nick and Alice on the Far East junket. He later became a poker pal of the Longworths until, one Sunday afternoon, Nick caught him with five kings. Years later, Alice told columnist Tom Braden that she took it upon herself to confront Curtis. She waited two days and then, "I called the Senator's office and made an appointment . . . and I walked up the stairs and into his office and there he was sitting there with his Indian eyes. . . . I said 'Senator, you are not going to play poker at our house anymore.' And he nodded and I turned around and walked out." [27]

toying with running for the Senate.) They felt that running Alice against her cousin Franklin would force him to stop trading off TR's name. Much as Alice wanted to stop FDR, she discouraged such talk, although the newspapers did take her possible candidacy seriously. One headlined, "Alice Longworth Political Topic: Boom for Vice Presidency Sufficient to Start Buzz in Capital." That same year Ohioans asked her to run for the Senate.[28]

When Franklin easily won the election, Alice was crazy with rage; so angry, she said later, that she could "grind my teeth and blow them out my nose." Personal vendetta aside, she was not alone in sneering at the notion of Franklin in the White House. "She grew up in that era which regarded Franklin as a real lightweight," columnist Nicholas von Hoffman explained. "It wasn't just her. People like Walter Lippmann when Roosevelt was nominated for the presidency just dismissed him as a complete Hyde Park ninny. . . . It was hard for her to really conceive that people were taking Cousin Franklin seriously."[29] Lippmann supported Newton Baker, describing FDR as "a pleasant man, who, without any important qualifications for the office, would very much like to be President."

Alice later claimed that she looked upon the plunging position of her branch of the family with a certain humor and "detached malevolence." "There we were, descendants of a popular president, and what happens? A fifth cousin comes along and gets into the White House. Can you think of anything more distressing?"[30]

People who knew Mrs. Longworth during that period claim that there was nothing detached about her malevolence. One longtime friend recalled her favorite put-down of the president—delivered at dinner parties among the nation's most influential: "My poor cousin, he suffered from polio so he was put in a brace; and now he wants to put the entire U.S. into a brace, as if it were a crippled country—that is all the New Deal is about, you know."[31]

She liked to contrast Franklin's philosophy of dependence on the government for personal security with her father's philosophy of self-reliance. What separated the two Roosevelts, she said, was that her father had overcome his physical disabilities through sheer spunk. The implication, which must have infuriated Franklin, was that had her father gotten polio he would have willed himself out of his wheelchair and onto his own two feet.

Alice nailed her cousin with the most vicious insult she could muster when she observed that he bore a "marked facial resemblance to Wilson."[32]

To nobody's surprise, shortly after FDR reached the Oval Office, he ousted Ted Jr. from his Hoover appointment as governor-general of the Philippines—a move that Ted, who had performed admirably in that post and as governor of Puerto Rico*, fully anticipated. Asked what relation he was to the new president, Ted quipped, "Fifth cousin about to be removed."

Alice smugly claimed that while Franklin had voted for her father (in 1904, when he said that TR was "a better Democrat than the Democrat"), "we never returned the favor and not one of our family ever voted for Franklin as far as I knew." She apparently chose to forget that while she, Ted Jr., and even the very private Edith campaigned for Herbert Hoover, cousin Corinne, a devout Republican, voted for FDR, attended his inauguration, and visited Eleanor in the White House. When Corinne came to Washington for a meeting of the obsessively anti-FDR Liberty League, Eleanor put her up at the White House.

Kermit's wife, Belle, and probably Kermit himself, voted for FDR. The handsome, blond, dashing, alcoholic Kermit, whom John Gable called "a closet Democrat," showed up at the Biltmore on election night to congratulate Franklin.[33] Belle, who came from a family of Southern Democrats—her father was Wilson's ambassador to Spain— was long out of the closet. After Kermit's death in 1943, Belle was often at the White House and worked actively for the Democrats in the forties.

TR's widow was not at all pleased that her favorite son, "the one with the white head and the black heart," as she put it, was so chummy with a man who she believed contributed to the political derailment of her eldest son. When Edith went to Manila in 1932 to visit lame duck Ted, the newspapers published reports that Kermit and Belle were cruising with FDR on his pal Vincent Astor's yacht. (FDR had befriended Astor after contracting polio. Franklin exercised in Astor's indoor, heated pool and during the thirties used his yacht as a presidential retreat.) The report embarrassed Ted because

---

*He solved some of Puerto Rico's health problems and put up $100,000 of his own money to avert a run on the banks. He was equally popular as governor-general of the Philippines, keeping the banks open during FDR's bank holiday.

he feared it might appear that Kermit was wooing Franklin to help his brother keep his job. When reporters asked Edith why she thought Kermit was palling around with Franklin, she snapped, "Because his mother was not there!"[34]

But most of the Oyster Bayers, who, trading off TR's name, had begun to prosper—mostly by managing other peoples' money—watched in horror as cousin Franklin pushed through what they considered socialistic policies. "I grew to be against Franklin in the thirties when I was in business," Bamie's son, Shef Cowles—the person to whom FDR confessed that not making the Porcellian was the biggest disappointment of his life—explained. "My wife and I used to go to the White House and stay with Franklin and Eleanor, but I felt that Franklin was letting our class down. I believed in business and I believed in the way America ran its business. That was as near a religion as I had and Franklin in my mind really busted it up. His anti-business policies were all part and parcel of his not being taken into the Porc. He was jealous and he took that out on the people who wouldn't accept him in his early years."[35]

At the time FDR became president, Philip J. Roosevelt, an Oyster Bayer, was managing Eleanor's money. He wrote FDR to ask what to do about a particular bond, and FDR wrote back to say that it was entirely his responsibility. "I put it into government bonds," Philip responded. "Now it's yours."

The thoroughly frustrated Alice Longworth was spending many evenings attacking Franklin with her Republican friends at the newly opened F Street Club. Laura Curtis had lost her money in the Depression. Rather than give up her house and the sparkling parties held there, her friends decided to turn it into a club where they could eat, drink, play poker (Alice had become a regular and skilled player), and belittle Franklin.* Alice, who, after Nick's death, became a sometime friend of Laura's, was a charter member. (According to Joe Alsop, the fact that Laura had promoted one of Nick's affairs "wasn't held against her at all.")[36]

As soon as Paulina was old enough, Alice started to destroy the

---

*The club, with its Waterford crystal chandeliers and eighteenth-century Chippendale mirrors, still exists, although somewhat diminished from the old days. Then it was the gathering spot for Washington's pedigreed Republicans, a place where political careers were launched or squelched, and where cabinet members who wanted to join had to furnish credentials that were carefully checked.

girl's warm memories of her father. When a playmate of hers discovered who her father was, he said to Mrs. Longworth, "I didn't know that Mr. Longworth was Speaker of the House." "Speaker of what House?" she hissed.[37] One friend recalled a family-dinner discussion of a political issue. When someone asked Alice to describe Nick's position, she said, as Paulina listened, "Nick was probably drunk or asleep."[38]

When Alice wasn't deriding Nick, she remained silent on the subject. Consciously or unconsciously, she was inflicting on her daughter the same cruelty that had been inflicted on her. But for Paulina, the silence was worse because she had known and loved Nick. (Alice's references to Nick later settled into, friends said, "a journalistic account." She talked about him "almost as if he were just another politician."[39] "While she talked about TR only with the greatest idolatry," said another friend, "she didn't speak of Nick with any dignity—always disparagingly, really as if he were unimportant to her life . . . dismissive."[40]

The fact that she and Nick shared a courtship and marriage that spanned nearly thirty years was nowhere evident in her memento-stuffed town house. But Theodore Roosevelt was everywhere—his hunting trophies (tiger, lion, and bear skins), a Sargent watercolor of the White House, Pennel's lithographs of the Panama Canal, a Flemish tapestry that had hung over the fireplace in the White House dining room, photographs of TR, etchings of TR, busts of TR, cartoons of TR. Of Nick Longworth and his colorful life and career there was barely a trace. "I don't remember a single thing in that house that would call to mind Nick Longworth," said Frank Waldrop, Alice's friend and former editor of the Washington Times-Herald.[41]

Nick would barely have recognized the little girl who had so charmed the Congress. Paulina began to consider herself a failure at an early age, and turned immensely shy. Marie Ridder, whose father, a New Deal economist, was a friend of Alice's and who, because Marie was the same age as Paulina, was constantly thrown together with her, explained that a pattern developed very early: "Paulina was always trying to please her mother. It was very sad."[42] Mrs. Longworth was the opposite of most parents, who naturally want to brag about their children. Paulina could never do anything right or interesting.

Alice showed an extraordinary lack of interest in her daughter's activities, even when these enthusiasms matched her own. Paulina, like her mother, loved to ride, but it was Waldie who took her to and picked her up from riding school. Mary Chewning, who took riding lessons with Paulina, recalled that she was an outstanding horsewoman but that Alice took no pleasure in Paulina's accomplishments. As Marie Ridder put it, "Mrs. Longworth didn't do much to amuse Paulina."[43] "I can't imagine anybody I'd sooner not have had as a mother than Mrs. Longworth," said one relative. "As a mother she was lethal. She was immensely selfish."[44]

Alice did take Paulina to a dude ranch in Sunlight Valley, Wyoming, every summer, but even there, on what should have been mutually enjoyable turf, Alice found fault. Marie, who vacationed at the same ranch with her parents, recalled Paulina as "an instinctive drip . . . She was inarticulate, not funny, she wasn't a good sportsman, she was the kind of girl that got the horse that stumbled and whose glasses fell off. But I don't even know if poor Paulina was as bad as all that or whether I think so because I didn't want to be stamped with the same imprimatur by her mother, so I separated myself from Paulina even then." She recalled Mrs. Longworth "in this great big cowboy hat up front while the rest of us trailed behind, turning around and belittling Paulina for whatever she happened, at the moment, to be doing wrong."[45] Said Sherry Geyelin, who was Paulina's schoolmate, "Mrs. Longworth had bullying qualities. . . . It must run in the family. Paulina couldn't stand up to that."[46]

At the opposite extreme was Waldie, who, according to her classmate Ruth Stevenson, "was always sort of clucking over her and worrying about, did she brush her teeth? did she brush her hair? did she take a bath? She did the best she could and she loved Paulina, but when you have just one chick you pick on it all the time."[47]

Even after the publication of *Crowded Hours* Alice had money worries. In 1934 she put her house up for sale, figuring that she and Paulina could live more cheaply in Virginia. She asked $70,000 for the house, which had been built in 1911,[48] but took it off the market when she couldn't get her price.

In August 1935, Alice took Paulina to Paris for the wedding of Clara's son, Rene. Much as Alice disliked the Longworths, she liked the de Chambruns, starting thirty years earlier with Charlie. Clara and Bertie's son, known in the family as "Bunny," was a favorite.

Bunny was marrying the daughter of then-French premier and later Nazi collaborator Pierre Laval. The wedding was the social event of that decade, and part of the next, as it was among the last great social affairs until after the war. *The New York Times'* Paris correspondent wired daily accounts: "Nearly every member of the French Cabinet, many diplomats and leaders in international society attended. Frenchmen lined the streets by the thousands, hoping to catch a glimpse of the wedding party." The marriage was seen as joining two nations. Laval, who had become premier two months earlier, walked his daughter down the aisle to meet the groom and his best man, General John J. Pershing. On their honeymoon in the United States and Canada, the newlyweds were greeted as visiting royalty.

Alice had been asked for years by newspaper and syndicate editors to write a column. Cissy Patterson, back in Alice's good graces for her incessant editorial battering of Franklin, was among them. She suspected that Alice could not transfer her talent for talking to paper. Indeed, faced with a blank sheet of paper, Alice turned self-conscious, stiff, even pompous. Part of the problem was that when she wrote she had to finish her sentences; when she spoke she could finish with the expressive gesture or shrug.

Cissy got the idea of having Alice come to her office and simply talk. Cissy would prompt and irritate Alice into her usual magnificently opinionated outpourings. Cissy's secretary, Margaret Barney, would record it all in shorthand. Cissy was convinced that a column could be fashioned from Alice's comments that would beat anything being written in Washington or elsewhere.

Unfortunately, Miss Barney's presence had the same effect on Alice as blank paper. She choked up; her conversation was bland. So Cissy got another idea—to seat Miss Barney behind a screen, hoping that Alice would forget that she was there. She wouldn't, and Cissy finally gave up. [49]

But other editors didn't and, because Alice needed the money, she began to listen—especially to her friend Frank Kent, a columnist and correspondent for the *Baltimore Sun*, who had once been a Wilsonian liberal but then, in his vastly influential column, "The Great Game of Politics," regularly attacked FDR. (FDR had once so admired Kent that he helped him to get his column syndicated—an effort FDR later regretted as Kent coined such New Deal put-downs as "Tax and tax, spend and spend, elect and elect.")[50] Kent urged Alice to sign with McNaught, the New York syndicate for which Will Rogers and Walter Winchell also wrote.

But what moved Alice most was the fact that in December 1935, cousin Eleanor started writing a column for United Feature Syndicate. The cousins were put in head-to-head competition—Alice's obsessively anti-New Deal "Capital Comment" often ran side-by-side with Eleanor's "My Day." *

At the start, neither column was much good. Had editors bothered to read Alice's bland memoirs, they would have known what to expect. "Why the hell do I roar hilariously when I'm with her and then only smile when her copy comes through?" a McNaught editor wondered. "Still, it's better to smile than read about Eleanor going from Pittsburgh to Cleveland to a CCC camp in Kentucky."[51]

Eleanor's column was a tedious mix of homely detail and comically inept writing. Columnist Westbrook Pegler, once an adoring fan of Franklin and Eleanor's—he called it "stingy" to describe Eleanor as the "most remarkable" and "most energetic" woman of her times and argued that she was quite simply "the greatest American woman"—had turned into a sharp critic.[52] His parody of Eleanor's column could easily have been mistaken for the real thing: "In the afternoon a group of young people arrived at the Little House and we plunged at once into a very interesting discussion of the duty of the citizen, not only toward his country but toward himself and his fellow man in relation to the past and the future ahead. One gentleman had rather strong ideas on the subject of nail-biting and while, of course, I realize there are two sides to this question. . . . I prefer what seems to me the more democratic way and proposed to approach it as a world problem since nail-biting is not a matter of race or creed."[53]

So careful was Eleanor not to say anything that might offend anyone that she wrote in an early column, "I think spring and autumn are my favorite seasons. There's beauty, of course, in every season."[54] Pegler later tried to have her kicked out of the Newspaper Guild because, he charged, if she were not the president's wife, no editor would give her valuable space on the editorial page. One reader wrote

---

* While Eleanor's column was known everywhere as "My Day," the title of Alice's column changed with the paper. In the *Toledo Blade* it ran as "Alice Longworth Says"; in the *San Francisco Chronicle* as "Alice in Blunderland"; in the *Washington Star* as "The National Scene"; in the *Reading Eagle* as "Chatting with Alice."

a letter to the *Pittsburgh Post Gazette* suggesting that "We have been paying our farmers for not raising hogs, cotton, corn, etc. I wonder if under the Constitution there is not some way of paying Mrs. Roosevelt for not writing her . . . amiable drivel." [55]

At the start Alice seemed to be winning the competition—with twice as many papers. She had a built-in audience of FDR-haters, such as a Baltimorean named Lulu Epler who wrote her, "Our capital is not related to the U.S., we are in the hands of foreigners . . ." A Mrs. Charles Moses of Savannah wrote: "I presume I am just one of the millions of Democrats who are literally fed up to the teeth with sanctimonious New Dealers all talking and acting like God. . . . And I'm sick of reformers with their big, bleeding hearts hanging out of their shirts." Lieutenant Colonel Warren Gould of Orlando, after praising TR, denounced FDR as a "fraud," and pointed out that TR's wife, "never butted in to every conceivable scheme to reform mankind." He then got around to what was really on his mind. Referring to "My Day," he said that he would not be surprised if Eleanor "preached in Yiddish to an Irish audience." [56]

But Alice's lead soon dwindled. Her carping at the New Deal got stale—not because there wasn't something to carp at, but because she did it in prose that was nearly as insipid as her cousin's. The associate editor of the Gannett newspapers wrote a letter to the chairman of McNaught complaining, "Frankly, I can't understand how so colorful an individual as I have always thought Mrs. Longworth to be can produce such conventional and uninteresting copy. It seems to me it has no value except the value of her name."

While Alice undoubtedly charmed terrific material out of her tea and dinner guests, it never found its way into print. Eleanor, who was out in the world, could only get better—especially once she grew beyond descriptions of family Christmases and gave vent to her opinions. Politicians and her fellow columnists began to read "My Day" avidly because, while it never became Franklin's mouthpiece, they knew that she often wrote about New Deal people and policies whose stars were on the rise.

When Franklin considered not seeking a third term and grooming Harry Hopkins as his successor, "My Day" readers knew it: "It was good to see Mr. Hopkins yesterday," Eleanor wrote in a 1938 column, "and to have him spend the night with us. He is one of the few people in the world who gives me the feeling of being absorbed in doing his job well. . . . He seems to work because he has an inner conviction that the job needs to be done and that he must do it. I think he would be that way about any job he undertook." [57]

Eleanor's column became so popular that she was soon making $75,000 a year, equal to her husband's salary, and giving it all to charity. Alice was soon making nothing, as the number of papers running her column dwindled and she and the syndicate reached a mutual agreement to part company.

For Alice, the most painful humiliation was yet to come. A couple of years earlier, she had signed to write a column for *Ladies' Home Journal*, published by the rabidly anti–New Deal Curtis Publishing Company. The magazine was losing readers and Alice's column was not helping to stem the losses, much less to attract new readers.

When Bruce and Beatrice Gould, a young and dynamic editing team took over, they offered Alice a settlement of $2000 to give up her column. That was bad enough, but the reason for their urgency was even worse. They were bidding for serial rights to Eleanor's autobiography and feared that the first lady would not look kindly on a magazine that published Alice.

The Goulds paid $75,000 to serialize Eleanor's *This Is My Story*. The excerpts set the magazine on an upward course, giving it the momentum to overtake its two major competitors. [58]

Years before when Eleanor visited Sagamore Hill, Edith wrote of the young girl: "Poor little soul, she is very plain. Her mouth and teeth seem to have no future. But the ugly duckling may turn out to be a swan." "Ugly duckling" was an image that took Eleanor nearly fifty years to shed. When the Goulds visited Alice to tell her that she was being cast aside for the world-respected Eleanor, Edith's comment came back: "I was the ugly duckling, not Eleanor," Alice said. [59]

As Eleanor's career blossomed, reporters began to point out the reversal. A writer for the *Nashville Tennessean* recalled that although Alice had been the center of the world, "it begins to look as if . . . Eleanor Roosevelt is going to make Alice . . . look like 'Alice-Sit-by-the-Fire.'" [60]

"Nobody got Alice as frantically jealous as did Eleanor," observed Nicholas von Hoffman. "After a certain point it had to have dawned on her [Alice] that regardless of Eleanor's politics that she was carving out a career. She was making something. And I think that had to in some sense have bothered her. I always felt that Mrs. L. would have been a politician had she been a man but she could make the excuse that the world that she was born into, her social position over which she had no control, would preclude her becoming a politician. Then along comes Eleanor, who in so many ways was so comparable in beginnings, and becomes really an important American political figure." [61] John Alsop, Joe's brother, put it bluntly: "She had been the local big shot. She got supplanted." [62] Ginny Blair, who knew both women, put it in terms that are frequently used to compare the cousins: "I think that Eleanor Roosevelt was a very great woman. I don't think that Alice could touch the hem of her gown." [63]

When the returns came in in 1932, giving Franklin his first term, Eleanor retreated to a corner and wept, "Now I will have no identity. I'll only be the wife of the president." Alice had heard this story from cousin Corinne and loved to tell it, complete with an uncannily accurate take-off of Eleanor. Eleanor responded to her insecurity by becoming the nation's preeminent do-gooder. Dame Rebecca West described her as a woman who had the tendency "to treat this country as a giant slum area." [64] Alice responded to her insecurity by showing off. She was, said one Washington reporter, "always doing something that left people gasping." [65]

Alice soon discovered that mimicking cousin Eleanor was a sure crowd-pleaser. Alice would tuck in her lower lip, heighten her voice and, said one admirer of Eleanor's, "No matter how much you loved Mrs. Roosevelt, you disloyally laughed." [66] One time, at the White House, having heard of Alice's popular performance, Eleanor asked to see it. Alice cheerfully complied, while Eleanor applauded. But behind the applause, Eleanor was hurt. Said her son Elliott, "Alice was the only person whom I have ever known who could make my mother break down and cry." He recalled inauguration night, 1933, a White House dinner for members of the family, including Alice: "The first thing she said when she swept into the White House was, 'Well, Eleanor, I wonder how you're going to be able to handle this.' I watched my mother that evening and Alice made several remarks that had my mother on the verge of openly crying right there at the dinner party." [67]

Alice dismissed Franklin as "two-thirds mush and one-third Eleanor." She suggested getting "the pants off Eleanor and onto Franklin"—a put-down fraught with meanness, considering the president's wasted legs and rumors that the first lady was having a lesbian relationship with a reporter. Franklin's sons, who were frequently involved in embarrassing business debacles, were easy targets for Alice. She accused them of "cashing in" on their father's position and joked about their stream of marriages, divorces, and scandals.

Eleanor, a glutton for punishment, continued to invite Alice to the White House. As Alice was leaving one reception, Franklin told her that he was about to sign a bill that would save the country $50 million. "That's a drop in the bucket compared to what you are costing the country," Alice answered.[68]

When Franklin took the country off the gold standard, Alice showed her disapproval by going to a White House reception draped in gold—gold earrings shaped like horns of plenty, a heavy gold chain from which dangled a gold frog, a gold watch, gold side combs in her hair. To the President's distress, she, not his monetary policy, was the center of press attention. (She also insisted on calling him "Franklin" in public. He invariably winced and so she did it often.)

At the reception, she spent the evening chatting with Will Rogers, trading quips about Franklin and Eleanor. At White House parties, Alice had become a magnet for everyone who was disgruntled with the New Deal. Still the invitations kept coming. Eleanor naively believed that eventually even Alice would be ashamed to show her face at the White House.

Alice never worked so hard for any candidate—aside from her father and brother—as she did for Robert Taft, whom she first supported for president at the 1936 convention. Given the animosity between their parents,* it is odd that the two became so personally and politically close. Bob had to forget Alice's imitations of his mother's "hippopotamus face" and the crack she made when Harding, in 1921, appointed Will Taft chief justice. When Taft remarked that he liked his new job so much he could hardly remember being president, Alice quipped, "Neither can the country."[69]

---

*Shortly before TR's death, the two former presidents heartily shook hands in the dining room of Chicago's Blackstone Hotel when they happened to stop there on the same day. Taft was told on his arrival that TR was dining alone and, showing himself to be the bigger man in more ways than one, immediately went to the dining room. When Theodore saw him, he threw down his napkin, rose, and extended his hand, to the cheers of the other diners. Taft would be seen weeping openly at Theodore's funeral six months later.

It was Taft's wife, Martha, who first drew Alice to this impossibly stodgy man whom the *New Republic* described as "about as magnetic as a lead nail." [70] (He was undeniably smart—first in his class at Yale and at Harvard Law School.) Sorbonne-educated Martha Bowers, the great-great granddaughter of Yale president Timothy Dwight, was a thoroughly charming, spirited, and witty woman. En route to a political rally she swerved to avoid hitting a dog. Her car turned over three times. She emerged uninjured, rushed to the meeting and opened her speech with, "Well, anyway, this ought to get us the Society for the Prevention of Cruelty to Animals vote." When Taft won his first United States Senate race, one Ohio newspaper headlined its story, "Bob and Martha Win." [71]

But even if Bob Taft had been married to a woman who devoted every weekday to turning down the corners of calling cards, Alice would have toiled to get Taft the nomination. His personality was a trial, but his politics were, in her mind, nearly perfect.

Unfortunately, the delegates didn't agree, and instead the nomination went to Alf Landon. Again there was talk of Alice for vice president—anything to dissipate Franklin's alarming popularity.

In August, with thoughts of four more years of Franklin in her mind, Alice went to Hollywood to tour 20th Century-Fox and MGM. She met Mae West, Norma Shearer, Cecil B. DeMille, Max Factor, Jean Arthur, and Gary Cooper, among many others. Leading men and leading ladies thrust scraps of paper at Alice and asked for her autograph.

FDR's first term was hideously frustrating for Alice because, given the magnitude of the problems he had to tackle, most of the country seemed to be with him and happy to forgive small errors. When, just at the start of his second term, he committed a big error, Alice pounced. FDR went to congressional leaders with a plan to "pack" the Supreme Court. He proposed increasing the number of justices from nine to as many as fifteen. If a justice did not retire six months after reaching age seventy, the president could appoint a new one. Roosevelt claimed to be concerned that the current court of "nine old men" was overworked. But his real concern was that four conservative members, with help from a fifth swing vote, had been able to declare unconstitutional much of FDR's New Deal legislation.

FDR ignored his usual sharp political instincts, infuriating congressional leaders by informing them of the plan just hours before he was to announce it to Congress. He also ignored several much less drastic plans that would have eliminated the need to pack the Court—such as giving the justices the opportunity to retire at full pay, which would have rid him of the two oldest conservatives, who wanted to retire but could not afford to.

FDR biographer Ted Morgan called this the "worst blunder of Roosevelt's peacetime presidency." [72] Not only was the legal profession against him—led by Chief Justice Charles Evans Hughes, himself seventy-five, who made it his mission to "save the Court"—but so were most of the nation's columnists and editorial writers.

Just as FDR released his plan, Marietta Tree and Edith Derby, school friends and both about seventeen, arrived at Alice Longworth's house for the weekend. "Hardly saying hello to us," recalled Marietta, "she bundled us off into this ancient car, ancient driver, and we went to call on everybody she could think of. . . . Of course she thought, 'Ha! this is where we get him.' She knew he'd made a fatal error and she was absolutely thrilled. . . . We went around and we saw other journalists, like Mark Sullivan and Arthur Krock and Joe Alsop . . . all absolutely thrilled because they were all [except Alsop] anti-Roosevelt. . . . I had the feeling that it wasn't of the deepest constitutional issue with her, simply a bad political mistake. And she was thrilled."

Later that weekend a very nervous Marietta and Edith attended one of Alice's famous dinner parties. "She was shouting down the table at everybody, making jokes," Marietta recalled. "She never let up on the Court-packing plan. She was obsessed by it." [73]

When the Senate held hearings on the plan, Alice got a front-row seat. She watched in glee as the Judiciary Committee sent "Court packing" into the history books as an example of what happens when a president forgets about separation of powers.

Although she admitted that her father would have leaped out of his grave had he known, that spring, still looking for a way to make some money, she endorsed Lucky Strike cigarettes. The April 12, 1937 issue of *Life* magazine featured a photo of Alice Longworth on the back cover, confiding, "I often lunch in the Senate restaurant at the Capitol and the number of Senators and Representatives I see with a package of Luckies is quite surprising. Off and on, ever since 1917, I myself have used Luckies for this sound reason: They really are a light smoke—kind to the throat. It's simply common sense that these Senators and Representatives, whose voices must meet the continuous strain of public speaking, should also need a cigarette that is considerate of their throats . . . a light smoke." Later she also endorsed cold cream.

A year later, she undertook the most improbable of her money-making schemes—she signed on with a lecture agency. Her friends were amazed, for Alice was known to be terrified of public speaking. She was so shy that, in 1936, when it was advertised at the Republican convention that she was going to give a speech, an overflow audience watched her step to the edge of the platform and say, "I'm sorry I don't speak."[74]

She signed with an agent named Harold Peat to lecture on "The American People and The American Government" for a reported $2500 per talk. She delivered her maiden speech in Akron, Ohio (she refused to be booked in towns where she knew people), addressing the subject "I Believe in America."[75]

By the time she reached Cleveland eight days later, she realized that public speaking was not for her. In that city she gave a talk on the cockroach: "How ancient is his history! In a straight line we can see it runs back so far into the past that it fairly takes your breath away."[76] She obviously was daring Mr. Peat to cancel her contract.

Arthur Krock was among many who urged Alice to give up lecturing. Krock, Washington bureau chief for *The New York Times* and probably the most influential journalist of that period, worshipped Alice Longworth. No matter how many Pulitzer Prizes he won—three during his career—and now many powerful contacts he had—he was the foremost repository of secrets about the powerful—prizes and power could not buy what Alice had as her birthright. Her father had been president; his was not only Jewish but a ne'er-do-well to boot. She was raised in Knickerbocker, New York; he in Tennessee. Krock, who frequently pointed out that his mother was not Jewish, was an active anti-Semite who would not hire Jewish reporters for the Washington bureau—even though he himself had been passed over for editorial page editor for the same reason by *The Times*'s publisher, also a Jew.

Alice did not mind Krock's anti-Semitism (in years to come some of her best friends were anti-Semites) or his pomposity (he did not permit his reporters to call him by his first name) because she loved his disdain for FDR, which he freely expressed at F Street Club dinners and in his column. Unlike Alice's dull attacks, Krock's columns left FDR reeling. The president once wrote a friend that he was "all in favor of chloroforming for certain newspaper men. Not Drew Pearson alone—but some of the more subtle murderers like Arthur Krock." [77]

For all Waldie's affection for Paulina, her cousins recalled that nobody would have mistaken Waldie for Mary Poppins. One cousin remembered her as "always telling Paulina what to do." [78] Another cousin said that she "never felt that Paulina had much fun because she was brought up by Miss Waldron, who was dreary and "a presence in the background that you felt was in complete control. I know Paulina loved her but it always seemed to us that Miss Waldron was kind of a dragon lady as far as allowing Paulina to romp and stomp and do all the things that we all did. . . . She had complete charge of her. . . . My idea was that she was really oppressed by Miss Waldron, worthy soul I gather, but certainly not a very cheerful type." [79]

But most of Paulina's friends felt that Waldie, in the words of one, "protected Paulina from her mother." [80] And, certainly, Paulina was sorely in need of a protector.

One of the more curious aspects of Alice as a mother was that she seemed to have forgotten her own rebellion and unconventionality. On the matter of clothes, for example, Alice had detested the prim white dresses that Edith made her wear. Yet she insisted that Paulina wear hand-made frocks with smocking, no waists, and matching panties; clothes that were positively Victorian and that stood out from those her friends wore like a short dress at a fancy ball.

Even Paulina's riding clothes were peculiarly out of style. "Paulina had this tacky safari outfit which . . . if you gave a fourteen-year-old that for the West now, it would be kind of camp," recalled Marie Ridder. "But we were all in blue jeans and Paulina had to wear this safari outfit. It was cruel somehow." [81]

Alice also refused to let Paulina have her hair bobbed, although Alice sported the new cut herself. When Alice sent Paulina away from home at age thirteen to board at the exclusive Madeira School in Virginia, Paulina arrived, Ruth Stevenson recalled, with long pigtails.

"She had not been allowed to grow up." She was unequipped to care for herself. "It took a bit of doing to get Paulina into shape," Ruth added. "She was pretty slovenly. I remember once we actually ganged up on her. She hadn't had a bath in quite a long while. We put her in the bathtub and scrubbed her. . . . I'm sure she was plunked in the bathtub every night by Waldie . . . and washed behind the ears and checked to see if she'd had her morning b.m., and she just totally rebelled . . . and didn't give a damn."[82]

Paulina boarded at Madeira from 1938 to 1942 and, away from her mother (and Waldie), she made several close friends, all somewhat older than she. With friends of her own for the first time, away from Waldie's smothering attention and her mother's painful inattention, Paulina thrived. Madeira had a wonderful faculty, especially in the subjects Paulina adored, literature and languages. These were to be the best years of Paulina's life.

Alice would often come to visit on Sunday afternoons. "My first cognizance of the fact that Paulie came from a rather unusual family," recalled classmate Lucille Tennant Flanagan, "was when another girl jabbed me in the ribs with her elbow and pointed at this enormous limousine that was out in front of Miss Madeira's [the school's founder] house and said, 'That's Paulie's mother.' Most parents didn't come in stretch limos with a chauffeur."[83] But then most didn't bring along the student's nanny, either. Alice always brought Waldie.

Allegra Maynard, then Madeira's headmistress, recalled that Alice would immediately head to the rooms of Susan Coyle—one of the assistant headmistresses and head of the English department—while Waldie attended to Paulina. Miss Coyle was a favorite of Alice's because, according to Miss Maynard, Alice "had never met anyone who knew as much about poetry as Miss Coyle knew."[84] Alice did not invite Paulina to join her at these sessions.

When she wasn't visiting with Miss Coyle, Alice was busy with her "great friend," Lucy Madeira Wing. They were both very bright, very witty. Lucy Madeira Wing was also a friend and great admirer of Eleanor Roosevelt. The liberal and democratic Lucy and the right-wing Alice would get into spirited discussions. The sparks flew while, in Mary Chewning's words, Alice "held court" and Paulina carefully kept out of her way.

"She wasn't a very attractive child," Mary Chewning added. "She

The Life of Paulina

didn't do anything to make herself more attractive"—like wash her hair.[85] Sherry Geyelin said that at dances she would think to herself, "Oh, that poor dreary girl. Her hair would be hanging down in greasy strings. I'd think, no one is going to ask her to dance. I was no great pick, but I felt great pity and compassion for her."[86]

Paulina's homely appearance resulted not so much from physical factors—other friends recalled her unusually beautiful green eyes: widely-spaced, slanted, and set in black lashes—as from emotional ones: a crippling lack of self-confidence. Her cousin Archie Roosevelt recalled her "sullen expression . . . no lightness or gaiety."[87] Marian Christie recalled her "exaggerated insecurity."[88] Katharine Graham, who was eight years older than Paulina, recalled her "as a rather sad girl, not terribly prepossessing and sort of pale and not done up."[89]

Paulina's emotional problems took a physical toll: severe stuttering, a handicap that particularly irritated Alice. For Alice Longworth to have a stutterer for a daughter was akin to a great musician having a tone-deaf child. A friend of Paulina, F. Reese Brown, recalled that at times—when Paulina was with people with whom she felt comfortable—she stuttered hardly at all. At other times—notably in the presence of her mother—she stuttered so badly that "she could hardly talk."[90] She was, said her cousin Archie, "absolutely struck dumb."[91]

10

The Right-Wing Years

Paulina Longworth had no more contact with William Borah than she had with Alice's other friends—which was very little. The senator's sudden death from a brain hemorrhage on January 19, 1940, meant little to Paulina, who likely was not privy to the rumors about her paternity. If Alice felt sorrow, she didn't show it. She was among the elite who attended Borah's funeral in the Senate chamber—thousands jammed the hall outside—but there were no dramatic scenes. The bouquet of faded violets in his hands had been placed there by Mary Borah. Alice did not go to Boise for the burial.[1]

Along with the rest of the political establishment, Alice was soon savoring some fascinating gossip. When Mary Borah opened her late husband's safe deposit box she found $200,000 in gold certificates. Borah was known as a skinflint, but not even the most dedicated skinflint could have socked away that much on a Senator's salary. The source of the money was never discovered, and what promised to be a delicious scandal soon faded. Among the conjectures was one that the Soviets had paid off Borah for his vigorous support of recognition of Russia. Another version of the payoff theory had the Nazis stuffing Borah's pockets in exchange for the senator's stalwart isolationism which, if Borah and his fellow isolationists (including Alice Longworth) had their way, would keep the United States from aiding the beleaguered British in their battle with the Nazis.

A few months before his death, Borah had assured Secretary of State Cordell Hull, "There is not going to be any war in Europe . . . Germany is not ready for it. All this hysteria is manufactured and artificial." A month later Russia and Germany signed a nonaggression pact and, a week later, German troops invaded Poland.[2]

In Alice's crowd, Borah's views were typical. Senator Robert Taft, who Alice hoped would get the Republican nomination the next summer, declared that the New Deal was a greater threat to American democracy than was Nazi Germany—and this was after Hitler had already swallowed Denmark, Norway, the Low Countries and France. He conceded that Hitler might swallow England next, but said he'd prefer a victory by Hitler to America getting mired in another war.[3]

So strongly did Alice agree with Bob Taft that he was the only person for whom she broke her cardinal rule of politics: "There is only one thing worse for a political candidate than to be wrong, and that is to be dull."[4] Although she privately mimicked Taft's leaden style, she wanted him in the White House and Franklin out. She wanted the United States to stay out of the war and to let Britain fight its own battles. She believed that Taft was the only Republican stubborn enough to stick to his isolationism—to keep his "feet . . . firmly on the ground" (a reminder of Franklin's inability to stand) and his "mind . . . on finding solutions to the national problems rather than becoming the shining hero of the undiscriminating masses."[5]

"What's the Matter With Bob Taft?" Alice asked in an article she wrote for the May 1940 issue of the *Saturday Evening Post*. Inadvertently, she answered her own question by describing a man whose personality was comically flaccid, and, in attempting to make him appear to be just-your-average-American, instead portrayed a man who, socio-economically, had much in common with Franklin. Alice described the Taft home in Cincinnati "on a hill overlooking the valley of the Little Miami River. It is a simple, unpretentious, American home surrounded by 60 or 70 acres of woods and grass. . . . It has no resemblance to the country estates modeled on the manorial tradition" (obviously referring here to Franklin's Hyde Park).[6]

She gritted her teeth as she watched Taft make a fool of himself. Wanting to appear to be an outdoorsman, Taft had himself photographed wearing a blue serge suit and holding a long-dead turkey that had been shot by somebody else. *Time* smirked that it was the silliest political picture since Calvin Coolidge was photographed in an Indian bonnet. *Life* dubbed him "the Dagwood Bumstead of American politics."[7]

Taft lost the nomination to Wendell Willkie, a utilities executive and Wall Street lawyer, who had never held an elective office and who, until the year before, was a registered Democrat. Alice was not impressed, especially because Willkie was as interventionist as any politician of the period. Much as Alice longed to see her cousin defeated, she could not keep to herself her contempt for Willkie. When Joe Alsop gazed around him at the Republican convention and observed the fervor of Willkie's supporters, Alsop said out loud that Willkie's support seemed to come from the "grass roots." To that Alice replied, "Yes, of course—from the grass roots of ten thousand country clubs." [8]

Although Alice never tired of Bob Taft's wife Martha, she preferred to spend her evenings with men, and during the 1940 campaign a particularly interesting one came into her life.

In 1880, four years to the day before Alice's birth, John L. Lewis was born in Iowa to immigrant parents, both from mining towns in Wales. He left school in the seventh grade and followed his father down into the mines, but he soon emerged to become the most powerful labor leader in American history. In 1920, he became president of the United Mine Workers. In 1935, as he watched dues-paying members flee the corrupt AFL in droves, he led miners out of the AFL into his newly founded CIO, in which workers were organized industry-by-industry rather than by craft. He originated the sit-down strike, he organized steel workers and auto workers and, of course, coal miners.

Coal miners, like Rough Riders, occupied a special place in Alice's heart, because they evoked such vivid memories of her father. As a young assemblyman, TR had been notably insensitive to labor. He opposed a minimum wage of two dollars a day for municipal workers, and he was about to oppose a bill, sponsored by the Cigarmakers' Union, that would have prohibited the manufacture of cigars in the filthy, pest-ridden tenements of immigrants. He changed his mind after another union leader, Samuel Gompers, took the young dandy to see how the immigrants lived and worked. TR never forgot the hovels, stuffed to near suffocation with two families, whose members, including children, ate, slept, and worked in one room. He saw tobacco stored beside "foul bedding" and mixed with scraps of moldy food. With the years, he became among the most pro-labor of American presidents.

In 1902 TR settled the coal miners' strike, becoming the first president ever to impartially intervene in a labor dispute: Up until then, it had been considered the government's duty to protect citizens against these dangerous unions. That same year he won a new convert to the Republican party named John L. Lewis. So popular was TR with the miners that, during his 1905 inauguration, they marched in the parade carrying a banner proclaiming, "WE HONOR THE MAN WHO SETTLED OUR STRIKE."

After he left the White House, TR began to sound like a labor activist. In August 1910, he gave a speech that shocked his wealthy supporters: "Labor is prior to and independent of capital . . . Labor is the superior of capital, and deserves much the higher consideration."[9] (After speaking those words, TR pointed out that he was quoting Abraham Lincoln.) He also called for a limitation of working hours, a graduated income tax (adopting an idea advanced by Karl Marx and Friedrich Engels), and declared, "I wish to see labor organizations powerful."[10]

Alice was introduced to John Lewis by Josephine Roche, a Vassar-educated Bull Mooser, Denver policewoman, coal mine operator, and disillusioned member of the FDR administration (as assistant secretary of the Treasury). She had remained in Washington to run the Welfare Fund, a joint venture of the union and the operators.

Josephine and Alice shared the same hairdresser, and, it turned out, an interest in John Lewis. John Hutchinson, a Lewis biographer, explained that Josephine "adored him greatly, but at a distance."[11]

After the gruff-spoken Lewis became a pet of Washington society, Alice admired him from a closer range, at Evalyn Walsh McLean's parties. The famous hostess, owner of the 44.5-carat Hope diamond, whose own father had been a miner who "struck it rich,"* found

---

* Evalyn married Edward "Ned" McLean, a ne'er-do-well friend of Alice. McLean's father, John, at whose home Nick and Alice spent their wedding night, left Ned the *Washington Post* and an income of half a million a year, which he and Evalyn squandered on alcohol, drugs, and dinners for two hundred—the sort, said Cissy Patterson, thrown by Moscow millionaires before the Revolution. Archie Butt described one McLean dinner at which "the table ornaments were gold and stood so high that no one could see the person opposite him or her."[12] Ned became a drinking and poker buddy of President Harding and was implicated in the Teapot Dome scandal. The *Post* became a shameless mouthpiece for Harding and was losing money. Meanwhile, Ned was carrying on an outrageously expensive affair with Rose Davies, sister of William Randolph Hearst's mistress Marion. Ned was finally institutionalized after suffering a nervous breakdown, and the *Post* was put up for auction. Evalyn longed to get control of it, but with what little power Ned had left, he thwarted her. Trying to pull off the scoop of the century and improve her chances of getting the paper, Evalyn

ALICE ROOSEVELT LONGWORTH

Lewis amusing and different and "took him up"—first with his wife Myrta, and, after her death in 1942, alone. "He was intelligent, powerful, and he had a great deal of charm," recalled Walter Trohan, long-time Washington bureau chief for the *Chicago Tribune*. "He was . . . the finest company in the world at a dinner party . . . a great Shakespearean, he was more or less self-educated, but he was a reader and . . . he was powerful." [14]

Although the bushy-eyebrowed Lewis was far from attractive, Alice was charmed. (In fact, Lewis looked like Borah. Both had big heads—literally and figuratively—coarse features, low hairlines, and both, in their builds and intense masculinity, resembled TR.) Hope Ridings Miller said she wasn't surprised. In her eyes, Lewis was "very attractive, very dynamic. He had charisma before we ever heard the word." [15] In Alice's own memory, what attracted her to Lewis was the same quality that attracted her to Borah—he was funny and he was *"never* boring. . . . We didn't pretend at all. We laughed at ourselves. We were suddenly fellow thieves. We could have come straight from the Arabian Nights." [16]

"She used to quote the Bible to him," recalled Hope Miller, "and he Shakespeare to her." [17] His conversation, like hers, was studded with references to poetry and the classics as well as to Shakespeare and the Bible. They used to dine together regularly, "sometimes at my home," Alice recalled, "sometimes at his house in Alexandria—just us." [18] Rumors that the two were having an affair started to fly.

During World War II, Drew Pearson and his second wife Luvie* were living on Drew's dairy farm. "It was very tricky to get around," Luvie recalled. "No gas. So you never went anyplace that you didn't say to your neighbor . . . 'I'm going to town, would you like a ride?'. . . . So this day I was walking [down] this little dirt road and a car comes. And it absolutely infuriated me because I think it's my neighbor. . . . So I stand in the middle of the road . . . and the car comes to a halt—naturally, or it would have run over me. It's Alice

dropped $104,000 into the hands of a swindler who promised to recover the kidnaped Lindbergh baby. At auction, the *Post* went to Eugene Meyer, father of its current chairman, Katharine Graham. In her later years, Evalyn became a joke hostess. Although she continued her massive parties, Evalyn was living in much reduced circumstances. When Maggie Cassini went to visit her she found the wallpaper peeling, but Evalyn still sporting the monstrous Hope diamond while two detectives sat nearby, their eyes fixed on it. [13]

*His first wife was Cissy Patterson's daughter.

The honeymoon—a trip to Cuba, where they toured the scenes of TR's triumph—was soon over. Nick started to show his preference for nights out with the boys—and the girls; and Alice started to show her preference—for her father. *(UPI/Bettmann Newsphotos)*

William E. Borah, head of the Senate Foreign Relations Committee and said to be the most powerful man in Washington, was Alice's close friend—and, many claimed, the father of her daughter. *(AP/Wide World Photos)*

After eighteen years of childless marriage, Alice shocked the nation by announcing she was pregnant. Rumor had anyone but Nick as the father, but Paulina, born on Valentine's Day 1925, and Nick—shown here in Atlantic City in 1929—adored one another. *(AP/Wide World Photos)*

A family portrait taken in 1931, about a week before Nick's death—a death from which Paulina never recovered. *(UPI/Bettmann Newsphoto)*

Alice and Paulina sailed to Europe in the summer of 1935 for the wedding of Alice's nephew to the daughter of French premier Pierre Laval. *(AP/Wide World Photos)*

Alice toured Hollywood in the summer of 1936. She met William Powell and Myrna Loy on the MGM set. The biggest movie stars thrust paper at Alice and asked for her autograph. *(AP/Wide World Photos)*

Nick's high living, drinking, and gambling had depleted most of his fortune, and, after his death, Alice undertook several schemes to raise money. She went so far as to endorse Lucky Strike cigarettes in ads that appeared in 1937 in *Life* and other magazines. *(AP/World Wide Photos)*

In 1938, falling deeper in debt, Alice put her house at 2009 Massachusetts Avenue on the market. But she was not able to get her price of $70,000 and continued to live there until her death in 1980. *(AP/Wide World Photos)*

Paulina at her debut in Cincinnati in 1942. She grew into an immensely shy young woman with a severe stutter. Two years later she made a spectacularly inappropriate marriage.
(UPI/Bettmann Newsphotos)

(above right)
Both John F. Kennedy and Robert F. Kennedy numbered Alice among their favorites. She especially enjoyed teasing the feisty Bobby, who called her "my favorite person in Washington" and shared a joke with her three months before he was assassinated. *(AP/Wide World Photos)*

Alice starred at the 1966 wedding of Luci Johnson—the first White House bride since Alice was married there—and Pat Nugent. LBJ once complained to Alice that her wide-brimmed hats made it difficult for him to kiss her. "That's why I wear them," she explained. *(UPI/Bettmann Newsphotos)*

(below right)
As she grew older, Alice became less interested in party and more in personality. The more outrageous a person's views and the more trouble he was likely to stir up, the more she liked him. Here she gives advice to Cuban premier Fidel Castro, whose photo she kept on her piano next to that of Senator Joe McCarthy. *(AP/Wide World Photos)*

Into her nineties, Alice remained the most popular and, some said, the most powerful woman in Washington. Presidents, including Richard Nixon, regularly dropped by for tea and came to pay tribute on her birthday. She died at home, shortly after turning ninety-six. *(UPI/Bettmann Newsphotos)*

The Right-Wing Years

Longworth and John L. Lewis. Everybody was really in shock, deep shock. . . . I couldn't pull myself together except to get out of the road. They were horrified at seeing Drew Pearson's wife. Then they sped on and that was the end of the story." [19]

Although many of Alice's friends believe that they did have an affair, Hutchinson was doubtful. "Lewis was very courtly, very gallant with women, and I imagine highly aware of the effect he had on them; but never in all his marriage to Myrta Lewis [they were married in 1907] was there a breath of scandal about him of any credibility, and by every account he was distraught when she died . . ." However, Hutchinson also says that Alice told him of Lewis' "tremendous animal appeal." [20]

"He loved making trouble and I loved watching him make it," Alice later recalled. "It was natural that we should get together." [21] She especially loved watching him make trouble for FDR—a man whom Lewis despised nearly as much as Alice did.

Although Lewis was a Teddy Roosevelt Republican, in 1932 he urged his members to vote for the other Roosevelt. The president's NRA act contained a collective-bargaining provision. FDR also supported the Wagner Act, which gave every worker the right to join a union. In 1936, Lewis again brought labor to FDR's side, making big labor, for the first time, a key element in FDR's coalition. Lewis also added a half million dollars to Roosevelt's campaign chest.

The alliance began to sour soon after the 1936 victory. "Lewis told the president," according to a recent FDR biographer, "that he expected to be consulted often on questions of national policy, and that the office of secretary of labor should be seen as a patronage plum for the CIO wing of the labor movement." In 1939, when FDR, frustrated by two years of sit-down strikes, refused to take sides in a steel strike, blurting, "A plague on both your houses!" Lewis roared his response: "It ill behooves one who has supped at labor's table and who has been sheltered in labor's house to curse with equal fervor and fine impartiality both labor and its adversaries when they become locked in a deadly embrace." [22]

In 1940 Lewis suggested to FDR that the one way to make a third term palatable to the American people was to put John Lewis on the ticket as candidate for vice president.* FDR complained to his labor

---

* To Alice's disgust, Cactus Jack Garner, who passionately opposed a third term for FDR, was one of a very few Democrats who were making noises about snatching the nomination from Franklin. Garner and FDR had come to hate one another so bitterly that the president

secretary, Frances Perkins, that the labor boss undoubtedly figured that the president wouldn't last another term, thus making way for Lewis to take over. FDR's coolness to Lewis's suggestion humiliated him. Later Lewis charged that the FBI, at FDR's instigation, had tapped his phone.

So, during that 1940 campaign season, as Alice watched in delight, John L. Lewis returned to the Republican fold, even if he supported that recent Democrat, Willkie. In a radio broadcast Lewis promised to resign the CIO presidency if Roosevelt beat Willkie. FDR and his advisers were stunned, for Willkie was the first of FDR's opponents who seemed to have a fair chance of defeating him. They feared that Lewis, in turning the election into a referendum on his leadership, could make the difference in key industrial states. Willkie promised Lewis that he would have a major voice in his administration—for openers, in the selection of a labor secretary. (To FDR's delight, Willkie promised in a speech that labor would choose the next labor secretary, "and it won't be a woman either.")

During the campaign, Alice noisily announced, "I'd rather vote for Hitler than vote for Franklin for a third term." Now, Alice Longworth and John Lewis had something major in common: they were driven by spite. As Ted Morgan, FDR's biographer, pointed out, "The radical labor leader, whose union was riddled with Communists, the originator of the sit-down strike . . . was backing the pure product of Wall Street, the candidate whose power companies had hired labor spies and promoted company unions. It was amazing what spite could make a man do." [24]

As was becoming all too predictable, FDR won his third term. Not only did he win the big industrial states, with the exception of Michigan, but he won every large city except Cincinnati. Later FDR would try unsuccessfully to nail Lewis on tax evasion. And Lewis reciprocated with wartime strikes in shipyards, auto plants and coal mines.

Despite Alice's remark about preferring Hitler to Franklin, Eleanor invited Alice to the diplomatic reception after the start of the third term. Presidential aide General Edwin "Pa" Watson bet the Presi-

implied that Garner, who made a practice of using his influence in Congress to sabotage his boss's policies, was the administration's Pontius Pilate. "The Vice-President is not here so we can talk freely," FDR said at one cabinet meeting. When Garner entered the race FDR joked at a cabinet meeting, "I see that the Vice-President has thrown his bottle—I mean his hat—into the ring." [23]

dent that Alice wouldn't dare to attend. As the guests' names were announced and Franklin heard, "Mrs. Nicholas Longworth," he nudged Eleanor and shouted, "Pa, you lose!"[25]

Eventually, at Franklin's behest, Eleanor wrote Alice a note: "Someone has told me that you say you have to go to the White House and that it is rather tough to go there so much, and I know that I never want you to come unless you want to come." Alice wrote back: "'How horrid people are, trying to make bad feelings. How can they say things like that, because I adore coming to the White House. I have such a good time.' I did, because there was always a sufficient number of people who didn't like Franklin and hovered around me."[26]

The invitations stopped. Franklin saw to that after one of her particularly vicious insults got back to him. "I never want to see that woman again," he thundered.

"If there is a war labor has to do most of the dying," Lewis bellowed during the 1940 campaign. After Franklin's victory, he stuck to that theme. He joined America First, an isolationist organization founded during that campaign year, which eventually grew to five hundred chapters and a membership of some 800,000.[27]

Next to Lewis and Charles Lindbergh, Alice Longworth was its most celebrated member. Colonel W. T. Bals, who investigated the group for military intelligence, explained its origins and purpose: "America First was set up because of the hatred for President Roosevelt and its purpose is to do everything possible to embarrass him. . . . America First has a lobby strictly anti-Roosevelt in Washington. [He here named Lewis, Alice, and William Castle as prominent members.] All are bitter enemies of the President. This group has figured out a way to reach the President with the most bitter attacks in the history of the world."[28]

While this report, recently declassified, sounds overblown, there's little doubt that the moving forces in America First—Lindbergh; Robert Wood, head of Sears, Roebuck; Senator Burton Wheeler and his wife; Senator Robert Taft and his; Henry Ford; Colonel Robert McCormick; John L. Lewis and his daughter Kathryn; Father Coughlin; and Alice—sometimes seemed to be battling FDR almost as much as they were battling involvement in the war. (Alice later cheerfully admitted that "a great deal [of her America First involvement] was entirely mischief and dislike of Franklin. . . . anything to annoy Franklin.")[29]

Other America Firsters had more lofty motives. The group was founded by a Yale law student, and its members included Chester Bowles, later Kennedy's undersecretary of state and ambassador to India; Kingman Brewster, then a Yale student, later the politically liberal president of Yale; June and the late Jonathan Bingham, a liberal congressman from the Bronx; Sargent Shriver, later a Kennedy in-law and head of the Peace Corps. These were genuine pacifists, naively ignorant of Hitler's motives and goals.

But most of them resigned after Charles Lindbergh's infamous speech, full of awful anti-Semitic arguments, at an America First rally in Des Moines. Lindbergh charged that warmongering Jews were among the "principal war agitators" and warned that "their greatest danger to this country lies in their large ownership and influence in our motion pictures, our press, our radio, and our Government." [30]

The speech sent moderates fleeing and left behind a hard core that apparently didn't mind associating with members of the Silver Shirts, the Bund, the Ku Klux Klan, and assorted fascist crackpots who were drawn to America First. Secretary of the Interior Harold Ickes denounced Lindbergh as the "number one Nazi fellow traveler" and the "first American to raise aloft the standard of pro-Nazism." Even the *Chicago Tribune* disavowed his remarks.

Alice Longworth's response to her friend Lindbergh's speech was to become an officer of America First's National Committee and a director of the Washington chapter. Although she still refused to speak before groups, she sat on the platform during rallies—there to distinguish the stage with her familiar face and all the connections it evoked to both TR and her popular husband. Printed on the left side of America First stationery, her name lent instant legitimacy. If America First was, as its critics charged, opposed to the United States aiding France and England out of a secret desire that Hitler win, how was it possible that Teddy's daughter would lend her name to it? If Teddy's daughter felt that staying out of the war was the course to take, there must be something to it. After all, her father had repeatedly proved himself to be the last person to flee a fight—unless fighting were so contrary to America's self-interest as to be positively un-American.*

---

*Still, there seemed an essential contradiction between TR, who was so eager to fight that he wrote Henry Cabot Lodge shortly before the Spanish-American War, "The clamor of the

The Right-Wing Years

At the same time Alice strengthened her ties to Lindbergh, she befriended a cast of anti-Semitic characters including Father Charles Coughlin, the radio priest from Royal Oak, Michigan. Coughlin too had begun as a New Deal supporter—"Roosevelt or Ruin"; "the New Deal is Christ's Deal"—then turned bitter critic. He was soon castigating Roosevelt as "Franklin Double-Crossing Roosevelt" and describing his backers as "the Jews [whose 'god is gold'], Communists, international bankers, and plutocrats."

In the Senate, Burton Wheeler, a Democrat from Montana and a former FDR admirer turned character assassin, took Borah's place. (Although there were rumors that Wheeler and Alice were having an affair, their friendship appears to have been fueled solely by hatred for Franklin. There were also rumors that the bulkily handsome senator had an affair with Cissy Patterson,† who somehow got away with inviting him to dinner minus his formidable wife.) Wheeler had been the first important Democrat to declare publicly for FDR in 1930, and went on to help the new president push through much of his regulatory legislation. Some slights involving Montana patronage, being passed over for attorney general and vice president, and Wheeler's genuine distaste for Roosevelt's Court-packing plan, turned the senator against FDR with a passion. The man who was once "a teacher's pet of the New Deal" [34] not only led the Senate charge against Court packing, but instigated the investigation of the allegedly shady business dealings of FDR's son Jimmy as well.

Wheeler's early years were remarkably like Borah's. Two years older than Alice, he was the tenth child of a Quaker shoemaker. After a childhood in Massachusetts and education in Michigan, Wheeler

---

peace faction has convinced me that this country needs a war. . . . I don't care whether our sea coast cities are bombarded or not; we could take Canada," [31] and his daughter, who was reluctant to fight Nazi Germany or Imperial Japan. Richard Nixon explained how his friend Alice could be true to her father and still spout isolationist views: "As a devoted admirer of her father, she was first, last, and always a nationalist. Her father, of course, was America's first truly internationalist President. He justified this internationalism in terms of America's self-interest." [32] The United States's entry into the Second World War might be in Britain's interest or in the "international bankers'" interest, but it wasn't in America's.

† Cissy was also an isolationist. She hinted that the accounts of Nazi slayings of Jews had been exaggerated by Jewish executives in the communications industry. On the floor of the House, a Pennsylvania Democrat attacked Cissy, her brother Joe Patterson, and her cousin Robert McCormick for "hating Roosevelt more than they hate Hitler." [33]

headed west. Legend has it that en route to Seattle he was passing through Butte when he lost every cent in a crooked poker game, and so was forced to stay.[35] He practiced law, all the time battling the copper interests as a courageous anticorporation lawyer. He entered politics as an insurgent Progressive. (He ran for vice president in 1924 on the Progressive ticket with Robert LaFollette.)

When Wheeler became an isolationist, he became, in the words of one historian, "the victim of obsession. He saw an 'international banker' (synonym for Jew) under every cot; he thought that England was Sodom and Gomorrah, and he hated one man, Franklin D. Roosevelt, with a fierce, fixed, vituperative and vindictive passion."[36] When FDR proposed his Lend-Lease, under which England would get guns and ships from the United States and the United States would get paid back after the war's end, not in dollars, but in kind, Wheeler led the fight against it. He charged that Lend-Lease would "plow under every fourth American boy" and, beginning to show signs of irrationality, claimed that the Army had ordered 1.5 million caskets.[37] He opposed selective service with equal fervor, warning, "If you pass this bill, you slit the throat of the last democracy still living."[38]

When William Dodd, U.S. ambassador to Germany, visited Washington and went to a dinner for some congressional leaders, he was horrified by Wheeler's Nazi-esque comments: "We shall soon be shooting up people here, like Hitler does." His world vision included U.S. domination of the Western Hemisphere, Japanese domination of the Far East, and German domination of Europe.[39] He believed that Germany would win the war and that America ought to be on the winning side.[40] Not surprisingly, stacks of America First mail franked with Wheeler's stamp were found in the office of a prominent American Nazi.

Although FDR desperately wanted the United States to enter the war against Hitler, he had his own deep-seated prejudices. According to a recent biographer, Ted Morgan: "When Burton Wheeler came to see him . . . FDR said, 'You know, Jack Garner wants to run for President, but he couldn't get the nigger vote.' Wheeler was startled that FDR had used the word 'nigger.' 'Farley wants Hull to run,' FDR went on, 'because of the fact that he wants to be Vice-President and he thinks Hull might not live and he'd become President. . . . You know, Burt, Mrs. Hull is part Jewish and you don't have to go back through your ancestors or mine to find out if there's any Jewish blood in our veins. We're either Dutch or English." Morgan described another incident: "In January 1942, Leo T. Crowley, a Catholic economist . . . witnessed an extraordinary outburst when he had lunch with the president. For no apparent reason, FDR started giving him the following lecture: 'Leo, you know this is a Protestant country, and the Catholics and the Jews are here on sufferance. It is up to both of you [Crowley and Treasury Secretary Henry Morgenthau, a Jew] to go along with anything that I want at this time.'" When Crowley told Morgenthau of FDR's remarks, Morgenthau said, "What am I killing myself for at this desk if we are just here by sufferance?"[41]

Mrs. Wheeler made her husband look moderate. A military intelligence report contained the following charge: "Mrs. Wheeler . . . is bitterly anti-Semitic. She is a stockholder of the *Chicago Tribune*. . . . Mrs. Wheeler . . . and Colonel McCormick are using America First as a sounding board for anti-Jewish propaganda."[42] An FBI report charged that the wife of a former German counselor was working in America First with Mrs. Wheeler to prepare an outline of Hitler's peace objectives.[43]

It was at William Castle's house that Alice, Mrs. Wheeler, and John Lewis's daughter Kathryn founded the Washington chapter of America First. Castle, who had been assistant secretary of state under Hoover, was branded by the FBI as the "alleged master mind behind Lindbergh . . ."[44]

Despite the acidic remarks about Alice—and Nick—that have since come to light in Castle's fifty-nine volume diary, he was an old friend of the Longworths. Like them he was a perpetual diner-out—a man who could afford to take a state department post and still live in high style on the gargantuan wealth he reaped from his missionary ancestors. His grandfather had gone to Hawaii to preach the gospel and stayed to take over so much of the island's wealth, including its pineapple fields, its gas company, and its street car company, that it is said that Queen Liliuokalani complained about him to the U.S. government.[45]

America First attracted other friends of Alice, such as Hamilton Fish. The Fishes and the Roosevelts had been close for generations; another Hamilton Fish had signed on as one of TR's Rough Riders and died at Las Guasimas in Cuba. Fish became the Republican congressman from Dutchess County (FDR's congressman, in fact), and, according to one FDR biographer, "a pro-German appeaser who had met with Nazi leaders in August 1939 and . . . was quoted in German newspapers as saying that Germany's claims were just . . ." Working up a crowd, Congressman Fish shouted, "Who made our foreign policy up, where did it originate from?" and the audience roared back, "The Jews, the Yiddles, the Kikes!" [46]

According to FBI documents, Hamilton Fish was among those invited to a luncheon of America First devotees at the Massachusetts Avenue house of another friend and neighbor of Alice's, Clarence Bussey Hewes—"Buzzy" to his intimates. Also there were Senator and Mrs. Wheeler and Senator and Mrs. Taft, as well as a friend of Buzzy's whose name remains classified but who later talked to the FBI and described the luncheon and his reasons for supporting America First. Alice couldn't make lunch but she came to tea. [47]

Buzzy's friend predicted that the British empire was about to break up and, he said, it deserved to. The German-dominated Europe that he hoped to see at war's end would not, he argued, pose a threat to the United States. A Russian victory, on the other hand, would pose a major threat. For eastern Europeans, he added, German socialism would be a far better deal than would Russian socialism. Should the United States help to defeat Hitler, he warned, it would be handing Russia complete control of Europe. [48]

Buzzy Hewes was a curious character, married only in the legal sense—he lived in Washington, his wife in New York, and they had a pact never to exchange visits. For years he had served as an extra man at Alice's dinner parties. A native Louisianian and a descendant of two signers of the Declaration of Independence, Buzzy came to Washington in 1917 to start his career in the foreign service. He served in various countries, including England and Germany, before retiring in 1933 to a life of attending and giving dinners and issuing opinions on matters of good taste and manners—for example, one must never answer an invitation with a ball-point pen and one must never attend a funeral unless one has dined in the dead person's house at least twice. [49]

Although he had profound admiration for British nobility (he entertained for the duke and duchess of Windsor when they visited the United States), he was unalterably opposed to the United States entering a war to rescue France and England from what he considered to be their own excesses. And so he joined America First and became, directly or indirectly, what seemed inevitable among those who stuck around long enough—a supporter of Hitler.

In the meantime, the honeymoon was over for Alice's beloved nephew, Rene "Bunny" de Chambrun, and his bride, Josee Laval. Pierre Laval had become deputy premier (under Marshal Petain) of Vichy France, and met with Hitler to lay the groundwork for a Hitler-Petain meeting. According to Hitler biographer John Toland, "At this time the Fuhrer planned to extend his program reducing France to complete vassalage. He hoped to do it with the willing help of the victims but was ready to use force and ruthless reprisals if necessary. . . . he hoped to gain Vichy France as an active ally against England. From Laval's attitude, Hitler was assured that this could be done . . ."[50] Paris newspapers later published a telegram, signed by Petain and Laval, congratulating the German commander in France "for the victory achieved by German troops which, by their defensive action, allowed the rapid mopping up of French soil." Laval made it plain that he was hoping for a German victory and a favored place for France in the new Europe that would result.[51]

It was said that Rene served his father-in-law as a sort of messenger boy to Hitler and Mussolini—"If you want anything from Pierre," you first had to "go to Rene." One of Laval's biographers wrote that "In 'Bunny,' Laval had what he thought was the perfect intermediary."[52]

Later there was strong sentiment in the United States to revoke Rene's American citizenship. (As a descendant of Lafayette he held dual citizenship.) FDR wrote a memo to Under Secretary of State Sumner Welles that referred to a "bill in Congress to take away the (American) citizenship of Rene de Chambrun. It might not be a bad idea to give it our blessing."[53] For some reason, Congress never acted.

Bob Taft, for whom Alice retained hope for 1944—surely Franklin couldn't be contemplating a fourth term—was stubbornly isolationist. In February 1941, ten months before Pearl Harbor, Taft declared, "It is simply fantastic to suppose there is any danger of an attack on the U.S. by Japan."

ALICE ROOSEVELT LONGWORTH

*   *   *

While Alice was trying her best to keep the United States out of the war, her brothers, Ted, Kermit, and Archie, couldn't wait to get in. In 1938, FDR had dispatched Vincent Astor and Kermit (on Astor's yacht) to the central Pacific to gather intelligence on Japanese war preparations.[54] In 1939, when war broke out in Europe but the U.S. was still neutral, Kermit, who had failed at business and who was only happy when on an adventure (the more dangerous the better), did what he had done in the first war—enlisted in the British army; this time directly offering his services to Winston Churchill. (He did this the first time in order to get into combat quickly without stopping for training.) He was commissioned a major and performed stunning acts of bravery; however, when he contracted malarial fever and dysentery, those, combined with the ravages of past drinking binges, left him pitifully weak. The army invalided him out. Kermit appealed directly to Churchill for reinstatement, but the prime minister reviewed Kermit's medical records and said no. In May 1941, he returned to the United States, disspirited and drinking more than ever.[55]

It was at this point that Kermit went off on a drinking binge, accompanied by a German-born masseuse. Kermit's wife and FDR feared that Kermit would die of cirrhosis of the liver. With physicians warning that he would not live more than three weeks without medical attention, Franklin ordered J. Edgar Hoover to find Kermit. On July 7, 1941, Kermit and his mistress showed up at the hospital. Archie later had his brother committed for treatment.[56] Like his Uncle Elliott before him, Kermit sued his brother for unjust incarceration.

In September 1941, three months before the devastating surprise attack by the Japanese at Pearl Harbor, Taft declared, "There is much less danger to this country today than there was two years ago, certainly less than there was one year ago."[57]

An old friend of Alice, Ethel Garrett, recalled Sunday lunch at Alice's on December 7, 1941, the day of the Japanese bombing: "Well, friends," Alice told her guests, "Franklin asked for it, now he's got it."[58]

*   *   *

According to Allegra Maynard, then headmistress of Madeira, "The night before Paulina's graduation [in June 1942] she kept the corridor in an uproar over a demonstration of herself in her pajamas, of her grandfather's charge up San Juan Hill until midnight, to the distress of the teacher who was in charge of the floor, who *unfortunately* was not amused!"[59]

What is remarkable about this prank is that Paulina committed it. She had begun to unfold at Madeira, but at Vassar—which appealed to her because her friend Lucille Tennant was already there—her old fears and inhibitions returned. Some friends say she was worried about boyfriends and marriage, which seemed beyond her reach and yet were necessary were she to escape her mother.

She left Vassar before completing her first year, for what were officially described as health reasons. Ever since, friends and relatives have whispered that she took too many sleeping pills, but the real story, according to Paulina's hallmate, Elizabeth Wadsworth, was that Paulina fell—or jumped—into Sunset Lake. College officials feared the latter and, said Elizabeth, "after that it was recommended that she have some psychological counseling. She never returned to Vassar."[60]

Paulina was miserable living at home with her mother, and her shyness and stuttering returned in full force. Elizabeth Wadsworth spent a Vassar vacation visiting Paulina in Washington. At lunch, "Mrs. Longworth was quoting somebody, it may have been one of the Alsops, laughingly said that either she was a terrible mother or had no talent at all for being a mother. . . . She laughed about . . . this disconcerting but probably true thing that somebody had said about her. At the time it didn't occur to me that that was something a little uncomfortable for a mother to say in front of her daughter. Paulina didn't say anything . . ."[61]

But worse was yet to come. Alice bragged to Paulina and Elizabeth, "'I haven't slept in a bed with a man for thirty years,' or maybe it was twenty-five, whatever it was, it was significantly older than Paulina." Elizabeth was surprised, not only that Alice would say such a thing to virginal girls, but that she would say it in front of Paulina.[62]

Even with her cousins, Paulina was remarkably shy. Edith Kermit Roosevelt recalled that "one had a great deal of difficulty getting anything out of her." Edith would sometimes ask Paulina to lunch, but getting her to talk was "like pulling teeth." [63] Tish Alsop's experience was identical: "I remember an agonizing couple of times when we had lunch together and went to a movie. There'd be total silence." [64]

Alice liked to recall her own childhood agony of shyness and awkwardness—"a shy, uncomfortable child;" [65] "a rather pathetic creature, terribly homely . . .," she described herself. [66] Yet if Alice felt any sympathy for Paulina, she never let on.

Showing a streak of cruelty as well as conventionality, Alice decided that she wanted Paulina to be the belle of the ball—a role as unsuited to Paulina as that of the dutiful daughter had been to Alice. "Paulina was withdrawn from everyone," recalled her cousin Edith. "Her mother was not the kind of person who could tolerate that. She wanted the kind of girl who was going out a lot, who was the talk of the town." [67]

Marietta Peabody Tree, a statuesque blond beauty several years older than Paulina, met Alice in the street one summer at Northeast Harbor, where the Peabody family vacationed.* " 'Marietta, I understand you know everybody and you're terribly popular,' Alice said. 'I wonder if you'd just do one thing for me. Introduce Paulina to some young men, some nice girls who will ask her around.' My heart sank because . . . I didn't think that Paulina was very attractive . . . and I knew that it would be a hard time putting her over. . . . But equally I was struck by the fact that Alice Longworth would ask me to help her in some area in which she was utterly helpless. It simply never occurred to me up to this moment that she could be helpless in any area, that she wasn't totally in control of everything she wanted to do." [68]

Being amused was always Alice's top priority, and Paulina was, in Alice's opinion, distinctly unamusing. "Had she been an extrovert she would have fascinated Mrs. Longworth," observed Marian Christie. "Had she only been somebody who was a very extreme kind of character who would have amused her . . ." [69] She wanted, said Marie Ridder, for Paulina to be funny. "I don't think she recognized

*Marietta's grandfather was Endicott Peabody, the founder and rector of Groton, where Alice's brothers and her cousin Franklin went before Harvard. Marietta calls herself a "vague cousin" of Alice, related through the Lees, who were first cousins to her grandparents. Marietta would become Eleanor Roosevelt's successor as U.S. representative to the United Nations Human Rights Commission.

that Paulina couldn't have been funny because every time she spoke a word her mother shut her up."[70]

But friends who saw her out of Alice's presence said that she had an intellect to rival her mother's—she could recite poetry ad infinitum—and, when she chose to reveal it, a marvelous dry wit. But she took some cultivating. She would not, in the Roosevelt style, shout her opinions. During a dinner party, recalled one friend, she remained silent. "Then the other guests would go and we'd begin to talk about them. Paulina in her quiet inimitable way would make the most acerbic comments. I remember her describing my roommate at Yale . . . as 'rather w-w-w-wet.' It's a very English expression. It hit it just right. That's exactly what he was. It meant kind of boring, well-meaning . . . and to be avoided at a cocktail party."[71] Another friend recalled another party: "Someone was talking about manners making the man. Paulina's remark was 'Manners are the morals of the epicene.'"[72]

The late Horace Taft (Bob Taft's son) once got into a discussion with Paulina, who was his contemporary and friend, about women in various professions. Horace argued that while women did pretty well in some things, "in the sciences they're just nowhere. I could name fifty prominent male scientists for every woman," he assured her. "Marie Curie. Name 50," she replied.[73]

Still, said Edith Roosevelt, "I would assume that the message had gotten across to Paulina that she was not exactly considered an asset to her mother's parties."[74] That was fine with Paulina, who wanted nothing to do with Alice's friends. Yet for her daughter's eighteenth birthday, on Valentine's Day, 1943, Mrs. Longworth invited Paulina's friend Ruth Carter Stevenson (whose father Amon Carter, a blustery Texan, art collector, friend of Will Rogers, and publisher of the *Fort Worth Star-Telegram*, was a favorite of Alice's) and filled the table with her own, much older friends, such as Arthur Krock, who must have been especially alarming to Paulina.[75]

Alice and Archie were helplessly watching Kermit drink himself to death when Archie got a call from FDR, asking, "What are we going to do about Kermit?" Franklin already knew the answer. Recognizing that Kermit longed for an adventure but that his health would not withstand the sort of service that Archie or Ted Jr. was performing,

FDR commissioned Kermit a major in the U.S. Army and sent him to Alaska.

That adventure was short-lived. The last threat to mainland America was soon eradicated. On June 4, 1943, fearing he had played out his final act of derring-do, Kermit shot himself through the head.*[76]

Around this time, a new Franklin-hater came into Alice's life, and became her closest friend during much of the forties and fifties. William C. Bullitt was FDR's ambassador to Moscow (1933–36), and later ambassador to Paris (1936–41) until the fall of France to the Nazis.† An old-line Rittenhouse Square Philadelphian whose grandfather had written the city's charter, Bullitt had the blood of Virginia's Patrick Henry in his veins but also, through his mother, the blood of Russian Jewish immigrants. He would have preferred to have forgotten about the latter. In a letter to a state department colleague he once described the man who would become the Soviet ambassador to the United States as "a wretched little kike. . . . It is perhaps only natural that we should find the members of that race more difficult to deal with than the Russians themselves."[77]

The incident that turned Bullitt violently against FDR involved Sumner Welles, FDR's number two man in the State Department. For all intents and purposes, Welles was really the number-one man. FDR ignored his secretary of state, Cordell Hull, and depended entirely on the brilliant, haughty,‡ secretly homosexual, and not-so-secretly alcoholic Welles. Hull had the title, but not the president's confidence or ear. Foreign diplomats would make courtesy calls on Hull and spend two hours with Welles.

Named for his great-uncle, abolitionist Charles Sumner, Welles was a product of Groton and Harvard and had been a page boy at FDR's wedding. His second wife was Mathilde Townsend, whose mother was *the* Mrs. Townsend who introduced Nick Longworth to Maggie Cassini. The Welleses lived in apparent blue-nosed harmony

---

*Elliott's mistress had shown up at his funeral. TR had remarked on how sincerely grieved she seemed and how decorously she behaved. Kermit's mistress came to his funeral. His relatives were outraged, especially when they discovered that he had left her money in his will.

†Bullitt had also been close to Woodrow Wilson, and was sent by the president on a secret postwar mission in 1919 to sound out Lenin.[78]

‡"It is a pity that he swallowed a ramrod in his youth," observed one British official.[79]

in a servant-stuffed mansion near Alice's on Massachusetts Avenue. Alice detested Welles and had added an imitation of him to her arsenal.

In September 1940 Speaker of the House William Brockman Bankhead, Tallulah's father, died. Welles was the State Department's representative at the funeral in Jasper, Alabama. On the return trip to Washington, Welles was downing whiskey after whiskey in a crowded dining car. On returning to his sleeping compartment, he lewdly propositioned the black porters who answered his service bell. One of them filed a complaint with Southern Railway Company headquarters in Philadelphia, where Bullitt, then out of the government, lived. Bullitt had several reasons for hating Welles, among them his jealousy over Welles's access to the president.

Bullitt told FDR of the complaint against Welles and also circulated copies among members of the Senate. With a congressional investigation threatened, Welles resigned. FDR was furious—with Bullitt. He knew of Welles's homosexuality and had planned to cover it up—not because of his old school ties to the undersecretary, but because he relied on Welles's foreign policy expertise.[80]

If Bullitt thought that he could step in to fill the gap left by Welles, he was sorely mistaken. FDR blackballed him from his club of advisers. Drew Pearson reported that when Bullitt called on FDR, the president told him: "If I were the Angel Gabriel and you and Sumner Welles should come before me seeking admission into the Gates of Heaven, do you know what I'd say? I would say, 'Bill Bullitt, you have defamed the name of a man who toiled for his fellow men, and you can go to hell.' And that is what I tell you to do now.'"[81] Humiliated and frustrated, Bullitt became one of FDR's most vicious enemies. He wrote books and articles that accused FDR of having lost the peace.

The man who had been so sympathetic to the Soviets that FDR had sent him to Moscow as ambassador to show U.S. support (Bullitt's first wife was Louise Bryant, the widow of Harvard-educated revolutionary John Reed, author of *Ten Days That Shook the World*, a sympathetic eyewitness account of the Bolshevik revolution) turned bitterly anti-Soviet, insisting that Russia was the United States's major postwar threat, that all of eastern Europe would ultimately fall under its control. Despite his Jewish roots, or perhaps because of them, Bullitt came to see the threat of Communism as much more pressing than the threat of fascism.

Alice not only agreed with Bullitt about the threat of Communism—as shown in her later championship of Richard Nixon and Joe McCarthy, who she believed would finally root out the Communists in the State Department—she admired his opinionated, hothead style. "Anyone who could say the things he said at the dinner table," remarked a friend of Alice's, "utter the violent political speeches, and occasional libels as he did, and raised the temperature, was someone whom Mrs. Longworth was amused by, and whom she encouraged to greater and greater verbal excesses."[82]

One of Alice's friends observed that if Bill Bullitt had had a son, Alice would have insisted that Paulina marry him. That way the domineering parents could have controlled their children. Despite Alice's desire to have a popular daughter, it seems almost unnecessary to mention that when a boyfriend for Paulina finally did appear, Alice didn't like him.

But Paulina did, drawn to him perhaps because he too was trying to escape a domineering mother, perhaps because of his obvious talents as an artist and a writer. Scribner's—also Alice's publisher—had already published two of his eccentric books, which crossed the line between children's and adult literature. He had written and illustrated both while a student at Yale. (*The Problem Fox* was published in 1941 and *Ambush to Zigzag* in 1942.)

But there was something else about the heavy-framed, pale-skinned Alexander McCormick Sturm that attracted Paulina. He had obvious contempt for the high-powered establishment types who frequented her mother's salon. He was not in awe of Alice.

Alex was the son of Katherine ("Kit") McCormick, a rich girl from Chicago whose father, Alexander McCormick, was a Chicago and Indiana publisher. Like her daughter-in-law-to-be, Kit had gone to Vassar, but graduated and, while there, met a Yale boy named Justin Sturm, whom she married in 1922.

Justin was a farm boy from Nehawka, Nebraska, who had been recruited as a scholarship student by Phillips Exeter Academy. From there he became Yale's all-American end and football hero. He married upon graduation, went to Chicago, tried conventional business jobs, failed, and, in 1926, retired to a life of novel writing, playwrighting, and sculpting in Westport, Connecticut.

Kit Sturm, a woman of consuming social ambitions, chose Westport, a community packed with publishing (friends claim that it was through Kit's contacts that her husband's and son's books got published) and theater people—just the environment she wanted to push her husband, and later her son, to fame.

It is unclear how Paulina and Alex met, although the person indirectly responsible for bringing them together was probably Ernst Franz Sedgwick Hanfstaengl, a Munich-born, Harvard-educated Nazi who later became one of Adolf Hitler's top aides. Ultimately Hanfstaengl, or "Putzi," as his friends called him, was arrested by the English and then "loaned" to the Americans, who hoped to pick his brain on the personal habits of top Nazis. Alex, who joined the OSS (the precursor to the CIA) on finishing college, was assigned to "guard" Hanfstaengl in a house in the Virginia countryside, twelve miles outside Washington.

Alice had met Putzi Hanfstaengl decades before when he was a guest at her father's White House. TR wanted to meet the young man, a classmate of his son, Ted Jr. Putzi had become renowned for using his extraordinary talent as a piano player to compose stirring football marches. After TR left office, Putzi claimed to have received regular invitations to Sagamore Hill.

An inveterate name-dropper, Putzi apparently cultivated the president's daughter. Among Alice Longworth's papers is a friendly letter from Putzi, dated March 20, 1936, when he was still in Hitler's employ, inviting Alice to go sailing ("When are you coming to Bavaria to have a sail with me on Lake Starnberg in my proud two-masted boat the *Perhaps* . . . Hoping to hear from you soon"). He also asked her for her recommendation on the best biography of George Washington.[83] (However, no American president would ever appeal to Putzi as much as TR. Hanfstaengl, who was one of Hitler's earliest supporters, later paid his führer his highest compliment by telling him that he reminded him of TR: "The former President had a vigor and courage, a vitality and familiarity with all manner of men . . . which had endeared him to the plain folk.")[84]

Presumably Alice visited Putzi, met Alex, and invited him to her house for tea—she would have been charmed by Alex's obvious brilliance and eccentricities. Alice was no longer charmed by Alex, however, when he showed an interest in her daughter. He was the kind of person whose tea-table conversation Alice would have enjoyed, but, as Campbell James (who grew up in Cold Spring Harbor near the

Oyster Bay Roosevelts and later befriended Alex at Yale) put it, "Sometimes you invite people to tea that you don't want to have in the family." [85]

According to David Mitchell, who roomed with Alex both at prep school and at Yale, Alice recognized in Alex a formidable foe. "One of the real reasons that Paulina was attracted to Alex was that she recognized that he could protect her against her mother. Alex would stand up to her mother. They had a sort of an armed truce all the time. . . . Mrs. Longworth might have felt that Alex wasn't a plain little boy that she could push around. . . . She knew there'd be trouble and there was trouble." [86]

11

The Death of Paulina

Alex sported a Henry VIII beard and Edwardian affectations, including a British accent, a beret, and an oversized cloak. Columnist Charles Bartlett, who was with Alex at Yale, recalled, "You'd get the feeling that he didn't give a damn about what anybody thought about the way he dressed. He had the marks of a very authentic individual."[1] He also had many bizarre political views, reinforced by his new-found friend and mentor, Putzi Hanfstaengl.

Nicholas Roosevelt, a cousin of Alice's who knew Putzi at Harvard, remembered the flamboyant German as "a tumultuous, gifted fanatic, with an exuberant passion for music. He would play the piano for me by the hour—largely from memory—Wagner, Strauss . . ."[2] Despite his nickname, which means "little fellow" in Bavarian country speech, he was a towering six feet four inches with an enormous head.

TR must have been fascinated by Putzi's background. He was born of an American mother whose father had been a general in the Union army, one of Abraham Lincoln's pallbearers and companion to Commodore Perry on his expedition to Japan. (Putzi's great-uncle, John Sedgwick, was also a Union general and is memorialized by a statue at West Point.) Putzi's German father and grandfather were connoisseurs and patrons of the arts in Munich, successful art publishers, and friends of Lilli Lehmann, Richard Strauss, and Mark Twain.

In the 1880s, Putzi's father established a Fifth Avenue branch of the family business. Putzi was sent to Harvard as preparation for running that branch, and he did so until 1920—catering to such customers as Pierpont Morgan, Toscanini, Henry Ford, Caruso, and William Randolph Hearst.

Things had gotten uncomfortable for Putzi, who was avidly pro-German, and, according to Nick Roosevelt, "convinced that the Germans were the master race."[3] One evening at the Harvard Club (Putzi was an active member and there befriended the young FDR) Putzi got himself punched in the nose when he loudly announced that he was glad the *Lusitania* had been sunk. He soon sold the store and returned to Munich where, in 1922, he discovered at a meeting, from which Jews were barred, a little-known street agitator named Adolf Hitler.

Hanfstaengl introduced Hitler to society and money in his crowd of wealthy patrons of the arts, which included Frau Bechstein (pianos) and Frau Winifred Wagner of Bayreuth.[4] Putzi also tried to smooth out Hitler's coarse manners. Hanfstaengl and his wife Helene—a beautiful American of German descent—suggested to Hitler that he learn to waltz. When Hitler protested that it was too effeminate a pastime for a statesman, Putzi pointed out that Washington, Napoleon, and Frederick the Great all enjoyed dancing.[5] Putzi worked on Hitler's appearance, which, he said, was "like a suburban hairdresser on his day off." Putzi worried, obviously to no effect, about Hitler's "stupid little moustache . . . which made him look as if he had not cleaned his nose."[6]

Most of all, Putzi soothed Hitler with his rousing rendition of Wagner's "Liebestod." Hanfstaengl's friends would later portray him as a naive and apolitical artist—a cross between court musician and jester. The truth is closer to that suggested by one columnist who called Putzi "one of the creators of the Nazi movement in Germany."

It was Hanfstaengl who gave Hitler the money to turn the weekly Nazi paper into a daily, lecturing him that it was the American newspapers with their "snappy headlines" that helped TR get his point across. Later Putzi helped Hitler edit *Mein Kampf*. Eventually Hanfstaengl became Hitler's foreign press chief, trying to sell men like William Randolph Hearst on Hitler as "an unbendable pure man of will and action,"[7] and claiming in news releases that Hearst had praised "Hitler's value to humanity."[8]

Even Putzi's talent for composing marches turned sinister. He played some of his Harvard marches for the führer, explaining how the music stirred thousands of Harvard men to roar, "Rah, rah, rah."

The Death of Paulina

Hitler was "fairly shouting with enthusiasm. 'That is it, Hanfstaengl, that is what we need for the movement, marvelous,' and he pranced up and down the room like a drum majorette." Hanfstaengl then wrote the march "that was played by the brownshirt columns as they marched through the Brandenburger Tor on the day Hitler took power. 'Rah, rah, rah!' became *'Sieg Heil, Sieg Heil!'*"

It is intriguing to imagine the course of history had Hitler not met Putzi and Helene, who, with Leni Riefenstahl, was the object of Hitler's greatest infatuation. One evening at the Hanfstaengl apartment, after Putzi played the piano and Hitler entertained the Hanfstaengls's young son Egon with a full rendition of battle noises followed by a tirade against the Jews, Hitler managed to get Helene alone, dropped to his knees, put his head in her lap, and moaned, "If only I had someone to take care of me."[9]

After the unsuccessful Beer Hall Putsch in 1923, Hitler fled to the Hanfstaengl home outside Bavaria. Hitler wanted to shoot himself rather than be arrested but Helene disarmed him with a judo grip and convinced him that the people needed him.[10] Putzi also saved Hitler's life, when, on a money-raising trip, they encountered a roadblock manned by Communists. Hanfstaengl showed his Swiss passport, claimed to be an American businessman, and introduced Hitler as his valet.[11]

Past favors forgotten, Hitler turned on Putzi in 1937 and the Nazi foreign press chief was forced to flee Germany for his life, eventually ending up in England. The British arrested him in 1939 as an enemy alien and interned him in Canada. They didn't believe Putzi's protests that he had broken with the Nazis and was ready to join the battle against them. (They figured it more likely that the Nazis had planted him as a phony refugee.)

It was the brainstorm of J. Franklin Carter, who, under the name "Jay Franklin," wrote a syndicated column and also ran a private intelligence service for FDR, to "borrow" his boss's Harvard Club friend from the English. The purpose would be to pick Putzi's brain for personal information about Hitler and his cronies—sexual perversions, preferences in women (or men), drug or alcohol use.

Putzi arrived in Washington in July 1942 and eventually was interned on a pre–Civil War estate, surrounded by a hundred and fifty acres of forest, at Bush Hill in Virginia. He was supplied with a high-powered radio that allowed him to listen to Goebbels's broadcasts and to interpret them for his interrogators, who included representatives of the military, the State Department, and the OSS.

This arrangement, known as the "S Project," was to be kept top secret. No contact between FDR and Putzi was ever to occur—although Putzi bragged that FDR supplied him with a grand piano. Carter, who had known Putzi in Germany, would be the go-between. FDR was afraid that details of this program, under which a crony of Hitler's was wined and dined in exchange for information of questionable value, would get into the arsenal of his political opponents.[12]

Putzi also bragged that his friend FDR supplied him with something more precious than a grand piano. From the start, the S Project's biggest difficulty was finding a suitable guard for Putzi. He later claimed that it was FDR's idea to assign Putzi's own son, Sergeant Egon Hanfstaengl, to guard him. (Egon had fled Germany soon after his father, later enrolled at Harvard and then in the U.S. Army.) But FDR could not ignore the strenuous objections of the British, and eventually OSS man Alex Sturm was assigned this unconventional guard duty. Carter felt that in order to get this moody, brilliant man to talk, he needed a cultured guard-companion—with the emphasis on the latter. Putzi liked Wagner, fine cigars, good wines, and the good life—and so did Alex.

According to his friends, Alex was enchanted with Putzi, who he felt represented the best in German culture. "Alex was," recalled Campbell James, "very, very Teutonic—German art, German literature, German this and that."[13] "He found Hanfstaengl to be a very amazing, marvelous personality," said William Ruger, later Alex's business partner. "Hanfstaengl had an immense influence on Alex."[14]

While Alex and Putzi were depleting Bush Hill's wine cellar, Theodore Roosevelt, Jr., already a World War I hero, was the oldest man among the forces training for the invasion of Normandy. On D-day, his performance at Utah Beach, where he fearlessly led his men through heavy fire, was so courageous that General Omar Bradley later called it the bravest he had ever seen. The brigadier general died of a heart attack a month later, in June 1944, while preparing for the next attack. He was buried with full military honors, Generals Patton and Bradley among the pallbearers. Although he had received every combat medal awarded by the U.S. Army, his Congressional Medal of

Honor—the recognition that his father had wanted so badly for his Rough Riding feats but that, for political reasons, had been denied him—was not awarded until nearly a year after his death. [15]

Alice and other members of the Oyster Bay clan accused Franklin of trying to hush up Ted's war heroics. They believed that FDR feared that were TR Jr.'s stunning record known, he, like his father during the Spanish-American War, might use that record as a springboard to the White House. The honor, Alice charged, was postponed until her brother's death took him out of the running.

Within a week of Ted's death, Alice was in Chicago for the Republican convention, still hoping to see Bob Taft win the nomination. Nineteen-year-old Paulina, who loathed politics, was also there, compliments of Arthur Krock, who every four years brought the child of one of his Washington friends or sources to see from the inside how a presidential convention worked. A now-prominent Washington reporter, then twenty-one and attending his first convention, recalled Paulina as the "shyest, most awkward human being I have ever met. In the course of the almost week we were there she never spoke to anybody except in response to a question which she'd answer in a monosyllable—yes or no. Painfully, painfully introverted. I sat next to her for most of the convention. She wouldn't even talk to me. That's not normal. . . . You'd meet someone who's nineteen, there'd be some laughter, some fun. She wasn't under attack or anything, but she acted as though she were." [16]

That summer the S Project was disbanded, not only because Putzi had proven a dry well, but also because Thomas Dewey, who had snatched the nomination from Taft, was known to be probing the project's financing.

As it became clear to Alex that his charge was about to be sent back to his captors,* Alex asked Paulina to marry him. The engagement was announced in the society pages on August 7, 1944, and the wedding date set for barely three weeks later on August 26.

Alice had reasons, in addition to her distaste for Alex, not to feel particularly festive. It was less than two months since Ted Jr. died and a bit more than a year since Kermit killed himself. If she had to give Paulina a wedding, then it would be a small and private one.

---

*In September 1944 Putzi was flown back to Canada and British custody. In the spring of 1946 he was transferred to Germany, interned for six months more, then released. He returned to Munich, where he died in 1975.

Alice's cousin, Katharine Fessenden Bigelow (her mother was one of Alice Lee's younger sisters) suggested that the reception be held at her family's summer home in Magnolia, Massachusetts, outside Manchester. Alice grabbed the offer. A small reception was planned at the Bigelow home for relatives and close friends. The ceremony would be held at the Emmanuel Episcopal Church in Manchester. The Right Reverend Oliver J. Hart, then Bishop of Pennsylvania, would officiate. Nineteen years before, when he was rector of the ultra-fashionable St. John's Episcopal Church in Lafayette Square, he had presided at Paulina's christening.

Elizabeth Wadsworth would be Paulina's only attendant. Alex's younger brother, Justin Jr., known in the family as Dusty, would be his best man. One of Ted Jr.'s sons, Lieutenant Cornelius V. S. Roosevelt, USNR, would give away the bride, an honor that would have gone to his father.

But first there was the matter of wedding presents, a topic that had so preoccupied Alice thirty-eight years earlier. While Alice salivated over the precious gifts and assigned the conventional ones to perpetual storage, Paulina showed no interest in any of them.

Alex, whose tastes were exotic and rigid, laughed as the traditional, and, in his opinion, bourgeois, sterling, crystal, and china arrived. He decided to rid himself and Paulina of these testaments to poor taste by tossing them down a well. The idea was Alex's, but Paulina happily assisted.[17]

Alex's friend F. Reese Brown recalled the arrival of champagne glasses from Baccarat: "They were beautiful, so thin they were flexible. Alex squeezed them repeatedly until they broke and wine [splashed] over everything."[18]

Elizabeth Wadsworth's parents had a summer home in Magnolia, which was about three blocks from the Oceanside Hotel, where Paulina, Waldie, and Alice stayed in the days before the wedding. Elizabeth noticed that Paulina was her usual "tense and melancholy" self. Alice was downright "testy." A New York designer had created her blue brocade gown and matching hat. "When the outfit arrived she took one look at the hat and hated it, threw it on the floor, didn't actually stamp on it, but behaved in a really tantrumish way."[19]

Alice had reason to be tense. An unpleasant task awaited her. According to members of the Roosevelt family and close friends of Paulina, on the eve of her wedding, Alice shared a perverse intimacy with her daughter. She told Paulina that Nick Longworth was not her father. Although at least one close relative claimed that Alice followed that revelation with the news that Senator Borah was her father, others say she didn't bother with the second half.

What led Alice to make such a confession on the night before Paulina was to step into her own life? Some relatives charged that it was simple vindictiveness. Alice didn't like this marriage and needed a way to hurt her daughter that would stand out from the multitude of hurts already inflicted. One relative claimed that Alice blurted, with no softening prelude, "You know you're illegitimate, of course." Others said that Alice had simply procrastinated until she could procrastinate no longer.

If Alice wanted to hurt Paulina as she had been hurt by Edith on her wedding night, she certainly succeeded. Actually, Alice was merely adding insult to injury, as some weeks earlier she had shared another confidence with Paulina, that, in a way, had left an even nastier wound.

Members of the Roosevelt family frequently mentioned how "strictly brought up" Paulina was. They recalled an engagement party at "21" and Paulina, in a white dress, escorted—chaperoned, really—by Waldie,[20] who was described by one acquaintance as looking like the "perfect New England nun."[21] When the drinking got heavy and the language coarse, Waldie took Paulina home.

Alice had told Paulina that the presumably maiden Miss Waldron, who had devoted most of her adult years to caring for Paulina, had in fact been married at age sixteen in Nova Scotia, given birth to a son, divorced, and apparently given up custody of that son.*

According to F. Reese Brown, Paulina would later bitterly complain not only about her mother's duplicity but also about Waldie's. "That was shattering because Waldie was her great friend. . . . It turned out that she was not as pure as the driven snow. Paulina would bemoan the fact that 'all life is a charade.'"[22]

As she started her marriage, friends said, she felt that both Waldie and her mother "had lived a lie." She could no longer depend on Waldie to protect her. She would now depend on Alex and he would fail her most grievously of all.

---

*Waldie's obituary made no mention of a former husband or a child. A month and a half later, Washington newspapers carried the story that a fifty-two-year-old man, who claimed to be Waldie's only child, petitioned to get her estate of some ten thousand dollars.

"He just did exactly what he pleased," said Bill Ruger, "and she fell in with everything." [23] When, after the wedding reception, Paulina changed into her conventional going-away costume of blue crepe with matching hat, bag, and shoes, he let her know that she looked like someone destined to pass her afternoons playing bridge at the country club. This sort of ensemble, which carried the stamp of Alice Longworth, would no longer be tolerated. Alex was interested in fabric and clothing design and he would later design or choose all his wife's clothes—to set off his own flamboyant style.

Alex's control was also evident in the wedding-night plans. The couple checked into an enormous suite at the Ritz in Boston, and Alex invited half a dozen friends to join them in dancing, dining, and drinking until dawn. Recalled Campbell James, "I forget how many bedrooms there were, but they used every single one." [24]

Campbell, whose friends called him "Zup," didn't say how he knew. Presumably he didn't spend the night with the newlyweds, although Alex would likely not have minded. Zup's comment was intended to dispel rumors, rampant in the Roosevelt family, that Alex was homosexual or bisexual. "There are no two ways about that," said one Roosevelt cousin. "That was fairly common knowledge." (David Mitchell, who roomed with Alex at boarding school and college, attributed the rumors to the Roosevelts' dislike of Alex. "I never saw any sign.")[25]

There was no question about Alex's intelligence. Zup may have gotten carried away when he placed Alex's adult IQ "slightly higher than Einstein's." But David Mitchell, who had a more balanced view of Alex, called him, "a genuine genius. One of the definitions of genius is eclectic knowledge. . . . He would have enormous knowledge of heraldry and also have a great knowledge of Egyptian history. He would also know a great deal about guns." [26]

Genius or not, Alex could not decide what he wanted to be when he grew up. "Alex had too many talents in too many different directions at too young an age . . . without any direction," explained F. Reese Brown.[27] He was thinking about writing another book. But, said Bill Ruger, "He wasn't built for the drudgery of writing a long book." [28] He was also doing some painting, some fabric design, some movie script writing, some cartooning for the *Saturday Review*.

But he was not making a living. He couldn't cut the purse strings that tied him to his mother. And so the newlyweds gave up their primitive house outside Westport (so primitive that it had an out-house) and moved into a small house on the Sturm property, where Alex entertained a steady stream of visitors.

To the Roosevelts, Alex seemed unsavory. Teddy would have been horrified, especially later when, still in his twenties, Alex's muscle (he swam and played polo at Yale) turned to flab. He looked, said a Roosevelt cousin, "fat, fat and white, a later Oscar Wilde." He kept all the curtains drawn—day and night. "He was very sensitive to light," recalled Zup, who visited the newlyweds nearly every weekend. "Never had daylight in there. . . . He preferred not to be out in the sunlight." [29]

Much as Alice wanted Franklin out of the White House, she still couldn't contain her talent for toppling the mighty with a single quip. "He looks like the little man on the wedding cake," she said of Dewey—a put-down wonderfully suited to the man with the "waxworks mustache and bland features" [30] who was so insecure about his short stature that he ordered an aide to keep taller men at a distance and prohibited newspaper photographers from taking unposed shots. (One photographer managed to catch Dewey sitting at his desk propped up on a telephone book.)

Franklin was in for four more years, and Lucy Mercer was back in the picture. When FDR died in Warm Springs, Georgia on April 12, 1945, Alice knew that Lucy was with him. Just a year earlier, Alice would have made it her business to be sure that Eleanor knew every humiliating detail. As much as Alice must have wanted to savor the story with her dinner guests, she kept quiet until, years later, it was revealed in a book.

In a left-handed way, Alice was now ready to pay Eleanor her due. Without her, Alice said, Franklin would have amounted to nothing. She made fun of Eleanor—she called her a "big dumb bunny"—but, as one of Alice's friends said, "one got the distinct impression that she was proud that Mrs. Roosevelt was a member of the family." [31]

She couldn't help but identify with Eleanor. It was reported that when Eleanor, in Washington, was informed that Franklin was dying in Warm Springs, she cheerfully followed the advice of her husband's aides to continue with her afternoon engagement. She went to the annual tea of the Thrift Shop at the Sulgrave Club on DuPont Circle.

A society reporter described Eleanor as "looking unusually smart and in soaring spirits." [32]

Alice even found it possible at war's end to feel sorry for Nick's sister Clara. It had been reported in both American and French newspapers that Rene was in hiding from the victorious Gaullists, who considered him Laval's right-hand man. * It was said that, except for his American citizenship, he would have joined his father-in-law before the firing squad.

On October 15, 1945, Laval went before the de Gaulle government's firing squad, despite the frantic efforts of Clara and Bertie who "tried vainly to move heaven and earth" to save the man who, she noted, was "the only man who could think straight in a world which had gone mad."

Laval left a note for his son-in-law: "My dear Bunny, I don't want to leave you without telling you of my deep affection, without embracing you . . . Be strong in adversity, my little bunny. I love you very much." [34]

Clara and Bertie were arrested, she clad only in her chemise, by agents of General de Gaulle. Clara's life was never the same. She visited the United States after the war and was shocked: "The crowds, a multicolored mass, packed the sidewalks and spilled far out onto the asphalt. Levant and Orient vied in the babble of tongues which seemed to include every language but English." The mere possession of naturalization papers, she added, could not transform an immigrant into an "American citizen of standing and repute. No official or government act can bestow on an alien . . . the spiritual treasure which came to my brethren as a birthright." [35]

Rene, who somehow escaped both arrest and loss of citizenship, became a regular visitor at Alice's—when he wasn't occupied defending his father-in-law against charges that he had sanctioned snatching Jewish children from their parents and deporting them to concentration camps.

Alex was not, said David Mitchell, an admirer of the Nazis but rather of the Germany of 1910, "the Kaiser and all of the finer

---

* De Chambrun denied ever having been Laval's envoy or ever having been sought by the French police. He told the *Washington Post* in 1976 that he worked tirelessly for the Allies during the war. [33]

qualities of the Germany of that period." [36] Bill Ruger recalled that Alex was "silent on the subject of Hitler, didn't say anything good or anything bad." [37]

"He liked the aristocrats," said Elizabeth Wadsworth. "I think that Alex had the authoritarian potential but I don't think that he was seriously interested in the Nazis. He was a royalist . . . attracted by aristocrats, wealth, nobility. His interests would have predated anything as crass as the Nazis." [38] Among his hobbies was collecting coats of arms.

After the war, Alex and Paulina went to Munich to visit Putzi. "My father liked Alex a good deal," recalled Egon. Alex and Paulina also called on Egon, who lived in New York after his discharge from the Army. "He [Alex] was voluble and engaging, spoke of my father with marked admiration, indeed with affection, and generally delighted in uttering unorthodox views and bizarre political notions." [39]

Most likely Alex shared Putzi's view on Jews, which seemed to be that Jews should be restricted in certain ways so as not to be so visible, but that they should not necessarily be slaughtered. (Or so Putzi claimed in his memoirs, although there was no record of his ever taking exception to Hitler's formulation of "the final solution.")

"Alex had a lot of Jewish friends," Reese Brown said, in arguing that his friend was not anti-Semitic. "My guess would be that he would be [anti-Semitic], if you're talking about the Seventh Avenue type [of Jew], I would say that's probably true, but then his friends were not 'Jew' Jews. But he was not an anti-Semitic person in the sense that he didn't like some particular subculture." [40]

Brown added that merchants were at the bottom of Alex's list of respectable occupations. "There were a couple of things that Alex approved of that one could do and in a gentlemanly sort of way—gun manufacturing, another was wines—if you were a wine merchant, this was in." [41]

Elizabeth Wadsworth summed up Alex's attitude toward the Jews as, "of course if we're going to talk to any Jews it had better be Rothschilds." She also recalled Alex thrusting a book on the evils of circumcision at her. "And I read a little bit . . . and was sort of scandalized because . . . the point of it was this is a useless and foolish procedure which the Jews have forced upon us. . . . There was an anti-Semitic twist to the whole argument." [42]

Alex had plenty of time to worry about such matters as circumcision. He was not working and his major occupation, besides drinking, was fending off his mother, who wanted to control the life of a son she was sure was destined for greatness.

Katherine "Kit" Sturm was pretty, although frumpily built, well dressed and groomed, witty, charming, urbane, and energetic. "Mostly," said Beth Moore, Henry Luce's sister and a friend of the Sturms, "you had a feeling of vigor and humor and being able to cope." [43]

And fortunately so, for Kit had her share of recalcitrant men to push. Her younger son, "Dusty," was obviously not going to blossom into another model of precociousness. Since childhood he was passionately interested in trucks. "The genius of the family was concentrated on Alex," Zup James explained. [44] "I don't think she was the kind of person who knew how to come to terms with Dusty," said Elizabeth Wadsworth. "She cared about achievement." [45] Eventually, recalled Beth Moore, "He married a great big Italian girl from Norwalk, from the trucking community, and this was a little hard for Kit to take." [46]

Kit's big problem was her husband, on whom she had lavished vast amounts of money and energy. She longed to be the power behind the genius. She understood that fame rested as much on contacts as on talent, and to that end she attracted to her house the elite of the publishing, art, theater, and film worlds. Richard Rodgers and his wife Dorothy were regulars at Kit's house. And so was an impressive array of the day's top stage and screen stars.

Justin, however, proved an unreliable host. He often failed to appear at his wife's parties. When he did appear, he was sure to make some "idiotic remark," in the words of Bill Ruger. [47] "I think she was trying to make him into a Noel Coward," said Reese Brown. "She was a real reverse Pygmalion." [48]

Justin, who had the face of a prizefighter, became a recluse and an alcoholic. "In all the years that I spent in Westport," recalled Zup, "even sleeping in their house rather than Alex and Paulina's, I never once laid eyes on him." [49] Still, remarked Beth Moore, "Kit handled her husband superbly. She held her head high no matter what he did. He drank an awful lot and he was in a couple of very serious automobile accidents." [50] He was, concluded David Mitchell, a "brooding, somewhat desperate, man." [51]

He published several novels, which, according to Bill Ruger, were "so awful that nobody could really read them. She paid to have them published." [52] He also had a couple of plays produced on Broadway,* and sculpted a variety of Hollywood and Broadway stars. But no matter how many works of "art" he created, the highlight of his life remained a feat he had achieved on his own: rising to all-American end on the Yale football team. "That," recalled Beth Moore, "was a story that would crop up quite often." (The jacket biography of *Index to Sybil*, a dreary novel published in 1951, twenty-nine years after his graduation, says: "He played football at Yale and was an all-American end.") [53]

His sculptures of the stars were, in David Mitchell's opinion, "bland." [54] Beth Moore dismissed them as "good likenesses but not art." [55] His sculptures of Nebraska farmers and scenes of his farm youth gave him not only the most pleasure but also the most critical praise. But those pieces did not excite his wife. She wanted him to be a sculptor to the stars, and he was soon sculpting and/or painting Katharine Hepburn, Gene Tunney, Ernest Hemingway, José Ferrer, and Lily Pons.

Alex, who knew that his father was producing commerce, not art, blamed his mother for, in Reese Brown's words, "wrecking his father. He never forgave her for that." [56] David Mitchell came away with a similar impression. "Justin Sturm was basically a captive of a rich wife all his life" [57]—a man both wiggling to get away and captivated.

Supported by his mother, Alex was also a captive, but rather than captivated, he was sneeringly disdainful. Reese Brown recalled that on Sunday morning, Kit would drop by her son's house "and she'd throw names around—Fredric March, Katharine Hepburn. That disturbed Alex. He couldn't stand it." Brown also recalled a birthday party Kit threw for Paulina. Among the guests were Mrs. Gene Tunney and Alice Longworth. "That was the damndest birthday party I have ever attended. Each one trying to up the other. . . . Paulina being so repressed . . . took it philosophically. Alex would sit there and glare." [58]

As her husband drifted further into his alcoholic stupor, Kit decided to become the power behind the real family genius, Alex. He resisted, much more effectively than did his father. But in shunning Kit's dream of mainstream success, he became increasingly unfocused

---

I Know What I Like (1939) and *One Eye Closed* (1954) both flopped.

and dilettantish. He let the ritual of living—elaborate dinner parties, elaborate conversation—entrap him. He spent his time planning menus, designing them, and later framing and hanging them on the wall. "My husband always felt he [Alex] lived in the wrong era," said Mitchell's wife Frannie.[59]

Although Alex had begun to drink at Yale, he was now drinking seriously, letting the ritual define his life. "If you'd go there for a weekend," recalled Reese Brown, "you'd have champagne for breakfast, have cocktails before lunch, choice of wines with lunch, and lunch would be postponed, so by the time you got through lunch, it was time for the cocktail hour, then dinner, nightcap."[60]

Alex seemed oddly proud of his dissipation and endlessly curious about the character of that other great American lush—Nick Longworth. He loved to amuse his guests with stories about the drinking prowess of Paulina's supposed father, a routine that left her feeling very uncomfortable.

Inevitably Paulina, a newcomer to alcohol, was drawn in. The birth of their daughter Joanna in 1946 seemed to make no difference. One cousin recalled them stopping by her house, "drunk and disheveled. . . . I could barely talk to them. They had the baby, too, and had to drive back in the car. . . . It was apparent that they had had lots to drink and it wasn't a time when you might have. . . . It was earlyish in the afternoon."[61]

The baby also did not do what babies usually do to new parents—routinize their lives. "Alex's drinking," recalled David Mitchell, "made his behavior at home more and more bizarre."[62] Although one cousin recalled that the house, its draperies drawn against the sun, was "filled with terrible messes and disorders . . . no clean sheets, no diapers for the baby,"[63] David Mitchell recalled a less extreme situation: "The visiting nurse would have found the place lacking certain standards. . . . It was certainly not a *House and Garden* household. It was a bizarre household. . . . Paulina was not a housekeeper, didn't really know how to be so. They had domestic help, a very nice cook who sort of kept them going and kept them in line."[64]

According to Bill Ruger, the cook would announce dinner, but before leading his guests in to eat, Alex would pour a round of drinks, then another. "This marvelous woman would just patiently keep dinner warm until he would condescend to sit down. Then usually he'd fall asleep over his dinner plate."[65]

If Kit Sturm liked houses that were done with just the right mix of bookish clutter and decorator chic—the sort of place that *House and Garden* or Ed Murrow might feature in a piece titled "Star Sculptor Finds Inspiration in Westport"—Alex preferred that his house be the sort of place that an editor, and Kit Sturm, would flee in horror.

A Roosevelt cousin recalled one weekend visit. "If they were talking to you and they didn't like the telephone, they just threw the telephone across the room. They'd get slightly irritated and they'd throw the beans . . . on the floor. . . . You have people who drink heavily and there's a small screaming child." [66]

But the screaming that most friends remembered came not from the baby, but from her father. "Paulina's such a slob," one cousin recalled Alex blurting. "She looks like hell."

Alex, on the other hand, despite the alcoholic flab and sickly white skin, always stood out. In his latest style—a great cloak, huge hat, cashmere suit, double-breasted vest, stick pin—he looked like a dandy from Edwardian England. Putzi Hanfstaengl's son Egon recalled that when the Sturms visited him, "He appeared as a flamboyant eccentric, resplendently dressed in a dramatic cape; his suit and colorful waistcoat were of the artistic-archaic variety; his behavior matched his attire; and his wife, who attended him, furnished the perfect foil; she looked and behaved like a drab little hen next to this magnificent bird of paradise." [67]

Alex was an ardent collector of guns and an admirer of their history and design. He, of course, did not hunt but he respected Bill Ruger, a hunter and outdoorsman, who had a design idea for a handgun that Alex immediately recognized as brilliant. The two men formed a business partnership—Ruger's job was the nitty-gritty work of running the company; Alex's was getting the financing, and he knew exactly whom to ask. His mother provided most of the money behind what became the Sturm, Ruger Company, which eventually grew to be among the two or three largest manufacturers of firearms—sporting, police, military—in the country.

Although Alex and Alice would never like one another, Alex's political views were not to blame. Some of Alice's friends spouted opinions that were easily as extreme as Alex's. One friend recalled a dinner party she attended at the F Street Club sometime in 1946. Among the guests were Alice, Bill Bullitt, and Buzzy Hewes. "Buzzy said he didn't believe all those stories about the Nazi atrocities. That was too much even for Mr. Bullitt. He got up and . . . left the club and slammed the front door." Nobody else, she said, expressed any disagreement with Hewes's opinion.[68]

That same year, Taft was calling the Nuremberg trials a "miscarriage of justice which the American people would long regret" and was deploring the death sentences.

Around this time Alice befriended and championed Ezra Pound, the American poet who had made viciously anti-Semitic broadcasts from fascist Italy. He called Jews "kikes," "sheenies," and "oily people." He also stated flatly, "The Jew is a savage." He signed his letters with "Heil Hitler" or a swastika.[69]

Alice regularly visited Pound after he was incarcerated in St. Elizabeths Hospital in Washington. (Pound had been indicted for treason in 1945, arrested by U.S. forces and placed in St. Elizabeths, a psychiatric hospital, after being declared unfit to stand trial by reason of insanity.) James Laughlin, Pound's student, his publisher for more than forty years, and his friend and defender, recalled that "Pound talked to me about Mrs. Longworth. . . . The gist of it was that she was a 'good' Roosevelt, not a stinker . . . like FDR and he wanted to establish contact with her to get his ideas into circulation in high places."[70]

Whether Alice relayed Pound's messages to any of her powerful friends is hard to tell. Some Pound scholars have attempted to soft-pedal Pound's anti-Semitism. Hugh Kenner of Johns Hopkins University, one of the foremost Poundians in the world, defined Pound's anti-Semitism as "almost wholly directed against international bankers who he thought placed their fellows' interests above the community's."[71] That was a message no different from America First's—one with which she was familiar and comfortable.

At the 1948 convention Alice again pulled strings for Taft—even after he nearly lost the support of the *Chicago Tribune*'s Colonel McCormick, who, in 1948, decided to go with Taft after General MacArthur removed himself from the race. A recent biography of McCormick describes the typically Taftian misstep: "On the eve of the convention, the Colonel and Mrs. McCormick gave a dinner for Taft and his wife at [their] house. Taft sat on Mrs. McCormick's right. Guests numbered about 20. The next day in Philadelphia Taft invited the McCormicks to a reception. Toward the end Taft asked the Colonel and a few others to come to his suite for a private discussion. The Colonel turned to Mrs. McCormick and said, 'Come along, darling.' Taft seemed surprised. 'She's my wife,' the Colonel said. 'Oh! I thought she was your stenographer.' 'Taft may have made a good president,' Mrs. McCormick said later, 'but he lacked the social graces necessary to win a national election.' " [72]

If Alice couldn't do anything for the hapless Taft in 1948, she could make her influence felt in a very different sphere. Arthur Krock was then a member of the Pulitzer Prize Advisory Board. Alice had recently read James Michener's collection of short stories, *Tales of the South Pacific*—Michener's first published fiction—and had decided that it deserved the Pulitzer. She was not, however, one of the fiction jurors, who were not so impressed and had ranked *Tales* fifth. The advisory board had decided against a fiction winner—until Krock got a call from Alice Longworth. He pushed his colleagues to choose Michener. The board was deluged with calls from book editors, who felt that Michener didn't deserve the Pulitzer, especially in competition with Saul Bellow and A. B. Guthrie, Jr., both of whom had novels in the running. Even Michener was amazed and said that a second call to retract the honor would not have surprised him. [73]

That was Alice's sole foray into literary wheeling and dealing. Politics was still her game and, in the words of David Mitchell, she had developed a "killer instinct as to who had or who would be able to achieve power." [74]

In 1948 an obscure congressman named Richard Nixon made headlines by investigating the alleged Communist affiliations of Alger Hiss, a former State Department official and adviser to FDR at Yalta. When Hiss appeared before the House Committee on Un-American Activities, Alice watched every day from a front-row seat. Nixon so impressed her that she began to invite the unpolished, shy, young Californian and his wife, then living in a four-room apartment in Park-Fairfax, Virginia, to dinner. The contacts Nixon made at her famous dinners, replete with senators, cabinet members, Supreme Court justices, and the cream of the Washington press corps (it was at Alice's house that Nixon first met J. Edgar Hoover) were invaluable in greasing his move to the Senate.

Nixon later said that Mrs. Longworth "did not attempt to affect political decisions. On the other hand, she had an enormous effect on the politicians with whom she came in contact. Her appraisal of them worked its way through the Washington gossip circles into the political columns." Nixon acknowledged that he was the beneficiary of her influence—that she "supported me in Washington social circles when I ran for the Senate in 1950, when I became a candidate for vice president in 1952." [75]

In those years, the private dinner party was at the height of its influence—and Alice was its most skilled practitioner. It used to be, said Bob Taft's son and namesake, himself a former senator, that "a lot of the fairly significant decisions on legislative strategy and maybe even on White House policy were discussed at dinners given by hostesses such as Alice Longworth." [76]

The violent partisanship of the FDR years continued until 1952, when Alice finally had to admit that her friend Bob Taft was out of business for good, defeated for the 1952 Republican nomination by the more moderate Eisenhower, who, to her mind, was merely a "nice boob." An almost final spark of party fervor came in her advice to Richard Nixon to grab the vice presidency if Ike offered it: "Someone will have to go on the ticket who can reassure the party regulars and particularly the conservatives that he won't take everyone to hell in a handcart and you are the best man to do it." What she liked best about Richard Nixon was that, unlike Ike, he had strong feelings.*

Although still a rock-ribbed Republican, she developed a curiously nonpartisan circle. Its members had one thing in common—power. "She aligned herself with anybody who was on the way up and cut herself off from anybody on the way down. She was really power hungry," [78] said F. Reese Brown.

Having fun became Alice Longworth's main concern, so much so that one acquaintance observed, "If the Communists take over the White House tomorrow, Mrs. L. would be one of the first people invited to dinner, and Mrs. L. would be the first person to accept the invitation." [79] Richard Nixon recalled that at Alice's dinners, political issues were often discussed "more in terms of the excitement of the

---

*Nixon said of Alice, "She delighted in egging on intelligent men who, in her view, were not fighting hard enough for their beliefs. Like her father, she liked fighters; she didn't like standpatters. Her goal was to make lions out of pussy cats." [77] At one point Alice Longworth noticed alarmingly pussy-catlike qualities in Nixon. She again goaded him to fight when Harold Stassen launched the "Dump Nixon" movement in 1956.

battle—who was going to win, etc. than in terms of which side *ought* to win." [80]

One friend recalled that she used to say, "'Stalin is my pin-up boy' and showed me a postcard of Stalin literally pinned up on her wall." [81] She met and was charmed by Fidel Castro and for years had his photo on her piano next to Joe McCarthy's. She admired the latter, said David Mitchell, because "he could maneuver people and was a killer." [82] She attended every one of the McCarthy hearings, and although she believed that there were Communists in the State Department—and was pleased when Hiss was indicted for perjury and later convicted—according to Larry Spivak, the creator and former moderator of *Meet the Press*, "she would root for either side that got a good punch in and smile and say, 'Good.' Pretty much like someone watching a wrestling match, as though she didn't care who got banged in the head as long as it was an exciting show." [83]

She began inviting Joe McCarthy over for tea. She was fascinated by his talent for stirring up trouble. "She would read about Joe McCarthy," explained Luvie Pearson, "and call him up and say, 'You're wonderful. Come to tea.'" [84] Said Kermit Roosevelt, Alice's nephew, "I think she was just interested in him because everyone else hated him so much. Because he was so objectionable. I think that was the kind of thing that intrigued her." [85]

When McCarthy turned from troublemaker to just plain drunk, Alice lost interest. She saw that he was a man doomed by his excesses. Not only did he drink too much, but, unlike Nixon, who she felt brilliantly managed his case against Hiss, McCarthy exaggerated his case and so did a disservice to the entire anti-Communist cause. He was, in other words, an inept player.

She needed to disassociate herself from him, and to do so publicly. An unexpected opportunity arose. After saying no repeatedly, she finally accepted a dinner invitation from Gwen Cafritz, a woman who, after her husband made a lot of money, worked doggedly to attract the powerful to her dinners. Consequently, Alice held her in high contempt as a parvenu who was long on pretentions and short on breeding. Alice was dressing—planning to go in her own car, as always—when Joe McCarthy, at Mrs. Cafritz's suggestion, showed up, orchid corsage in hand, to "escort" her to the party. "Dear Senator McCarthy," she told him, "I always go in my own car." When he handed her the orchid, she declined, "How sweet of you, but I never wear orchids." Seated between McCarthy and Bob Hope at dinner, she spoke only to the comedian and, after dinner, strolled with Hope around her hostess's house making fun of her furniture.

Several weeks later, McCarthy approached Alice at a party, put his arm around her and, with a kind of "yokel jocularity," announced, "Since you were my blind date, from now on I'm going to call you Alice." "No, Senator McCarthy," she answered, "you are *not* going to call me Alice. The truckman, the trashman, and the policeman on the block may call me Alice, but you may call me Mrs. Longworth." [86]

David Mitchell began to drift away from Alex and Paulina. As "an earnest young banker," Mitchell explained, "I was leading a more conventional life, joining boards of nonprofit organizations," and immersing himself in other conscientious, socially acceptable activities. Alex and Paulina were "traveling a kind of frivolous road . . . leading a kind of Evelyn Waugh life. I could see the overtones of possible tragedy." [87]

Within the Roosevelt family and Alice Longworth's circle of friends, it is said that Alex Sturm committed suicide. His friends hotly deny that assertion and they are right—but only technically. He drank himself to death.

On October 18, 1951, Alex checked in to the hospital in Norwalk. He had had an earlier bout with hepatitis and, according to friends, his doctor had warned him to stop drinking. He didn't, and not quite a month later, on November 13, he died of cirrhosis of the liver, caused by heavy drinking and malnutrition. For despite Alex's insistence on serving his guests the most sophisticated fare, he ate little, concentrating instead on filling his guests' glasses and, always, his own.

Paulina was devastated. The three people who had been most important in her life—Nick Longworth, Waldie,* and Alex—were all dead. Paulina and Joanna, then five, were on their own.

Marriage had not improved Paulina's relationship with Alice. It was, said Zup, "quite alienated," [88] and Paulina could not bring herself to move back into her mother's house. She stayed in the house

---

*Waldie remained in Alice's employ until her death in 1946, in Alice's home. Her later role was undefined. Some people felt that Alice kept on the baby nurse after the baby got married because Waldie knew too much for Alice to let her go.

she had shared with Alex, becoming increasingly depressed and reclusive. Several months later, she and Joanna returned to Washington, renting a tiny house in Georgetown at 1220 Twenty-eighth Street. Paulina's mood did not improve.

The late Clare Boothe Luce, a friend of Alice's, recalled Paulina at this time as "very, very morbid . . . suffering from an extraordinary amount of depression, and, I'm told, alcoholic."[89] Edith Roosevelt occasionally met her cousin for lunch. ". . . Paulina would never order a drink. It was a serious kind of drinking, not social drinking. Paulina wasn't a gay drinker. The kind . . . who drink at parties. She was a sad kind of drinker. She only drank alone."[90]

On May 7, 1952, six months after Alex's death, Paulina made what appeared to be a second suicide attempt. A maid found her unconscious in her room at the Alrae Hotel in New York. She was rushed by police to Roosevelt Hospital and released in the care of her psychiatrist.

Although Paulina had been christened and married in the Episcopal church, religion played no part in her life. Her mother, who, said Kermit Roosevelt, called herself a "pagan" with justification—"she certainly wasn't a Christian"—would not have allowed it. Alice had nothing but contempt for the Episcopalian sermons of her youth— "the dumbest things that ever were . . . sheer voodoo, most of it."[91]

"I don't think she believed in anything,"[92] Selwa Roosevelt said of Alice. But Paulina desperately needed to believe in something. She and Alex had flirted with the intellectual side of Catholicism and were great fans of Catholic writer and critic Hilaire Belloc. But Alex, who fancied himself a Bellocian figure, was much more interested in the man—an outrageous, witty commentator on English society of the twenties—than in his religion. Alex called himself a "born-again agnostic"[93] and used to love to maintain that "there was nothing better than to be a cardinal in the Greek church back in 1500, when high church officials were privileged, luxurious people."[94]

After Alex's death, Paulina needed not an intellectual attachment, but an emotional one. She was, said Tish Alsop, a "rootless"[95] person. She was looking for comfort, for the home she never had, and she found that home in the Catholic church. "Exhaustion . . . is a good word to express the overall impression I have of Paulina," recalled Elizabeth Wadsworth. "She was a person in retreat from events that were, over and over again, too much for her. I suppose that the

Catholic church was attractive to her, at least in part, because it had a tremendous energy of support for the failing spirit." It was also attractive to her, Elizabeth added, because it was "something that her mother would *not* have joined."[96]

Clare Boothe Luce, who had enormous disdain for what she called "Alice's high Anglican agnosticism,"[97] had converted to Catholicism in 1946. When Paulina told Mrs. Luce that she wished to follow her example, she introduced Paulina to the late Father Edward Bunn, then president of Georgetown University. Father Bunn guided her through the conversion.

But it was another converted Catholic, Dorothy Day, who almost made the difference for Paulina. Day, a radical reformer and journalist who converted from socialism to Catholicism at age thirty, was the sort of do-gooder who would never have gotten by Alice's butler. And despite Alex's theoretical interest in Catholicism, he would have considered Dorothy and her Catholic Workers to be among the untouchables.

Dorothy Day was first arrested in 1917 for demonstrating for women's suffrage outside the White House.* After her conversion, she cofounded the Catholic Worker Movement. The Movement ran "houses of hospitality" that fed and sheltered the poor in twenty cities, and also published a monthly newspaper, *The Catholic Worker*, which was dedicated to reconstructing the American social system.

In the summer of 1952, shortly after her apparent suicide attempt, Paulina discovered the charismatic Dorothy Day. Paulina had just read Day's autobiography, *The Long Loneliness*, and wrote to tell her how inspiring she found it. With her letter she included, in Day's words, "a large gift." Having put Joanna in summer camp, Paulina visited Day's Chrystie Street hospitality house on New York's Lower East Side and stayed six weeks.

Paulina had finally found a home, among the city's most impoverished and hopeless. "She loved to go into the room filled with knicknacks that Hatty and Veronica have," Dorothy Day recalled, "and where they serve coffee to all and sundry. Veronica takes care of all the linens and blankets. . . . Her side of the room is filled with potted plants around a little shrine. Hatty has an old curiosity shop

---

*Day was last arrested in 1973 for protesting at the side of Cesar Chavez and his United Farm Workers.

and I'm always threatening to walk off with the tiny vases and animals which cover the dresser and what-not. . . . So they are always there, and for a shy person like Paulina, it was nice to go up and sit with them and have coffee."[98]

Paulina pitched in in a way that puzzled her mother. She handed out leaflets with Dorothy and when Dorothy was arrested for protesting compulsory air raid drills, Paulina paid her bail. (Paulina would have joined the picket line, Day said, except for her responsibility to Joanna.) Paulina stood on street corners with a *Catholic Worker* editor and, although she was too shy to hawk the papers herself, she held them while her comrade hawked.

Frannie and David Mitchell recalled that Paulina would sometimes stop by their house for dinner and a bath and then return to Chrystie Street for a round of bed making and floor washing.

In 1955 Paulina joined Dorothy for a retreat in Newburgh, New York. "She slept in her station wagon under the old apple tree by the side of the house," Dorothy recalled, "right under the dormitory window; I could look down on her from my attic window. She spent most of her time reading, and the retreat was in silence, of course." (Later she gave her station wagon to the Catholic Worker movement.)*[99]

Not even Dorothy Day could help Paulina. During this period Paulina had what friends called a "nervous breakdown." There were also, according to two close friends, shock treatments during three periods of institutionalization in upstate New York. Presumably the shock therapy was aimed at pulling Paulina out of her depression and was, friends said, approved by her mother.

No matter how morbid Paulina became, Alice insisted that she occasionally attend dinner parties. Many of the men who frequented Alice's parties—some Alice's age but many closer to Paulina's—remember drawing Paulina as an unbearably silent dinner partner.

---

* Both Dorothy Day and Alice Longworth died in 1980, powerful and egotistical to the last. They both had one daughter, about the same age. Neither had husbands in the house during their daughters' formative years (Dorothy's common-law husband deserted her), and both shipped their daughters off to boarding school. Although both were uncomfortable parents—Dorothy insisted that her daughter call her by her first name—they were idolized by other women's daughters. Shy, neglected, inarticulate, and unable to please their mothers, both girls escaped them by marrying unsuitable men. There was, however, in David Mitchell's opinion, one big difference between Dorothy and Alice: "One used power for the good and the other for . . ."[100]

Bill Walton recalled her as "sad looking. . . . [with] acne that comes from emotional upheaval. . . . She'd always look sort of blotchy as if she'd been crying, sort of puffy, very unhappy looking and insecure. You could just read her shaking insecurity." [101]

Nancy Dickerson recalled once going to the prize fights with Alice, who insisted that Paulina come also. This was another of Alice's interests that was inherited from her father, who had shocked society by receiving the "pugilist" John L. Sullivan at the White House. Alice regularly bought tickets to the fights and usually asked Turner, her black chauffeur, to join her.

Occasionally she assembled a group of her fancy friends—one night including Nancy Dickerson, Congressman Kenneth Keating, Joe Alsop, Walter Robertson (who was in the State Department), cave dweller-socialite Virginia Bacon—and Paulina. Nancy Dickerson recalled her own aversion to the bloody bout, but at least she enjoyed the social hoopla surrounding it. Paulina enjoyed none of it. Nancy described watching as "teeth came out, blood, we're in the second row . . . every time there was a hefty blow I'd look at Mrs. L. and she'd yell, 'Bully, bully,'"* And then Nancy turned to Paulina, who looked like she would rather be anywhere else. [102]

In 1956, seventy-two-year-old Alice had her first major illness. A lump on her breast was diagnosed as malignant and she underwent a mastectomy. Not even her closest relatives knew and she managed to keep any hint of illness from the newspapers. The next year brought a tragedy that she could not keep private.

On Sunday, January 27, 1957, Paulina sent Joanna, then ten, to play at a friend's house. When Joanna returned home at about 5:30, she found her mother upright on the living-room couch with her head thrown back. Joanna couldn't wake her.

---

*As demands for a ban on boxing increased, Rep. Keating suggested that the country needed a "czar of boxing" and he recommended Alice Longworth. She certainly would not have been acceptable to the antiboxing crowd for, according to her nephew Cornelius, she was never happier than when watching someone's nose get smashed or skin get grazed off. She and Cornelius used to visit a man named Harold Lee in Hong Kong, who owned the Mandarin Hotel, along with a sizable chunk of the city. Leaving his wife at home, Lee loved to escort Alice to the fights. As Cornelius described it, "no holds are barred. They're allowed to kick and one of the devastating blows is to stand on one foot and kick and turn and catch your opponent . . . on the side of the head with the side of your foot. They also have their lower arms wrapped in hemp rope and no gloves and very often the abrasion of the hemp rope will remove big patches of skin. My aunt was thoroughly fascinated by all of this." [103]

The Death of Paulina

She called her mother's school friend and then neighbor, Lucille Flanagan. "She said she was worried that Mommy wasn't moving," Lucille recalled. Her husband Bob called the Fire Department rescue squad and then, with his wife, rushed over. Lucille took Joanna home with her while Bob, who could not determine whether Paulina was dead or alive, waited for the ambulance.[104]

Paulina Longworth Sturm, thirty-one, was taken to the George Washington University Hospital, where she had recently started to volunteer.* She was pronounced dead on arrival.

The next day newspapers across the country reported that homicide investigators had found an empty bottle, apparently a sleeping pill container, near the couch on which Paulina was found.[105] Investigators also learned that she had bought forty-eight tranquilizer tablets and twelve barbiturate tablets from two drugstores the day before her death, and that she had apparently washed down all of them with hard liquor. The combination was lethal. When questioned by police, Paulina's doctor said that he had prescribed the drug in small quantities to combat insomnia.[106]

The coroner announced that he would withhold a death certificate until the Department of Public Health could analyze tissues from the internal organs and determine the cause of death.[107]

Although some six weeks later he would rule the death accidental†—he didn't say how she happened to swallow sixty tablets accidentally—few people who knew Paulina doubted that she had killed herself. "I certainly never had any question about it," said P. James Roosevelt.[109] "Paulina committed suicide," said Mrs. William Howard Taft III.[110] "I certainly think she intended to take an overdose when she did," said Elizabeth Wadsworth. "Her mother was too much for her."[111]

Wadsworth saw Paulina as suffering from a kind of psychic exhaustion: "I don't think she had a big will to live. I don't think she had a will to be someone herself. She had gone through the motions of living, and I think it was not a pleasurable process for her."[112]

By the time of the requiem mass, three days later, at a Catholic church in Georgetown, Alice had steeled herself against any public

---

*She also volunteered at the Washington Home for Incurables.

†He declared that death was due to the "synergistic action" of three non-narcotic depressants—a barbiturate, a tranquilizer, and alcohol—none of which, if taken separately, would have caused death.[108]

display of grief. Although Dorothy Day and some of her Catholic Worker comrades were there, the small church was packed with dignitaries, including Vice President Richard Nixon, who served as a pallbearer. Nancy Dickerson recalled Alice Longworth walking out of church "almost as if she had practiced holding her chin way up—so far up it looked like it would have hurt her back."[113]

The burial was in Washington's Rock Creek Cemetery, rather than next to her "father" in Cincinnati, or next to her husband, who was buried in Westport.

Those who saw Alice Longworth in the hours and days following saw an as yet unexposed side. Marian Christie rushed to Alice's house and stayed with her until relatives arrived. (Lucille Flanagan had called Cornelius Roosevelt, who twelve years earlier had walked Paulina down the aisle, and asked him to tell Alice.)

"It nearly killed her, it nearly killed her, it really did," Mrs. Christie recalled. "She kept saying, 'I wonder, I wonder, is it all my fault? Could it be my fault?'"[114]

So crushed was Alice over the death that friends noted that when Ken Keating called to pay his respects, she kissed him as she thanked him for coming. The last time she had made such an affectionate gesture was some forty years earlier when she embraced Senator Lodge as he left the Senate floor after killing the League of Nations.

Alice immediately focused on "taking over," as she put it, Joanna. One old family friend recalled visiting Alice three days after Paulina's death: "She was distraught, she was self-blaming and she was also thrilled at the chance to raise Joanna. . . . It's as though . . . God had said to Mrs. Longworth, 'You have a second chance.'" Alice Longworth confessed to her visitor, who recalled that this was "the only day I ever heard her say anything personal," that as a girl she "hadn't been sure that she was loved. She conveyed the distinct feeling that she was terribly aware of her failure and . . . that she of all people should have known better. It's the only time I've ever seen her . . . shaken, ashamed . . . stricken, remorseful."[115]

"I think Mrs. L. realized what a destructive mother she'd been," said David Mitchell, "how much her own vanity and pride had been pushed on this really very nice person . . . and what an impossible mother she'd been, and therefore she was much more careful with Joanna, which was her second chance."[116]

Seizing her second chance meant hard work for a woman just a couple of weeks shy of her seventy-third birthday and only recently recovered from major cancer surgery. Also, not surprisingly, Joanna wanted nothing to do with her grandmother. "She had been brought up with horror stories about Gammy," recalled June Bingham. "Joanna entered the household with fear and trembling that Mrs. L. was an ogre." [117]

Actually, Joanna did not enter the household immediately. It was clear to Lucille and Bob Flanagan—it was Bob who told Joanna that her mother was dead—that Joanna would muster every weapon in a ten-year-old's arsenal to resist living with her grandmother. "At that time, Joanna hated her grandmother," Lucille explained, "and she felt that in some way her grandmother was responsible for her mother's death. . . . She could see that her mother was always tense around Mrs. L." [118]

The Flanagans, who had a daughter about Joanna's age and a baby on the way, decided to keep Joanna for the time being, knowing that Mrs. Longworth would be wise enough to go along with the plan—so long as she knew it wasn't permanent. Joanna stayed with the Flanagans for about six months. "She was," recalled Lucille, "terrified that her grandmother would take her." [119]

Alice devoted herself to alleviating that fear. She stopped by the Flanagans almost every day to amuse Joanna by turning handstands and imitating animal noises. "Mrs. L. just knocked herself out to make Joanna like her," recalled Lucille, "playing games in the living room and trampling up over the back of sofas . . . and shouting with laughter." [120]

Alice would always insist that Paulina's death was an accident. She told Ann Perin, a relative of Nick's, that "Paulina had become a Catholic and she was sure she would never have done it but she was drinking quite a lot and taking tranquilizers." [121] She told Elizabeth Wadsworth that because the church buried Paulina, "one could infer that they didn't think it was a suicide and there was an overdose but it was not witting." [122] Some of Paulina's friends agreed. "She was very pious and pious people don't commit suicide unless they've got terrible cancer," said Zup James. [123] "Can you imagine a brand-new convert to Catholicism committing suicide?" asked Lucille Flanagan. "You know the saying that there's no one so enthusiastic as a new convert." [124]

Alice was furious with the *Washington Post* for reporting the death as a suicide. Mrs. Graham, whose own husband committed suicide six years later, recalled Alice's anger, but shrugged her shoulders and said, "I never heard anyone doubt that [Paulina committed suicide]. . . . Nobody ever wants suicides in a family, and I don't blame her, but you know it is our policy that you have to say." * 125

What most puzzled Paulina's friends was how she could have abandoned her daughter Joanna, to whom, all agreed, she was devoted. Friends wondered especially how she could have put herself in a situation in which Joanna would be the one to find her dead or near death. "No way could I imagine Paulina would willingly do something so Joanna would find her," said Frannie Mitchell. 129 "She absolutely adored Joanna," said Lucille Flanagan. "She wouldn't have hurt Joanna for anything in the world." 130

The probable explanation is that Paulina, who felt so thoroughly inadequate, believed that Joanna deserved a better mother. In Paulina's addled mind, by ending her misery she would be doing Joanna, as much as herself, a favor. Given Paulina's feelings about her mother, who under normal circumstances would get custody, this made sense only when the will was read. Paulina had indeed left custody of Joanna to her mother, but, said friends, she did so only for

---

*Alice had grown accustomed to kindly treatment by reporters who prized her for her witty remarks, opinions on nearly every subject, and accessibility—she answered her own phone. The papers carried only veiled hints of Nick's infidelities and none of the humiliating details. When Kermit killed himself, the cause of death was never reported. There was, remarked John Gable, "a kind of gentleman's agreement not to report it." 126 On the subject of Paulina, the press, including the *Post*, had been servile—one report claimed, "She loves her child more than her life"—so Alice was stunned by the *Post*'s report of Paulina's death as a suspected suicide. The late Washington *Star*, at that time Washington's society paper, was much more considerate in reporting Paulina's death: Although its editors would run news of Alice's new hat on page one, they ran news of her daughter's death deep in the paper, at the bottom of the second page of obituaries. The *Star* was adhering to a long tradition. When Nick and Alice married in 1906, it had piously rebuked its competition for invading the newlyweds' privacy: "There is a certain section of the public, and it includes some news correspondents of the yellow-type, who always want to push their inquiries concerning notable people to the point where legitimate interest becomes impertinence." In Alice's obituary, the *Post* again raised the subject of Paulina's death: "Paulina was a shadowy, pathetic child, considered 'desperately shy' and completely overshadowed by her mother," wrote a *Post* reporter in her front page story. "She was raised by a governess; Mrs. Longworth had little patience, understanding or interest in children in those days. Paulina married . . . was widowed at age 26 and died from an overdose of drugs when she was just 31." 127 The *Star*'s coverage of Alice's death contained the following description of Paulina: "Paulina, later the wife of the late Alexander McCormick Sturm, died in 1956 [sic]." 128 That was it, no mention of suicide.

form's sake. Paulina had someone else in mind tờ raise Joanna and felt secure, positive, that her mother would refuse custody. If her mother was "for any reason, unwilling or unable to accept such appointment" as guardian, then Paulina left custody to "my dear friend," another convert to Catholicism, Clare Boothe Luce. Paulina mistakenly assumed that her mother would grab the out that the will left her. It never occurred to her that her mother would want the child.

Paulina found Mrs. Luce appealing because a personal tragedy had led her to seek solace in Catholicism. The year that Paulina married Alex Sturm, Mrs. Luce's only child was killed in a car accident. "Nothing would have given me greater joy than to have had Joanna," recalled Mrs. Luce. "I would have reveled in it." [131]

"Reveled" was not the word to describe Alice's reaction to Mrs. Luce's suggestion that Paulina had really wanted her to have Joanna. According to Mrs. Luce, Alice would not hear of any such arrangement. She was determined to raise Joanna—a determination that surprised many of Alice's friends, who were well aware of her indifference toward children. She was so determined that Mrs. Luce declined to pursue the matter: "I'm a practical woman and it was quite clear . . . Alice Longworth [was not] going to give up that child." *[132]

"Finally I made Joanna go there," Lucille recalled. Despite Alice's efforts, Joanna wasn't ready. Lucille described this time as a "black period." [135]

An old family friend, Bazy Tankersley, stepped in. Bazy, the daughter of Alice's friend Ruth Hanna McCormick Simms (Ruth had later married Congressman Simms) suggested that Joanna spend most of her time at the family's Arabian horse farm in Maryland. Bazy had a daughter around Joanna's age and horses that delighted the young girl.

Relatives and friends said that the relationship evolved so that, in effect, Bazy became Joanna's mother, leaving Mrs. Longworth to assume the easier and more natural role of eccentric grandmother. "Bazy raised Joanna for Mrs. L. and helped give Joanna a proper environment," recalled Selwa Roosevelt. [136] Mostly Joanna spent

---

*In a note to the author, Joanna Sturm called Mrs. Luce's recollection of events "inventive." [133] Joanna and Mrs. Luce rarely saw one another. According to Mrs. Luce, "Alice told Joanna [of] . . . her mother's desire to have her in my custody. . . . I was told by friends that she told Joanna that I had refused custody of her because I really didn't like children very much." [134]

weekdays at Bazy's and on weekends went to her grandmother's house in Washington, or Alice came out to stay at the Tankersleys'.

The arrangement worked, although a cousin and close friend of Joanna's, Robin Roosevelt, described Bazy as something of a "stern figure." [137] Relatives recalled a letter Bazy sent to the as yet undisciplined Joanna requiring that she abide by certain house rules. (At Alice's house there were no rules. Anna Roosevelt, a cousin, recalled a visit to the Massachusetts Avenue house. She and Joanna filled balloons with hot water and dropped them from the top-floor window onto the heads of the unwitting people at the bus stop below. The drenched targets were not amused, but Alice was. "We didn't get punished. It wasn't really her role," [138] Anna explained. Alice's niece, Grace McMillan, recalled walking with Alice into the library for tea. "Joanna was sitting in a big armchair and just waved her foot at us as we came in. And my aunt just accepted that.") [139]

Today, added Robin, Joanna and Bazy see little of one another. Joanna has a left-wing slant to her politics, whereas Mrs. Tankersley is sharply right-wing—"a little to the right of Attila the Hun," according to one friend of Alice. [140] Bazy was known as the hostess who promoted Joe McCarthy in Washington; with her considerable fortune (her uncle was Col. Robert McCormick), she was the senator's chief "financial and moral supporter." She stood up for him at his wedding and, despite her claustrophobia, which was so severe that it kept her from getting into elevators, she rushed to Walter Reed Hospital when McCarthy had his heart attack and took an elevator to be at his side. In May 1957, she supported Mrs. McCarthy at her husband's funeral. [141]

Despite the time Joanna spent at Bazy's, nobody disputed that she was Mrs. Longworth's top priority. "I never heard Alice being serious about anything—except Joanna," said Mrs. William Howard Taft III. [142] "In those early years," recalled Marie Ridder, "Mrs. Longworth turned her life upside down for Joanna. Everything centered around Joanna." [143]

"Whatever Joanna did Mrs. Longworth was interested in and knew about," said a friend, Lilly Guest. [144] She was there when Joanna learned to ride and jump, and trailed Joanna to horse shows all over the world. If Paulina could do nothing right, Joanna could do nothing wrong. Joanna had been living with Alice for barely six months when she told a reporter for the *Washington Evening Star* how proud she was of her eleven-year-old granddaughter, who had made for Alice's birthday "the very best porkchops I've ever eaten, wrapped in cornflakes and done in a pressure cooker." [145]

Said Marie Ridder, "All through Joanna's childhood I remember my parents commenting, 'If only Alice had been able to treat Paulina the way she does Joanna. . . . Had Paulina had that gay, enthusiastic, gung-ho kind of life that she gave Joanna . . .'" [146] Eventually the affection was mutual: "It came to be one of the most touching relationships I've ever known, on both sides," said Bill Walton. "Both of them had nobody else. But usually you would find them locked in hate. Not them. Each thought the other was the funniest person who ever moved. They each gave the other great space, no crowding, it was a remarkable way to grow up." [147]

Clare Boothe Luce claimed that it was at her insistence that Joanna was sent to Catholic schools—she went to Stone Ridge, the Sacred Heart day school in Bethesda, Maryland, and from there to a Sacred Heart college in Newton, Massachusetts. Perhaps, but Mrs. Longworth was totally supportive of that education. She even refrained from expressing her disdain for religion and she involved herself with Joanna's schooling in a way that she never did with Paulina's.

Nearly every afternoon, Mrs. Longworth's driver pulled her ancient black Cadillac to the Stone Ridge entrance. Mrs. Longworth sat reading in the back seat, usually in the lotus position. Often Turner would drop Joanna at the Tankersleys' horse farm, but Alice thought it important that she go along for the ride.

Although Alice did not particularly like Joanna's other grandmother, Kit Sturm, and although she actively disliked Justin Sturm, she remained cordial to them, for Joanna's sake. (Kit Sturm had wanted custody of Joanna, but, like Clare Boothe Luce, backed down in the face of Alice's resolve.) Kit turned up at Alice's election-night parties, to which invitations were a prized commodity. (Justin died in 1967 and Kit in 1971.)

Later Alice dealt with her feelings about Paulina's death by simply avoiding the subject completely—moving on, just as her father had done in his grief over her mother's death. Alice's last word on Paulina came five months after her death, in response to a condolence note from cousin Eleanor: "For months after Paulina died, whenever I tried to write, I simply crumpled." June Bingham was one of many of Mrs. Longworth's friends in later years who said that she had no idea what Paulina looked like. There was not a single photo or portrait of Paulina in the house.

12

"The Other Washington Monument"

Alice Longworth supported Richard Nixon for the presidency in 1960, but when John Kennedy won, she learned how amusing and attractive Democrats could be. There was a tremendous injection of life into Washington. The Eisenhower administration had been elderly and boring. "The Kennedys met her," recalled Kay Graham, "and were enchanted by her. She was very spoiled by them. She got asked to dinner and put on Jack's right. They treated her with great respect, admiration, and affection. . . . It's enchanting to have a president court you."[1] Parties and ideologies began to take a back seat to personalities. Politics became a spectator sport.

The Nixons paid a farewell call on Mrs. Longworth. "It was one of the few times we saw her . . . let her hair down," the former President recalled. "She told Mrs. Nixon that she hoped that after we got to California we would not think that she was no longer a friend because she would be attending events at the White House. She put it very bluntly that she simply couldn't bear being out of the swing of things and that while she had supported me and opposed Kennedy, she would welcome their invitations."[2]

Alice did not forget Nixon, who she believed had life in him yet. During his exile she invited him to dinner at least once a year.

But at least once a month she was enjoying herself with the Kennedys, especially with Bobby, the brash younger brother of the president. She got a kick out of his combativeness: "He was like a tiger always ready to spring and fight," recalled Larry Spivak.[3] Bobby, in turn, declared the seventy-plus-year-old "my favorite person in

Washington." At dinner parties, he insisted that she sit at his right.

In Bobby Kennedy she recognized what she described in herself as "a certain monkey-like quickness for 'catching on.'"[4] But Alice Longworth, who could recite from memory Longfellow's "Saga of King Olaf" or Hadrian's "Animula vagula, blandula" at the drop of a hat, could not let Bobby forget that by her standards he was laughably unread—as rough in education as he was in demeanor.

Unlike his brother John, who loved the verbal sparring matches with Mrs. Longworth, Bobby did not like to be teased. He had a certain pretentiousness about him that Alice was born to prick. He also did not like to be reminded of his not-too-distant roots. So of course Alice told him immediately what her blue-blooded father—the seventh generation of Roosevelts born on Manhattan Island—had to say about those red-faced Irish politicians with whom he deigned to serve during his days in the New York Assembly. "The Democrats," TR sneered in 1882, "include six liquor sellers, two bricklayers, a butcher, a tobacconist, a pawn broker, and a typesetter. . . . Worse yet, 25 are Irish." The typical Irish politician, he added, is "stupid, sodden, vicious. . . . equally deficient in brains and virtue."[5]

When Bobby, then his brother's attorney general, and Interior Secretary Stewart Udall climbed Mt. Kennedy in Canada, Alice couldn't wait to let him know how measly she considered his accomplishment, especially when compared to her father's ascent of the Matterhorn. Bobby and a cast of notables had barely settled themselves at her dinner table when she pounced: "We have all watched with bated breath," she began in her clipped, upper-class voice (she described it as "the voice of one of the pompous old ladies on the cover of the *New Yorker* surrounded by frilly maids").[6] "We have picked up our newspapers each morning to learn about your progress. It is marvelous to have made it all that way, and then to cap it all to have the brilliant idea of naming the mountain after yourself. Have you thought what you will do next? How about running around Kennedy Airport?"[7] Bobby's face turned red with embarrassment and anger.

It had been noted in newspaper accounts that Bobby carried a flag to place at Mount Kennedy's peak. Alice had this in mind when she continued to mock him by quoting from a poem of Longfellow's about "A youth who bore, through / snow and ice, / The banner with a strange / device—Updi, Upda, Excelsior!" Bobby's banner, she said later, "looked as though it had three leprechauns on it" and "had been invented . . . apparently, at the request of the Kennedy family."

"Bobby then looked angrier still," she recalled. After some further teasing, "I'd seen Bobby saying to himself—he was back in his grandfather's saloon—saying, 'Put that face in the sawdust. How shall I get even with her?'" He tried by asking Mrs. Longworth, "What arrangements have you made for your funeral?" Mrs. Longworth, a self-proclaimed pagan, answered that she would like to be thrown into a volcano in Hawaii. "You *would* say that when you know cremation is against my faith," Bobby replied. "Well, anyway, who are you going to have for pallbearers?" he asked. Mrs. L. shot back, "I have not made up my mind . . . but I have decided who I'll have in the front pew, and it's going to be you and Dick Nixon."[8]

Alice never made it to John Kennedy's funeral service because her decades of smoking had left her with emphysema and she could not tolerate the uphill walk or the crowds. The next day her houseguests, Tom and Joan Braden—close friends of the Kennedys and of Alice—decided to go to see JFK's grave. Alice insisted on joining them on that rainy day. As they walked toward the grave, a reporter for the *New York Times* recognized Alice and said, "Oh, Mrs. Longworth, you've come to visit Kennedy's grave." "Oh no, no, no," she answered. "I'm not out here at all for that, my young man. I've just been to see the Lee Mansion. You know my friends the Bradens. I'm showing them the Mansion." Then she turned to Tom and whispered, "Imagine if it got into the papers. I could hear them now down in Long Island. 'The old lady's gone dotty. Grave sitting in the rain.'" At that point she returned to the car, with the Bradens, whose mission was frustrated, in tow. "Really Joanie," she said as the door closed, "to have it printed that I'm grave sitting would be . . . ridiculous, [I] couldn't do that."[9]

In 1964 she went to Atlantic City to watch LBJ grab the Democratic nomination. (She had been going to Republican and Democratic conventions since 1908 and considered them the only thing more exciting than a good boxing match, horse race, or poker game.) She wanted to see her new friend Bobby get the nod for vice president, and, according to one report, "spent a lot of time scooting around town digging up the latest inside information which she thought might be helpful."[10]

Party loyalty became so unimportant to her that in 1964 she voted for Lyndon Johnson and wondered aloud whether the DAR would revoke her voting privileges.[11] She found Goldwater impossibly dull. He certainly failed the amusing-dinner-companion test miserably. In October 1963 she sat next to him at a birthday party for former President Eisenhower. William Miller, chairman of the Republican National Committee and soon to be Goldwater's running mate, made the after-dinner speech: "He assured us that when the Eisenhowers were in the White House no one did the twist in the historic East Room and no one had been thrown into the pool fully clad. I thought to myself: 'This is where I came in.' I told Goldwater of the criticism of my father's use of the East Room for far more violent and vigorous activity such as Judo and singlestick. And regarding the comment on people going into pools with their clothes on, I mentioned that in 1905 I was on a steamer going across the Pacific; a canvas tank was rigged up on the deck. One day I appeared in a linen coat and skirt and some friend dared me to go in like that. I said, 'Let me take off my shoes,' and I dived in. . . . His only response was a murmur.'"[12]

She thought LBJ exhaustingly colorful and a brilliant player in the political arena. "I've watched him for years, from the Senate gallery," she explained. "He is a masterful man, the greatest I've ever seen at getting things done, and I've seen them all."[13] She never said how she felt about his Great Society programs or his increasing involvement in Vietnam. Her interest in Vietnam seemed limited to watching the antiwar crowd give the establishment a bad case of heartburn. Stewart Alsop's daughter Elizabeth recalled stopping for tea at Alice's during the march on the Pentagon. "Mrs. L. decided she wanted to go see the march. . . . Daddy and Mrs. L. and I got in the car with Turner driving and he drove us out to the Pentagon. . . . The two of them were having the time of their lives. Daddy would knock on the glass, Turner would open it and say, 'Yes, Sir!' . . . Daddy would say, 'Well, approach them from the left flank.'"[14] Mrs. Longworth shrieked with pleasure, as if she had the best seat in the house for an amusing play.

The only thing she didn't like about LBJ was his tendency to touch. He tried to kiss her under her broad-brimmed hat and, finding the logistics impossible, said in exasperation, "I can't kiss you under that hat." "That's why I wear it," Alice replied.

At a White House dinner, he moved a beautiful young woman from her assigned seat next to his and substituted Mrs. Longworth. When an aide chortled that the president didn't know what he was missing, Johnson replied, "Ah, but I know what I'm getting." [15]

Richard Nixon heartily agreed. He called Alice "the most interesting dinner partner I ever had in Washington. Generally, sitting between a couple of women at a Washington dinner party, or any place else for that matter, is a pretty boring experience. The subjects for conversation are usually family, fashion, food, sometimes the weather. I can never recall Alice Longworth spending more than a minute on such mundane subjects." [16]

Unlike Nixon, Bill Bullitt could not accept Alice's flirtations with the Camelot crowd. Bullitt, who had a reputation for choosing his friends and lovers on the basis of political or social advantage—it was said that he had seduced FDR's secretary, Missy LeHand, in order to improve his access to her boss [17] and that he had an affair with Cissy Patterson, ten years his senior, to give him access to her newspaper— was a genuine friend of Alice's. When the insurance companies did not want to pay on Paulina's policies because of the possibility of suicide, he worked things out. [18] When friends worried about Alice's declining financial health, Bullitt told them not to, as he would "always take care of her and see that she didn't lack anything." [19]

But, with Bullitt haranguing her on her choice of friends, they began to feud. She called him and tried to patch it up, saying it was absurd for an old man and an old woman to fight. He'd have none of it, and their friendship died several years before he did in 1967.

In her later years, Alice's power could be defined as what is known today as "networking:" "Washington's a town in which yak yak and gossip prevail," said former *Washington Times-Herald* editor Frank Waldrop. "She knew everybody on God's earth. If you went there you'd meet somebody. That's what it all came down to." He added that while she "couldn't fix a parking ticket, she could precipitate animosities between people by saying something that wounded or . . . by pure happenstance have a couple of people in for tea who hit it off and the result was a genuine change in direction somewhere." [20] "Could she get a bill passed which was very important to her?" Marietta Tree asked rhetorically. "No, but every president came to do honor to her. They came to her house for dinner, which I don't think most presidents do, go out to private houses for dinner." [21]

"The Other Washington Monument"

Despite Alice's complaint that her debut was the sort that Edith Wharton would have scoffed at, that disgruntled debutante grew into a woman who, in Washington writer Judy Waldrop Frank's words, "always managed to confer an imprimatur of 'Edith Wharton would have approved of this tea party.' I think people have a deep yearning to be given that stamp of approval." Alice Longworth's invitations also bestowed the stamp of "old money," particularly, said Judy Frank, "on Johnny-come-latelies, people who were kind of on the fence and wanted to be thought of as old-line something or other." [22]

Mrs. William Randolph Hearst, Jr. ("Bootsie"), who was a columnist for the *Washington Times-Herald* at the time she married the press magnate's son,* counted Alice among the women in Washington (Cissy Patterson was another) "whose power far exceeded most men's. In that period, more than now, it was very important to be invited to the right places. . . . I suppose you could compare it to the court of Louis XVI. The important hostesses had much more influence because they could carry a big stick. They could cut you out of their parties and that would cut you out of a lot of information that you could gather—as a newspaper man, as a member of Congress. . . . A man in Congress had his public to think about and to be ostracized by one of the important hostesses was like being sent to Siberia." [23]

Why would Robert McNamara, mired in Vietnam, stop for tea at Alice's? Because, he claimed, he could speak "very freely" with her "without any feeling that what one said was going to be repeated to the press the next morning." [24] Judy Frank suggested another reason: "For the same reason that Henry Kissinger used to dig Jill St. John. Because it got him a certain kind of publicity he could never have gotten another way." [25]

After her daughter's death, Alice befriended several young women who were around Paulina's age—but who were also outgoing, flamboyant, and successful. She made these women into surrogate nieces or grandnieces, offering them advice, listening to their problems (so long as they were amusingly scandalous), letting them shine at her dinner parties, and so inestimably upping their cache.

One of her favorites during the Kennedy years was Joan Braden,

---

* Bootsie's first husband was Marguerite Cassini's son, the gossip columnist Igor, also known as "Cholly Knickerbocker."

who was chairman of Bobby's presidential campaign in California. She regularly flouted convention, and reporters never tired of alluding to assorted public affairs and pranks. She probably reminded the octogenarian Mrs. Longworth of her own naughty youth. "Joanie" fast became Mrs. L.'s favorite.

When Bobby Kennedy was assassinated, Joan and Tom again stayed with Alice while attending the funeral. "The next morning," Joan recalled, "there was a call for me from Nelson Rockefeller," for whom she had worked as a young woman. She instructed the maid to say she was not at home because she knew why "Nelson" was calling. In the wake of Bobby's death, Rockefeller was going to make a run for president and wanted Joan to co-chair his campaign. "I adored Nelson. He was my mentor, my best friend. . . . But Bobby's death was a tragedy that was unbelievable. I was terribly close to him. So I just couldn't call Nelson back and I didn't. Mrs. L. was fascinated by this.

"Finally I took the call. Nelson asked if he could fly down and see me. I said 'of course'. . . . We sat down in Mrs. L.'s sitting room and he said that he would like to carry on the flag for Bobby and that it would mean a great deal to him if I would be co-chairman of his campaign.

"The funny thing about it was that Mrs. Longworth was behind the draperies. She . . . wanted to know what was happening . . . not eavesdropping in the evil way. . . . It was simply that she was interested in me and interested in Nelson, interested in what was going on." [26]

Asked if Alice showed any sadness at Bobby's death, Tom Braden observed, "I don't remember Mrs. Longworth ever showing any emotion except humor." She had planned to go to the 1968 Democratic convention in Chicago to root for Bobby. Part of her disappointment at his death was that she would miss a match between the pugnacious Bobby and the coolly arrogant Eugene McCarthy. [27]

When Nixon was elected in 1968, Alice was again the center of White House attention. She was among the ten invited to the Nixons' first dinner party, held in the room that had once been her bedroom but was then the first family's private dining room. Her energy seemed limitless.

Then in 1970, at age eighty-six, she had a second mastectomy. She

"The Other Washington Monument"

called a startled Jane Childs from the hospital at 2 A.M. and announced, "Well, isn't it lucky it's me and not Brigitte Bardot."[28] Undoubtedly she meant to shock the listener into silence, for she certainly had no intention of discussing her surgery or allowing anyone to feel sorry for her. She refused to discuss her aches and pains with others, and had no desire to hear about theirs.

Even her closest friends and most relatives didn't know that she was having cancer surgery. She told them that, like an old car, she was going into the hospital "for an overhaul." Illness to Alice was a nuisance, like a flooded basement or a kitchen fire.* So when Stewart Alsop was in the hospital with the leukemia that eventually killed him, she wrote him a note, "Stew—what a nuisance—love from your aged coz." Alsop wondered, "Acute leukemia—a nuisance?"[29] but then decided the note was just right, and so were her telephone calls—filled with the social gossip they both loved—instead of hospital visits. Alice would have been more likely to visit a dead friend in the morgue, for the eerie interest, than a sick one in the hospital.

Franz Bader recalled Alice coming to his bookstore with a nurse hidden in the back seat of her car. Alice got out alone—to be seen in the company of a medical attendant was unthinkable[30]—to search for a book on her latest enthusiasm, which might have been astronomy, Greek grammar, anthropology, bats, quasars, quarks, or flying saucers.

She had developed an interest in physics and, to that end, began a friendship with Edward Teller, the man who is revered or reviled as the father of the hydrogen bomb. Teller gave her one of his books to read, and the next time he came to dinner, she alerted him to a couple of mistakes in his mathematical calculations.[31]

Alice had a lot of time for reading because she kept clear of the occupation of most Washington dowagers—charity committees. Her

---

*This was all a matter of childhood training and example. The people she most respected did not dwell on their ills. Her father, during his senior year at Harvard (just after his engagement to Alice Lee) had been warned by the college physician that his heart was so weak that unless he led a sedentary life—he even advised against climbing stairs—he would not live long. "Doctor," Theodore replied, "I'm going to do all the things you tell me not to do. If I've got to live the sort of life you have described, I don't care how short it is." Typically, Theodore told no one, including Alice or his diary, of this alarming news. He simply made sure that his physical activity included not only climbing stairs but also mountains. It was on his honeymoon that he climbed the Matterhorn. Scaling its 15,000-foot peak, he wrote, was "like going up and down enormous stairs on your hands and knees for nine hours."

friends were amazed in 1971 when she agreed to serve on one. Alice strode in to the first meeting, held at Joan Braden's, and announced to the fourteen committee ladies already gathered: "I'm not going to do any work" and "There's a boa constrictor loose in this house." The ladies went into "instant hysterics" as Alice explained that the Bradens' fifteen-year-old daughter had misplaced her pet, Ben Boa. "He is only eight feet long," reported the eighty-seven-year-old who, at a Braden dinner party a few days earlier, had wrapped Ben Boa around her neck. (That antic had so unnerved another guest, Israeli ambassador Yitzhak Rabin, that several guests later reported that they saw him reach for what they assumed to be a gun in an effort to save the old lady who, it seemed, was being strangled by a snake.) Once the snake was recovered, she wrapped it around her neck and stroked it, causing an early adjournment, which was exactly what she had in mind.[32]

Even after becoming what she called "the topless octogenarian," Alice dressed with flair and originality—never in the old lady, comfortable-shoes way into which, with age, most women settle. Her dresses were timeless—she joked that she hadn't bought a new one since she was eighty—and some were made from the empress dowager's 1905 tribute of gold brocade. The patterns were subtle. If her dressmaker slipped, Alice let her know about it. She once described her dress to a visitor as looking like "uncomfortable vegetables." When a few minutes later her dressmaker called, she complained, "I wore that dress with the stripes going round. I looked like a striped barrel. . . . No, I don't want it let out. Unfortunately, it fits."[33]

Hope Ridings Miller said that Alice "felt above fashion, like Smith girls, like well-bred Englishwomen."[34] She wore a shawl that effortlessly and gracefully hung off her arms, but her signature was her wide-brimmed hat, which she first wore as a girl in the White House. Back then her hats sported flowers, fruit, feathers, and even a dead bird or two (one congressional wife described Alice in 1906 wearing a hat laden with a "white cock's breast and plume"),[35] but eventually she stripped them of all but a grosgrain ribbon band and a bow. The hats were as predictable as her dresses—in the spring, black, brown, and navy straw; and in the fall, the same colors in felt. "They were replaced," she said, "only when they got worn and fell off my head." When asked where she got her hats, she replied, "I don't get my hats, I have my hat."[36]

Tea at Alice Longworth's was an event that those so honored never forgot. And it was not the glamorous surroundings that made the occasion memorable.

Alice stayed in her Dupont Circle neighborhood when it turned from fashionable to funky. Other dowagers moved up and away and donated their mansions to assorted good causes, but Alice stayed. She claimed to enjoy the clashes between hippies and police, the mix of pushers, students, and even the radical Weathermen, who, when they stormed the South Vietnamese embassy near her home, got sprayed with tear gas. Alice deliberately stuck her head out to get a whiff. "It clears my sinuses," she explained.[37]

She stayed when the houses next door came down for the Embassy Row Hotel. (When that was being built, her bedroom wall caved in, and when the head of the construction company came to apologize, she complained, "But you didn't even knock.")

She even stayed after her house was burglarized while she attended Truman Capote's masked ball at New York's Plaza Hotel. The burglar, a potbellied neighbor, got in by cutting a hole in the glass pane of the door. He scooped up her diamond-studded bracelets with Kaiser Wilhelm's miniature and her father's Rough Rider souvenir medal.*

In front of her house was a bus stop. Few of the working people who waited, practically on her front lawn, knew that Teddy Roosevelt's daughter lived beyond the aluminum fence, the garbage blowing in the wind, and the poison ivy crowding the walkway.

Getting to her front door, recalled National Gallery director J. Carter Brown, was "a little bit like an Amazonian adventure."[39] When Tish Alsop pointed out to Alice that poison ivy was covering her lawn,

---

*Luvie Pearson saw Alice soon after. "Stewart [Alsop] and I were about to make a grand slam with diamonds and at that moment the doorbell rang and it was Alice and she was all dressed up and carrying this enormous bag. . . . Stewart asked her, 'What's in the bag?' and she said, 'Oh, when I go out to dinner it's in the paper and then the robbers come and rob me. . . . So I never go to dinner anymore without my jewels."[38] At age eighty-two, she testified against the burglar in U.S. District Court. At first he pleaded guilty to a lesser charge, but later he sued Mrs. Longworth for $250,000 for disrupting his trial. He claimed that she was hiding in her "mansion," dodging process servers. In truth, she was always asleep when the sheriff called in midmorning.

Alice claimed not to have deliberately cultivated it, "but what a good idea!"[40] She refused to allow it to be pulled out.

Guests who survived the passage entered a large anteroom on the ground floor where they left their coats. The kitchen and maids' dining room were also on this level, and food was sent upstairs via dumbwaiter. One floor up were the drawing room and the dining room, and, on the third floor, her bedroom and sitting room—in which reigned the famous pillow embroidered with, "If you haven't got anything good to say about anyone, come and sit by me." On the top floor were guest bedrooms.

Every shelf, window sill, table, and nearly every square inch of floor in Alice's bedroom and sitting room were piled high with books and newspapers—so high that relatives called her "Aunt Collyer" after the recluse Collyer brothers of New York who never threw anything away. A stack of her books once fell on Joanna's pet hamster. When it was found two years later, it was mummified. "Presumably a strange smell didn't mean anything to anybody," said Cornelius Roosevelt.[41] When Alice's maid informed her that the burglar had ransacked her bedroom, she asked, "Are you certain? How can anyone tell in my room? It always looks ransacked."

The house, friends remarked politely, "didn't have that decorated look." It had, said J. Carter Brown, a "wonderful shabbiness." Joe Alsop was typically less polite: "The interior of the house was extremely . . . unsmart. It was a decorator's nightmare." It looked, Alsop added, like the "Fall of the House of Usher."[42] The relics of her father's big-game-hunting days hung moldering on the stairwell walls in ratty, disintegrating shreds. When Stewart Alsop playfully shook hands with the paw of a tiger skin, the paw came off in his hand.[43]

The Sargent watercolor of the White House rested casually on a chair. On one wall was a huge Flemish tapestry that had hung in the White House dining room and on another wall were scrolls given to her in 1905 by the empress dowager of China. There was a begging bowl, made from the top of a human skull and used by a Buddhist priest. There was a pair of rhinoceros hooves, and, standing in the corner, a narwhal tusk. Under glass was a Japanese Kabuki actor's headdress, left by its owner after he arrived for tea in full costume. One of her most prized possessions was a bronze model of the Statue of Liberty, given to her as a wedding present by the widow of the sculptor Bartholdi. Over Miss Liberty's crown and face she had placed a native mask from Upper Volta. (She told Julie Nixon Eisenhower that it was her "version of black power!")[44]

Scattered about were photos of everyone from the empress of Japan to Fidel Castro and originals of cartoons that she particularly liked, such as the Batchelor cartoon of Eleanor and Franklin captioned, "All this . . . and Truman too" and another, titled "The Holy Family of the GOP," in which Bob Taft as the Virgin Mary cradles Ike as the Infant Jesus in his lap, while McCarthy as St. Joseph hovers above.

Some regular visitors claimed that the house was downright unsafe. "You had to have life insurance before you went down the stairs," said June Bingham.[45] "There wasn't a sofa which you could sit down on safely," observed Joe Alsop.[46] Joe's step-daughter, Anne Crile, recalled, "You did have the feeling in her living room that at any time the ceiling would cave in."[47]

Still the guests happily came and jostled for the sturdiest seats around the drawing-room table, where tea was served every afternoon at five. Those who had been by previously didn't wait to be asked. They simply dropped in, and invariably she'd be there with a cast in attendance for which most hostesses would have hocked their best crystal. "It's nice to be invited to the White House but the real social coup is tea at Alice Roosevelt Longworth's," observed a reporter for *60 Minutes*.

Central to the event was the process of brewing tea, strictly controlled by Mrs. Longworth. Her maid, Janie, arrived with the tea tray, on which rested bread and butter,* homemade sugar cookies, and a silver kettle over a burner that Alice would light herself.

Guests knew that it would be bad form to prod her to pour, or, worse yet, to offer to pour themselves. "Everybody's hair would have gotten straight," June Bingham recalled, "because she'd have forgotten to turn off the flame under the boiling water. You would not be able to say, 'Mrs. L., would you turn off the flame before my hair falls out?' because she wouldn't have appreciated it."[48]

The tea was always Earl Grey from Jackson's in Piccadilly, a blend

---

* When the Kennedy Center compiled a cookbook with recipes solicited from artists who had performed there and from first ladies, Alice Longworth was the only person asked to contribute who fit neither category. Her recipe was titled "Bread and Butter": "Get very good unsliced bread, butter it with sweet butter then cut it into very thin slices with a very sharp knife and repeat."

that she had drunk since childhood. The very strong tea—her friends
quipped that it was no wonder she went to bed at dawn—was served
in tall glasses with silver holders, or sometimes in Rose Medallion
porcelain cups. But hers was always served Russian-style, with heap-
ing teaspoons of brown sugar. When Bob Hope and his wife Dolores
came for tea, he was shocked to hear the eighty-year-old admit that
she had smoked "reefers." As he was leaving, he asked his wife what
she thought of the tea. "Well, the tea was a little strong." "Strong?"
Hope replied. "I don't think she smokes pot. I think she *drinks it!*"[49]
(It turned out that by "reefers" Alice meant corn silks.)*

Guests were expected to sing for their supper—to join in a sort of
conversational Olympics. "Everybody was on their own," recalled a
cousin, Margo Hornblower. "It was survival of the fittest."[51] Nancy
Dickerson recalled that "Everybody had their little arsenal. . . . You
didn't go to sit around and be a lump or to sit on the sofa and have
somebody else entertain you. You were on stage. You were expected
to be witty, clever and amusing. . . . She didn't have any old dolts
around her."[52]

Alice could attract anyone she wanted to her dinners. A typical
party would include an admiral or two, an important and/or controversial member of each house of Congress, a Supreme Court justice.
"Now, let's see David, you're a banker," she said to David Mitchell,
whom she had just invited to dinner. "I'll get a banker for you." So
she "got" Federal Reserve Board Chairman William McChesney
Martin, Jr.[53] Lucille Flanagan recalled once getting into a good-
natured argument about small airplanes with a guest. "I took a rather
strong stand. . . . it turned out that the man who was smilingly dis-
agreeing with me was the secretary of the Air Force."[54]

Dinner was always called for 8:00 P.M., and at 8:30 sharp she took
the guest-of-honor by the arm and led the way into the dining room.
Drinking disgusted her—she took only an occasional glass of sherry or
wine—and she deliberately kept the cocktail time short so that her
guests would take their places relatively sober. Jane Childs, another
young friend of Alice, recalled Alice walking into Jane's Georgetown
house one day and finding Jane and Lorraine Cooper—wife of Sen.

*In 1905, Grandpa Lee wrote Alice to congratulate her on her engagement to Nick, who, he
hoped, had "enough strength of character to make you . . . leave off cigarettes, cigars and
hogtails."[50]

John Sherman Cooper of Kentucky—drinking Bloody Marys before lunch. "You two just make me sick," Alice berated them, "so stupid to sit there and drink." [55]

"If a guest was late," recalled Richard Nixon, "the dinner went ahead without them. As a result very few were late." [56] The Nixons' daughter Julie told how her parents "would sit in their car until exactly two minutes past eight if by chance they arrived early for one of Mrs. Longworth's dinner parties." [57] (Alice's insistence on punctuality was a reaction to Nick Longworth, who, because he had his own cocktail hours at home and at his club before dining out, was habitually late. The Longworths reputation got so bad that hostesses would tell them that dinner was at seven when it was really at eight. Soon after Nick's death, a hostess asked Alice for seven and was in the bathtub when the maid announced Mrs. Longworth. The embarrassed woman hastily dressed and rushed to the top of the stairs. "It was Nick who was always late," Alice shouted up.) [58]

Alice Longworth had very good—very appropriate-to-her-background—manners. She could, for example, forgive Joe McCarthy for ruining reputations, but she could never forgive him for his "easy manners of a perfect jay." [59] "She would not and could not tolerate familiarity, particularly from political figures," explained Richard Nixon, whose "Mrs. L." was as familiar as he ever got. [60] She noticed if a younger man neglected to rise when an older one entered the room.* Friends said that she never forgave Leonard Bernstein for going to her dining table with his cigarette still lit. (However, Alexandra Roosevelt recalled that Alice, most decorously dressed, would often sit cross-legged at the table, pick up a chicken bone in her hand or even pick her teeth.) [62]

She sat eighteen to twenty guests around her table, the men in black tie, white-gloved waiters stationed behind the chairs. The menu, which rarely changed, got rave reviews. "It was not like anybody's else's food at all," explained Joe Alsop. "She had old-fashioned grand American food. She had the most wonderful crab soup, saddle of lamb . . . wonderful consommé. . . . It's also very expen-

---

* It seemed perfectly appropriate to her that her father based his dislike of Winston Churchill on his bad manners. "He never liked Churchill," she explained. "Churchill was here in about '99 after the war in Cuba. . . . My father was then Governor of New York. . . . He didn't get up when older men came in or when women came in. And he puffed on a cigar, and was generally obnoxious." [61]

sive. . . . It depends on things you can't get anymore, like terrapin*
and heavy cream and new fresh local vegetables."[64] The wines were
the finest and the dessert was usually her cook's specialty, crème
brûlée.

Food was first on no one's mind who came to 2009. Guests anticipated the contacts, conversation, and theatrics—especially the latter.
While an ordinary hostess would be horrified if two guests got into a
shouting match at her table, to Alice that was a sign of success. She
would deliberately seat political or social enemies next to one another. She claimed not to give a damn about seating protocol: "I put
people next to each other who are going to fight, who are disagreeable
to one another."[65] She would regularly seat Vice President Nixon on
one side of her and the Senate minority leader, William Knowland, on
the other because she knew they hated one another. And then, recalled David Mitchell, "She would goad them: 'Dick, you said this
and it doesn't seem to fit with what Bill said . . .' Sometimes she
would take bets: 'Let's have a bet on it, let's have a bet on it.'"†[66]

She invited both Bob Taft and John Lewis to one dinner party.
Given Taft's sponsorship of the Taft-Hartley Law (passed in 1947, it
forbade unions to force employees to become members and allowed
employers to replace striking workers), she knew sparks would fly.
When her nephew Cornelius dropped by to show her a new recorder
he was using in the Navy, she asked him to set it up behind the couch
so she could record the brawl. She changed her mind when she realized that if it were to get out that she was bugging her own dinner
parties, spontaneity might suffer.[68]

After dinner, in keeping with her generally traditional manners,
men and women briefly separated. As the evening drew to a close
Alice would sometimes do her imitation of Eleanor—for Richard
Nixon, who found it "outrageously funny,"[69] and for Kay Graham,
who noted that Alice would do it "at the drop of a pin," and that it
was "very funny" at the same time as it was "really awful."[70] (She

---

*At Christmas, Frank Kent gave her, according to Joe Alsop, "a substantial quantity of
terrapin from the Maryland Club, and she invariably consumed it all herself.[63]

†The fact that Alice had someone to dinner did not mean she liked him. Knowland, for
example, she found terribly pretentious. She used to imitate him lying on the couch with his
hands over his chest, his eyes closed, saying, "Alice, do you think I would make a good
president?"[67]

once did it during tea at the White House for Lady Bird Johnson, who marveled, "What an actress, a really accomplished performance!")[71]

On her ninetieth birthday, in the midst of Watergate, Alice hosted—for herself, her special guest Richard Nixon, and two hundred friends—one of the most extraordinary birthday parties in Washington history. Besides Nixon, she invited such luminaries as Henry Kissinger, Joan Kennedy, Averell Harriman, Robert McNamara, Margaret Truman Daniel, as well as Mary McGrory, Art Buchwald, and nearly every other reporter in town who was salivating for Nixon's scalp. So eager was she for the fun to start that relatives couldn't keep her from peering out the window at the crowd of reporters and people-watchers gathering below.

Senator Hugh Scott, who had just read the transcripts of the White House tapes, arrived early to announce that the president was in the clear: "Time will prove me right when these things come out," Scott promised, as Alice, then still transported by the breaking Watergate story, listened with delight, and as members of the press listened with undisguised skepticism. As the onslaught of secret service men signaled the arrival of the president and the first lady, a group of reporters retreated to another room, vowing not to lower themselves by going into the same room with Nixon.

Nixon later said that he wasn't at all miffed by Mrs. Longworth's choice of guests—although he added that "Bill Bullitt probably would have walked out if he had seen some of the people who were there!"[72] At the time he couldn't restrain himself from lecturing the press, using his hostess to make his point: "Mrs. Longworth has kept young by not being obsessed by the Washington scene. If she had spent all her time reading the *Post*, she'd have been dead by now. . . . She stays young by not being obsessed by miserable political things all of us unfortunately think about in Washington instead of the great things which will affect the future of the world."[73]

In fact, thinking about those things, rubbing her hands in glee over Watergate and other scandals, is precisely what kept her young.

The friendship waned after Watergate, not because she was offended by Nixon's abuse of power—she said she had seen much worse in her time—but because he, who had so brilliantly handled Hiss, was now, like Joe McCarthy, playing the game so ineptly. "Dick is a weaker man than I thought him. Weak, weak, weak!

Kennedy *never* would have shilly-shallied the way Nixon is doing. The tapes should have been destroyed and enough of this nonsense!" [74]

Marie Ridder, working on a story about Watergate, went to tea at Mrs. Longworth's. Knowing of Alice's long friendship with the president, she didn't expect much in the way of spicy quotes. While Marie was there, Mary McGrory also stopped by. "I remember we walked out and we were so pleased with the mean things Mrs. Longworth said." Marie recalled Alice being "really rude about Nixon . . . a man with no background and no sense of himself. The utter insanity of his line . . ." *[75]

For Alice, Nixon's fate as a friend and a politician soon was lost in her fascination with the daily drama of the Watergate hearings, which she called "good, unclean fun." [77] But later she felt that the hearings should have been canceled due to terminal redundancy. "It was getting to the point where it was about to become very boring," she complained. [78]

"She was irritated by bad performances by people," said Charles Bartlett. "In the last two decades of her life, I don't think issues grabbed her too much. . . . She really looked at the performers with the objectivity of a critic. She was just looking at them for their style and the way they carried it off." [79]

Alice awarded no stars to Dick Nixon for the final scene of his presidency. As he said good-by to his staff, the emotionally overwrought, suddenly former president quoted TR's tribute to his dead wife, Alice Lee: "When my heart's dearest died, the light went from my life forever." Nixon continued, pointing out that "that was TR in his twenties. He thought the light had gone from his life forever—but he went on. He not only became president, but as an ex-president he served his country always in the arena, tempestuous, strong, sometimes wrong, sometimes right, but he was a man."

How did Alice respond to her fallen friend's tribute to her parents? On the day after Nixon left Washington in utter humiliation, the *Washington Post* ran a story, on the front page of "Style," in which the

*Later Alice even got nasty about Nixon's daughters. While being interviewed by Sally Quinn for an article marking Mrs. L.'s ninetieth birthday, Alice agreed with Joanna's comment that Julie Nixon Eisenhower's tribute to Alice, then running in the *Saturday Evening Post*, was "totally inane." She added that she liked Julie, but that "I've never been able to get on with Tricia. She seems rather pathetic, doesn't she? I wonder what's wrong with her." [76]

reporter noted that on hearing Nixon's words, "Mrs. Longworth let out a laugh." She also coldly pointed out—in a comparison that had all the compassion of a reporter noting that a death-row inmate was ill groomed en route to the electric chair—that "I don't know why my father's recovery from my mother's loss gave President Nixon heart. My father was a very young man, at the very start of his life. President Nixon is in his 60s." [80]

Nixon was not the last president to pay homage to Alice. "They all went and bowed to her," [81] in Kay Graham's words. Most of them made a regular pilgrimage to her house, as if they needed to prove that although they were from Texas or Ohio, they were still in the Washington in-crowd. "Presidents come to Washington as outsiders," explained Robin Roosevelt, "even if they've been in Congress for years. They're still outsiders compared to her." [82] It would have been impossible to invent a woman with a more impressive Washington history than Alice. In 1901, the seventeen-year-old daughter of the president sat in the East Room, no doubt planning the escapades to come later that night, listening to a young Spanish cellist named Pablo Casals—second on the bill of a White House concert. Sixty years later she sat in the same East Room at the invitation of President and Mrs. Kennedy and again heard Casals. It was a fact that did not escape the graceful young president, and he asked Alice to come forward and take a bow.

Another reason that presidents courted Alice was, in Bob Taft, Jr.'s words: "If she liked you you were less in danger of being pinioned." [83] It was probably for that reason that Gerald Ford, Nixon's appointed successor, when facing election to his own term, came to pay tribute on her ninety-second birthday in 1976, bearing a crystal bowl embellished with the presidential seal. For his trouble he got hit in the head by the balloon-bopping, four-year-old Kermit Roosevelt III.

He also got the clear message that Alice Longworth didn't know who he was—and didn't much care. Joanna decided that her grandmother should sit on a two-man settee and that President Ford would be brought up and seated next to her. To keep her grandmother focused and polite, Joanna pinned a note on the arm of the settee that said, "#1—The President's name is Ford. #2—Do not talk about bumping his head," and so on. Bill Walton, who was watching with

Joanna from the door, described the scene: "They brought him in and he was very pleased to be there and he sat down and started to chat with her. She glanced at the paper and turned to him and announced, 'The President's name is Ford. Do not talk about bumping his head.' He collapsed in laughter. . . . The President was doubled up laughing and everybody else was trying not to notice. She was having the time of her life. . . . He was not a great intellect but he was a very attractive person, an easy person. Carter would have probably knelt and prayed." [84]

Alice called herself "Washington's only perambulatory monument." Like a monument her friends somehow assumed that this woman with her straight back and her uplifted chin was around to stay. "You'd see her walking in the room . . . at the age of eighty-eight . . . [she would] square her shoulders, stride in like a young woman," said Joe Alsop. [85] She bounded up stairs, two at a time, and was offended at the offer of a helping arm. Tom Braden recalled her once walking down treacherous brick stairs. When he offered his arm, "she shunned it." [86]

Eventually even Alice Longworth got old. Just past age ninety-two, she suddenly seemed an old woman. Said June Bingham, "Mrs. Longworth never seemed old until she was half dead." [87] The signs started two years earlier when she went to a dinner party and was exhausted all the next day. Her final White House function was the bicentennial dinner for Queen Elizabeth, which prompted much speculation in the press: Would Alice curtsy to the Queen or the Queen to Alice? (They shook hands.) The managing editor of the *Economist* was staying at her house, and when he returned there in midafternoon, he answered a ringing telephone. On the other end was an anxious White House aide inquiring if Mrs. Longworth could be expected that evening. The editor rushed upstairs to her. She answered, "Oh, I suppose so." "That was the first time," recalled Fred Holborn, "when she felt that she'd really gotten old and she felt it was a bit of an exertion to go to the White House." [88] She even stopped going to bookstores.

A year later, Jimmy Carter, the quintessential outsider, tried to court the quintessential insider, but went about it the wrong way—by making ninety-three-year-old Alice come to him. The new president invited Alice to witness the Theodore Roosevelt Association's presentation of a set of TR's collected works to the White House library.

John Gable, P. James Roosevelt, Ethel Derby, and Ethel's daughter Sarah Gannett were to pick up Alice at 11:00 A.M. en route to the White House. Despite the fact that Alice was never known to be dressed before 2:00 P.M., when they arrived, according to P. J. Roosevelt, "she was up, she was dressed, she was sitting on a couch. . . . And when we started to talk about Carter, she started to talk about Coolidge. The first thing I said was, 'Oh damn, another senile one. . . . Then as I sat and watched . . . I thought, 'The hell she's senile. She doesn't want to go. She doesn't want to be rude. This was her stunt. . . . We said, 'Come and meet the president with us,' and she said, 'Oh, yes, Coolidge, a lot of people don't think he's doing a very good job. What do you think?'"[89]

When they saw that she had no intention of joining them, they went without her, much to Jimmy Carter's embarrassment, and to P. James Roosevelt's, who had promised the president that his famous relative would be there. When the network camera crews learned that Alice had, in effect, stood up the President, they shut off their cameras. They had little interest in Teddy Roosevelt's other daughter, Ethel.

That was the last time that Alice saw her half-sister. Ethel Roosevelt Derby* died that year. Now Alice and Archie (who would die in 1979), were the only two of TR's six children still living.

Many friends remember Alice as looking beautiful well into her nineties. Not only did she have an extraordinarily animated and intelligent face, she had, as they say, good bones. "That's the one thing about a great beauty," said Alice's niece Grace. "Her chinline held up through the years."[90] With age, the bones became more prominent, the straight nose a bit beaky.

"The frame of her face allowed her beauty still to transpire in her," said Egidio Ortona, the former Italian ambassador to the United States. "I rarely saw in a woman of that age such a capacity of attrac-

---

*Ethel spent her life working in her community (she lived for more than fifty years in a house four miles from Sagamore) on a staggeringly large number of good causes; she headed the Red Cross during World War II. She cared little for gradations of education, breeding, or culture, though she had them all in abundance. TR used to tell her, "If you look hard enough you'll find good in everybody." Ethel lived by that, making her nearly the opposite in personality of her sister. Having had such a loving relationship with her father, Ethel had a devoted, productive, half-century marriage to Richard Derby, a surgeon who started and nurtured the hospital that became the major medical center for the North Shore.

tion."[91] To Sheffield Cowles, who saw her at a family wedding at age ninety-four, she "had all of those looks. She was perfectly astonishingly beautiful."[92] Her wide-spaced aquamarine eyes remained glittering and clear, and until her dying day she never wore glasses or a hearing aid or false teeth. Her teeth were white and strong, her skin transparent and devoid of age spots, her makeup limited to lipstick and powder.

She dyed her hair a pale ash blond, but retained streaks of gray. She continued to pin it up and friends began to notice that it was increasingly thin, barely covering her scalp. Evangeline Bruce recalled her once becoming "absolutely enraged" when LBJ sneaked up behind her and "tried to ruffle these few thin strands. She only had about three thin strands of white hair pulled across her pate."[93]

Because her posture had been so perfect—she carried herself like a model—in the last few years friends were shocked at her stooped, shrunken appearance. At under ninety pounds, she was so tiny that she was almost cadaverous. She suffered from emphysema, and prehaps malnutrition. P. James Roosevelt recalled that when he came to collect her for the visit to the Carter White House, "It did appear that if anybody opened the window and let in a puff of air, she might blow away."[94] She suddenly seemed too fragile to support her hats.

She had started eating nothing at dinner parties, explaining that she had eaten at home first. Even at home Joanna had to bully her into eating.* She preferred to cut her food into small pieces and feed it to her newly acquired cat. She never liked vegetables and she soon stopped eating the meat course, as if she were simply tired of ninety-plus years of downing the stuff. She even lost her taste for caviar, which she used to eat for "breakfast" (mid-afternoon) with a spoon. (Her favorite ninetieth-birthday gift had been two jars of Iranian caviar from the Nixons.)

And then, somewhere after her ninety-second birthday, she became, in Bill Walton's words, "mad as a hare and incorrigible too."[95] She would ask her guests if Eleanor Roosevelt was still alive. "Some ghastly thing came over her. I don't know whether it was Alzheimer's," said Kay Graham. "She literally didn't recognize you or she knew who you were one minute but not the next."[96] "She would

---

*She was unlike TR who, for breakfast, would down a whole loaf of bread, an entire platter of liver and bacon, and a half gallon of heavily sugared coffee.

slightly focus but there was no sense of when you had seen her last," recalled Fred Holborn, "no connecting tissue at all." *[97]

The biggest surprise to her friends came when she began to denigrate her father. Previously, she hadn't allowed even the most good-natured criticism to be made in her presence. Tom Braden recalled once saying something "mildly derogatory" and having her "really put me down. . . . She let me know with . . . the kind of cold stare you might give to a seven-year-old who just spilled his milk on the dining room rug."[99] She had once told a reporter that, while she disdained "good causes," she was always available to plant trees and dedicate bridges and monuments in honor of TR because "he was a cause for me." But now her father, whom she had taken to calling a phony, "much more of a poseur than a man of substance," pompous, and "such a bore," was fair game—as was everyone else.

June Bingham brought Marie Ridder to tea, and, to the great embarrassment of both, Mrs. Longworth kept looking at Marie, whom she didn't recognize, and insisting, "You've gotten fat." Then she would talk to June Bingham, whom she did recognize, and then turn again to Marie and repeat, "You've gotten fat."[100] Bill Walton recalled Joanna inviting four of her friends to tea, hoping that they would cheer up her grandmother. "Mrs. Longworth was a tiny figure in a great big chair. And she leaned over to me and said, 'Who's that one across the room with the big fat legs?' This is audible to the whole room. I said, 'It's one of Joanna's friends.' She said, 'Not too attractive, do you think?' I said, 'Oh, I think she's quite attractive.' 'What does she do?' 'She's a lawyer.' 'What are they talking about?' 'Not much.' 'I thought so.'. . . Then she turned to me and said, 'What are you defending her for? Just for good manners? I will not have good manners in my house.'"[101]

"She simply got bored with being alive," Robin Roosevelt explained. "She was finding life less interesting. She didn't much like President Carter."[102] Indeed, her inability to follow politics hastened

---

* Her long-term memory, however, continued to be good. Cornelius brought a friend to tea who was researching an article on early Washington race tracks. "She began to discuss the racetrack at Anacostia which is no longer in existence. She remembered the exact layout of it and where the bookies were located and the one that she favored . . . My friend was quite astounded. He had familiarized himself with all of that and here she was without any previous warning just dredging it up out of her memory and very accurately and in splendid detail."[98]

her mental deterioration. This inveterate newspaper reader had to stop because of glaucoma. (She had never liked television, which she blamed for "murdering the English language.")

Not even the fate of her father's Panama Canal excited her interest. During the 1977 congressional hearings, a reporter called Alice, expecting that she would be outraged at the prospect that Jimmy Carter was about to give her father's canal to the Panamanians: "I don't care what they do with the canal," she told the reporter. "Who cares? It's there and I don't give a damn. Nothing could bore me more." [103]

As she disintegrated, so did the house. What was once eclectic charm turned into gloomy and dirty disrepair. "In the final years, the place itself was very sad," said a close friend and relative of Alice. "There was nothing you could sit down on safely. She didn't notice, she couldn't see it." [104] To writer Stephen Birmingham, the house seemed to be "just falling down. . . . It was a catastrophe. The paint was flaking, great stains on the ceilings, water was leaking. You couldn't tell whether the furniture was any good because it was all covered with plastic sheets . . . the carpets were threadbare, the curtains were falling apart." [105]

The yellowing plastic covers were installed by Janie, who was trying to keep what little was left of the furniture from the claws of Alice's blue-eyed, cross-eyed Siamese cat, named simply, "Cat." Alice liked Cat's "to hell with it" attitude and its zaniness. It was "positively crazed," said Sherry Geyelin who came over regularly to trim Cat's claws, because Alice refused to have it declawed. [106] Consequently, said Marian Christie, Cat "tore all the furniture to pieces, [it] hung in strips. She thought that was absolutely lovely." [107] Cat, said June Bingham, "really delivered the coup de grace." [108]

Friends also began to notice that the house was, by anyone's standards, dirty. "Before you sat down," said one old friend, "you'd have a tendency to kind of dust it off a little bit." [109] P. J. Roosevelt noticed that "the servants weren't cleaning the place. . . . You couldn't be sure when you left that the cook and the maid would give a damn about Mrs. L. . . . whether she was going to get fed or what or when." [110] Adding to the disarray was an obscure Melville poem about slimy serpents that Joanna had painted on the wall. Joanna, who also liked to write slogans on the walls, painted the front window sills a "ghastly red." [111]

2009 Massachusetts Avenue had lost its cachet. Most of the people who, five years earlier, had never found that business pressures kept them from stopping by at 5:00, were suddenly too harassed at the office to find time. Joanna had to phone old friends and beg them to visit: "How about coming by and pepping up my grandmother?" Joanna never forgave some, such as Joan Braden, who claimed to be too busy to make it. Bill Walton, who was one of those who continued to visit, explained, "Joan had been one of the most constant visitors—social mileage—and then, Bingo, gone, which was very unwise of her." * [112]

"Joanna feels that people coasted on her grandmother," explained Charles Bartlett, "sort of made their social reputation." [114] Bazy Tankersley also put out the call for visitors. In the fall of 1979, she gave a dinner at the F Street Club. Everybody wanted to know how Alice was. "She isn't bad," Bazy said, "but her problem is that she's really lonely. If she just had people to come in and talk to it would do her a lot of good." [115]

Some came, but most didn't. Marie Ridder continued to visit even after Mrs. Longworth's insults. "Eventually the shoe was on the other foot," Marie reflected, "and you came to visit her because you didn't want her to think you'd forgotten her. And she was so sensitive to that turnabout and very appreciative. After all, in the years when she was still the cat's meow, having us to dinner was a great treat for us. It was one of the honors of Washington." [116]

June Bingham came and so did Lorraine Cooper and Kay Halle, an old friend and Churchill scholar, and Michael Teague. Joe Alsop visited only occasionally. Many, such as Nancy Dickerson, said they stopped coming because "Mrs. Longworth never wanted to impose on anybody and I didn't want to impose on her. It's one of my regrets. I'm sorry that I didn't call on her more." [117] Indeed, in recalling her last visit, Jane Childs said, "The end was just tragic. She lost everything. . . . You felt that you were looking at something like a great piece of art that had decayed . . . it was just tragic. . . . People who had seen her were so shocked that they'd relay it." [118]

---

* Joan Braden recalled Joanna tearfully pleading with her to visit: "You're the only person who gives my grandmother pleasure," Joanna told her. "I believed and hoped that Mrs. Longworth would think that I did as much as I could," Mrs. Braden said, seven years after Alice's death. "I never had a dinner party, ever, that I didn't invite her [to]. . . . I think Mrs. Longworth would have hated being as she was at the end, as we all would. All of us would say, 'Don't let this happen to me, do something.' . . . I wrote Joanna a long letter which she never answered." [113]

Larry Spivak recalled his last visit, made at Bazy's urging. "I really did not want to see her in that condition because I had always thought of her as so vibrant." Another visitor had a baby and Alice was holding it. To Spivak, who knew how much she disliked babies, it was strange and sad that she would get so much pleasure from playing with a baby.[119]

Alexandra Roosevelt, then staying at the house to watch over Alice while Joanna was out of town, also recalled Spivak's last visit: "He had no idea how to talk to her because for him the whole connection with her had been poker or conversation about politics. He made one comment about the president and didn't get a response and didn't know what else to say. I think that was the problem with some people. They thought, 'I can't go anymore and talk about politics.' It was terrifying to them. Instead of saying, 'What a great old girl, still has charm at ninety-six,' they would say, 'Oh how tragic!' which was selfish."[120]

Alice's lifelines were Joanna and an ever-changing group of friends and cousins who stayed with her and, when Alice was ready to be lucid, talked to her. That was typically around 2 A.M., when suddenly she became almost her old self. She might recite poetry or gossip, and they were there to respond. "Joanna had a crowd of pleasant young people who were always around, sort of circling around Joanna," Joe Alsop explained. "I don't know how it all worked or what everybody's relations were but they were always there. . . . She wasn't asleep in bed, she was always in the middle of some kind of life going on." After thinking about his cousin's last years, Alsop added, "I can't imagine a luckier end for anyone who has to live so long."[121]

There was nothing conventional about the way Alice spent her final years. Ethel's daughter, Sarah Gannett, said that Joanna's approach with her grandmother was probably more "suitable than the way my sister and I agonized over our mother, tried to make everything perfect. Joanna would say, 'Granny never went to bed, so I'd just dump the chair off and she'd fall on the floor and then we'd get her to bed.' Very different approach."[122] (Alice did not want maids or nurses staying overnight and, until a month or two before her death, there was no around-the-clock nurse.)

"It was just moving to see how much of her own life Joanna sacrificed to Auntie Sister's," Sarah Gannett added. "Joanna took care of her, made sure she was comfortable, protected her, tried to make life cheerier so she could be comfortable in her own home." [123]

For about a month before her ninety-sixth birthday party—which included just a couple of friends, arranged, as all her later birthdays were, by Joanna—she pretty much lived in her bedroom. After her birthday, she never left again.

She had moments of lucidity, and in one of those moments, within a few weeks of her death, she told Joanna that Nick Longworth was not her grandfather. [124] Joanna had already heard.

The day after her birthday Alice caught a cold that, over the weekend, developed into pneumonia. She died the following Ash Wednesday, February 20, 1980, of what was officially described as cardiac arrest and bronchial pneumonia. Joanna was at her bedside. So was Joanna's boyfriend, Robert Hellman, who told a reporter that just before Alice died she stuck out her tongue at him—and perhaps at God and at death. [125]

She was strangely detached about death. "She wasn't worried about death or scared of death," said Robin. [126] Death held no mystery, no terror, and certainly no romance. When she went to a birthday party President Nixon gave her at the White House, she remarked, "So gruesome. Everyone looks at you and wonders if she'll last another year." She said there were two things she loathed— "Going to funerals and going to parties with anyone her own age." [127]

President Carter immediately issued a eulogy, made poignant by her earlier rejection: "She had style, she had grace and she had a sense of humor that kept generations of political newcomers to Washington wondering which was worse—to be skewered by her wit or to be ignored by her."

Alice managed to shock her friends in death as she had in life. She had instructed Joanna that there should be no funeral, not even a memorial service. Then came the telephone calls from Alice's friends: "There should be a big funeral," they said. "The president should come to it." Bill Walton believed that Joanna did the right thing in standing firm: "The fact that Alice was an atheist was the reason there was no funeral. She didn't want one and was very adamant about it. She wanted no priests or anybody else around." Walton argued that some of her friends wanted a service because "they were all planning their own roles at the funeral. Joe Alsop would have liked to have been the chief mourner as head of the family and have had all the world there. Mrs. Longworth knew that well in advance. She wouldn't have had a funeral just to frustrate Joe."[128] Robin Roosevelt agreed. "A lot of people . . . wanted to put on their Sunday best and go to an event. She was simply carted out of the house and that was that."[129] She was cremated and her ashes buried next to Paulina, whose religion forbade cremation. When the mortician asked how to list her occupation on the death certificate, Joanna's boyfriend, Robert Hellman, suggested "Gadfly."[130]

No sentiment, no pompous eulogies, certainly no prayers. But to some of her friends, such as June Bingham, the decision still feels wrong: "I think it was a great mistake. . . . It was hard on everybody. Particularly hard on Joanna. She may have done it because that's what Gammy wanted . . . but Gammy sometimes asked for things half tongue-in-cheek. Maybe she didn't want people to say pompous things about her. But I think when someone is not given a farewell you have a terribly uneasy feeling of their spirit hovering. It's as if a piece of music stopped before the final chord."[131]

Indeed, one Roosevelt niece described Alice's house as a "sort of coo-coo boarding house." She claimed that a younger Roosevelt who lived in the house after Alice's death and who slept in Alice's bedroom, "was fairly well convinced that my aunt's ghost was walking."[132]

Joanna was no longer living in the house, having moved into the Georgetown house she bought from Bill Walton, but she was renting rooms, at very nominal rates, to out-of-work artists and assorted bohemians. "There were a lot of Auntie Sister's clothes around," one relative reported, "and people would put them on and traipse around in them—sort of like Carson McCullers' *Member of the Wedding*. . . . It was so badly run that there were still even stuff like cosmetics around . . . her night clothes in the closet—the moths and the dirt."[133]

When Alice Longworth died, "they retired the crown,"[134] quipped Sally Quinn. Richard Nixon argued that "many have tried" to take Alice's place but that the major hostesses in Washington today "are primarily noteworthy from the standpoint of fashion, family, food and gossip tidbits. From what I have read of such events, I would have no desire to be in attendance. After attending one of Mrs. L.'s dinners, everything else would be second cabin."[135]

"The Other Washington Monument"

Alice Longworth would be amused to know that many who scooped up her dinner invitations now pronounce her passé, a tart-tongued anachronism. Today, they declare, women have so many more opportunities—in the professions, in elective politics. Pamela Harriman, they say, certainly qualifies by background, marriage, and intelligence to be a successor to Alice Longworth, but she would consider such a role contemptible. Instead of using her salon for tea parties, the wife of Averell Harriman uses it to run one of the country's most powerful Political Action Committees on behalf of liberal causes and candidates.

Alice Longworth would have wished Mrs. Harriman good luck and then joked about another Harriman, Alice's own contemporary, Daisy—a suffragist, manager of the New York State Reformatory for Women, organizer of the wartime Woman's Motor Corps, and envoy to Norway. Alice would have described Daisy's insistent tapping of her spoon against a glass, in hopes of leading her dinner guests into lofty discussions of the day's issues. And Alice undoubtedly would have used that to launch into a funny story about Cousin Eleanor.

In death, as in life, Alice was doomed to be compared to Eleanor; to be criticized for contributing about as much to society as might be expected from the Washington monument she had become. "I'm a hedonist," she declared on her ninetieth birthday. "I have an appetite for being entertained. Isn't it strange how that upsets some people?" [136]

Eventually she felt that she came out on the winning end of that comparison. When people are asked if they admired Alice, they usually say "No," eulogize Eleanor, and then, as they think about Alice, cannot help but smile. "She was such fun. She was one of the few people in Washington—a city of deceptions and images—who was willing to say what she thought."

Her cousin, Joe Alsop, described her ability "to use language with more precision than anyone I have ever met." [137] It was this quality that prompted Nixon to call her "the most fascinating conversationalist of our time." [138]

Paulina's friend, Elizabeth Wadsworth, responded to that question in a way that Alice would have appreciated. Elizabeth, who saw the blackest side of Alice's character, saw no need to moralize before saying, "Oh, yes, I did admire her. . . . I admired her intelligence and her energy and her honesty. . . . What made the naughtiness, the raffishness acceptable is that she did try to be honest. She cared about that." [139]

In the end, Alice Longworth's most striking quality was herself. "The more I think of it," said Larry Spivak, "the greater the wonder that somebody could come along who wasn't a political star or literary star or a movie star to make such a place for herself. It wasn't her social standing, it wasn't her money, or her father who had been long dead. All of the other presidents' children have just faded away. It is extraordinary to become almost mythological in a city of this kind, just by being yourself." [140]

By a "city of this kind," he meant Washington's notoriety for chewing up celebrities—in Washington that means politicians—and spitting them out. Somehow Alice persisted.

"She was a woman in a million," Diana Vreeland said. How to respond to the criticism that she didn't do anything? "I wouldn't respond. I'd crack them in the jaw." [141]

When Svetlana Alliluyeva, Stalin's daughter, appeared on *Meet the Press* in September 1969, Larry and Charlotte Spivak gave a luncheon party in her honor. Guests included former senator Eugene McCarthy, Eric Goldman (a writer and professor of history at Princeton), and the eighty-five-year-old Alice Longworth. "Even in her eighties she could steal the show," Spivak recalled. "Both Professor Goldman and Senator McCarthy were vying for Alice's attention (and ignoring the guest of honor), so my wife and I talked to Svetlana"—a woman who, Spivak added, was "still a person who was in the news and created a great deal of excitement wherever she went."

After the others had gone, Stalin's daughter, who was a house guest of the Spivaks', asked her hosts, "Who was that woman who was here at lunch?" "We told you," Larry answered. "She's the daughter of the late President Teddy Roosevelt." "I know you told me," Svetlana snapped. "But who is *she?* What has *she* ever done?" [142]

Notes

The Alice Roosevelt Longworth Collection of diaries and letters at the Library of Congress is referred to by the abbreviation ARL-LC.

1 Alice's Parents

1. Lilian Rixey, *Bamie* (New York: McKay, 1963), pp. 10, 12.
2. Alice Roosevelt Longworth, *Crowded Hours* (New York: Scribner's, 1933), p. 20.
3. David McCullough, *Mornings on Horseback* (New York: Simon and Schuster, 1981), pp. 66–67, 245.
4. Corinne Roosevelt Robinson, *My Brother Theodore Roosevelt* (New York: Scribner's, 1921), p. 18.
5. Quoted in Edmund Morris, *The Rise of Theodore Roosevelt* (New York: Coward, McCann, 1979), p. 120.
6. Cleveland Amory, *The Proper Bostonians* (New York: Dutton, 1947), p. 19.
7. Both descriptions are quoted in Edmund Morris, *Rise of Theodore Roosevelt*, pp. 84, 99.
8. Both Mittie's description and Theodore's confidence to Corinne are quoted in Ibid., pp. 64, 130.
9. Ibid., pp. 47–48.
10. Ibid., pp. 88, 110.
11. Classmate's fiancée's observations are quoted ibid., p. 88, and in McCullough, *Mornings on Horseback*, p. 215.
12. Quoted in McCullough, *Mornings on Horseback*, p. 370.
13. Quoted in Sylvia Morris, *Edith Kermit Roosevelt* (New York: Coward, McCann, 1980), p. 93.
14. Quoted in Edmund Morris, *Rise of Theodore Roosevelt*, p. 117.
15. Ibid., p. 119.

ALICE ROOSEVELT LONGWORTH

16. Ibid.
17. Ibid., p. 120.
18. Ibid., pp. 121–122.
19. Ibid., p. 122.
20. McCullough, *Mornings on Horseback*, pp. 222–223, 208.
21. Edmund Morris, *Rise of Theodore Roosevelt*, p. 122.
22. Ibid.
23. TR's diary, quoted in James Brough, *Princess Alice* (Boston: Little, Brown, 1975), p. 26.
24. Quoted in Edmund Morris, *Rise of Theodore Roosevelt*, p. 121.
25. Quoted in Gore Vidal, *The Second American Revolution* (New York: Random House, 1982), p. 216.
26. McCullough, *Mornings on Horseback*, p. 223.
27. Amory, *The Proper Bostonians*, p. 15.
28. Quoted in McCullough, *Mornings on Horseback*, p. 223.
29. Ibid., p. 224.
30. Quoted in Edmund Morris, *Rise of Theodore Roosevelt*, p. 125.
31. Ibid., pp. 123, 125.
32. Letter from TR to Corinne quoted in Rixey, *Bamie*, p. 31.
33. Letter from TR to Alice, quoted by permission of the Houghton Library, Harvard University.
34. Account of Fanny Smith, quoted in Sylvia Morris, *Edith Kermit Roosevelt*, p. 64.
35. Edmund Morris, *Rise of Theodore Roosevelt*, p. 135.
36. McCullough, *Mornings on Horseback*, p. 231.
37. Quoted in Edmund Morris, *Rise of Theodore Roosevelt*, p. 136.
38. Quoted in Brough, *Princess Alice*, p. 28.
39. Quoted by permission of the Houghton Library, Harvard University.
40. McCullough, *Mornings on Horseback*, p. 234.
41. Ibid., p. 246.
42. Owen Wister, *Roosevelt: The Story of a Friendship* (New York: Macmillan, 1930), p. 24.
43. Edmund Morris, *Rise of Theodore Roosevelt*, p. 154.
44. Quoted in Rixey, *Bamie*, p. 33.
45. Quoted by permission of the Houghton Library, Harvard University.
46. Robinson, *My Brother*, p. 118.
47. McCullough, *Mornings on Horseback*, p. 254.
48. Ibid., pp. 21–22.
49. Edmund Morris, *Rise of Theodore Roosevelt*, p. 159.
50. Quoted in McCullough, *Mornings on Horseback*, p. 279.
51. Isaac Hunt recollection and description of TR's appearance by John Walsh both from Edmund Morris, *Rise of Theodore Roosevelt*, pp. 166, 162.
52. Quoted in Sylvia Morris, *Edith Kermit Roosevelt*, p. 69.
53. Edmund Morris, *Rise of Theodore Roosevelt*, p. 162.

54. Quoted by permission of the Houghton Library, Harvard University.
55. Quoted in Rixey, *Bamie*, p. 42.
56. Ibid., p. 43.
57. Quoted in Brough, *Princess Alice*, p. 30.
58. Quoted by permission of the Houghton Library, Harvard University.
59. Quoted by permission of the Houghton Library, Harvard University.
60. Quoted in Edmund Morris, *Rise of Theodore Roosevelt*, p. 233.
61. Quoted by permission of the Houghton Library, Harvard University.
62. Quoted by permission of the Houghton Library, Harvard University.
63. Edmund Morris, *Rise of Theodore Roosevelt*, p. 240.
64. Quoted by permission of the Houghton Library, Harvard University.

2 The Death of Alice Lee

1. David McCullough, *Mornings on Horseback* (New York: Simon and Schuster, 1981), p. 283.
2. Ibid.
3. Quoted by permission of the Houghton Library, Harvard University.
4. Edmund Morris, *The Rise of Theodore Roosevelt* (New York: Coward, McCann, 1979), p. 241.
5. Ibid, p. 243.
6. Author interview with Salim Mujais, M.D.
7. Edmund Morris, *Rise of Theodore Roosevelt*, p. 242.
8. Quoted in McCullough, *Mornings on Horseback*, p. 286; and Edmund Morris, *Rise of Theodore Roosevelt*, p. 247.
9. Sylvia Morris, *Edith Kermit Roosevelt* (New York: Coward, McCann, 1980), p. 77.
10. Ibid., p. 83, and Edmund Morris, *Rise of Theodore Roosevelt*, p. 314.
11. Author interview with a member of the Roosevelt family; anonymity requested.
12. Quoted by permission of the Houghton Library, Harvard University.
13. Quoted in McCullough, *Mornings on Horseback*, p. 164.
14. "Society Topics of the Week," *New York Times*, August 29 and September 5, 1886, as quoted in Sylvia Morris, *Edith Kermit Roosevelt*, pp. 89–90.
15. TR letter to Bamie in Sylvia Morris, *Edith Kermit Roosevelt*, pp. 90–92; ARL quoted in Michael Teague, *Mrs. L: Conversations with Alice Roosevelt Longworth* (Garden City, N.Y.: Doubleday, 1981), pp. 10, 12.
16. Alice Roosevelt Longworth, *Crowded Hours* (New York: Scribner's, 1933), p. 4.
17. Edmund Morris, *Rise of Theodore Roosevelt*, p. 315.
18. Ibid.
19. Longworth, *Crowded Hours*, p. 4.
20. Teague, *Mrs. L*, p. 42.

ALICE ROOSEVELT LONGWORTH

21. Edmund Morris, *Rise of Theodore Roosevelt*, p. 373.
22. Quoted in Lilian Rixey, *Bamie* (New York: McKay, 1963), p. 68.
23. Author interview with a member of the Roosevelt family; anonymity requested.
24. McCullough, *Mornings on Horseback*, p. 359.
25. Teague, *Mrs. L*, pp. 12–13.
26. Ibid., p. 12.
27. Edmund Morris, *Rise of Theodore Roosevelt*, pp. 243–244.
28. Quoted in McCullough, *Mornings on Horseback*, p. 288.
29. Teague, *Mrs. L*, p. 18.
30. Sylvia Morris, *Edith Kermit Roosevelt*, p. 133.
31. Teague, *Mrs. L*, p. 109.

3 Life with Father—and "Mother"

1. Michael Teague, *Mrs. L: Conversations with Alice Roosevelt Longworth* (Garden City, N.Y.: Doubleday, 1981), pp. 28, 37.
2. Alice Roosevelt Longworth, *Crowded Hours* (New York: Scribner's, 1933), p. 2.
3. Michael Teague, *Mrs. L*, p. 167.
4. Quoted in Sylvia Morris, *Edith Kermit Roosevelt* (New York: Coward, McCann, 1980), p. 119.
5. Longworth, *Crowded Hours*, p. 17.
6. Sylvia Morris, *Edith Kermit Roosevelt*, p. 112.
7. Teague, *Mrs. L*, p. 36.
8. Sylvia Morris, *Edith Kermit Roosevelt*, p. 113.
9. Teague, *Mrs. L*, pp. 13, 18.
10. Ibid., p. 13.
11. Longworth, *Crowded Hours*, p. 12.
12. Ibid.
13. Teague, *Mrs. L*, pp. xii, 13.
14. Quoted in James Brough, *Princess Alice* (Boston: Little, Brown, 1975), p. 51.
15. David McCullough, *Mornings on Horseback* (New York: Simon and Schuster, 1981), p. 141.
16. Nathan Miller, *The Roosevelt Chronicles* (Garden City, N.Y.: Doubleday, 1979), p. 163.
17. Sylvia Morris, *Edith Kermit Roosevelt*, p. 399.
18. Ibid., pp. 137–138, 140.
19. Ibid., p. 138.
20. Longworth, *Crowded Hours*, pp. 3, 8.
21. William Manners, *TR and Will* (New York: Harcourt, Brace & World, 1969), p. 34.
22. Teague, *Mrs. L*, p. 42.

23. Ibid.
24. Longworth, *Crowded Hours*, p. 17.
25. Brough, *Princess Alice*, p. 81.
26. Longworth, *Crowded Hours*, p. 5.
27. Teague, *Mrs. L*, p. 42.
28. Brough, *Princess Alice*, p. 80; Teague, *Mrs. L*, pp. 36–37.
29. Author interview with Grace McMillan.
30. Teague, *Mrs. L*, p. 73.
31. Ibid., p. 22.
32. Lilian Rixey, *Bamie* (New York: McKay, 1963), p. 80.
33. Quoted in Sylvia Morris, *Edith Kermit Roosevelt*, p. 278.
34. Ibid., p. 153.
35. Rixey, *Bamie*, p. 82.
36. Brough, *Princess Alice*, p. 64.
37. McCullough, *Mornings on Horseback*, p. 249.
38. Joseph Alsop, *FDR: A Centenary Remembrance* (New York: Viking, 1982), p. 39.
39. Joseph Lash, *Eleanor and Franklin* (New York: Norton, 1971), pp. 51–52.
40. Joseph Alsop, *FDR*, p. 40.
41. Edmund Morris, *The Rise of Theodore Roosevelt* (New York: Coward, McCann, 1979), p. 485.
42. Brough, *Princess Alice*, p. 79.
43. Manners, *TR and Will*, p. 36.
44. Teague, *Mrs. L*, p. 52.
45. Sylvia Morris, *Edith Kermit Roosevelt*, p. 170.
46. Teague, *Mrs. L*, pp. 52–53.
47. Ibid., p. 57.
48. Quoted by permission of the Houghton Library, Harvard University.
49. Archibald Butt, *The Letters of Archie Butt*, edited by Lawrence F. Abbott (Garden City, N.Y.: Doubleday, Page, 1924), p. 146.
50. Longworth, *Crowded Hours*, p. 26.
51. Karl Fleming and Anne Fleming, *The First Time* (New York: Simon and Schuster, 1975), p. 178.
52. Betty Beale, *Washington Star*, October 22, 1967.
53. Longworth, *Crowded Hours*, p. 30.
54. Ibid., p. 12.
55. Author interview with Edith Kermit Roosevelt.
56. Longworth, *Crowded Hours*, pp. 26–27.
57. Ibid., p. 34.
58. Ibid., p. 33.
59. Sylvia Morris, *Edith Kermit Roosevelt*, pp. 203, 205.
60. H. H. Kohlsaat, *From McKinley to Harding* (New York: Scribner's, 1923), p. 89.
61. Longworth, *Crowded Hours*, p. 36.

ALICE ROOSEVELT LONGWORTH

4 The President's Daughter

1. Alice Roosevelt Longworth, *Crowded Hours* (New York: Scribner's, 1933), pp. 36–37.
2. Henry Brandon, "A Talk with an 83-Year-Old Enfant Terrible," *New York Times Magazine*, August 6, 1967.
3. Michael Teague, *Mrs. L: Conversations with Alice Roosevelt Longworth* (Garden City, N.Y.: Doubleday, 1981), p. 61.
4. Quoted in Lilian Rixey, *Bamie* (New York: McKay, 1963), p. 145.
5. Quoted in Sylvia Morris, *Edith Kermit Roosevelt* (New York: Coward, McCann, 1980), p. 205.
6. Edith Kermit Roosevelt diaries, quoted in *TRA Bulletin*, Spring/Summer 1986, edited by A. Richard Boera.
7. Teague, *Mrs. L*, p. 62.
8. Jean Vanden Heuvel, "The Sharpest Wit in Washington," *Saturday Evening Post*, December 4, 1965.
9. Longworth, *Crowded Hours*, p. 42.
10. ARL-LC.
11. Teague, *Mrs. L*, p. 72.
12. Ibid., p. 76.
13. Longworth, *Crowded Hours*, p. 47.
14. Countess Marguerite Cassini, *Never a Dull Moment* (New York: Harper and Bros., 1956), p. 192.
15. Teague, *Mrs. L*, p. 76.
16. Daisy Cleland, "A Half Century of Debutante Parties in Washington," December 18, 1955, newspaper unidentified.
17. Cassini, *Never a Dull Moment*, p. 166.
18. Longworth, *Crowded Hours*, p. 47.
19. Quoted in Ted Morgan, *FDR: A Biography* (New York: Simon and Schuster, 1985), p. 81.
20. Quoted in James Brough, *Princess Alice* (Boston: Little, Brown, 1975), p. 126.
21. ARL-LC.
22. Quoted in Nicholas von Hoffman, "Snap-Shots at a Hot Shoppe," *Washington Post*, Februrary 26, 1967.
23. Quoted in Morgan, *FDR*, p. 75.
24. Joseph Alsop, *FDR: A Centenary Remembrance* (New York: Viking, 1982), p. 36.
25. Quoted in William Manners, *TR and Will* (New York: Harcourt, Brace & World, 1969), p. 5.
26. Quoted in Sylvia Morris, *Edith Kermit Roosevelt*, p. 274.
27. From ARL's White House diaries, as quoted in Sylvia Morris, *Edith Kermit Roosevelt*, p. 544.
28. Quoted by permission of the Houghton Library, Harvard University.

Notes

29. ARL-LC.
30. ARL-LC.
31. Quoted in Howard Teichmann, *Alice: The Life and Times of Alice Roosevelt Longworth* (Englewood Cliffs, N.J.: Prentice-Hall, 1979), p. 49.
32. Brough, *Princess Alice*, p. 143.
33. Anonymous, *Boudoir Mirrors of Washington* (Philadelphia: John C. Winston, 1923), p. 29.
34. Quoted in Sylvia Morris, *Edith Kermit Roosevelt*, p. 273.
35. W. R. Hearst, "Alice Roosevelt's Suitors," May 2, 1902; newspaper unidentified.
36. Longworth, *Crowded Hours*, p. 48.
37. Lucille McArthur, "Idle Moments of a Lady in Waiting," *Saturday Evening Post*, September 19, 1931.
38. Brough, *Princess Alice*, p. 135.
39. Sylvia Morris, *Edith Kermit Roosevelt*, p. 235; Teague, *Mrs. L*, p. 68.
40. Cassini, *Never a Dull Moment*, pp. 102, 140, 166.
41. Quoted in Edmund Morris, *Rise of Theodore Roosevelt*, p. 328.
42. Brough, *Princess Alice*, pp. 143–144.
43. Cassini, *Never a Dull Moment*, p. 11.
44. Quoted in Alice Albright Hoge, *Cissy Patterson* (New York: Random House, 1966), p. 24.
45. Ralph G. Martin, *Cissy* (New York: Simon and Schuster, 1979), p. 63.
46. Cassini, *Never a Dull Moment*, pp. 188–190.
47. Teague, *Mrs. L*, p. 151.
48. Brough, *Princess Alice*, p. 161.
49. Owen Wister, *Roosevelt: The Story of a Friendship* (New York: Macmillan, 1930), p. 87.
50. Longworth, *Crowded Hours*, p. 61.
51. ARL-LC.
52. Archibald Butt, *Taft and Roosevelt: The Intimate Letters of Archie Butt*, 2 vols. (Garden City, N.Y.: Doubleday, Doran, 1930), vol. 1, p. 275.
53. Brandon, "A Talk."
54. Quoted in Sylvia Morris, *Edith Kermit Roosevelt*, p. 271.
55. ARL-LC.
56. ARL-LC.
57. Longworth, *Crowded Hours*, p. 54.
58. From ARL'S White House diaries, quoted in Sylvia Morris, *Edith Kermit Roosevelt*, p. 273; Teague, *Mrs. L*, p. 109.
59. Quoted in Brough, *Princess Alice*, p. 77.
60. Irwin Hood "Ike" Hoover, *Forty-two Years in the White House* (Boston: Houghton Mifflin, 1934), p. 34.
61. Author interview with Sarah Alden Gannett.
62. Quoted in Brough, *Princess Alice*, p. 113.
63. Longworth, *Crowded Hours*, p. 65.

64. ARL-LC.
65. Quoted in Sylvia Morris, *Edith Kermit Roosevelt*, p. 222.
66. Longworth, *Crowded Hours*, p. 44.
67. Teague, *Mrs. L*, pp. 109–110.
68. Brandon, "A Talk."
69. Edmund Morris, *Rise of Theodore Roosevelt*, p. 9.
70. Author interview with Edith Williams.
71. Author interview with John Gable.
72. Quoted in Sylvia Morris, *Edith Kermit Roosevelt*, pp. 126, 268, 278.
73. Longworth, *Crowded Hours*, p. 63.
74. Cassini, *Never a Dull Moment*, pp. 188, 189–191, 199–200.
75. Ethel Barrymore, *Memories: An Autobiography* (New York: Harper and Bros., 1955), p. 131.
76. ARL's White House diaries, quoted in Sylvia Morris, *Edith Kermit Roosevelt*, p. 274.
77. Cassini, *Never a Dull Moment*, p. 200.
78. Longworth, *Crowded Hours*, pp. 64, 37–38.
79. Quoted in Rixey, *Bamie*, p. 258.
80. Quoted in Brough, *Princess Alice*, p. 152.
81. Told to the author by Elizabeth Mahony, who read her grandmother Corinne Alsop's diary while researching a book she is now writing.
82. Sylvia Morris, *Edith Kermit Roosevelt*, p. 289.
83. Teague, *Mrs. L*, p. 157.
84. Ibid., p. 129.
85. Quoted in Manners, *TR and Will*, p. 11.
86. Clara de Chambrun, *The Making of Nicholas Longworth* (New York: Ray Long and Richard R. Smith, 1933), p. 193.
87. Teichmann, *Alice*, p. 41.
88. Longworth, *Crowded Hours*, pp. 74–75, 89.
89. Teague, *Mrs. L*, p. 119.
90. ARL-LC.
91. Longworth, *Crowded Hours*, p. 72.
92. Ibid., pp. 77–78.
93. Brough, *Princess Alice*, p. 173; Teichman, *Alice*, p. 203.
94. George Rothwell Brown, "Nick Longworth: His Life and Romance," *Washington Herald*, April 17, 1931.
95. Longworth, *Crowded Hours*, pp. 79–80.
96. Brough, *Princess Alice*, p. 178.
97. Longworth, *Crowded Hours*, p. 105.
98. Teichmann, *Alice*, pp. 43–44.
99. Longworth, *Crowded Hours*, p. 88.
100. Brough, *Princess Alice*, p. 174; ARL's White House diaries, quoted by Sylvia Morris, *Edith Kermit Roosevelt*, p. 546.
101. ARL-LC.

Notes

102. Longworth, *Crowded Hours*, p. 96.
103. Gore Vidal, *The Second American Revolution* (New York: Random House, 1982), p. 221.
104. Longworth, *Crowded Hours*, pp. 99–100.
105. Ibid., pp. 106–107.
106. Ibid., p. 108.
107. Ibid.
108. Karl Fleming and Anne Fleming, *The First Time* (New York: Simon and Schuster, 1975), p. 181.
109. "Alice Roosevelt's Wedding, 1906: Six Great Moments in the White House," *This Week Magazine*, January 19, 1964.

5 The Longworth Family

1. Clara de Chambrun, *The Making of Nicholas Longworth* (New York: Ray Long and Richard R. Smith, 1933), p. 8.
2. Author interview with Landon Wallingford.
3. de Chambrun, *Making of Nicholas Longworth*, pp. 27–28.
4. Ibid., p. 30.
5. Denny Carter Young, "The Longworths: Three Generations of Art Patronage in Cincinnati," in Kenneth R. Trapp, editor, *Celebrate Cincinnati Art: In Honor of the 100th Anniversary of the Cincinnati Art Museum, 1881–1981* p. 30.
6. Ibid.
7. Author interview with Muriel de Chambrun.
8. Michael Teague, *Mrs. L: Conversations with Alice Roosevelt Longworth* (Garden City, N.Y.: Doubleday and Co., 1981), pp. 137–138.
9. Young, "The Longworths, p. 36."
10. Clara de Chambrun, *Making of Nicholas Longworth*, pp. 157–159.
11. Author interview with Landon Wallingford.
12. Author interview with Muriel de Chambrun.
13. de Chambrun, *Making of Nicholas Longworth*, pp. 148–150.
14. Author interview with Frank Waldrop.
15. Clara de Chambrun, *Making of Nicholas Longworth*, pp. 201–202.
16. Ibid., p. 115.
17. Ibid.
18. Ibid., p. 162.
19. Nicholas Longworth Papers, Library of Congress.
20. Edmund Morris, *The Rise of Theodore Roosevelt* (New York: Coward, McCann, 1979), p. 84.
21. de Chambrun, *Making of Nicholas Longworth*, p. 162.
22. Nicholas Longworth Papers, Library of Congress.
23. Author interview with Joseph Alsop.

24. de Chambrun, *Making of Nicholas Longworth*, p. 165.
25. Corinne Roosevelt Robinson, *My Brother Theodore Roosevelt* (New York: Scribner's, 1921), p. 118.
26. de Chambrun, *Making of Nicholas Longworth*, p. 181.
27. Teague, *Mrs. L*, p. 139.
28. Joseph Alsop, *FDR: A Centenary Remembrance* (New York: Viking, 1982), p. 34.
29. Archibald Butt, *Taft and Roosevelt: The Intimate Letters of Archie Butt*, 2 vols. (Garden City, N.Y.: Doubleday, Doran, 1930.
30. de Chambrun, *Making of Nicholas Longworth*, p. 29.
31. Ibid., p. 116.
32. Alice Roosevelt Longworth, *Crowded Hours* (New York: Scribner's, 1933), pp. 67–68.
33. de Chambrun, *Making of Nicholas Longworth*, p. 191.
34. Longworth, *Crowded Hours*, p. 68.
35. Author interview with a member of the Roosevelt family; anonymity requested.
36. Ted Morgan, *FDR: A Biography* (New York: Simon and Schuster, 1985), p. 80.
37. Karl Fleming and Anne Fleming, *The First Time* (New York: Simon and Schuster, 1975), p. 181.
38. Author interview with William Sheffield Cowles.
39. Sylvia Morris, *Edith Kermit Roosevelt* (New York: Coward, McCann, 1980), p. 303.
40. Teague, *Mrs. L*, p. 114.
41. Author interview with Timothy Dickinson.
42. James Brough, *Princess Alice* (Boston: Little, Brown, 1975), pp. 155–156.

6 The White House Wedding

1. Howard Teichmann, *Alice: The Life and Times of Alice Roosevelt Longworth* (Englewood Cliffs, N.J.: Prentice-Hall, 1979), pp. 54–55.
2. Taken from accounts in Alice Roosevelt Longworth, *Crowded Hours* (New York: Scribner's, 1933), p. 110, and Michael Teague, *Mrs. L: Conversations with Alice Roosevelt Longworth* (Garden City, N.Y.: Doubleday, 1981), pp. 128–129.
3. Longworth, *Crowded Hours*, p. 110.
4. Irwin Hood "Ike" Hoover, *Forty-two Years in the White House* (Boston: Houghton Mifflin, 1934), p. 35.
5. Author interview with Selwa Roosevelt.
6. Quoted by permission of the Houghton Library, Harvard University.
7. Archibald Butt, *The Letters of Archie Butt*, edited by Lawrence F. Abbott (Garden City, N.Y.: Doubleday, Page, 1924), p. 329.
8. "On a Sun-Kissed Day in Room Abloom, the Eyes of the World Beholding

Alice Roosevelt, the President's Fair Daughter, Becomes Mrs. Nicholas Longworth," *Washington Post*, Februrary 18, 1906.

9. "Happy the Bride the Sun Shines On/Brilliant Ceremony in the East Room of the White House/Miss Roosevelt and Mr. Longworth/The President's Daughter United to the Man of Her Choice/Bishop Satterlee Officiates/A Distinguished Company Witnessed the Marriage—the Elaborate Toilets of the Ladies—the Reception Afterward—Congratulations and Good Wishes," *Washington Evening Star*, February 17, 1906.

10. Lady Bird Johnson, *A White House Diary* (New York: Holt, Rinehart & Winston, 1970), p. 65.

11. Karl Fleming and Anne Fleming, *The First Time* (New York: Simon and Schuster, 1975), p. 183.

12. Clara de Chambrun, *The Making of Nicholas Longworth* (New York: Ray Long and Richard R. Smith, 1933), p. 196.

13. Sylvia Morris, *Edith Kermit Roosevelt* (New York: Coward, McCann, 1980), p. 305.

14. Ibid., pp. 288–289.

15. Ibid., pp. 304–305.

16. Teague, *Mrs. L*, p. 123.

17. Ibid., p. 123.

18. Ibid., pp. 123, 128.

19. Sylvia Morris, *Edith Kermit Roosevelt*, p. 307.

20. Jonathan Daniels, *The Time Between the Wars* (Garden City, N.Y.: Doubleday, 1966), p. 90.

21. Longworth, *Crowded Hours*, p. 115.

22. Quoted in Sylvia Morris, *Edith Kermit Roosevelt*, p. 303.

23. Teichmann, *Alice*, p. 63.

24. Ibid., p. 66.

25. Longworth, *Crowded Hours*, p. 117.

26. ARL-LC.

27. Ibid.

28. Ibid.

29. Ibid.

30. Ibid.

31. William Manners, *TR and Will* (New York: Harcourt, Brace & World, 1969), p. 46.

32. Ibid., p. 182.

33. Bess Furman, *White House Profile* (Indianapolis: Bobbs-Merrill, 1951), p. 266.

34. Longworth, *Crowded Hours*, p. 125.

35. Archibald Butt, *Taft and Roosevelt: The Intimate Letter of Archie Butt*, 2 vols. (Garden City, N.Y.: Doubleday, Doran, 1930), vol. 1, p. 226.

36. de Chambrun, *Making of Nicholas Longworth*, pp. 169–170.

37. Longworth, *Crowded Hours*, p. 127.

ALICE ROOSEVELT LONGWORTH

7 A *Marriage Made—and Unmade—in Washington*

1. Quoted in Howard Teichmann, *Alice: The Life and Times of Alice Roosevelt Longworth* (Englewood Cliffs, N.J.: Prentice-Hall, 1979), p. 67.
2. Alice Roosevelt Longworth, *Crowded Hours* (New York: Scribner's, 1933), pp. 135–136.
3. Teichmann, *Alice*, p. 67.
4. Quoted by permission of the Houghton Library, Harvard University.
5. Quoted in Lilian Rixey, *Bamie* (New York: McKay, 1963), p. v.
6. Longworth, *Crowded Hours*, p. 148.
7. Karl Fleming and Anne Fleming, *The First Time* (New York: Simon and Schuster, 1975), p. 182.
8. Marguerite Cassini, *Never a Dull Moment* (New York: Harper and Bros., 1936), p. 200.
9. Quoted in Sylvia Morris, *Edith Kermit Roosevelt* (New York: Coward, McCann, 1980), p. 303.
10. Archibald Butt, *Taft and Roosevelt: The Intimate Letters of Archie Butt*, 2 vols. (Garden City, N.Y.: Doubleday, Doran, 1930), vol. 2, p. 792; *The Letters of Archie Butt*, edited by Lawrence F. Abbott (Garden City, N.Y.: Doubleday, Page, 1924), p. 316.
11. Butt, *Letters*, p. 25.
12. Longworth, *Crowded Hours*, pp. 157–158.
13. Butt, *Letters*, p. 234.
14. Irwin Hood "Ike" Hoover, *Forty-two Years in the White House* (Boston: Houghton Mifflin, 1934), p. 275.
15. William Manners, *TR and Will* (New York: Harcourt, Brace & World, 1969), pp. 6, 44, 47.
16. Teichmann, *Alice*, p. 75.
17. Sylvia Morris, *Edith Kermit Roosevelt*, p. 343.
18. Longworth, *Crowded Hours*, p. 159.
19. Butt, *Taft and Roosevelt*, p. 159.
20. Ibid.
21. Clara de Chambrun, *The Making of Nicholas Longworth* (New York: Ray Long and Richard R. Smith, 1933), p. 186.
22. Butt, *Taft and Roosevelt*, p. 341.
23. "You Can't Help Liking Nick," *The Literary Digest*, November 21, 1925.
24. Ellen Maury Slayden, *Washington Wife* (New York: Harper & Row, 1962), p. 131.
25. Longworth, *Crowded Hours*, p. 180.
26. Butt, *Taft and Roosevelt*, pp. 467, 478.
27. Longworth, *Crowded Hours*, p. 116.
28. Teague. *Mrs. L*, p. 119.
29. Butt, *Taft and Roosevelt*, p. 83.
30. Ibid., p. 143.

31. Slayden, *Washington Wife*, pp. 156–157.
32. Anonymous, *Boudoir Mirrors of Washington* (Philadelphia: John C. Winston, 1923), p. 22.
33. Teague, *Mrs. L*, p. 57.
34. Longworth, *Crowded Hours*, p. 186.
35. Butt, *Letters*, p. 343.
36. Longworth, *Crowded Hours*, p. 192.
37. Quoted in Sylvia Morris, *Edith Kermit Roosevelt*, p. 378.
38. Manners, *TR and Will*, p. 233.
39. Ibid., p. 248.
40. Longworth, *Crowded Hours*, pp. 202–203.
41. Ibid., p. 203.
42. Ibid., pp. 211–212.
43. Ibid., p. 213.
44. Quoted in Richard B. Cheney and Lynne V. Cheney, *Kings of the Hill* (New York: Continuum, 1983), p. 141.
45. Longworth, *Crowded Hours*, p. 134.
46. Author interview with a member of the Roosevelt family; anonymity requested.
47. Teague, *Mrs. L*, p. 158.
48. Jean Vanden Heuvel, "The Sharpest Wit in Washington," *Saturday Evening Post*, December 4, 1965.
49. Manners, *TR and Will*, p. 290.
50. Ibid., p. 269.
51. Ibid., p. 232.
52. Ibid., p. 291; and de Chambrun, *Making of Nicholas Longworth*, p. 205; Manners, *TR and Will*, p. 291.
53. Longworth, *Crowded Hours*, pp. 186, 194.
54. Quoted in Sylvia Morris, *Edith Kermit Roosevelt*, pp. 390, 394.
55. Ibid., pp. 395, 398.
56. James Brough, *Princess Alice* (Boston: Little, Brown, 1975), pp. 230–231; and Howard Teichmann, *Alice*, p. 96.
57. Author interview with William Sheffield Cowles.

8 A Love Affair with Borah

1. Ralph G. Martin, *Cissy* (New York: Simon and Schuster, 1979), p. 190.
2. Michael Teague, *Mrs. L: Conversations with Alice Roosevelt Longworth* (Garden City, N.Y.: Doubleday, 1981), p. 170; and Alice Roosevelt Longworth, *Crowded Hours* (New York: Scribner's, 1933), p. 322.
3. Longworth, *Crowded Hours*, pp. 323–324.
4. Ibid., p. 242.
5. William Manners, *TR and Will* (New York: Harcourt, Brace & World,

ALICE ROOSEVELT LONGWORTH

1969), p. 297; and Sylvia Morris, *Edith Kermit Roosevelt* (New York: Coward, McCann, 1980), p. 408.

6. Jonathan Daniels, *Washington Quadrille* (Garden City, N.Y.: Doubleday, 1968), pp. 116–117.

7. Ted Morgan, *FDR: A Biography* (New York: Simon and Schuster, 1985), pp. 205–206.

8. William R. Castle, Jr., unpublished diary, Harvard University.

9. Teague, *Mrs. L,* p. 160.

10. Morgan, *FDR,* p. 206.

11. Joseph Alsop, *FDR: A Centenary Remembrance* (New York: Viking, 1982), p. 66.

12. Joseph Lash, *Eleanor and Franklin* (New York: Norton, 1971), p. 215.

13. Longworth, *Crowded Hours,* pp. 258–259.

14. Teague, *Mrs. L,* p. 162.

15. Ibid.

16. Joseph Alsop, *FDR,* p. 67; and Teague, *Mrs. L,* pp. 162–163. The former account includes May Ladenburg's name; the latter does not. Alsop confirmed his published account in an interview with the author, in which he said that Alice Longworth herself had told him the story. Marietta Tree, Nathan Miller, Fred Holborn, and Frank Waldrop also confirmed the story during interviews with the author.

17. Lash, *Eleanor and Franklin,* p. 214.

18. Nathan Miller, *The Roosevelt Chronicles* (New York: Doubleday, 1979), pp. 131–133.

19. Longworth, *Crowded Hours,* p. 285.

20. Interview with Arthur Link.

21. Alice's pivotal role in the League defeat was described not only in her own memoirs, but in interviews the author conducted with Joseph Alsop, John Alsop, and Frank Waldrop.

22. Teague, *Mrs. L,* p. 156.

23. Alfred Steinberg, *Mrs. R: The Life of Eleanor Roosevelt* (New York: Putnam's, 1958), p. 118.

24. Quoted in Morgan, *FDR,* p. 229.

25. Author interview with Tom Braden.

26. Longworth, *Crowded Hours,* p. 324.

27. Hiram Johnson, *The Diary Letters of Hiram Johnson,* edited by Robert E. Burke (New York: Garland, 1983), 7 vols., unpaginated; letter dated September 23, 1921.

28. Ibid., September 23, 1921.

29. Drew Pearson and Robert Allen, *Washington Merry-Go-Round* (New York: Horace Liveright, 1931), pp. 217–218.

30. Longworth, *Crowded Hours,* p. 281.

31. "Longworth Nears Death of Pneumonia," *Washington Herald,* April 9, 1931.

32. Author interview with William Sheffield Cowles.
33. Karl Fleming and Anne Fleming, *The First Time* (New York: Simon and Schuster, 1975), p. 180.
34. Pearson and Allen, *Washington Merry-Go-Round*, p. 24.
35. Clara de Chambrun, *The Making of Nicholas Longworth* (New York: Ray Long and Richard R. Smith, 1933), p. 268.
36. Author interview with a member of the Roosevelt family; anonymity requested.
37. Ibid.
38. Author interview with Tish Alsop.
39. Author interview with Hope Ridings Miller.
40. Author interview with John Gable.
41. Author interview with Robert Maddox.
42. Hiram Johnson, *Diary Letters*, unpaginated, letter of September 23, 1921.
43. Author interview with Robert Maddox.
44. Author interviews with Marian McKenna and Leroy Ashby.
45. Author interview with Harry Shellworth.
46. Author interview with Marian McKenna.
47. Anonymous, *Boudoir Mirrors of Washington* (Philadelphia: John C. Winston, 1923), p. 121.
48. Author interview with Marian McKenna.
49. Author interview with Leroy Ashby.
50. Forest History Society, *Oral History Research Office, Weyerhaeuser Project, the Reminiscences of H. C. Shellworth;* and author interview with Harry Shellworth.
51. Author interview with Leroy Ashby and Fred Kohlmeyer.
52. Ralph Martin, *Cissy*, p. 189.
53. Alice Albright Hoge, *Cissy Patterson* (New York: Random House, 1966), pp. 71–72.
54. Ibid., pp. 73–74.
55. Author interviews with Elliott Roosevelt and Deborah Dows.
56. Author interview with Marian Christie.
57. Author interview with Elliott Roosevelt.
58. ARL's remark is quoted by permission of the Theodore Roosevelt Collection, Houghton Library, Harvard University; Gore Vidal's is from a letter to the author.
59. Teague, *Mrs. L*, p. 139.
60. de Chambrun, *Making of Nicholas Longworth*, pp. 219–220.
61. Pearson and Allen, *Washington Merry-Go-Round*, p. 25.
62. Gore Vidal, *The Second American Revolution* (New York: Random House, 1982), p. 222.
63. Author interview with Jane Childs.
64. Marion Elizabeth Rodgers, *Mencken and Sara* (New York: McGraw-Hill, 1987), p. 361.

65. Longworth, *Crowded Hours*, p. 316.
66. Corinne Roosevelt Robinson, *My Brother Theodore Roosevelt* (New York: Scribner's, 1921), p. 285; Sylvia Morris, *Edith Kermit Roosevelt* (New York: Coward, McCann, 1980), pp. 339, 456; Joseph Alsop, *FDR*, p. 39; author interview with Elizabeth Mahony.
67. Sylvia Morris, *Edith Kermit Roosevelt*, pp. 419, 511.
68. Mrs. Theodore Roosevelt, Jr., *Day Before Yesterday* (Garden City, N.Y.: Doubleday, 1959), pp. 147–156.
69. Eleanor Roosevelt, *The Autobiography of Eleanor Roosevelt* (Boston: G.K. Hall, 1984), p. 143.
70. Howard Teichmann, *Alice: The Life and Times of Alice Roosevelt Longworth* (Englewood Cliffs, N.J.: Prentice-Hall, 1979), p. 127.
71. Sylvia Morris, *Edith Kermit Roosevelt*, pp. 462–463.
72. Author interviews with Elizabeth Wadsworth and Mary Chewning.
73. Author interview with a member of the Roosevelt family; anonymity requested.
74. Author interview with Mary Chewning.
75. Author interview with Walter Trohan.
76. *Chicago Sun-Times*, October 19, 1983.
77. Teague, *Mrs. L*, pp. xiv–xv.
78. Author interview with Hope Ridings Miller.
79. AP Biographical Service, July 1, 1957.
80. Author interview with Marian McKenna.
81. Author interview with Mrs. William Howard Taft III.
82. Author interview with Marian Christie.
83. Author interview with David Mitchell.
84. Author interview with June Bingham.
85. Drew Pearson and Robert Allen, "More Merry-Go-Round: Another President's Daughter," *Cosmopolitan*, February 1932.
86. Lucille McArthur, "Idle Moments of a Lady in Waiting," *Saturday Evening Post*, September 19, 1931.
87. Ibid.
88. Ibid.
89. Author interview with Neil MacNeil.
90. "Paulina Plays in Ignorance of 'Daddy's' Death," UP, April 10, 1931.
91. Letter to author from Raymond W. Smock.
92. Neil MacNeil, *Forge of Democracy: The House of Representatives* (New York: McKay, 1963), pp. 81–83.
93. William "Fishbait" Miller, as told to Frances Spatz Leighton, *Fishbait: The Memoirs of the Congressional Doorkeeper* (Englewood Cliffs, N.J.: Prentice-Hall, 1977), p. 55.
94. Author interview with Neil MacNeil.
95. Author interview with Tom Braden.
96. Miller, *Fishbait*, pp. 103–104.

97. Teichmann, *Alice*, p. 138.
98. de Chambrun, *Making of Nicholas Longworth*, pp. 289, 310.
99. Author interview with Marian McKenna; Helena Huntington Smith, "The Lady of the Legend: Mrs. Nicholas Longworth," *Boston Evening Transcript*, July 26, 1930.

9 The Life of Paulina

1. Lucille McArthur, "Idle Moments of a Lady in Waiting," *Saturday Evening Post*, September 19, 1931.
2. Bess Furman, *Washington By-Line* (New York: Knopf, 1949), p. 95.
3. "You Can't Help Liking Nick," *The Literary Digest*, November 21, 1925.
4. William R. Castle, Jr., unpublished diary, Harvard University.
5. "Longworth Nears Death of Pneumonia," *Washington Herald*, April 9, 1931.
6. Author interview with Nancy Dickerson.
7. Author interview with Virginia Blair.
8. Drew Pearson and Robert Allen, *Washington Merry-Go-Round* (New York: Horace Liveright, 1931), p. 24.
9. Jonathan Daniels, *Washington Quadrille* (Garden City, N.Y.: Doubleday, 1968), p. 238.
10. Gore Vidal, *The Second American Revolution* (New York: Random House, 1982), p. 222.
11. Letter to author from Gore Vidal.
12. Author interview with Marian Christie.
13. ARL-LC.
14. Author interview with Marian Christie.
15. Alice Roosevelt Longworth, *Crowded Hours* (New York: Scribner's, 1933), p. 19.
16. "Alice Is Urged to Seek Seat of Longworth," Universal Service, April 11, 1931.
17. Sally Quinn, "Alice Roosevelt Longworth at 90," *Washington Post*, February 12, 1974.
18. Ann Crutcher, ". . . and Many of Them, Mrs. L.," *Washington Star News*, February 12, 1974.
19. Helen Fetter Cook, "A Glimpse of Alice Longworth," *The Senator*, March 18, 1939.
20. Author interview with Landon Wallingford.
21. Author interview with Joseph Alsop.
22. Howard Teichmann, *Alice: The Life and Times of Alice Roosevelt Longworth* (Englewood Cliffs, N.J.: Prentice-Hall, 1979), p. 158.
23. Walter Lippmann, *Public Philosopher: Selected Letters of Walter Lippmann*, edited by John Morton Blum (New York: Ticknor & Fields, 1985), pp. 313–314.

24. Teichmann, *Alice*, p. 160.
25. Alice Roosevelt Longworth, *Crowded Hours*, p. 229, and Michael Teague, *Mrs. L: Conversations with Alice Roosevelt Longworth* (Garden City, N.Y.: Doubleday, 1981), pp. 138–139.
26. Ted Morgan, *FDR: A Biography* (New York: Simon and Schuster, 1985), p. 352.
27. Author interview with Tom Braden.
28. James Brough, *Princess Alice* (Boston: Little, Brown, 1975), pp. 287–288; Teichmann, *Alice*, p. 151; "Alice Longworth Political Topic: Boom for Vice Presidency Sufficient to Start Buzz in Capital," October 28, 1931, newspaper unidentified.
29. Author interview with Nicholas von Hoffman.
30. Henry Brandon, "A Talk With An 83-Year-Old Enfant Terrible," *New York Times Magazine*, August 6, 1967.
31. Letter to author from a friend of Alice Longworth, anonymity requested.
32. Longworth, *Crowded Hours*, p. 340.
33. Joseph P. Lash, *Eleanor and Franklin* (New York: Norton, 1971), p. 377.
34. Sylvia Morris, *Edith Kermit Roosevelt* (New York: Coward, McCann, 1980), p. 480.
35. Author interview with William Sheffield Cowles.
36. Author interview with Joseph Alsop.
37. Author interview with John Gable.
38. Author interview with a friend of Alice Longworth; anonymity requested.
39. Author interview with Fred Holborn.
40. Author interview with William Waltor.
41. Author interview with Frank Waldrop.
42. Author interview with Marie Ridder.
43. Ibid.
44. Author interview with Tish Alsop.
45. Author interview with Marie Ridder.
46. Author interview with Sherry Geyelin.
47. Author interview with Ruth Carter Stevenson.
48. Genevieve Forbes Herrick, "Worth Millions in Memories, Longworth Home Goes on Sale," North American Newspaper Alliance, November 11, 1934.
49. Author interview with Frank Waldrop.
50. Nathan Miller, *FDR: An Intimate History* (Garden City, N.Y.: Doubleday, 1983), pp. 347, 445.
51. Quoted in Teichmann, *Alice*, p. 161.
52. Lash, *Eleanor and Franklin*, p. 428.
53. Alfred Steinberg, *Mrs. R: The Life of Eleanor Roosevelt* (New York: Putnam's, 1958), p. 258.
54. Ibid.
55. ARL-LC.

56. Ibid.
57. Steinberg, *Mrs. R*, p. 271.
58. Lash, *Eleanor and Franklin*, pp. 430–432.
59. Brough, *Princess Alice*, pp. 64, 293.
60. Quoted in Lash, *Eleanor and Franklin*, p. 356.
61. Author interview with Nicholas von Hoffman.
62. Author interview with John Alsop.
63. Author interview with Virginia Blair.
64. Teague, *Mrs. L*, p. 160.
65. Author interview with Sally Quinn.
66. Author interview with June Bingham.
67. Author interview with Elliott Roosevelt.
68. Teague, *Mrs. L*, p. 161.
69. Teichmann, *Alice*, p. 117.
70. Quoted in John Gunther, *Inside U.S.A.* (New York: Harper and Bros., 1947), p. 434.
71. Ibid., p. 432.
72. Morgan, *FDR*, p. 478.
73. Author interview with Marietta Tree.
74. Teichmann, *Alice*, p. 169.
75. Cook, "A Glimpse of Alice Longworth."
76. "Cockroach Interests Mrs. Alice Longworth," AP, October 28, 1938.
77. Quoted in Morgan, *FDR*, p. 561.
78. Author interview with a member of the Roosevelt family; anonymity requested.
79. Author interview with Sarah Alden Gannett.
80. Author interview with David Mitchell.
81. Author interview with Marie Ridder.
82. Author interview with Ruth Carter Stevenson.
83. Author interview with Lucille Tennant Flanagan.
84. Letter to author from Allegra Maynard.
85. Author interview with Mary Chewning.
86. Author interview with Sherry Geyelin.
87. Author interview with Archibald Roosevelt, Jr.
88. Author interview with Marian Christie.
89. Author interview with Katharine Graham.
90. Author interview with F. Reese Brown.
91. Author interview with Archibald Roosevelt, Jr.

10 The Right-Wing Years

1. Marian C. McKenna, *Borah* (Ann Arbor: University of Michigan Press, 1961), pp. 373–374.

2. Jonathan Daniels, *The Time Between the Wars* (Garden City, N.Y.: Doubleday, 1966), p. 313.

3. Steve Neal, *Dark Horse: A Biography of Wendell Willkie* (Garden City, N.Y.: Doubleday, 1984), p. 75.

4. Written answers to the author's questions from Richard Nixon.

5. Alice Longworth, "What's The Matter With Bob Taft?" *The Saturday Evening Post*, May 4, 1940.

6. Ibid.

7. Neal, *Dark Horse*, p. 62.

8. Joseph Alsop, *FDR: A Centenary Remembrance* (New York: Viking, 1982), p. 202.

9. Sylvia Morris, *Edith Kermit Roosevelt* (New York: Coward, McCann, 1980), p. 367.

10. William Manners, *TR and Will* (New York: Harcourt, Brace & World, 1969), p. 179.

11. Letter to the author from John Hutchinson.

12. Archibald Butt, *Taft and Roosevelt: The Intimate Letters of Archie Butt*, 2 vols. (Garden City, N.Y.: Doubleday, Doran, 1930), vol. 2, p. 837.

13. Marguerite Cassini, *Never a Dull Moment* (New York: Harper and Bros., 1956), pp. 348–349.

14. Author interview with Walter Trohan.

15. Author interview with Hope Ridings Miller.

16. John Hutchinson, "What Alice Said About John at Tea," *Boston Globe*, August 17, 1975.

17. Author interview with Hope Ridings Miller.

18. Hutchinson, "What Alice Said About John at Tea."

19. Author interview with Luvie Pearson.

20. Letter to the author from John Hutchinson.

21. Hutchinson, "What Alice Said About John at Tea."

22. Ted Morgan, *FDR: A Biography* (New York: Simon and Schuster, 1985), p. 483.

23. Ibid., pp. 518–519.

24. Morgan, *FDR*, p. 538.

25. Alfred Steinberg, *Mrs. R: The Life of Eleanor Roosevelt* (New York: Putnam's, 1958), p. 276.

26. Henry Brandon, "A Talk with an 83-Year-Old Enfant Terrible," *New York Times Magazine*, August 6, 1967.

27. Ralph G. Martin, *Cissy* (New York: Simon and Schuster, 1979), p. 404; Morgan, *FDR*, p. 581.

28. Documents obtained under the Freedom of Information Act (FOIA).

29. Brandon, "A Talk."

30. Morgan, *FDR*, p. 582.

31. Quoted in Lilian Rixey, *Bamie* (New York: McKay, 1963), p. 97.

32. Written answers to the author's questions from Richard Nixon.

33. Alice Albright Hoge, *Cissy Patterson* (New York: Random House, 1966), p. 195.
34. Morgan, *FDR*, p. 472.
35. John Gunther, *Inside U.S.A.* (New York: Harper and Bros., 1947), p. 176.
36. Ibid., p. 175.
37. Morgan, *FDR*, p. 579.
38. Neal, *Dark Horse*, p. 139.
39. Morgan, *FDR*, p. 414.
40. Gunther, *Inside U.S.A.*, p. 175.
41. Morgan, *FDR*, pp. 509, 553.
42. Documents obtained under the Freedom of Information Act (FOIA).
43. Morgan, *FDR*, p. 582.
44. Documents obtained under the Freedom of Information Act (FOIA).
45. Drew Pearson and Robert Allen, *Washington Merry-Go-Round* (New York: Horace Liveright, 1931), pp. 152–153.
46. Morgan, *FDR*, p. 554.
47. Documents obtained under the Freedom of Information Act (FOIA).
48. Ibid.
49. From a portrait written for the fiftieth anniversary of the Sulgrave Club by Eleanor Waldrop.
50. John Toland, *Adolf Hitler* (New York: Doubleday, 1976), p. 635.
51. Herbert R. Lottman, *Petain, Hero or Traitor: The Untold Story* (New York: Morrow, 1985), pp. 283–284, 285.
52. Karen DeYoung, "Lafayette's Kin Called Inappropriate for '76—Lafayette Kin Denounced," *Washington Post*, January 23, 1976; Lottman, *Petain*, p. 135.
53. Karen DeYoung, "Lafayette's Kin Called Inappropriate."
54. Thomas Heinen, "Hoover used FBI to do favors, scholar finds," *Milwaukee Journal*, May 13, 1984.
55. Ibid.
56. Ibid.
57. Howard Teichmann, *Alice: The Life and Times of Alice Roosevelt Longworth* (Englewood Cliffs, N.J.: Prentice-Hall, 1979), p. 184.
58. Author interview with Ethel Garrett.
59. Letter to author from Allegra Maynard, August 4, 1985.
60. Author interview with Elizabeth Wadsworth.
61. Ibid.
62. Ibid.
63. Author interview with Edith Kermit Roosevelt.
64. Author interview with Tish Alsop.
65. Alice Roosevelt Longworth, *Crowded Hours* (New York: Scribner's, 1933), p. 2.
66. Sally Quinn, "Alice Roosevelt Longworth at 90," *Washington Post*, February 12, 1974.

67. Author interview with Edith Kermit Roosevelt.
68. Author interview with Marietta Tree.
69. Author interview with Marian Christie.
70. Author interview with Marie Ridder.
71. Author interview with David Mitchell.
72. Author interview with Campbell James.
73. Author interview with Robert Taft, Jr.
74. Author interview with Edith Kermit Roosevelt.
75. Author interview with Ruth Carter Stevenson.
76. Sylvia Morris, *Edith Kermit Roosevelt*, p. 507.
77. Morgan, *FDR*, p. 498.
78. Martin, *Cissy*, p. 217.
79. Morgan, *FDR*, p. 678.
80. Description of Welles incident is taken from Ibid., pp. 677–686.
81. Ibid., p. 686.
82. Letter to author from friend of Alice Longworth's; anonymity requested.
83. ARL-LC.
84. Ernst Hanfstaengl, *Unheard Witness* (New York: Lippincott, 1957), p. 55.
85. Author interview with Campbell James.
86. Author interview with David Mitchell.

11 The Death of Paulina

1. Author interview with Charles Bartlett.
2. Nicholas Roosevelt, *A Front Row Seat* (Norman, Okla.: University of Oklahoma Press, 1953), p. 212.
3. Ibid.
4. Dorothy Thompson, "Putzi's Cautious Adieu: Hitler's Former Confidant Loses Favor, But Not His Life—Yet," April 16, 1937.
5. John Toland, *Adolf Hitler* (Garden City, N.Y.: Doubleday, 1976), p. 212.
6. Ernst Hanfstaengl, *Unheard Witness* (New York: Lippincott, 1957), pp. 22, 69.
7. Documents obtained under the Freedom of Information Act (FOIA).
8. Alice Albright Hoge, *Cissy Patterson* (New York: Random House, 1966), p. 117.
9. Hanfstaengl, *Unheard Witness*, p. 53; Toland, *Adolf Hitler*, pp. 135, 204.
10. Hanfstaengl, *Unheard Witness*, p. 113.
11. Ibid., p. 59.
12. Documents obtained under the Freedom of Information Act (FOIA).
13. Author interview with Campbell James.
14. Author interview with William Ruger.
15. Sylvia Morris, *Edith Kermit Roosevelt* (New York: Coward, McCann, 1980), p. 510; Mrs. Theodore Roosevelt, Jr., *Day Before Yesterday* (Garden City, N.Y.: Doubleday, 1959), p. 455.

16. Source requested anonymity.
17. Author interview with Edith Kermit Roosevelt.
18. Author interview with F. Reese Brown.
19. Author interview with Elizabeth Wadsworth.
20. Author interview with a member of the Roosevelt family; anonymity requested.
21. Letter to the author from Allegra Maynard.
22. Author interview with F. Reese Brown.
23. Author interview with William Ruger.
24. Author interview with Campbell James.
25. Author interview with a member of the Roosevelt family; anonymity requested; interview with David Mitchell.
26. Author interview with David Mitchell.
27. Author interview with F. Reese Brown.
28. Author interview with William Ruger.
29. Author interview with Campbell James.
30. Steve Neal, *Dark Horse: A Biography of Wendell Willkie* (Garden City, N.Y.: Doubleday, 1984), p. 60.
31. Author interview with Tom Braden.
32. Jonathan Daniels, *Washington Quadrille* (Garden City, N.Y.: Doubleday, 1968), p. 312.
33. Karen DeYoung, "Lafayette's Kin Called Inappropriate for '76—Lafayette Kin Denounced," *Washington Post*, January 22, 1976.
34. Clara de Chambrun, *Shadows Lengthen: The Story of My Life* (New York: Scribner's, 1949), p. 266.
35. Ibid., p. 270.
36. Author interview with David Mitchell.
37. Author interview with William Ruger.
38. Author interview with Elizabeth Wadsworth.
39. Letter to the author from Egon Hanfstaengl.
40. Author interview with F. Reese Brown.
41. Ibid.
42. Author interview with Elizabeth Wadsworth.
43. Author interview with Beth Moore.
44. Author interview with Campbell James.
45. Author interview with Elizabeth Wadsworth.
46. Author interview with Beth Moore.
47. Author interview with William Ruger.
48. Author interview with F. Reese Brown.
49. Author interview with Campbell James.
50. Author interview with Beth Moore.
51. Author interview with David Mitchell.
52. Author interview with William Ruger.
53. Justin Sturm, *Index to Sybil* (Philadelphia: Dorrance, 1951).

ALICE ROOSEVELT LONGWORTH

54. Author interview with David Mitchell.
55. Author interview with Beth Moore.
56. Author interview with F. Reese Brown.
57. Author interview with David Mitchell.
58. Author interview with F. Reese Brown.
59. Author interview with Frannie Mitchell.
60. Author interview with F. Reese Brown.
61. Author interview with a member of the Roosevelt family; anonymity requested.
62. Author interview with David Mitchell.
63. Author interview with a member of the Roosevelt family; anonymity requested.
64. Author interview with David Mitchell.
65. Author interview with William Ruger.
66. Author interview with a member of the Roosevelt family; anonymity requested.
67. Letter to author from Egon Hanfstaengl.
68. Author interview with a friend of Alice Longworth's; anonymity requested.
69. E. Fuller Torrey, *New York Times Book Review*, December 8, 1985, letter to the editor; author interview with Torrey.
70. Letter to the author from James Laughlin.
71. Letter to author from Hugh Kenner.
72. Gwen Morgan and Arthur Veysey, *Poor Little Rich Boy* (Carpentersville, Ill.: Crossroads Communications, 1985), pp. 408–409.
73. John P. Hayes, *James A. Michener: A Biography* (New York: Bobbs-Merrill, 1984), pp. 81–82; Robert Bendiner, *McCall's* magazine, 1966.
74. Author interview with David Mitchell.
75. Written answers to author's questions from Richard Nixon.
76. Author interview with Robert Taft, Jr.
77. Written answers to author's questions from Richard Nixon.
78. Author interview with F. Reese Brown.
79. Quoted in Howard Teichmann, *Alice: The Life and Times of Alice Roosevelt Longworth* (Englewood Cliffs, N.J.: Prentice-Hall, 1979), p. 214.
80. Written answers to author's questions from Richard Nixon.
81. Letter to the author from a friend of Alice Longworth's; anonymity requested.
82. Author interview with David Mitchell.
83. Author interview with Larry Spivak.
84. Author interview with Luvie Pearson.
85. Author interview with Kermit Roosevelt.
86. "Yokel jocularity" is from Michael Teague, *Mrs. L* (Garden City, N.Y.: Doubleday, 1981), p. 199. The McCarthy account is from several sources, primarily an author interview with Jane Childs.
87. Author interview with David Mitchell.

88. Author interview with Campbell James.
89. Author interview with Clare Boothe Luce.
90. Author interview with Edith Kermit Roosevelt.
91. Author interview with Kermit Roosevelt; Karl Fleming and Anne Fleming, *The First Time* (New York: Simon and Schuster, 1975), p. 178.
92. Author interview with Selwa Roosevelt.
93. Author interview with F. Reese Brown.
94. Author interview with William Ruger.
95. Author interview with Tish Alsop.
96. Author interview with Elizabeth Wadsworth.
97. Author interview with Clare Boothe Luce.
98. *The Catholic Worker*, February, 1957.
99. William D. Miller, *Dorothy Day: A Biography* (San Francisco: Harper & Row, 1982), p. 448; *The Catholic Worker*, February, 1957.
100. Author interview with David Mitchell.
101. Author interview with William Walton.
102. Author interview with Nancy Dickerson.
103. Author interview with Cornelius Roosevelt.
104. Author interviews with Lucille Flanagan and Bob Flanagan.
105. "Mrs. Paulina Sturm Dies: Longworths' Daughter," newspaper unidentified, January 28, 1957.
106. "Paulina Sturm Death is Declared Accidental," *Washington Post*, March 7, 1957.
107. "Sturm Death Certificate is Withheld," *Washington Post and Times Herald*, January 29, 1957;
108. "Paulina Sturm Death is Declared Accidental," *Washington Post*, March 7, 1957; "Mrs. Sturm Death Ruled an Accident," newspaper unidentified, March 6, 1957.
109. Author interview with P. James Roosevelt.
110. Author interview with Mrs. William Howard Taft III.
111. Author interview with Elizabeth Wadsworth.
112. Ibid.
113. Author interview with Nancy Dickerson.
114. Author interview with Marian Christie.
115. Author interview with Marie Ridder.
116. Author interview with David Mitchell.
117. Author interview with June Bingham.
118. Author interview with Lucille Flanagan.
119. Ibid.
120. Ibid.
121. Author interview with Ann Perin.
122. Author interview with Elizabeth Wadsworth.
123. Author interview with Campbell James.
124. Author interview with Lucille Flanagan.

125. Author interview with Katharine Graham.
126. Author interview with John Gable.
127. Myra MacPherson, "'Princess' Alice Roosevelt Longworth; Dominated Society Nearly a Century," *Washington Post*, February 21, 1980.
128. Richard Slusser, "Alice Roosevelt Longworth Dies at 96," *Washington Star*, February 21, 1980.
129. Author interview with Frannie Mitchell.
130. Author interview with Lucille Flanagan.
131. Author interview with Clare Boothe Luce.
132. Ibid.
133. Note to author from Joanna Sturm.
134. Author interview with Clare Boothe Luce.
135. Author interview with Lucille Flanagan.
136. Author interview with Selwa Roosevelt.
137. Author interview with Robin Roosevelt.
138. Author interview with Anna Roosevelt.
139. Author interview with Grace McMillan.
140. Author interview with Fred Holborn.
141. Author interview with John Gable.
142. Author interview with Mrs. William Howard Taft III.
143. Author interview with Marie Ridder.
144. Author interview with Lilly Guest.
145. Jane Kottmeier, "Princess Alice Recalls the President's Table," *Washington Evening Star*, March 11, 1958.
146. Author interview with Marie Ridder.
147. Author interview with William Walton.

12 *"The Other Washington Monument"*

1. Author interview with Katharine Graham.
2. Written answers to author's questions from Richard Nixon.
3. Author interview with Larry Spivak.
4. Alice Roosevelt Longworth, *Crowded Hours* (New York: Scribner's, 1933), p. 46.
5. Quoted in Howard Teichmann, *Alice: The Life and Times of Alice Roosevelt Longworth* (Englewood Cliffs, N.J.: Prentice-Hall, 1979), p. 11.; Edmund Morris, *The Rise of Theodore Roosevelt* (New York: Coward, McCann, 1979), p. 162.
6. Unidentified newspaper article, July 5, 1968.
7. Author interviews with Tom Braden.
8. Henry Brandon, *New York Times Magazine*, August 6, 1967.
9. Author interviews with Joan Braden and Tom Braden.
10. Lee Belser, "Teddy Roosevelt's Daughter Speaks Out," *Coronet*, April, 1966.

11. Teichmann, *Alice*, p. 206.
12. Jean Vanden Heuvel, "The Sharpest Wit in Washington," *Saturday Evening Post*, December 4, 1965.
13. Maxine Cheshire, "Princess Alice Presides Half a Century in GOP Politics," *Washington Post*, July 12, 1964.
14. Author interview with Elizabeth Mahony.
15. Myra MacPherson, "'Princess' Alice Roosevelt Longworth: Dominated Society Nearly a Century," *Washington Post*, February 21, 1980.
16. Written answers to author's questions from Richard Nixon.
17. Ted Morgan, *FDR: A Biography* (New York: Simon and Schuster, 1985), p. 679.
18. Written answers to author's questions from Richard Nixon.
19. Author interview with Marian Christie.
20. Author interview with Frank Waldrop.
21. Author interview with Marietta Tree.
22. Author interview with Judy Frank.
23. Author interview with Mrs. William Randolph Hearst, Jr.
24. Author interview with Robert McNamara.
25. Author interview with Judy Frank.
26. Author interview with Joan Braden.
27. Author interview with Tom Braden.
28. Author interview with Jane Childs.
29. Stewart Alsop, *Stay of Execution: A Sort of Memoir* (Philadelphia: Lippincott, 1973), p. 66.
30. Author interview with Franz Bader.
31. Author interview with Jane Childs.
32. "Snake Charmer," *Washington Post*, October 10, 1971; "How to Squeeze Most out of a Committee," newspaper unidentified, September 28, 1971.
33. Quoted in Teichmann, *Alice*, p. 240.
34. Author interview with Hope Ridings Miller.
35. Ellen Maury Slayden, *Washington Wife* (New York: Harper & Row, 1962), p. 90.
36. Author interview with Mrs. William Randolph Hearst, Jr.
37. Teichmann, *Alice*, p. 216.
38. Author interview with Luvie Pearson.
39. Author interview with J. Carter Brown.
40. Author interview with Tish Alsop.
41. Author interview with Cornelius Roosevelt.
42. Author interview with Joe Alsop.
43. Author interview with Tish Alsop.
44. Julie Nixon Eisenhower, "Teddy Roosevelt's Daughter at 90," *Saturday Evening Post*, March 1974.
45. Author interview with June Bingham.
46. Author interview with Joe Alsop.

47. Author interview with Anne Crile.
48. Author interview with June Bingham.
49. Maxine Cheshire, *Washington Post*, March 15, 1970.
50. ARL-LC.
51. Author interview with Margo Hornblower.
52. Author interview with Nancy Dickerson.
53. Author interview with David Mitchell.
54. Author interview with Lucille Flanagan.
55. Author interview with Jane Childs.
56. Written answers to author's questions from Richard Nixon.
57. Julie Nixon Eisenhower, "Teddy Roosevelt's Daughter at 90."
58. As told to author by John Gable.
59. Michael Teague, *Mrs. L: Conversations with Alice Roosevelt Longworth* (Garden City, N.Y.: Doubleday, 1981), p. 197.
60. Written answers to author's questions from Richard Nixon.
61. Jean Vanden Heuvel, "The Sharpest Wit in Washington."
62. Author interview with Alexandra Roosevelt.
63. Letter to author from Joseph Alsop.
64. Author interview with Joseph Alsop.
65. Quoted in Teichmann, *Alice*, p. 237.
66. Author interview with David Mitchell.
67. Author interview with Tom Braden.
68. Author interview with Cornelius Roosevelt.
69. Written answers to author's questions from Richard Nixon.
70. Author interview with Katharine Graham.
71. Lady Bird Johnson, *A White House Diary* (New York: Holt, Rinehart & Winston, 1970), p. 770.
72. Written answers to author's questions from Richard Nixon.
73. Jeannette Smyth, "Bearing Gifts & Criticisms," *Washington Post*, February 13, 1974.
74. Quoted in Teichmann, *Alice*, p. 225.
75. Author interview with Marie Ridder.
76. Sally Quinn, "Alice Roosevelt Longworth at 90," *Washington Post*, February 12, 1974.
77. Quoted in Teichmann, *Alice*, p. 226.
78. Dorothy McCardle, "A Daughterly Vantage," *Washington Post*, August 10, 1974.
79. Author interview with Charles Bartlett.
80. Dorothy McCardle, "A Daughterly Vantage."
81. Author interview with Katharine Graham.
82. Author interview with Robin Roosevelt.
83. Author interview with Robert Taft, Jr.
84. Author interview with William Walton.
85. Author interview with Joe Alsop.

86. Author interview with Tom Braden.
87. Author interview with June Bingham.
88. Author interview with Fred Holborn.
89. Author interview with P. James Roosevelt.
90. Author interview with Grace McMillan.
91. Letter to author from Egidio Ortona.
92. Author interview with William Sheffield Cowles.
93. Author interview with Evangeline Bruce.
94. Author interview with P. James Roosevelt.
95. Author interview with William Walton.
96. Author interview with Katharine Graham.
97. Author interview with Fred Holborn.
98. Author interview with Cornelius Roosevelt.
99. Author interview with Tom Braden.
100. Author interview with June Bingham.
101. Author interview with William Walton.
102. Author interview with Robin Roosevelt.
103. "People" column, *Washington Post*, October 17, 1977.
104. Interview with a Roosevelt relative; anonymity requested.
105. Author interview with Stephen Birmingham.
106. Author interview with Sherry Geyelin.
107. Author interview with Marian Christie.
108. Author interview with June Bingham.
109. Interview with a friend of Alice; anonymity requested.
110. Author interview with P. James Roosevelt.
111. Author interview with June Bingham.
112. Author interview with William Walton.
113. Author interview with Joan Braden.
114. Author interview with Charles Bartlett.
115. Author interview with Glen Elsasser.
116. Author interview with Marie Ridder.
117. Author interview with Nancy Dickerson.
118. Author interview with Jane Childs.
119. Author interview with Larry Spivak.
120. Author interview with Alexandra Roosevelt.
121. Author interview with Joe Alsop; letter to the author from Joe Alsop.
122. Author interview with Sarah Alden Gannett.
123. Ibid.
124. Source wishes to remain anonymous.
125. Author interview with Betty Beale.
126. Author interview with Robin Roosevelt.
127. Myra MacPherson, "'Princess' Alice Roosevelt Longworth; Dominated Society Nearly a Century."
128. Author interview with William Walton.

129. Author interview with Robin Roosevelt.
130. Author interview with Alexandra Roosevelt.
131. Author interview with June Bingham.
132. Author interview with a member of the Roosevelt family; anonymity requested.
133. Ibid.
134. Author interview with Sally Quinn.
135. Written answers to author's questions from Richard Nixon.
136. Sally Quinn, "Alice Roosevelt Longworth at 90."
137. Author interview with Joe Alsop.
138. Julie Nixon Eisenhower, "Teddy Roosevelt's Daughter at 90."
139. Author interview with Elizabeth Wadsworth.
140. Author interview with Larry Spivak.
141. Author interview with Diana Vreeland.
142. Author interview with Larry Spivak.

Bibliography

Books

ABELL, GEORGE, and EVELYN GORDON. *Let Them Eat Caviar.* New York: Dodge, 1936.

ALSOP, JOSEPH. *FDR: A Centenary Remembrance.* New York: Viking, 1982.

ALSOP, STEWART. *Stay of Execution: A Sort of Memoir.* Philadelphia: J.B. Lippincott, 1973.

AMORY, CLEVELAND. *The Proper Bostonians.* New York: E. P. Dutton, 1947.

ANONYMOUS. *Boudoir Mirrors of Washington.* Philadelphia: John C. Winston, 1923.

ASHBY, LEROY. *The Spearless Leader: Senator Borah and the Progressive Movement in the 1920s.* Champaign, Ill.: University of Illinois Press, 1972.

BARRYMORE, ETHEL. *Memories: An Autobiography.* New York: Harper and Bros., 1955.

BEER, THOMAS. *Hanna.* New York: Alfred A. Knopf, 1929.

———. *The Mauve Decade: American Life at the End of the Nineteenth Century.* New York: Alfred A. Knopf, 1926.

BROUGH, JAMES. *Princess Alice: A Biography of Alice Roosevelt Longworth.* Boston: Little, Brown, and Co., 1975.

BUTT, ARCHIBALD. *The Letters of Archie Butt,* edited by Lawrence F. Abbott. Garden City, N.Y.: Doubleday, Page, and Co., 1924.

———. *Taft and Roosevelt: The Intimate Letters of Archie Butt,* 2 vols. Garden City, N.Y.: Doubleday, Doran, and Co., 1930.

CASSINI, COUNTESS MARGUERITE. *Never a Dull Moment.* New York: Harper and Bros., 1956.

CHENEY, RICHARD B., and LYNNE V. CHENEY. *Kings of the Hill: Power and Personality in the House of Representatives.* New York: Continuum, 1983.

CURTIS, CHARLOTTE. *The Rich and Other Atrocities.* New York: Harper and Row, 1976.

ALICE ROOSEVELT LONGWORTH

DANIELS, JONATHAN. *The Time Between the Wars.* Garden City, N.Y.: Doubleday and Co., 1966.

————. *Washington Quadrille: The Dance Beside the Documents.* Garden City, N.Y.: Doubleday and Co., 1968.

DE CHAMBRUN, CLARA LONGWORTH. *The Making of Nicholas Longworth.* New York: Ray Long and Richard R. Smith, 1933.

————. *Shadows Lengthen: The Story of My Life.* New York: Charles Scribner's Sons, 1949.

————. *Shadows Like Myself.* New York: Charles Scribner's Sons, 1936.

DE CHAMBRUN, RENE. *Pierre Laval: Traitor or Patriot?* New York: Charles Scribner's Sons, 1984.

DICKERSON, NANCY. *Among Those Present: A Reporter's View of Twenty-five Years in Washington.* New York: Random House, 1976.

FERRELL, ROBERT H. *Woodrow Wilson and World War I, 1917–1921.* New York: Harper and Row, 1985.

FLEMING, KARL, and ANNE FLEMING. *The First Time.* New York: Simon and Schuster, 1975.

FURMAN, BESS. *Washington By-Line: The Personal History of a Newspaperwoman.* New York: Alfred A. Knopf, 1949.

————. *White House Profile.* Indianapolis: Bobbs-Merrill, 1951.

GARDNER, JOSEPH L. *Departing Glory: Theodore Roosevelt as Ex-President.* New York: Charles Scribner's Sons, 1973.

GIZYCKA, ELEANOR. *Glass Houses.* Minton, Balch, 1926.

GREEN, CONSTANCE MCLAUGHLIN. *Washington: Capital City, 1879–1950.* Princeton, N.J.: Princeton University Press, 1963.

GUNTHER, JOHN. *Inside U.S.A.* New York: Harper and Bros., 1947.

HAGEDORN, HERMANN. *The Roosevelt Family of Sagamore Hill.* New York: Macmillan, 1954.

HALBERSTAM, DAVID. *The Powers That Be.* New York: Alfred A. Knopf, 1979.

HANFSTAENGL, ERNST. *Unheard Witness.* New York: J. B. Lippincott, 1957.

HARBAUGH, WILLIAM HENRY. *Power and Responsibility: The Life and Times of Theodore Roosevelt.* New York: Farrar, Straus, and Cudahy, 1961.

HAYES, JOHN P. *James A. Michener: A Biography.* New York: Bobbs-Merrill, 1984.

HEALY, DIANA DIXON. *America's Vice-Presidents.* New York: Atheneum, 1984.

HEWITT, DON. *60 Minutes: Minute by Minute.* New York: Random House, 1985.

HOGE, ALICE ALBRIGHT. *Cissy Patterson.* New York: Random House, 1966.

HOOVER, IRWIN H. *Forty-two Years in the White House.* Boston: Houghton Mifflin, 1934.

HOWAR, BARBARA. *Laughing All the Way.* New York: Stein and Day, 1973.

JOHNSON, CLAUDIUS O. *Borah of Idaho.* New York: Longmans, Green, 1936.

JOHNSON, HIRAM. *The Diary Letters of Hiram Johnson,* edited by Robert E. Burke. 7 vols. New York: Garland, 1983.

JOHNSON, LADY BIRD. *A White House Diary.* New York: Holt, Rinehart, and Winston, 1970.

KELLY, TOM, *The Imperial Post.* New York: William Morrow, 1983.

Bibliography

KILIAN, MICHAEL, and ARNOLD SAWISLAK. *Who Runs Washington?* New York: St. Martin's, 1982.

KOHLSAAT, H. H. *From McKinley to Harding.* New York: Charles Scribner's Sons, 1923.

KROCK, ARTHUR. *Memoirs: Sixty Years on the Firing Line.* New York: Funk and Wagnalls, 1968.

LASH, JOSEPH P. *Eleanor and Franklin.* New York: W. W. Norton, 1971.

LIPPMANN, WALTER. *Public Philosopher: Selected Letters of Walter Lippmann,* edited by John Morton Blum. New York: Ticknor and Fields, 1985.

LONGWORTH, ALICE ROOSEVELT. *Crowded Hours.* New York, Charles Scribner's Sons, 1933.

LOOKER, EARLE. *The White House Gang.* New York: Fleming H. Revell, 1929.

LORANT, STEFAN. *The Life and Times of Theodore Roosevelt.* Garden City, N.Y.: Doubleday and Co., 1959.

LOTTMAN, HERBERT R. *Petain, Hero or Traitor: The Untold Story.* New York: William Morrow, 1985.

MCCULLOUGH, DAVID. *Mornings on Horseback.* New York: Simon and Schuster, 1981.

MCKENNA, MARIAN C. *Borah.* Ann Arbor, Mich.: University of Michigan Press, 1961.

MACNEIL, NEIL. *Forge of Democracy: The House of Representatives.* New York: David McKay, 1963.

MADDOX, ROBERT JAMES. *William E. Borah and American Foreign Policy.* Baton Rouge, La.: Louisiana State University Press, 1969.

MANNERS, WILLIAM. *TR and Will: A Friendship That Split the Republican Party.* New York: Harcourt, Brace and World, 1969.

MARTIN, RALPH G. *Cissy: The Extraordinary Life of Eleanor Medill Patterson.* New York: Simon and Schuster, 1979.

MEYER, AGNES E. *Out of These Roots: The Autobiography of an American Woman.* Boston: Little, Brown, and Co., 1953.

MILLER, NATHAN. *FDR: An Intimate History.* Garden City, N.Y.: Doubleday and Co., 1983.

———. *The Roosevelt Chronicles.* Garden City, N.Y.: Doubleday and Co., 1979.

MILLER, WILLIAM D. *Dorothy Day: A Biography.* San Francisco: Harper and Row, 1982.

MILLER, WILLIAM "FISHBAIT," as told to Frances Spatz Leighton. *Fishbait: The Memoirs of the Congressional Doorkeeper.* Englewood Cliffs, N.J.: Prentice-Hall, 1977.

MILLER, ZANE L. *Boss Cox's Cincinnati.* Chicago: University of Chicago Press, 1968.

MOONEY, BOOTH. *Mr. Speaker: Four Men Who Shaped the United States House of Representatives.* Chicago: Follett, 1964.

MORGAN, GWEN, and ARTHUR VEYSEY. *Poor Little Rich Boy.* Carpentersville, Ill.: Crossroads Communications, 1985.

MORGAN, TED. *FDR: A Biography.* New York: Simon and Schuster, 1985.

MORRIS, EDMUND. *The Rise of Theodore Roosevelt*. New York: Coward, McCann, and Geoghegan, 1979.

MORRIS, SYLVIA JUKES. *Edith Kermit Roosevelt: Portrait of a First Lady*. New York: Coward, McCann, and Geoghegan, 1980.

NEAL, STEVE. *Dark Horse: A Biography of Wendell Willkie*. Garden City, N.Y.: Doubleday and Co., 1984.

NIXON, RICHARD. *RN: The Memoirs of Richard Nixon*. New York: Grosset and Dunlap, 1978.

PARKS, LILLIAN ROGERS, and FRANCES SPATZ LEIGHTON. *My Thirty Years Backstairs at the White House*. New York: Fleet, 1961.

PARTRIDGE, BELLAMY. *The Roosevelt Family in America*. New York: Hillman-Curl, 1936.

PEARSON, DREW, and ROBERT ALLEN. *Washington Merry-Go-Round*. New York: Horace Liveright, 1931.

———. *More Washington Merry-Go-Round*. New York: Horace Liveright, 1932.

PECK, HERBERT. *The Book of Rookwood Pottery*. New York: Crown, 1968.

PERRINE, MARY LOUISE. *Elephants and Donkeys: The Memoirs of Mary Borah*. Moscow, Idaho: University of Idaho Press, 1976.

PILAT, OLIVER. *Drew Pearson: An Unauthorized Biography*. New York: Harper's Magazine Press, 1973.

PRINGLE, HENRY F. *Theodore Roosevelt: A Biography*. New York: Harcourt Brace, 1931.

PUTNAM, CARLETON. *Theodore Roosevelt, the Formative Years, 1858–1886*. New York: Charles Scribner's Sons, 1958.

RIXEY, LILIAN. *Bamie: Theodore Roosevelt's Remarkable Sister*. New York: David McKay, 1963.

ROBINSON, CORINNE ROOSEVELT. *My Brother Theodore Roosevelt*. New York: Charles Scribner's Sons, 1921.

RODGERS, MARION ELIZABETH, editor. *Mencken and Sara: A Life in Letters*. New York: McGraw-Hill, 1987.

ROOSEVELT, ELEANOR. *The Autobiography of Eleanor Roosevelt*. Boston: G. K. Hall, 1984.

ROOSEVELT, ELLIOT, and JAMES BROUGH. *An Untold Story: The Roosevelts of Hyde Park*. New York: G. P. Putnam's Sons, 1973.

ROOSEVELT, FELICIA WARBURG. *Doers and Dowagers*. Garden City, N.Y.: Doubleday and Co., 1975.

ROOSEVELT, NICHOLAS. *A Front Row Seat*. Norman, Okla.: University of Oklahoma Press, 1953.

ROOSEVELT, THEODORE. *An Autobiography*. New York: Charles Scribner's Sons, 1925.

———. *Theodore Roosevelt's Letters to His Children*, edited by Joseph Bucklin Bishop. New York: Charles Scribner's Sons, 1919.

ROOSEVELT, MRS. THEODORE, JR. *Day Before Yesterday*. Garden City, N.Y.: Doubleday and Co., 1959.

ROSS, ISHBEL. *An American Family: The Tafts*. Cleveland, Ohio: World, 1964.

Bibliography

RUSSELL, FRANCIS. *The Shadow of Blooming Grove: Warren G. Harding in His Times.* New York: McGraw-Hill, 1968.

SCHRIFTGIESSER, KARL. *The Amazing Roosevelt Family, 1613–1942.* New York: Wilfred Funk, 1942.

SCOTT, GEORGE. *The Rise and Fall of the League of Nations.* New York: Macmillan, 1974.

SLAYDEN, ELLEN MAURY. *Washington Wife: Journals of Ellen Maury Slayden, 1897–1919.* New York: Harper and Row, 1962.

STEINBERG, ALFRED. *Mrs. R: The Life of Eleanor Roosevelt.* New York: G. P. Putnam's Sons, 1958.

STOKES, THOMAS L. *Chip Off My Shoulder.* Princeton, N.J.: Princeton University Press, 1940.

STURM, JUSTIN. *Index to Sybil.* Philadelphia: Dorrance, 1951.

SWANBERG, W. A. *Whitney Father, Whitney Heiress.* New York: Charles Scribner's Sons, 1980.

TEAGUE, MICHAEL. *Mrs. L: Conversations with Alice Roosevelt Longworth.* Garden City, N.Y.: Doubleday and Co., 1981.

TEICHMANN, HOWARD. *Alice: The Life and Times of Alice Roosevelt Longworth.* Englewood Cliffs, N.J.: Prentice-Hall, 1979.

THAYER, WILLIAM ROSCOE. *Theodore Roosevelt: An Intimate Biography.* Boston: Houghton Mifflin, 1919.

TOLAND, JOHN. *Adolf Hitler.* Garden City, N.Y.: Doubleday and Co., 1976.

TRAPP, KENNETH R., editor. *Celebrate Cincinnati Art: In Honor of the 100th Anniversary of the Cincinnati Art Museum, 1881–1981.* Cincinnati: 1981.

TROHAN, WALTER. *Political Animals: Memoirs of a Sentimental Cynic.* Garden City, N.Y.: Doubleday and Co., 1975.

VIDAL, GORE. *The Second American Revolution.* New York: Random House, 1982.

WALDROP, FRANK C. *McCormick of Chicago.* Englewood Cliffs, N.J.: Prentice-Hall, 1966.

WARD, GEOFFREY C. *Before the Trumpet: Young Franklin Roosevelt, 1882–1905.* New York: Harper and Row, 1985.

WERNER, M. R., and JOHN STARR. *Teapot Dome.* New York: Viking, 1959.

WISTER, OWEN. *Roosevelt: The Story of a Friendship, 1880–1919.* New York: Macmillan, 1930.

WRIGHT, WILLIAM. *The Washington Game.* New York: E. P. Dutton, 1974.

Unpublished Documents and Archival Collections

CASTLE, WILLIAM R. Diary. Harvard University.

DOCUMENTS OBTAINED UNDER THE FREEDOM OF INFORMATION ACT: Federal Bureau of Investigation, U.S. Naval Intelligence, War Department Military Intelligence Service.

FOREST HISTORY SOCIETY. Oral History Research Office, Weyerhaeuser Project. Reminscences of H. C. Shellworth.

ALICE ROOSEVELT LONGWORTH COLLECTION. Library of Congress.

NICHOLAS LONGWORTH PAPERS. Library of Congress.
THEODORE ROOSEVELT COLLECTION. Houghton Library, Harvard University.

Interviews and Personal Communications

ALSOP, JOHN. Interview. July 15, 1985.
ALSOP, JOSEPH. Interview. February 26, 1985.
————. Letter to the author. August 30, 1987.
ALSOP, TISH. Interview. February 26, 1985.
ASHBY, LEROY. Interview. September 5, 1985.
BADER, FRANZ. Interview. April 6, 1985.
BARTLETT, CHARLES. Interview. April 1, 1985.
BEALE, BETTY. Interview. February 27, 1985.
BINGHAM, JUNE. Interview. May 14, 1985.
BIRMINGHAM, STEPHEN. Interview. September 13, 1984.
BLAIR, VIRGINIA. Interview. April 6, 1985.
BRADEN, JOAN. Interview. April 5, 1985.
BRADEN, TOM. Interview. June 19, 1985.
BROWN, F. REESE. Interview. June 4, 1985.
BROWN, J. CARTER. Interview. April 8, 1985.
BRUCE, EVANGELINE. Interview. April 4, 1985.
CHEWNING, MARY. Interview. July 3, 1985.
CHILDS, JANE. Interview. June 3, 1985.
CHRISTIE, MARIAN. Interview. June 19, 1985.
COWLES, WILLIAM SHEFFIELD. Interview. May 17, 1985.
CRILE, ANNE. Interview. June 4, 1985.
DE CHAMBRUN, MURIEL. Interview. June 11, 1985.
DICKERSON, NANCY. Interview. February 24, 1985.
DICKINSON, TIMOTHY. Interview. January 24, 1985.
DOWS, DEBORAH. Interview. November, 15, 1985.
ELSASSER, GLEN. Interview. October 10, 1985.
FLANAGAN, BOB. Interview. December 23, 1985.
FLANAGAN, LUCILLE TENNANT. Interview. October 28, 1985.
FRANK, JUDY. Interview. June 27, 1985.
GABLE, JOHN. Interview. May 15, 1985.
GANNETT, SARAH ALDEN. Interview. August 21, 1985.
GARRETT, ETHEL. Interview. June 18, 1985.
GEYELIN, PHILIP. Interview. June 18, 1985.
GEYELIN, SHERRY. Interview. June 24, 1985.
GRAHAM, KATHARINE. Interview. June 20, 1985.
GUEST, LILLY. Interview. April 3, 1985.
HANFSTAENGL, EGON. Letter to the author. February 8, 1986.
HEARST, MRS. WILLIAM RANDOLPH, JR. Interview. May 16, 1985.

HOLBORN, FRED. Interview. February 28, 1985.
HORNBLOWER, MARGO. Interview. May 8, 1985.
HUTCHINSON, JOHN. Interview. October 3, 1985.
———. Letter to the author. November 15, 1985.
JAMES, CAMPBELL. Interview. April 5, 1985.
KENNER, HUGH. Letter to the author. November 26, 1985.
KOHLMEYER, FRED. Interview. October 3, 1985.
LAUGHLIN, JAMES. Letter to the author. November 30, 1985.
LINK, ARTHUR. Interview. September 19, 1985.
LUCE, CLARE BOOTHE. Interview. March 29, 1985.
MCKENNA, MARIAN. Interview. September 6, 1985.
MCMILLAN, GRACE. Interview. March 1, 1985.
MCNAMARA, ROBERT. Interview. June 24, 1985.
MACNEIL, NEIL. Interview. July 24, 1985.
MADDOX, ROBERT. Interview. September 6, 1985.
MAHONY, ELIZABETH. Interview. June 4, 1985.
MAYNARD, ALLEGRA. Letter to the author. August 4, 1985.
MILLER, HOPE RIDINGS. Interview. February 28, 1985.
MITCHELL, DAVID. Interview. May 16, 1985.
MITCHELL, FRANNIE. Interview. May 16, 1985.
MOORE, BETH. Interview. June 4, 1985.
MUJAIS, SALIM, M.D. Interview.
NIXON, RICHARD. Written answers to the author's questions. November 27, 1985.
ORTONA, EGIDIO. Letter to the author. July 24, 1985.
PEARSON, LUVIE. Interview. February 24, 1985.
PERIN, ANN. Interview. April 11, 1985.
QUINN, SALLY. Interview. April 2, 1985.
RIDDER, MARIE. Interview. June 17, 1985.
ROOSEVELT, ALEXANDRA. Interview. May 14, 1985.
ROOSEVELT, ANNA. Interview. May 2, 1985.
ROOSEVELT, ARCHIBALD, JR. Interview. February 28, 1985.
ROOSEVELT, CORNELIUS. Interview. February 27, 1985.
ROOSEVELT, EDITH KERMIT. Interview. February 26, 1985.
ROOSEVELT, ELLIOTT. Interview. July 11, 1985.
ROOSEVELT, KERMIT. Interview. February 28, 1985.
ROOSEVELT, P. JAMES. Interview. May 15, 1985.
ROOSEVELT, ROBIN. Interview. April 2, 1985.
ROOSEVELT, SELWA. Interview. June 20, 1985.
RUGER, WILLIAM. Interview. April 8, 1987.
SHELLWORTH, HARRY. Interview. September 13, 1985.
SMOCK, RAYMOND W. Interview. April 1, 1985.
———. Letter to the author. October 7, 1985.
SPIVAK, LAWRENCE. Interview. April 3, 1985.

STEVENSON, RUTH CARTER. Interview. September 5, 1985.

STURM, JOANNA. Note to the author. April 23, 1985.

TAFT, ROBERT, JR. Interview. April 3, 1985.

TAFT, MRS. WILLIAM HOWARD III. Interview. February 27, 1985.

TORREY, E. FULLER. Interview. November 22, 1985.

TREE, MARIETTA. Interview. June 5, 1985.

TROHAN, WALTER. Interview. January 30, 1986.

VIDAL, GORE. Letter to the author. June 13, 1985.

VON HOFFMAN, NICHOLAS. Interview. July 25, 1985.

VREELAND, DIANA. Interview. May 31, 1985.

WADSWORTH, ELIZABETH. Interview. February 24, 1986.

WALDROP, ELEANOR. Interview. April 2, 1985.

WALDROP, FRANK. Interview. February 25, 1985.

WALLINGFORD, LANDON. Interview. July 10, 1985.

WALTON, WILLIAM. Interview. May 16, 1985.

WILLIAMS, EDITH. Interview. August 20, 1985.

Index

Index